Materiality and Popular Culture

"Conceptually eclectic and empirically wide-ranging, this book provides an expansive and sophisticated exploration of the complex, shifting and emergent relations between the material and the popular."
—*Mike Michael, University of Sydney, Australia*

"Approaching the growing research field of material and popular culture from a range of perspectives and through many relevant and up-to-date case studies, this anthology adds to our understanding of the materiality of our everyday encounters with the popular."
—*Karin Fast, Karlstad University, Sweden*

This book critically approaches contemporary meanings of materiality and discusses ways in which we understand, experience, and engage with objects through popular culture in our private, social, and professional lives. Appropriating Arjun Appadurai's famous phrase—"the social life of things"—with which he inspired scholars to take material culture more seriously and, as a result, treat it as an important and revealing area of cultural studies, the book explores the relationship between material culture and popular practices, and points to the impact they have exerted on our coexistence with material worlds in the conditions of late modernity.

Anna Malinowska is Assistant Professor at the Institute of English Cultures and Literatures (IECL), University of Silesia, Poland. Her research interests embrace critical theory, popular culture, material culture, and love studies. She is particularly interested in the formation of social and cultural norms and social-aesthetic codes of cultural production.

Karolina Lebek is Assistant Professor at the Institute of English Cultures and Literatures (IECL), University of Silesia, Poland. She specializes in early modern studies, specifically in the study of objects as well as material cultures—that is, theorizing and representing things in cultural and literary practices.

Routledge Research in Cultural and Media Studies

For a full list of titles in this series, please visit www.routledge.com.

83 **Reviving Gramsci**
Crisis, Communication, and Change
Marco Briziarelli and Susana Martinez Guillem

84 **Motherhood in the Media**
Infanticide, Journalism, and the Digital Age
Barbara Barnett

85 **The Pedagogies of Cultural Studies**
Edited by Andrew Hickey

86 **Intimacy on the Internet**
Media Representation of Online Intimacy
Lauren Rosewarne

87 **The DIY Movement in Art, Music and Publishing**
Subjugated Knowledges
Sarah Lowndes

88 **Advertising and Public Memory**
Social, Cultural and Historical Perspectives on Ghost Signs
Edited by Stefan Schutt, Sam Roberts and Leanne White

89 **Postfeminist Celebrity and Motherhood**
Brand Mom
Jorie Lagerwey

90 **Technologies of Consumer Labor**
A History of Self-Service
Michael Palm

91 **Performing Ethnicity, Performing Gender**
Transcultural Perspectives
Edited by Bettina Hofmann and Monika Mueller

92 **Materiality and Popular Culture**
The Popular Life of Things
Edited by Anna Malinowska and Karolina Lebek

Materiality and Popular Culture
The Popular Life of Things

Edited by
Anna Malinowska
and Karolina Lebek

NEW YORK AND LONDON

First published 2017
by Routledge
711 Third Avenue, New York, NY 10017

and by Routledge
2 Park Square, Milton Park, Abingdon, Oxon OX14 4RN

Routledge is an imprint of the Taylor & Francis Group, an informa business

© 2017 Taylor & Francis

The right of the editors to be identified as the authors of the editorial
material, and of the authors for their individual chapters, has been asserted
in accordance with sections 77 and 78 of the Copyright, Designs and
Patents Act 1988.

All rights reserved. No part of this book may be reprinted or reproduced or
utilized in any form or by any electronic, mechanical, or other means, now
known or hereafter invented, including photocopying and recording, or in
any information storage or retrieval system, without permission in writing
from the publishers.

Trademark notice: Product or corporate names may be trademarks or
registered trademarks, and are used only for identification and explanation
without intent to infringe.

Library of Congress Cataloging-in-Publication Data

Names: Malinowska, Anna, 1979– editor. | Lebek, Karolina.
Title: Materiality and popular culture: the popular life of things /
edited by Anna Malinowska and Karolina Lebek.
Description: New York; London: Routledge, 2016. | Series: Routledge
research in cultural and media studies; 92 | Includes bibliographical
references and index.
Identifiers: LCCN 2016014250
Subjects: LCSH: Material culture.
Classification: LCC GN406 .M384 2016 | DDC 306.4/6—dc23
LC record available at https://lccn.loc.gov/2016014250

ISBN: 978-1-138-65780-9 (hbk)
ISBN: 978-1-315-62116-6 (ebk)

Typeset in Sabon
by codeMantra

Contents

List of Figures	ix
Acknowledgments	xi

Introduction: The Popular Life of Things   1
ANNA MALINOWSKA AND KAROLINA LEBEK

PART I
Theorizing *the Popular* and *the Material*

1 Culture: The 'Popular' and the 'Material'   13
JOHN STOREY

2 Cultural Materialisms and Popular Processes of Late Modernity   25
ANNA MALINOWSKA

3 The Secret Life of Things: Speculative Realism and
the Autonomous Object   41
GRZEGORZ CZEMIEL

PART II
From Material Media to Digital Materiality

4 The Representation of Book Culture in *It-Narratives*   55
JOANNA MACIULEWICZ

5 The Intimacy of Writing—Lost in a Digital Age?   65
MAYANNAH N. DAHLHEIM

6 Popular Digital Imaging: Photoshop as Middlebroware   76
FRÉDÉRIK LESAGE

7 When You Are Not What You Do Not Have: Some Remarks
on Digital Inheritance   88
MARCIN SARNEK

vi *Contents*

PART III
The Agency of Things and the Negotiation of Meaning

8 I See Faces: Popular Pareidolia and the Proliferation
of Meaning   105
JOANNE LEE

9 From Piss-Communication to GraffARTi: Hegemony,
Popular Culture, and the Bastard Art   119
DAVID WALTON

10 From Performance to Objects and Back: London's *InterAction*   132
LUCIA VODANOVIC

11 Bohemian Bourgeoisie and Subversive Commodities   143
BARTOSZ STOPEL

PART IV
Popular Narratives and Material Culture

12 Objects Don't Lie. The Truth and Things in
Detective Stories   157
JOANNA SOĆKO

13 Emotional Territories: An Exploration of Wes Anderson's
Cinemaps   167
NICOLÁS LLANO LINARES

14 The Poetics of Objects in *True Detective*   179
KAROLINA LEBEK

15 Mapping the Daytime Landscape: World-Building on
U.S. Soap Operas   193
C. LEE HARRINGTON AND BYRON MILLER

PART V
Material Culture and the Creative Self

16 In Reverse: Declining Automobility and the Accidents
of Progress   213
MARCIN MAZUREK

17 Living Dolls—A Food Studies Perspective   225
NINA AUGUSTYNOWICZ

Contents vii

18 Contemporary Toys, Adults, and Creative Material Culture:
From *Wow* to *Flow* to *Glow* — 237
KATRIINA HELIAKKA

19 From Stuff to Material Civilization—Toward a Materiality
of Childhood — 250
DAVID JAMES

Contributors — 261
Index — 265

List of Figures

9.1	Graffiti as marking territory, Cieza, Murcia. (Photo by Margarita Navarro Pérez.)	127
9.2	Squat and double appropriation in Madrid. (Photo by Ana Rull.)	127
9.3(a) and (b)	The street answers back. Details: Mother Teresa and Kofi Annan. (Photos by David Walton.)	128
18.1	Blue toys in photoplay. (Photo by Katriina Heliakka.)	246
18.2	Seiren of the sea—artistic photoplay. (Photo by Katriina Heliakka.)	246
18.3	Toys in a game session within a diorama. (Photo by Katriina Heliakka.)	247
19.1	Framework for a materiality-informed study of childhood.	257

Acknowledgments

This book owes thanks to many people and things: colleagues, friends, family members, life partners, places, objects of everyday use, objects of extraordinary use—all of whom and all of which have inspired our thinking about the project.

Our gratitude goes first to Jacek Mydla, director of the Institute of English Cultures and Literature at the University of Silesia in Poland, who supported the idea of the Popular Life of Things Conference, where the themes of the book were first rehearsed. Also, we would like to thank John Storey, who provided an incentive for the conference to happen and Felisa Salvago-Keyes at Routledge for her invaluable help with the manuscript.

Special thanks must also be given to all the contributors for their engagement and trust in the project, followed by advice on the collection's shape and content, as well as for their patience with the long preparation stage.

From Karolina a deep expression of gratitude to Jesion Kowal, as he took care of things when she couldn't. And from Anna to anyone and anything that taught her things.

Introduction
The Popular Life of Things

Anna Malinowska and Karolina Lebek

The interest of this volume is in material reality, and its purpose is twofold: first and in general, it wants to examine recent changes in the meanings, perception, and studies of material cultures; second, and on a more specific note, it intends to provide a further and detailed insight into the relationship between materiality and popular culture as rehearsed in de Certeau's claim that "the actual order of things is precisely what 'popular' tactics turn to their own ends [...]" (1984, 26; after Fiske 1989a, 17).

Material culture, just like the idea of materiality itself, is not a self-sufficient occurrence, but rather one that arises at the intersection of a variety of cultural movements. The study of objects and that of materiality itself is, therefore, never an isolated process but one that contextualizes other phenomena of culture to redefine one through another in relation to their real-life and theoretical interactions. The belief shared in the current volume is that a phenomenon that perhaps best resonates materiality in a cultural setting is popular culture. It is mainly due to the direct link between manifestation forms, products, and production modes that both, *the popular* and *the material*, coalesce under the common label of *materialism*.

Popular culture dominates in exercising and theorizing cultural change as it embraces practices ranging from daily life to manufactures of entertainment. Vast and diverse, popular culture allows for an extensive methodological and practical analyses of the life of things in the current cultural environment. The trajectories of things tracing their 'social life,' as Arjun Appadurai claims in his opening essay to *The Social Life of Things. Commodities in Cultural Perspective* (1986), relied for him on the commodification of things and their exchange in social contexts. Since the publication of his text, not only did those trajectories become much more convoluted and complex, but also the very idea of exchange underwent a significant complication.

Ian Hodder speaks of the growing need "to explore how society and thing are co-entangled" (2012, 3) by advancing a few programmatic statements for a study of this inter-relatedness: things are interdependent and relational; things are vibrant and unstable despite their seemingly inert material presence; things and technologies endure through time, accumulate, and assembly in polychronic configurations of matter; "things often appear as

2 Anna Malinowska and Karolina Lebek

non-things" (5) because of our cognitive limitations, cultural situatedness and blindness generated by habit. He then offers a complex model of thinking about things through different spatially and temporally conceptualized frameworks: the relation of dependence (humans on things, things on other things, things on humans), entanglement, fittingness (whereby elements cohere and resonate), evolution, and patterns of co-emergence, sequencing, and directionality.

Interestingly, the processes of popular culture could be conceived of in similar metaphorical terms, which encourages a thought that the intuitions behind this book could have their contribution to the understanding of matter through the study of popular materialism. This also stresses the belief that the social life of things in contemporary culture cannot be separated from the popular life of things. This, however, requires a tentative spectography of the problems of (popular) materiality through the analytical dispersal offered by the prism of *the popular*.

Methods (of) Matter

Materiality is a modern concept of a wide range of postmodern meanings, each depending on our experiences with material reality. In a basic sense, materiality means the substantial quality of things: their presence, function, and performative volume; in relation to manufacture modes, it stands for "the physical manifestation of making" (Attfield 2000, 41), or conversely, "the merely apparent, behind which lies that which is real" (Miller 2005, 1). A lot of what we understand by 'materiality' and 'material experience' derives from how they have been defined for us in cultural representation. Part of this representation owes to scholarly debate and ways it has rehearsed the 'praxis of matter' in abstract interpretations.

Modern humanist theories rest on two main, arguably conflicted paradigms of materiality: a cultural method that binds the existence of objects to social experience, and New Materialism that rejects this social ontology to the advantage of enchanting vitalism, "ascribing agency to the inorganic phenomena such as electricity grid, food, and trash, all of which enjoy a certain efficacy that defines human will" (Coole and Frost 2010, 9). The first paradigm emerged from materialist thinking rooted in the ideologization of human activities that acknowledged the priority of the socioeconomic factors over the natural predispositions of things (Bourdieu 1984; Williams 1980). The cultural method reads materiality in terms of the role of social agency for objects' affordances and general disposition, seeing *the material* as an indicator of the status of things used for contextualizing their usability into particular social settings and vice versa (Chapter 1). It assumes the transcendence of social symbolism over the 'nature' of everyday objects and, following Durkheim's sociology of collective consciousness (2014), links the meaning of things with the signifying rituals of modern societies (Featherstone 1991, 119f), and informs us that "value is never an

Introduction 3

inherent property of objects but is a judgement made about them by subjects" (Appadurai 1986, 3).

The cultural thinking about materiality is part of the poststructural code born from the 'semiotic turn' in the late 1960s. That code, as Strinati observes, has read the life of stuff in terms of hegemonic causalities, seeing materiality as an element of a political agenda of high capitalism:

> Semiology argues that material reality can never be taken for granted. It is always constructed and made intelligible to human understanding by culturally specific systems of meaning. This meaning is never 'innocent,' but has some particular purpose or interest lying behind it, which semiology can uncover. Our experience of the world is never 'innocent' because systems of meaning make sure it is intelligible. (2014, 100)

Recent debates on materiality have increasingly rejected this social determinism; they have accused culturalism of the "ignor[ance of] the power of matter" (Coole and Frost 2010, 1) and proclaimed it a method with "a tendency to treat culture as something that exists either in the heads of people or their social relations with one another, and to disregard the role that *material* culture plays in shaping our lives" (Graves-Brown 2000, 1). Dissatisfaction with this approach ignited a turn into scientific methodologies, specifically in disciplines such as archeology, anthropology, psychology, and medicine (Latour 2000; Graves-Brown 2000). These disciplines have seemed to allow for a theoretical balance by offering a focus on the nature of things per se (Chapter 3, this volume). In a groundbreaking essay on the perception of objects in young autistic patients, Emma Williams and Alan Costal explain how the concentration on the social signification of things may limit other affordances of matter. They write:

> Artefacts such as a child's toothbrush or potty provide a means by which the child appropriates new action schemes, and in so doing enters into the shared practices of society (Volpert 1985). The very form of objects constrains our possible activities with them, drawing us into common actions. Indeed, objects intended specifically for children [...] are often specially designed to further constraints and guide the infant's activity [...]. [This] has not only deflected attention away from the role of other people in the mediation of object use, but also from the psychological significance of objects themselves.
> (Williams and Costal 2000, 99)

This turn to things, although it entails a departure from traditional cultural approaches, does not denunciate their methods; rather, it provides a missing perspective in analyzing our material interactions, offering a complementary insight into the material experience by reconceptualizing the issue of human–object agency. As such, it opens space for other possible readings of

4 Anna Malinowska and Karolina Lebek

materiality, reaching for cultural anthropology and studies in modernization (Chapter 2) whose contexts diagnose the condition of the material world in broader theoretical and practical settings.

Popular culture provides a theoretical framework for the study of material cultures that combines diachronic and transdisciplinary approaches for a more inclusive assessment of the material world today. The experiences of materiality we get through *the popular* unveil a myriad of aspects of our personal and social interactions with objects on local and global scales. Social connections between *the popular* and *the material* prove the inherent entanglement of the two as well as point to how fundamental this entanglement is for the shape (and shaping) of our being in the world. On a general level, popular culture conceptualizes materiality with respect to structures of everydayness and our daily lives. As such, it explains the meaning of materiality through the lenses that identify the essence of things with social involvement and practical contexts (Chapter 1).

When approached comparatively, in relation to other fields of cultural production (*lowbrow*, *highbrow*), or with respect to the entity of cultural condition, popular culture shows idiosyncrasies for a specific study of things. The starting point for such a study is an observation that the experience of materiality in popular culture is processually and aesthetically peculiar to this field. The term this volume proposes to explain this idiosyncrasy is *popular materialism* that becomes a method for the analysis of our material experience as formed specifically through popular culture (Chapter 2). This particularization does not, however, intend to breach the universality of cultural experiences; rather, it seeks an opportunity in aesthetic and developmental factions to provide a more focused and precise examination of our coexistence with matter.

Pointing to the multitude of materialisms for explaining the material condition, this volume sets materiality against general cultural processes to distinguish their popular counterparts and identify mechanisms that impact the experience of the material world in 'late modernity.' Such temporal and methodological perspective allows for developing a bridging method in materiality and for noticing the reciprocal character of the object–subject interaction, pronounced by New Materialism studies (Speculative Realism), which approaches objects in relation to the hierarchy of categories (human vs. material), providing a revision of notions such as creativity, identity, dependence, and other in light of object-oriented philosophy (Chapter 3).

Substance

Part of the interest in materiality today focuses on a change in the constitution of the material world caused by ever advancing technological progress. The increasingly digital organization of life and the impact it has on the substance of things (objects, activities) restructures the ways we perform

Introduction 5

and interact in material reality. This restructuring shows perhaps most in the change of the nature of these performances and interactions; over the past few decades, many basic activities, among them writing, reading, or talking, have changed their 'substance,' becoming more 'intangible' (i.e., less physically involving). It is mainly due to the development of new media and its effect on the operational mode of many practices today. For example, the electronic book or digital communication has made intangibility a dominant mode of our lives and a new reference for theorizing and understanding materiality.

The awareness of the substance of things is not a recent occurrence, but rather one that has been present in the literary examples of anthropomorphization of things since ancient and medieval cultures. It is, however, in the eighteenth century when the voice of things is made to express the consciousness of matter in the context of growing industrialization, commodification, consumption, and distribution. The very modern anxieties about ephemerality, originality, and distinction (responsible for the aura of things) see expression in the literature of that period (Chapter 4). Novels featuring personal belongings and items, narrated from the perspective thereof, show a contemporaneous preoccupation with the physicality of things and our tangible physical engagement in activities they entail.

Seen from this perspective, the transition from tangible matter to the intangible material seems a rather acute intervention in the signification of many activities. This is well demonstrated in today's reading and writing cultures, whose production technology enforced a new kind of intimacies in man-to-man and man-to-object interactions. For example, the status of a personal letter in the era of a gradual disappearance of handwriting in favor of digital communication reveals a drastic change in the physical act of writing (Chapter 5). Our epistolary exchanges are no longer the effect of a manual labor but rather system-ridden acts determined by the possibilities behind given hardware and software solutions of the computer market. This raises questions about how haptic presences are being negotiated in a cultural space and to what extent their status impacts our understanding of matter in a digitally infused social environment.

More radical instances of the 'substantial shift' relate to issues of appropriation, ownership and inheritance of (im)material objects. Uses of Photoshop, for example, inform about the problem of resurrecting cultural commodities by means of digital tools for the production of other commodities of culture fetishized toward ideals that lack a material form (Chapter 6). As a cultural practice facilitated by new technologies, Photoshop represents an advancement in cultural manufacture and points to the manner in the production of artifacts, which rests on and explores the ephemeral *popular* for the generation of digital commodities. Apart from changing the substance of many practices, digital applications or software problematize issues of authorship and copyrights as they are behind the emergence of a different—immaterial—kind of heritage (Chapter 7).

6 *Anna Malinowska and Karolina Lebek*

This, in turn, opens a discussion on digital ownership and digital inheritance, inquiring after the unsettled legal status of immaterial artifacts in consumer culture and indicating the challenges that digitalization poses to our relationship with stuff and our notion of possession.

Signification of Matter and Signifying Material

Popular culture is an arena of a reciprocal or two-way exchange of material signification, where objects gain and provide meanings in an interaction between the external contexts of their use (society) and the internal environments that objects impact the society through the constant evolution of their affordances. This signifying reciprocity has been theorized by Fiske in an observation on the nonsubordinate working of *the popular*:

> Popular culture is made from within and below, not imposed from without or above as mass cultural theorists would have it. There is always an element of popular culture that lies outside social control, that escapes or opposes hegemonic forces. Popular culture is always a culture of conflict, it always involves the struggle to make social meanings that are in the interests of the subordinate and that are not those preferred by the dominant ideology.
>
> (Fiske 1989b, 2)

When it comes to meanings generated from the signifying practices of the social, a great many of them arise from subversive rereadings of things and their material practice. A good example here would be contemporary urban cultures, characterized by novel ways in connoting matter. The popular urban area is where the meanings of things emerge from ongoing changes in the organization and reappropriation of the living space, and where things and 'objectified locations' have been explored and adapted to transcend, often revolutionarily, their original purposes and denotations. *The popular* emerges, therefore, where the current pursuit for significance is variously identified with the desire to reinterpret the already existing 'signs' and to read meaning into things (Chapter 8); the need to oppose cultural hegemonies that restrict the uses and meanings of things (Chapter 9); the performative uses of public spaces and community engagement (Chapter 10); and the tendency to hybridize (or reconnote) cultural constructs, which, as the critique of the bohemian bourgeoisie in Chapter 11 shows, gives rise to new social practices and new consumerist behaviors.

The signifying affordance of objects is particularly revealed in their (re)incarnations in popular narratives. Objects get produced or appropriated to meet the discursive demands of various genres, aesthetic conventions, and material media in order to tell stories and build worlds. Material assemblages accrued in narratives reiterate and disseminate whole contexts of use for creators, fictional characters, and fans. This repetition and spreading

Introduction 7

extend both through space (globalization, cultural transfer, customization) and time (serialization, recycling), contributing to the spawn of hybrids and reboots. The ever expanding popular archives therefore hold rich collections of everyday objects, fantastic artifacts, and curious and monstrous specimens, as well as a whole range of cooking utensils, instruments of torture, and laboratory equipment. Intimate knowledge of all those materials, exercised by forensic fandom (Mittell 2015), builds popular culture literacy.

Those collections are often constituted by and explored for the development of generic forms in response to anxieties and hopes afforded by our dependence on things in everyday life for both cognition and agency. This has most obviously been true in the case of detective fiction (Chapter 12). The roles popular narratives bestow on material culture turn things into complex narrative artifacts with multiple poetic functions, which in turn depend on media-specific formats. Such artifacts may take part in construction of characters, plot development, concretization of landscapes and places, or aesthetic elaboration (Chapters 13 and 14). The extensive possibilities of transmedial world-building and the growth of the phenomenon of popular fandom create spaces for further engagement with popular artifacts in active reception and extension of story worlds (Chapter 15). Those popular phenomena influence our understanding of matter in everyday contexts and allow for a further elaboration of the entangled trajectories of human-objects relations, in that they channel desire, determine patterns of consumption, shape tastes, and afford the exercise of identity.

Identity and Function

The popular lives of things (i.e., their coentanglement with the human as well as their material agency) complicate the distinction between the apparently stable categories of subjects and objects, of activity and passivity, of a thing and person. The functioning of one set of things or technologies in social life is predetermined by historical changes and cultural shifts in other material domains; this influences in turn the role afforded to humans in the context of use. Individuals are forced to surrender their agency in the name of comfort and technological progress (which passes for an extension of social agency) to the working of things, whose intensely digitalized operations carry a catastrophic potential (Chapter 16).

The ambiguity of the exact allocation of object and subject positions allows the fashioning of selves through depersonifying of self (Chapter 17). In other words, *the popular* affords the exercise of one's agency through subsuming an objecthood, which in turn exposes and subverts major cultural constructs such as power relations across social divisions (gender divisions, class divisions, and geographical divisions); social and cultural myths (like the body ideal); and the ever persistent duality of mind and matter. This positional ambiguity is also reenacted in the cultures of play, which invite affective engagement of subjects with personified objects (Chapter 18).

8 *Anna Malinowska and Karolina Lebek*

The fashioning of objects as subjects in play involves popular aesthetic processes that entail building narratives for personal histories, multiple-media reenactments of narratives, customization of mass-produced toys, collecting, and exchange. The creative outcomes of those processes are also shared and distributed in communities, generating social identification.

The material ecosystem of things concretizes the spaces and places of social reality and therefore participates in the production (Lefebvre 1984) of material infrastructures with which humans engage. Such engagement assumes interactions with social objects through their practical and expressive potential (Harré 2002) brought about through narrativization. In light of the idea of human–thing codependence—the making of narratives charged with responsibility of turning things into social objects (Harré 2002)—may be understood as constituted not prior to but rather during a performative engagement with material environment. In this sense, some aspects of this codependence may be nurturing and mutually enabling, whereby objects and humans shape one another (Chapter 19).

The popular life of things is the expression of the necessity to see the connection between the social and aesthetic aspects of cultural production. It proves that the valence of things is not the effect of cultural codes imposed from above but rather of the working of environmental conditions and material affordances in which all objects commingle. This volume suggests that the method for reading materiality through the lens of popular culture reflects on how the valences of things arise from the resonance between the external cultural conditions and internal capacities of matter that contribute to the shaping of objects and our entanglement with material reality in *the popular*.

References

Appadurai, Arjun. 1986. "Introduction. Commodities and the Politics of Value." In *The Social Life of Things. Commodities in Cultural Perspective*, edited by Arjun Appadurai, 3–63. Cambridge: Cambridge University Press.

Attfield, Judy. 2000. *Wild Things. The Material Culture of Everyday Life*. Oxford and New York: Berg.

Bourdieu, Pierre. 1984. *Distinction. A Social Critique of the Judgement of Taste*. Cambridge, MA: Harvard University Press.

Coole, Diana, and Samantha Frost. 2010. "Introducing the New Materialisms." In *New Materialism. Ontology, Agency, and Politics*, edited by Diana Coole and Samantha Frost, 1–46. Durham and London: Duke University Press.

Durkheim, Emile. 2014. *The Division of Labor in Society*. New York, London, Sydney, and New Delhi: Free Press.

Featherstone, Mike. 1991. *Consumer Culture and Postmodernism*. London: Sage.

Fiske, John. 1989a. *Reading the Popular*. London: Routledge.

———. 1989b. *Understanding Popular Culture*. London: Routledge.

Graves-Brown, Paul. 2000. "Introduction." In *Matter, Materiality and Modern Culture*, edited by Paul Graves-Brown, 1–9. London and New York: Routledge.

Harré, Rom. 2002. "Material Objects in Social Worlds." *Theory, Culture and Society* 19 (5/6): 23–33.

Hodder, Ian. 2012. *Entangled. An Archeology of the Relationships between Humans and Things*. London and New York: Wiley–Blackwell.

Latour, Bruno. 2000. "When Things Strike Back: A Possible Contribution of 'Science Studies' to the Social Sciences." *British Journal of Sociology* 51 (1): 107–123.

Lefebvre, Henri. 1984. *The Production of Space*. Oxford: Blackwell.

Miller, Daniel. 2005. "Materiality: An Introduction." In *Materiality*, edited by Daniel Miller. Durham, NC: Duke University Press.

Strinati, Dominic. 2014. *An Introduction to Theories of Popular Culture*. London: Routledge.

Volpert, Walter. 1885. "Epilogue." In *Goal Directed Behavior. The Concept of Action in Psychology*, edited by Michael Frese and John Sabini, 357–365. Hillsdale, NJ: Erlbaum.

Williams, Emma, and Alan Costall. 2000. "Taking Things More Seriously. Psychological Theories of Autism and the Material–Social Divide." In *Matter, Materiality and Modern Culture*, edited by Paul Graves-Brown, 97–111. London and New York: Routledge.

Williams, Raymond. 1980. *Culture and Materialism*. London: Verso.

Part I

Theorizing *the Popular* and *the Material*

1 Culture
The 'Popular' and the 'Material'

John Storey

This chapter seeks to problematize the two key concepts of the book, the 'popular' and the 'material.' Both concepts have helped produce two general categories, popular culture and material culture. In the course of my analysis I will try to show some of the complexities and contradictions that can arise if we treat either of these categories as self-evident. I will argue that it is impossible to really understand the texts and practices of what we call 'popular culture' without a critical engagement with the different concepts of popular culture. In order to do this, I will outline five ways in which popular culture has been theorized and show how each theorization carries with it a different understanding of what we are doing when we engage in the study of popular culture. In the second part of the chapter I will approach the concept of *the material* in a slightly different way. Rather than present a critical discussion of the definitional difficulties we might encounter with competing concepts, I will tighten the critical focus to the materiality of popular culture. This will inevitably involve a discussion of what cultural studies means by culture and how this connects to its understanding of *the material*.

Popular Culture

An obvious starting point in any attempt to define popular culture is to say that it is simply culture that is well liked by many people. We could examine sales of books, CDs, and DVDs. We could also examine attendance records at concerts, sporting events, and festivals. We could also scrutinize market research figures on audience preferences for different television programs or genres of cinema. The difficulty with the coming together of culture and popular in this way is that we are required to agree on a figure over which something becomes 'popular culture' and below which it is just 'culture.' Unless we can agree on such a figure, we might find that 'well liked' by many people might include so much as to be virtually useless as a conceptual definition of popular culture. Despite this problem, what is clear is that any definition of popular culture must include a quantitative dimension. The 'popular' of popular culture would seem to demand it. What is also clear, however, is that, on its own, a quantitative index is not enough to provide

14 *John Storey*

an adequate definition of popular culture. Another way of defining popular culture is to suggest that it is what is left over after we have decided what is culture. Popular culture, in this definition, is a residual category, there to accommodate texts and practices that are unable to meet the required standards to qualify as culture. In other words, it is a definition of popular culture as inferior or failed culture. Those who deploy this definition generally insist that the division between popular and 'real' culture is absolutely clear. Moreover, not only is this division clear, it is transhistorical—fixed for all time. This latter point is usually insisted on, especially if the division is dependent on supposed essential textual qualities. But even a little knowledge of cultural history should make us skeptical of such claims. In the UK and U.S., for example, the work of William Shakespeare is now seen as the very epitome of 'real' culture, yet as late as the nineteenth century, before the plays became poetry on the page rather than scripts to be performed on the stage, they were very much a part of popular theatre (Levine 1988). Similarly, since its invention in the late sixteenth century, opera has been both popular and exclusive culture (Storey 2010). Many who challenge the supposed certainties of popular culture as a residual category often do so from a position heavily influenced by the work of the French sociologist Pierre Bourdieu (1984, 2009). Contrary to most definitions, this position argues that there is no 'essential' difference between culture and popular culture; rather, the difference has to be produced and reproduced—'culture' and 'popular culture' are social constructions and social categories. The content of these categories continually changes but it is the categories that matter, not their content. The difference between the two marks and maintains a social difference between two types of consumer: elite and nonelite. Bourdieu argues that cultural distinctions of this kind are often used to support class distinctions. Taste is a deeply ideological category: it functions as a marker of 'class' (using the term in a double sense to mean both a social economic category and the suggestion of a particular level of quality). The function of the division between culture and popular culture (based on this argument) is to make, mark, and maintain social difference—what Bourdieu calls "social distinction." As he explains, the division is, ultimately "predisposed [...] to fulfil[l] a social function of legitimating social difference" (2009, 503). In other words, the division is always part of an attempt to mark differences between people. Therefore, if something becomes too popular it ceases to have what Bourdieu calls its "cultural capital"; lacking 'cultural capital' it loses its ability to produce 'social distinction.' When this happens, elite groups will reject it, as consuming it no longer marks them out as different (i.e., the perception of themselves as superior). Therefore, the general point of this perspective is that, 'culture' and 'popular culture' are empty categories; the content of these categories can and does change, but the distinction between them must be maintained, must be policed in the interests of social exclusivity. The first really sustained and detailed intellectual linking of popular and culture was developed in Europe in the late eighteenth century as a result of a growing interest in the culture of the so-called 'folk' (Storey 2003, 2016). In the late eighteenth century and throughout the nineteenth century and into the early part of the twentieth century, different groups of intellectuals, working under the different banners of nationalism, Romanticism, folklore, and, finally, folksong, 'invented' the first 'intellectual' concept of popular culture. For these groups, popular culture is culture that originates from 'the people' (i.e., the 'folk'). This produces a definition of popular culture as something that spontaneously emerges from 'below'—something communal and self-made. According to this definition, the term 'popular culture' should be used only to indicate an 'authentic' culture of the people. One problem with this approach is the question of who qualifies for inclusion in the category 'the people.' The intellectuals involved in the 'discovery' of the folk distinguished between two versions of the people—the 'rural folk' and the 'urban masses'—and only the 'folk' were producers of popular culture. Another problem with this definition is that it evades any significant discussion of the commercial nature of many of the resources from which popular culture as folk culture is produced. For example, many of the folksongs collected were later discovered to be versions of once popular 'commercial' songs.

The 'discovery of the folk' not only produced a concept of popular culture as folk culture, but it also helped to establish the intellectual tradition of seeing the urban working class as masses consuming mass culture. This is because the 'discovery' of the rural folk was accompanied, and no doubt driven, by the 'discovery' of the urban masses. If the folk represented a disappearing 'positive' popular, the new urban masses represented an emerging 'negative' popular. As Cecil Sharp, one of the leading figures in the English 'folksong' movement, made clear in 1907,

> [f]lood the streets [...] with folk-tunes, and those, who now vulgarise themselves and others by singing coarse music-hall songs, will soon drop them in favour of the equally attractive but far better tunes of the folk. This will make the streets a pleasanter place for those who have sensitive ears, and will do incalculable good in civilising the masses. (quoted in Storey 2003, 12)

Sharp is clearly working with two versions of the people (rural folk and urban masses) and two versions of popular culture (folk and mass). This way of thinking, premised on the idea that the rural folk were being replaced by the urban masses, gradually produces a concept of popular culture as commercial culture, mass-produced for mass consumption, with an audience of nondiscriminating consumers. The culture itself is seen as formulaic and manipulative (to the political right or left, depending on who is doing the analysis). It is a culture that is consumed with brain-numbed and brain-numbing passivity. But as John Fiske (1989) points out, "between 80 and 90 per cent of new products fail despite extensive advertising [...]

16   *John Storey*

many films fail to recover even their promotional costs at the box office" (31). Simon Frith (1983, 147) also points out that about 80 percent of singles and albums lose money. Such statistics should clearly call into question the notion of consumption as an automatic and passive activity and, in so doing, undermine one of the key claims of this definition.

Finally, analysis informed by Antonio Gramsci's concept of hegemony (1971, 2009) tends to see popular culture as a terrain of ideological struggle between dominant and subordinate classes. Popular culture in this usage is not the imposed culture of the mass culture theorists, nor is it an emerging from below, spontaneously oppositional culture of 'the people.' It is a terrain of exchange and negotiation between the two: a site of struggle between the 'resistance' of subordinate groups and the forces of 'incorporation' operating in the interests of dominant groups—in other words, a terrain of the production and reproduction of hegemony. The texts and practices of popular culture move within what Gramsci calls a "compromise equilibrium" (2009, 76)—a balance that is mostly weighted in the interests of the powerful. For example, the music of the counterculture helped mobilize people against America's war in Vietnam, but the profits from the music could be used to support the war. This contradiction is captured in Keith Richards's discovery of the actions of his record label:

> We found out, and it wasn't for years that we did, that all the bread we made for Decca was going into making black boxes that go into American Air Force bombers to bomb fucking North Vietnam. They took the bread we made for them and put it into the radar section of their business. When we found that out, it blew our minds. That was it. Goddamn, you find out you've help kill God knows how many thousands of people without even knowing it. (quoted in Storey 2010, 28–29)

The music worked like 'folk culture' in that it articulated an oppositional, communal politics, but it also worked like 'mass culture' in that it made profits for a capitalist culture industry that could use the money to undermine the very politics promoted by the music.

So far, I have discussed popular culture as a concept, but what each of these different formulations has in common is that they all depend on materiality. In other words, however we define popular culture, we are defining a social practice that entangles meaning and materiality. Thinking this idea critically will be the focus of the next section.

Materiality

Popular culture always takes material form. Even a few random examples should make this point: mobile phones, clothes, greetings cards, toys, bicycles, CDs (discs and players), DVDs (discs and players), cars, game consoles, televisions, radios, sporting equipment, computers, computer tablets (including the iPad), magazines, books, cinemas, football grounds, nightclubs, and pubs. Youth subcultures are an obvious example of the visibility of materiality in popular culture. How we know a youth subculture is always through the materiality of what it consumes. There is always a drug of choice, a particular dress code, social spaces that are occupied, a particular music providing an aural landscape. It is the combination of these different forms of materiality that makes a youth subculture visible to the wider society. But this is not just the case with youth subcultures; most people's lives are filled with material objects. We interact with material objects in many ways: we produce and consume them, we exchange them, we talk about them and admire them, and we use them to say things about ourselves. I type these words on my computer and you read them in the book you hold in your hands. These different forms of materiality have enabled our communication. If I know you, I might send you an e-mail from my laptop and you might respond with a text message from your mobile phone. We may then travel by bus, train, or taxi to a pub and have a few bottles of beer or share a bottle or two of wine. In these different ways our encounter is enabled and constrained by the materiality that surrounds us.

Sometimes the material capacities of an object are such that they transform what we do. The car is an obvious example. It has helped bring about a fundamental change in the popular culture of shopping—not only how we shop, but also who shops. It has reshaped both the social practice of shopping and the built materiality of the shopping areas of towns and cities. Without the widespread use of the car, it is very difficult to imagine the success of the out-of-town shopping center, which always has as much space for cars as there is for shops and shoppers. Another obvious example is the mobile phone, which has changed many aspects of everyday life. For example, it is now impossible to walk down the street of any town or city and not see people using mobile phones to talk, text, take photographs, or listen to music. Text messaging has also significantly changed the development of romantic relationships (see Storey 2014). The mobile phone's camera has 'democratized' the self-portrait—making possible the so-called 'selfie.'

Material objects surround us and we interact with them and use them to interact with others. They accompany us through the shifting narratives of our lives, becoming the material of our emotions and our thoughts. But they always do this from within a particular regime of realized signification (Williams 1980, Storey 2014). Popular culture is never just the materiality of things; it is always a simultaneous entanglement of meaning, materiality and social practice. This admixture can take various forms: a text message written on an iPhone, musical sounds produced by the human body, graffiti painted on a wall, a toy loved by a child. When Roland Barthes writes about other similar examples, he says that what they have in common is that they are signs (1995, 157). "When I walk through the streets—or through life— and encounter these objects, I apply to all of them, if need without realizing

18 *John Storey*

it, one and the same activity, which is that of a certain reading" (157). In other words, the material objects Barthes encounters are also signs to be read. They have materiality, but they also have meanings. Cultural studies shares with Barthes the insistence that "[a]ll objects which belong to a society have a meaning" (182); that is, they have been transformed by the fact that "humanity gives meaning to things" (179). In this way, then, the material objects that surround us do not issue their own meanings; they have to be made to mean, and how they are made to signify informs how we think about them, value them, and use them.

Although material objects are always more than signs, more than symbolic representations of social relations, what they are for us is inconceivable outside a particular culture that entangles meaning, materiality, and social practice. They are never things in themselves, but always objects that are articulated in relation to a particular regime of realized signification, enabling and constraining particular types of social practice. A mobile phone, a dress, a football, a wooden table, a CD, an ad in a magazine—what they all have in common is materiality and meaning produced by social practice. It is this combination that makes them examples of culture. Culture is not therefore something we 'have'; rather, it is something we 'do'—the social production and reproduction of meanings realized in materiality and social practice. Meanings are not in the materiality of things, but rather in how things are constructed as meaningful in social practices of representation. The world and its contents have to be made to signify; this is not a denial of the reality of material things but it is an insistence that such things are mute until made to signify in social practices of representation. This claim is sometimes misunderstood (often deliberately and mischievously) as a denial of the materiality of things. But to be absolutely clear, the material properties of an object are not culturally constructed; what is constructed is its inscription and location in culture. Materiality is mute and outside culture until it is made to signify by human action. However, saying materiality is mute is not the same as saying it does not exist, nor is it the same as saying that it does not enable and constrain how it might be made to signify. In other words, culture is a social practice that entangles meaning with materiality.

It is sometimes claimed that cultural studies reduces material objects to a simple matter of meanings. The opposite is in fact true: the material object is not reduced; it is expanded to include what it means in human culture. Cultural studies has always been interested in the use of things, and this interest has always involved a consideration of their materiality. For example, if I pass a business card to someone in China, the polite way to do it is with two hands. If I pass it with one hand, I may cause offence. This is clearly a matter of culture. However, the culture is not simply in the social act, in the materiality of the card, or in the meaning of the card and act—it is in the entanglement of meaning, materiality, and social practice. Moreover, the passing and/or receiving of a business card in China is not simply a symbolic

Culture 19

performance in which meaning is represented; rather, it is a performative event in which meaning is enacted and realized.

Material objects have to be realized as meaningful by social practice. It is this process—human acts of making things mean—that transforms them into cultural objects. In other words, they have to be culturally constructed. But as I said earlier, what is meant by cultural construction is often misunderstood. To be absolutely clear, it does not mean the making real of something. For example, nature is a cultural construct, but this does not mean that culture brings into actual being the things we call trees, rivers, and mountains. What we refer to as trees, rivers, and mountains have a real material existence outside of how they are constructed culturally. They are not cultural constructions in the sense that they only exist once framed within culture. Before its encounter with human culture, the tree did not exist as a tree, but it did exist as a living organism. What was culturally constructed was not this living organism, but rather its conceptualization as a tree. Over the years this conceptualization has grown deeper and richer as a result of, for example, the discourses of artists, novelists, botanists, and poets. Cultural construction, therefore, does not mean the bringing into being of a material object; rather, it points to how material objects are made meaningful and understood as meaningful in the particular regimes of realized signification we call culture. The material world is always framed by culture (this determines our experience of it, our understanding of it, and the questions we ask when we encounter it—in this sense, it is a cultural construct), but the ontology of the material world is not in doubt (this is not a cultural construct).

I live near a woods and it is a magical place to walk and daydream. But I do not think this magic is something intrinsic to the trees themselves. I have no doubt that their type, size, and shape enable and constrain this magic, but I do not think they produce it. In my view the magic is a result of the entanglement of trees with human culture. The magic depends on the existence of the woods, but it is only really made to happen because of how woods in general have been made to signify, how they have been realized in signification—fairy tales, children's adventure stories, gothic horror, historical romance, etc. Although they exist outside culture, woods are cultural constructs. However, what is constructed is not the trees themselves, but rather what the trees signify. This means that, when we go into a wood, we encounter it as already entangled with meaning—even the simple idea that a wood is a good place to relax is a cultural construct. So when we say something is a cultural construct, we are not saying that culture brought it into being—we are saying that there is nothing natural about what it means and how it is understood as meaningful; this is always the result of the work of a particular culture: realized signification. However, to repeat, material reality is not an effect of signification; it can exist perfectly well without being made to mean and being understood as meaningful, but for us it always exists realized in signification, and it is this entanglement of

20   *John Storey*

signification and materiality enabled by a social practice that cultural studies calls culture.

To describe the moon as a cultural construct might sound slightly ridiculous. Surely it is a natural satellite in synchronous rotation with the earth? Yes, it is, but from the beginning of human history people have looked up at the moon and inscribed meaning on it, and in this way it has also become a cultural object represented in, for example, songs, poetry, stories, paintings, mythologies. It is this ascription of signification that has culturally constructed the moon as an entanglement of meaning and materiality. But these representations, these modes of signification, did not construct the moon's material existence, an existence that predates human beings by more than four billion years. Similarly, the universe as the *universe* is a cultural construct. It is human culture that gives it meaning as *the universe*. However, this is not to deny that what we call the universe has an existence outside signification. In other words, what we call the universe exists prior to its realization in signification, but it does not exist as *the universe*. (i.e., as an aspect of human culture). When thinking critically about a material object, we have to distinguish between its undeniable materiality and its variable meanings. Moreover, to focus our critical gaze on its variable meanings does not in any way deny its undeniable materiality. This is not to conflate culture with the material reality of the world. The materiality of the moon can exist just fine without human culture. To describe the moon as a cultural construct is not to claim that it is culture that brought it into being. Rather, the claim that what the moon signifies and how this signification helps organize our relations with the moon is always a matter of culture. The moon is real enough, but for us its reality is entangled with signification and this signification frames out interactions with the moon. Once it is caught in the human gaze, it becomes a cultural object—a significant object in human culture. It existed perfectly well before this moment, but it is only with this moment that it begins to exist as a part of human culture.

Those working in material culture studies often accuse cultural studies of ignoring the materiality of things to focus instead on their meanings. Contrary to cultural studies, they seem to think that objects exist in the world as meaningful before they are made meaningful by human practice. Material culture studies seem to take for granted the material object as only ever a thing in itself. What is missing from this analysis is the recognition that the material object always exists for us in terms of how it has been realized in culture and that realization always involves signification. The human making of meaning is presented by material culture studies as a secondary process that always occurs after a natural meaning has been constituted. But there are no natural meanings, only meanings produced by human practice. Meaning is not found waiting to be discovered; it is a human production.

Paul Graves-Brown, in what I take to be a misplaced critique of cultural studies, makes this claim, "If meaning is only ever 'read into' things, there can be no common basis for understanding" (2000, 4). He seems to assume that our common basis for understanding is produced by the materiality of things—they produce their own meanings. But materiality is always mute until made to signify in a particular social practice. Therefore, any common basis for understanding cannot emerge from muteness; it can only emerge through a shared regime of realized signification within which the material object is situated and made meaningful. In other words, our common basis for understanding derives from the regime of realized signification in which the object and we exist. Moreover, regimes of realized signification are always structured by power. But these meanings, meanings that organize and regulate social practice, do not come from the materiality of things; rather, they come from those with the power to make things mean in particular ways. Material culture studies seem to think that things just signify in themselves or that signification is just not that important. Both positions are very unhelpful if we are trying to understand the relations between culture and power.

In Daniel Miller's little manifesto for material culture studies (Miller 2010), he uses "The Emperor's New Clothes" as a means to demonstrate why semiotics (which seems to be code for cultural studies) is incapable of really understanding materiality. First published in 1837, "The Emperor's New Clothes" is a story by Danish writer Hans Christian Andersen, in which two swindlers present themselves as master weavers and promise to make the emperor a beautiful set of clothes that will be "invisible to anyone who was unfit for his office, or who was unusually stupid." Of course it quickly becomes clear that the clothes do not exist. People therefore have a choice: either acknowledge the emperor's nakedness or pretend he is wearing beautiful clothes. Out of fear of seeming unfit for office, the emperor and the court officials admire the beautiful clothes. Not wishing to seem stupid, the town's people choose the same option. It is only the little boy who shouts out that the emperor is in fact naked.

According to Miller, semiotics believes that clothes represent "a real or true self which lies deep within us" (2010, 13). Semiotics supposedly sees clothing "as the surface that represents, or fails to represent, the inner core of true being" (13). Heroically challenging the idea of an inner self, Miller concludes that the real meaning of the story is this: "But what was revealed by the absence of clothes was not the Emperor's inner self but his outward conceit" (13). Therefore, what we have is "a morality tale of pretentiousness and vanity" (13).

I am not sure which semioticians actually believe in an inner self that is represented by clothes, but I think it is possible, from the perspective of cultural studies, to produce a very different reading of Andersen's story.

With the exception of the little boy's recognition of the emperor, the court officials, and the townspeople are all trapped in the 'common sense' of a realized signifying system in which the emperor's position of power is simply taken for granted. However, to recognize that he is naked (as a result of his own stupidity) is to threaten the legitimacy of this power. As Karl Marx observed, "One man is king only because other men stand in the relation of

22   *John Storey*

subjects to him. They, on the contrary, imagine that they are subjects because he is king" (1976, 149). The emperor's absence of clothes threatens to break this relationship and end the misrecognition that sees being an emperor as a gift of nature and royal subjecthood as a natural consequence of this gift. What is revealed is the fact that the emperor really is naked, in that there is no natural substance to his authority to command. As Slavoj Žižek explains,

> 'Being-a-king' is an effect of the network of social relations between a 'king' and his 'subjects'; but—and here is the fetishistic misrecognition—to the participants of this social bond, the relationship appears necessarily in an inverse form: they think that they are subjects giving the king royal treatment because the king is already himself outside the relationship to his subjects, a king; as if the determination of 'being-a-king' were a 'natural' property of the person of a king. (1989, 20)

In other words, the emperor's nakedness threatens this misrecognition. Clothing, here and elsewhere, is cultural not because it represents an inner self (whatever this might be) but rather because it is part of how the self is produced and reproduced. In order to understand this we have to pay attention not just to meanings or materiality, but also to how meanings and materiality are entangled together by social practice. Moreover, to focus only on materiality or only on meanings would blind us to the many ways the entanglement is structured by relations of power.

Miller argues that "in material culture we are concerned [...] with how things make people" (2010, 42). Although I would not disagree—"clothes maketh the man"—this making is always, and fundamentally, inseparable from realized signification and social practice. We have seen this already in the case of the emperor. In other words, using an object is always entangled with the meaning of the object. But Miller remains quite adamant that "we cannot regard clothing as a form of representation, a semiotic sign or symbol of the person" (40). While it is true that we cannot regard clothing as *just* a form of representation, a semiotic sign or symbol of the person, it is also always true that clothing *is* a form of representation, a semiotic sign, a symbol of the person. It is never a question of either one or the other; it is always both. Again, we have to recognize the entanglement of meaning, materiality, and social practice. Miller's dress code as a student is a clear example of the need to fully recognize this entanglement. He provides the example of what he was routinely wearing when he met his wife at Cambridge University: "[w]hen I met my wife as fellow students, my trousers were held up at the top with string and their hem at the base with staples" (14). Miller's mode of dress at Cambridge means something quite specific. It is a visible identification with the rather conservative and middle class idea that intellectuals are too concerned with matters of the intellect to be bothered about what they wear. To dress in this way is not a sign of casual neglect; it is a sign of a very studied disrepair—identification with a very old image of the serious student as would-be intellectual. But this dress code can also be found in less privileged places. It is not difficult to find in any city men who dress in a way similar to how Miller dressed at Cambridge—but here we will find not studied disrepair but rather an increasing inability, through lack of alternatives and the imperatives of drugs and alcohol, to pay attention to how one looks. In both cases the dress code seems the same, but in each example the cultural significance, the entanglement of materiality, meaning, and social practice is literally worlds apart—the same dress code but very different meanings. If we pay attention only to the materiality of the clothes, we would not be able to understand the difference between the privileged culture of a Cambridge student and the often inescapable hopelessness of being what George Orwell called "down and out" (2001). To pay attention to only the materiality of the clothes, without locating their materiality in a particular realized regime of signification, would produce a very impoverished understanding. Moreover, by paying attention to the entanglement of materiality, meaning, and social practice, we are at the start of an analysis that can expand from dress code to wider questions of why students dress the way they do and why the fourth richest country in the world should have people sleeping rough on its streets.

It is, therefore, only partly true to say that "[c]ulture comes above all from stuff" (Miller 2010, 54). When culture does come from stuff it is always stuff entangled in meaning and social practice. Material culture studies' endless descriptions of the materiality of stuff are always accompanied by the claim that addressing questions of meaning is superficial. The irony here, of course, is that all the interesting things it has to say about materiality are always about its meaning. For example, in an attempt to explain why, in so many rooms allocated to au pairs, the furniture of choice is white melamine IKEA furniture, Miller moves quickly away from mute materiality to matters of meaning:

> Just like the au pair herself, white melamine from IKEA is generally seen as inexpensive; generically European in a young, modern poise, characterized by cleanliness, functionality and efficiency. Hopefully reasonably long-lasting, and quite easy to replace. (90)

Regardless of what we might think of this analysis, it is dependent on a series of assumptions about what white melamine IKEA furniture signifies. Put simply, it is an analysis of the au pair's room that depends on the entanglement of materiality, meaning, and social practice.

Conclusion

Writing from the perspective of cultural studies, what I hope I have demonstrated is two things: first, that popular culture is not a self-evident category and any analysis of popular culture must first begin with the concept itself and, second, that, while attention to materiality is absolutely vital to serious

24   John Storey

cultural analysis, it has to begin with a full recognition that it is mute until articulated by culture. Things may exist without needing to be made to signify, but as things in human culture they are always a part of a realized signifying system. Culture is about making the world signify. It matters because signification helps organize and regulate social practice. Such a concept of culture does not deny the existence of the materiality of things, but it does insist that this materiality is mute, it does not issue its own meanings, and it is therefore always made meaningful by human agency entangled in relations of power. Although how something is made meaningful is always enabled and constrained by the materiality of the thing itself, culture is not a property of mere materiality; it is the entanglement of meaning, materiality, and social practice—variable meanings in a range of different contexts and social practices. In other words, culture is never merely mute materiality; it is always social, material, and semiotic.

References

Barthes, Roland. 1995. *The Semiotic Challenge*. Berkeley: University of California Press.

Bourdieu, Pierre. 1984. *Distinction: A Social Critique of the Judgment of Taste*. London: Routledge.

———. 2009. "Distinction and the Aristocracy of Culture." In *Cultural Theory and Popular Culture: A Reader*, edited by John Storey, 498–507. London: Routledge.

Fiske, John. 1989. *Understanding Popular Culture*. London: Unwin Hyman.

Frith, Simon. 1983. *Sound Effects: Youth, Leisure and the Politics of Rock*. London: Constable.

Gramsci, Antonio. 1971. *Selections from Prison Notebooks*. London: Lawrence & Wishart.

———. 2009. "Hegemony, Intellectuals, and the State." In *Cultural Theory and Popular Culture: A Reader*, edited by John Storey, 75–80. London: Routledge.

Graves-Brown, Paul. 2000. *Matter, Materiality and Modern Culture*. London: Routledge.

Levine, Lawrence. 1988. *Highbrow/Lowbrow: The Emergence of Cultural Hierarchy in America*. Cambridge, MA: Harvard University Press.

Marx, Karl. 1976. *Capital*. Vol. 1. Harmondsworth, England: Penguin.

Miller, Daniel. 2010. *Stuff*. Cambridge, England: Polity.

Orwell, George. 2001. *Down and Out in Paris and London*. Harmondsworth, England: Penguin.

Storey, John. 2003. *Inventing Popular Culture: From Folklore to Globalisation*. Malden, MA: Blackwell.

———. 2010. *Culture and Power in Cultural Studies: The Politics of Signification*. Edinburgh: Edinburgh University Press.

———. 2014. *From Popular Culture to Everyday Life*. London: Routledge.

———. 2016. "Class and the Invention of Tradition: The Cases of Christmas, Football, and Folksong." In *The Making of English Popular Culture*, edited by John Storey, 197–212. London: Routledge.

Williams, Raymond. 1980. *Culture and Materialism*. London: Verso.

Žižek, Slavoj. 1989. *The Sublime Object of Ideology*. London: Verso.

2 Cultural Materialisms and Popular Processes of Late Modernity

Anna Malinowska

Studies in materiality are at a moment of a conceptual shift from a cultural to speculative paradigm. This shift developed from conflicts over the agency of things—a standpoint that the speculative materialism proclaims and the cultural method defies—which has opened space for the revision of approaches to material culture as well as for new methodological frames to conceptualize materiality in modern contexts. This chapter offers a method in the study of materiality that draws on cultural materialisms (mainly the culturalist and anthropological ones) and combines their research tools to speak of popular culture as a lens for analyzing material reality. It uses the culturalist idea of field (popular culture) and discusses it in terms of cultural infrastructure to show that most of our material experience is an effect of the working of processes, specific for each cultural domain. My thinking of popular culture in terms of processes was inspired by studies in modernization (Fornäs, Giddens, Beck, Lash), which describe contemporary cultural conditions with respect to procedures (rather than effects). Following this approach, this chapter distinguishes and theoretically systematizes processes typical for popular culture and studies them in relation to 'the life of things.' The temporal frame of my analysis is late modernity with a focus on the latest experience of popular and material cultures. A binding notion for the study of both is popular materialism—a concept I coin to reflect on the plurality of the materialist approach. It helps consolidate the popular method and outline a wider perspective for defining materiality in culture today.

Popular Materialism

According to Daniel Miller, the study of matter requires an insight into "the diversity of material domains" (1998, 5ff). He claims that "the generality of materiality" provides too little information about "the material quality of artefacts, commodities, aesthetic forms and so forth" and must be supported with a more local, specific perspective (i.e., "complemented by another strategy that looks to the specificity of material domains and the way form itself is employed to become the fabric of cultural worlds" (5ff). Popular culture is a domain where matter begets material variety that is specific in comparison to other cultural domains. As such, it is a specific materiality of objects and

26 *Anna Malinowska*

a form of materialism that respectively regulate and explain functionality of things in culture.

The material significance of popular culture is measured by ways this culture integrates objects in aesthetic interaction. This interaction is rather intense since, as Storey observes, "a great deal of popular culture takes material form" (2015, 225). Material objects populate every aspect of what we define as popular culture; they permeate daily routines, mass entertainment, leisure, mainstream art, and economic and political structures. Things are a fundamental part of the popular décor and popular system of life. In this way, popular culture accommodates the majority of our experiences with things and is a main source of knowledge on material reality. Also, it preconditions most of how we see matter and deal with it in our customary and subversive, direct and secondary, active and receptive interplays.

The accumulation of things in *the popular* results from its nature. Hebdige (1988) defines it as "a set of generally available artefacts, films, records, clothes, TV programmes, modes of transport etc." (after Strinati 2014, xiv). Moore rehearses a term, 'material popular culture,' in a curatorial context when talking about *the popular* as a source of "spurious masterpieces" and "spurious artefacts" (2000, 3–4ff). Also, Linda S. Katz refers to popular culture as "specific types of *materials*" (1992, 2; italics mine) that people produce, explore, collect, and recycle along or against their formal (natural) affordances. In comparison to other cultural uses of materiality—which are either minimalist, selective, or overly metaphorical—popular culture offers a vast and usually highly approachable array of material interactions. Unlike other areas of culture, it does not alienate objects in symbolized representations but metaphorizes them for a number of possible readings. These readings are usually integral to objects' affordances and do not depart from their developmental trajectory but rather extend their material potential. This feature of popular culture is known as *polysemy* and stands for the ability to grant objects a multitude of meanings that open them to a multitude of possible interpretations. For example, a ring in a fantasy story (like in *The Lord of the Rings* by J. R. R. Tolkien) is a different kind of ring from the one in a jewelry shop. Even if it may essentially be exactly the same object, its nature and functionality change with context. In a fantastic narrative, a ring may be an independent artifact with an agency spreading over a story world as a prop in charge of its own usability. In a jewelry store, a ring is a commodity that renders a number of 'cultural facts' such as conditions of the metals market, corporate or individual entrepreneurship, artistry of crafts, social trends, and fashion styles—let alone the entire social symbolism of class, prosperity, or love and relationships. All these 'values' may spread on other cultural denominations and undergo further, often subversive placement to extend the popular symbolism (e.g., pride rings in homosexual minorities). None of them, however, changes the integrity of the ring as a round metal object.

Following Miller's domain-oriented thinking of materiality, I propose the term *popular materialism* to distinguish popular culture from other cultural

Cultural Materialisms and Popular Processes of Late Modernity 27

materialisms and claim it as separate but one of many spheres of material activity. I link *popular materialism* with the development of specific aesthetics affordances of objects, and define it as a set of processes behind the formation of 'cultural infrastructure' we identify as essentially popular. Fundamental parts of this infrastructure are popular processes which allow for the study of things and their cultural lives as shaped by popular culture and in relation to other cultural domains. By no means, however, does popular materialism, detach itself from other materialisms that have so far theorized cultural-material relations (e.g., historical materialism). Rather, it focalizes the theoretical debate on a given cultural context. In this way, popular materialism shares the materialist concentration on "a processually holistic and globally comparative scientific research [...]," which is "concerned with diachronic and synchronic, long term and short term, emic and etic, and behavioral and semiotic phenomena [...]" that "prioritize material, behavioral, and etic conditions and processes in the explanation of divergent, and parallel evolution of human sociocultural systems" (Harris 1999, 141)—but in relation to popular culture.

The Infrastructure of Things in Late Modernity

Popular materialism relies on "the principle of infrastructural determinism" also defined as the "primacy of infrastructure" (Harris 1999, 141). Like other materialist methods, it prioritizes the role of production and reproduction for shaping human condition in cultural structures (see Harris 1999, 144) and points to the importance of cultural processes for the establishment and functioning of sociocultural systems. The principle of infrastructural determinism comes from anthropological thinking proposed by Marvin Harris (1979), who distinguished between three layers of social organization: structure, infrastructure, and superstructure. As defined by Harris, these layers refer respectively to local, external, and symbolic patterns of social systems, and they represent: "demographic, economic, technological and environmental variables (infrastructure), "domestic patterns, political organization, and economic relations" (structure), and "values, aesthetics, rules, beliefs, symbols, rituals, religions, philosophies and sciences" (superstructure) (1999, 141; Ferguson 1995, 23). Infrastructure is the leading sphere of cultural organization with impact on the overall development of the sociocultural system (Ferguson 1995, 23). In other words, social, technological, and economic processes determine experiences of given societies and what the societies have become during their structural and superstructural evolvement.

I am adopting Harris's notion of infrastructure for the study of popular materialism as it allows for concentrating on processes rather than effects of human–material experiences. I, however, broaden his definition of infrastructure, understood as a separate and dominating layer of culture, and propose a more democratic approach in which all the layers form one

28 *Anna Malinowska*

organizing system that I will collectively refer to as 'infrastructure.' This modification is dictated by methodological choices of popular materialism that, although based on an anthropological method, stem from culturalism and its reliance on the idea of field. The rule of infrastructural primacy can be true for analyzing popular culture only when, by infrastructure, we mean the convergence of all cultural elements with a special role given to the superstructural sphere. As an aesthetic domain of social consequences, popular culture relates to a sociocultural system mainly on the aesthetic level. Therefore, popular materialism accommodates the notion of infrastructure in aesthetic terms—that is, only if aesthetic codes, narrative patterns, representations, etc. are considered of an equal value to 'solid' technologies in the formation of broader cultural processes as well as those specifically connected with popular culture.

The infrastructural thinking about the role of cultural processes for the study of popular material reality derives from the framework of postmodernity studies (Giddens 1991; Beck 1992; Fornäs 1995). Theories that represent this framework offer a set of diagnoses on the structure and progress of contemporary advanced societies as triggered by *modernization*—that is, the tendencies of change over a given historical period—from the industrial era onwards—that "shape a specific temporal logic of fundamental transformations in the development of social, cultural and psychological patterns" (Fornäs 1995, 25). Modernizing processes break down into two main types: one called *simple* or *orthodox* modernization, responsible for the shift from the feudal to industrial system, and the other called *reflective modernization* (late modernity)—the one we experience now (Beck, Giddens, and Lash 1994, 2; italics mine).

As a critical notion, *late modernity* marks the continuum of modernizing processes in opposition to the antithetical distinctions into the *modern* and the *postmodern*; late modernity 'sees itself' as another stage—a 'new phase' in modern chronologies—and is regarded "more as a radicalization and an intensification of modernity than as its demise" (Fornäs 1995, 38). This intensity shows in the advancement and rapidness of the change, caused by "irreversible dynamization," "ambivalent rationalization," and "differentiating universalization" (Fornäs 1995, 18–31). These three main powers of modernity conjugate and climax through *globalization*—the source of new patterns for time, space, and identity (individual as global, local as global, and vice versa). This in turn becomes a source of a new late modern awareness and practice. As Giddens explains:

> In all cultures, social practices are routinely altered in the light of ongoing discoveries which feed into them. But only in the era of modernity is the revision of convention radicalized to apply (in principle) to all aspects of human life, *including technological intervention into the material world*. (1991, 38–39; italics mine)

Cultural Materialisms and Popular Processes of Late Modernity 29

As Giddens observes, through the reflexive impact, late modernity becomes an arena of change in a material practice and its environmental contextualization. In other words, late modernity brings a radical transformation of many spheres of human life: daily activities, communication forms, communication tools, and general organization patterns—changing, perhaps forever, the so-far-valid (solid) routines and rhythms of existence (liquid modernity). Most of the transformation takes place in popular culture; late modernity may be defined as a group of given processes responsible for the emergence of a particular cultural infrastructure, part of which is identified as inherently popular, and thus responsible for what I will provisionally call the 'popular material' (the popular quality of things).

Popular Processes

Popular culture accommodates a number of processes that generate a certain type of cultural infrastructure. This infrastructure conditions the changes of materiality as it prepares a background—a cultural habitat—for things to 'live' and interact. Popular processes come in two types and are distinguished by their aesthetic and distributive dispositions. The aesthetic type relates to practices responsible for the emergence of the popular style based on a group of narrative-representational devices, technologies, and strategies we identify as popular art (see 'popular aesthetics' in Kaplan, 1966, or Shusterman, 1992). The distributive type, bred of technological progress, comprises processes that generate the so-called 'deployment modes' (I borrow this term from IT jargon) responsible for the circulation of 'cultural stuff' within or across societies. They are connected with media forms and temporalities of communication today and relate as well to the ever changing norm of social interactions.

Aesthetic Processes

The first type consists of four major processes that exist in the center of popular culture as defining tropes of its aesthetics. I will specify them, moving from those I find most fundamental to those that, although equally important, reflect on more recent, and therefore more specific, tendencies within the popular style.

Customization. The founding quality of popular culture is its appeal, measured by the enthusiasm with which people approach and respond to 'popular outcome.' Culture theorists define *the popular* as something widely appreciated (Williams 1983), which points to a certain kind of attractiveness (on the product level) and to a very particular sort of satisfaction (on the audience level); popular culture must assure in order to work on a large scale. Appreciation in popular culture effectuates from procedures aimed to customize raw cultural forms (objects, representations, facts) into

30 *Anna Malinowska*

aesthetically pleasing and approachable materials. Smith relates this to the market conditions of late capitalism, which shape the public demand and at the same time respond to it (2005, 152). In aesthetic terms, customization is simply the familiarization of cultural content toward a given cultural domain in ways that allow people to identify with the content on many levels. Identification is a central effect of this process as it opens matter for a number of 'practical rereadings' that alter and verify the matter's original functions. Identification sets up a relationship between an object (text, content, etc.) and a user in which the material potential of the latter undergoes far-reaching explorations. Throughout this relationship, objects become rediscovered for new cultural uses as well as establish new contexts for people and their engagement with the material world. Fiske describes such (re)appropriations in terms of "trickery and tenacity" performed on things of everyday use. In his description of shopping malls, he speaks of youths who alter the mall space into subversive playgrounds or pedestrians who use the space for leisurely exploration ("mall walkers"; 1989, 17). Customization may be, therefore, seen as a market-to-object or user-to-object process with agency on the part of the social. Also (but this is missing from Fiske's description), this "trickery and tenacity" may proceed from a thing to 'the social' and express an object's impact on the user and the market respectively (object-to-market customization and object-to-user customization). Fan cultures, which entirely depend on the cultural stuff, are an excellent example of appropriations that work both ways as they operate on the market-to-object-to-user trajectory that, in the course of fan practices, transforms into an object-to-use-to-market procedure. Fan objects stimulate the development of fans' engagement with artifacts, texts, and representations to dominate the choices behind these appropriations. To reverse Sandvoss's stance, although they "correspond with the fundamental meaning structure through which these [things] are read," [...] fan objects "form a *field of gravity*" (2014, 65) with power to determine the social material practice.

Serialization. According to recent studies on popular culture, serialization is "an endemic feature of our twenty-first-century, hyper mediated world" that "has become much more than a trend in contemporary cultural practice (Lindner 2014, ix). Allen and van den Berg observe that serialization "is not just a production and publication logic but a narrative form that performs important cultural work and has profound aesthetic and ideological consequences" (2014, 3). As a market process, serialization relates to the proliferation of goods that followed the technological turn in the nineteenth century. Ever since, we have been exposed to the multiplication of objects (things, texts, etc.) with intensity exceeding, and drastically transforming, the idea of functionality in ways that never occurred before. The rise of material presence through serialization has generated an impression of the universal availability of things. This, in turn, inspired the utopia of abundance and indispensability—both becoming a sealing power behind the human–object relationship.

Cultural Materialisms and Popular Processes of Late Modernity 31

Aesthetically, serialization renders the accumulation of narrative contents and styles, achieved by means of sequencing and reproduction. Seriality, which is a feature of 'texts' produced in series (the so-called 'serials'), reflects on two conflicting tendencies of popular manufacture (i.e., repetitiveness and modification). Sarah Schaschek contends that, as a derivative of the Latin *series* ('row,' 'chain') and *serere* ('join' or 'combine'), seriality "impl[ies] the paradoxical principle on which all serial works are based; there are always at the same time aspects of repetition and difference, scheme and variation, to the extent that one cannot be separated from the other" (2014, 7). This paradox was first brought to modern awareness by Kierkegaard in the dilemma of repetition and originality. Later criticism theorized it under the notions of copy (Benjamin), simulacrum (Baudrillard), second-time event (Jameson), rediscovery of identity (Freud), and *différance* (Derrida)—all pointing to dubious effects of reproductivity for the material world to suggests that serialized matter is both novelty and reproduction (Jameson 2005, 123; Schaschek 2014, 7; Lindner 2014, x).

In popular culture, repetition connotes the sense of iterability, implying an agreement between duplicity and difference. Popular texts, or popular matter in general, values repetition for its pleasure potential. Consumers of popular culture are characterized by the passion for reliving the same narrative patterns; in every popular text and thing, they seek the same aesthetic elements: objects, contents, contexts, tropes, etc. that would allow for the reexperience of what is familiar yet at the same time distant and unrealistic. In her studies on romantic love (the practice and trope), Eve Illouz remarks that "popular classes tend to identify emotionally and in a participatory mode with cultural products" (1997, 258). At the same time, however, these products must be exotic enough not to spoil the utopia of life they are consumed for. The accumulation of effects and repetition of sensations produced in popular texts—be it a book or a movie—allow objects, practices, activities, etc. that participate in their construction to extend (or complete) their pragmatic function by glamorized contexts or uses. In this way objects transform their usual mundaneness into material glitter.

Recycle and *hybridization.* A constitutive and requisite part of popular culture today is pastiche, which critics define as a main mechanism for the making of popular products and the main power behind their actual popularity (Jameson 1984; McRobbie 1994; Storey 2003). Pastiche is an inherently postmodern form of adaptive processes preoccupied with rearranging and localizing cultural variety through the circulation of different stylizations, patterns, tropes, etc. As such, it is representative of a distinct aesthetic style dubbed "the new sensibility" (Sontag 2013). *Recycle* and *hybridization* are two reverse processes of pastiche aimed at modifying the already existing cultural content and its customization for the popular use. They differ in operational mode, which for *recycle* is 'transformation by processing' and for *hybridization* is 'transformation by combining.' Based on the cross-pollination of aesthetics, they are both a response to globalizing

32 *Anna Malinowska*

tendencies characterized by the dynamic mingle of societies and markets. Aesthetically, they have been seen as a strategy of mass entrainment and the effect of marketizing popular art, enhanced by the influx of inspirations from different cultural contexts (e.g., Bollywood films). In a broader meaning, *recycle* and *hybridization* are part of cultural 'tapestry' woven from practices connoting appropriation, accommodation, negotiation, borrowing, mixing, and second-handedness.

Despite this 'resurrecting potential,' recycle has been critically seen as a sign of cultural depthlessness (Jameson 1984)—a consequence of a creativity crisis in consumerist societies (McRobbie 1994, 142). As early as in MacDonald (1957), Greenberg (1961), or Adorno (1970), we observe a discriminating critique of cultural reproduction, reflected in concepts such as parasitism, homogenization, and aesthetic regression, which have been a source of major stereotypes about the general cultural condition and popular culture itself. Recent diachronic insights into the progression of popular aesthetics, however, have reprehended these views and have conceptualized *recycle* in terms of beneficial retrospections: "re-writing," "re-viewing," "reactivation," "reconfiguration" (Brook and Brook in Storey 2003, 71). These new theories have reestablished *recycle* as a process that adds to the cultural experience rather than impoverishes it. Also the manifestations of recycle-like remix (in music), reboot (in film), or adaptation (all media) have helped verify these old cultural diagnoses; once considered "parasitic, cancerous on the body of High Culture" (MacDonald 1957, 59), popular culture has long been a source of inspiration for 'sophisticated art markets.' Good demonstrations of this reversal are the entire idea of Pop Art, nobilitation of kitsch (e.g., art of Jeff Koons or Pierre&Gilles), or classic adaptations of popular songs (e.g., "Hip-Hop History Orchestrated" by JIMEK). All these examples make hybrid forms conceived from the mixture of styles and aesthetic clashes. They show how local conventions (ones within one integral style or genre) become 'invaded' by external stylizations for the production of new aesthetic forms: texts, things, content. Also, *hybridization* shows many pragmatic uses visible in quasi-artistic or nonartistic objects or practices. Architecture is a source of many hybrid artifacts (Bruke 2009); cuisine is an arena where cultural experiences mingle and hybridize (e.g., chopstick forks or Asian fast food). In other examples, the mobile phone is a hybrid of various technologies and items (telephone, camera, voice recorder, calculator, organizer, music player, computer, and what not). All of them have impacted our perception of things and provided new notions of functionality for everyday life and the material world.

Distributive Processes

This other type of popular process specifies operational and communication mechanisms behind contemporary social relations and the general organization of life. Although all of them reflect to all spheres of cultural activity,

Cultural Materialisms and Popular Processes of Late Modernity 33

I discuss them in relation to *the popular*, where they often originate or acquire their full form.

Mediatization. As defined by Johan Fornäs, mediatization "refers to the process whereby media increasingly come to saturate society, culture, identities and everyday life" (1995, 1). It is connected with the growing presence, variety, and importance of media forms (television, print, radio, telecom, and Internet), as well as "social changes" affecting "almost all areas of social and cultural life in late modernity" (Lundby 2009, 1). Although mediatization impacts all forms of art, its role for popular culture is rather fundamental due to the inherent connection of the latter with a variety of media forms. Popular culture is, to a large extent, media culture since, to repeat after Fornäs (2014), "mediatization is almost synonymous with popularization" (490).

Mediatization reforms our realities by binding the 'popular life' with its representations in popular media. Since the rise of print, radio, and television, we have been constantly immersed in two, rather incompatible dimensions of living where our experiences have been invariably confronted with and appropriated by the images of life offered in feature films, soap operas, newscasts, commercials, day shows, blog entries, etc. that have paralleled the experiences in time and space. In effect, our interactions with the material world have occurred on two levels: that of the media and that of a real life. Consequently, the authentic matter—real-life houses, real-life belongings, real-life equipment, and real-life relations—have coalesced with their counterparts in equivalent media realities. In other words, mediatization makes us accommodate the material world through the constant exchange between the mediated (virtual, symbolic) and the real (authentic).

Recent digitalization of life complicates this situation by changing the 'substance' of many practices and instances of our daily routines. Activities once regarded as tangible (i.e., ones involving physical marks or presence (conversations, writing, reading, making love) have altered in physical character, impacting the entire procedure or practice their significations have traditionally entailed. The change of manner in many activities (e.g., writing on a computer rather than by hand, dating on Tinder rather than in real life) has begot new forms of tangibility. These forms have been already theorized with respect to commodity fetishism, defined as "the domination of society by 'intangible as well as tangible things' [...]" which come together in a social spectacle "where the tangible world is replaced by a selection of images which exist above it, and which at the same time are recognized as the tangible par excellence" (Debord 1970, 36). The contemporary miens of tangibility and intangibility are, however, much more advanced as they stand for a fetish much more powerful and effective—the one of the media.

Transfer. The concept of cultural transfer developed from translation studies and a focus on the cultural load in world literature. It was introduced in the 1980s by Michel Espagne and Michael Werner (1985) as a model for analyzing aspects and natures of cultural exchange (Stockhorst 2010), but

34 *Anna Malinowska*

it quickly turned into a method for describing larger changes in a growingly global environment. In a broader perspective, transfer is a process that denotes the transmission of cultural content and its transferability into new cultural settings (Malinowska 2014). As a cultural occurrence, transfer entails 'cultural mobility'—a process that Stephen Greenblatt (2010) associates with the increasing transnational and transcultural flow of objects, texts, habits, languages, customs, etc. and the exchange of practices that effectuate from a cultural merge.

Transfer is not a new process, but rather something that has accompanied global social formations since the rise of navigation, railway, print, etc. Its scale moved up during the colonial conquests of the modern era and migration waves at the beginning of the twentieth century. But even then it operated on a macroscale, affecting only given communities, states, nations, or minorities. Now, following rapid technological progress, transfer is a defining process for cultural development whereby the issues of difference and sameness, locality and periferiality, in-rootedness and out-rootedness determine the cultural practice. Effects of transfer imprint in our social reality by reflecting on the origins, identities, and heritages of many practices and things as well as by showing how these practices and things extend beyond their political geographies. Transfer is a 'witness' and record of the trajectories of things on the global move, and it is through the study of transfer that we get an insight into "hidden as well as conspicuous movements of peoples, objects, images, texts, and ideas" as well as "moments in which cultural goods are transferred out of sight, concealed inside cunningly designed shells of the familiar or disguised by subtle adjustments of color and form" (Greenblatt 2010, 250–251). This also relates to "[t]he physical, infrastructural, and institutional conditions" that 'enable' the movement of things in schematized social systems: "the available routes; the maps; the vehicles; the relative speed; the controls and costs; the limits on what can be transported; the authorizations required; the inns, relay stations and transfer points; the travel facilitators [...]" (Greenblatt 2010, 250). Important part of these infrastructures are new communication tools and technologies with the entire new sense of 'physicality' and 'material presence' they beget. Nonlimitedness and far-reachingness are now the new signifiers for time and space, which, as Morley and Robins (2002) observe, are constantly reformulating our geographical thinking as well as imposing new spatial and temporal matrixes of life:

> We are seeing the restructuring of information and image spaces and the production of a new communication geography, characterized by global networks and an international space of information flows; [...] Our senses of space and place are all being significantly reconfigured [...]. Increasingly we must think in terms of communication and transport networks and of the symbolic boundaries

Cultural Materialisms and Popular Processes of Late Modernity 35

of language and culture—the "spaces of transmission" defined by satellite or radio signals—as providing the crucial, and permeable, boundaries of our age. (1)

In these new geographies, cultures are in convergence (i.e., are on a constant exchange via "multiple media platforms") (Jenkins 2006a, 2). The movement of cultural content, now possible due to communication unlimitedness, promotes a search for cultural variety, which is perhaps best seen in "the cooperation of multiple media industries" as well as in "the migratory behavior of media audiences who will go almost anywhere in search of the kind of entertainment experiences they want" (Jenkins 2006a, 2). As Jenkins points out, convergence is not only about a technological change, but about the new "relationship between existing technologies, industries, markets, genres, and audiences" (2006b, 155). The dynamics of this relationship generates specific environments in which culture clash becomes an arena for aesthetic and social negotiation rather than conflict.

Although transfer is the condition spreading on the entire culture, most of its instances take place in *the popular*. In other words, popular culture is where most cultural exchange happens on a large scale as facilitated by social, economic, and aesthetic practices that popular culture monopolizes and controls. The form in which *the popular* accommodates the processes of transfer is pop-cosmopolitanism, understood as "the ways that transcultural flows of popular culture inspires [*sic*] new forms of global consciousness and cultural competency" (Jenkins 2006b, 156). As a concept, pop-cosmopolitanism emerged from an ethnographic insight into some popular content with an interest to provide information on their social and aesthetic genealogies. Although the method confirms the pancultural character of *the popular*, it also challenges the critical premise of its homogeneity. For example, American popular culture, seen as imperial and model to other (local) popular aesthetics (Americanization, McDonaldization), is in fact a (bri)col(l)age of cross-continental influences (Asian, Indian, etc.) that have contributed to the structure of its matrix for decades. As Jenkins remarks, the notion of American popular culture has been a fake construct that developed along economic and political domination of the U.S. (see Jenkins 2006b, 158). Of course, impacts of American popular culture remain constitutive for most international popular practices. A relatively recent example of this impact in the film industry, for instance, is Korean romantic comedy, a genre bringing an inherently Western aesthetics to the Orient setting, including the model of modern courtship, soundtrack, and narrative patterns (e.g., *Seducing Mr. Perfect*, 2006; *2000 Pounds Beauty*, 2006). Those influences, however, happen to be more democratic than we are used to thinking, and less universalizing than we believe. As Arjun Appadurai points out, difference is a dominant category of culture today: not as a substantive but rather a comparative quality in things. Difference

36 *Anna Malinowska*

(not sameness) unveils "the [full] dimensionality of culture" and "permits our thinking of culture less as a property of individuals or group and more as a heuristic device that we can use to talk about difference" (2005, 13) and on the condition of things in new global infrastructures.

Acceleration. In *On Waiting*, Harold Schweizer observes that "[p]ost-modernity is characterized by an ever-accelerating contraction of duration" (2008, 6). What he specifically means is that "we no longer live in linear time but in 'the light of speed'" (Schweizer 2008, 6). "The light of speed" is a concept by Paul Virilio (2005) to name the simulacra of time and our experience of the alternating tempo of life. Acceleration, which is a leading paradigm of culture today, translates the complexity of our 'being in time' with all temporal moods, modes, and effects that this complexity exerts on our private and social functioning.

Contemporary theories of culture speak of acceleration with regard to three main problems: the parallel existence of different temporalities, the impact of the quickening social pace on individual lifestyles, and immediacy as a new temporal system (Tomlinson 2007; Urry 2010; Rosa 2013). Temporal plurality (with its biological, psychological, social, and physical varieties) as confronted with "the tempo of our time" has significantly constrained "the psychological make-up of the individual" (see Rosa 2013, 7). Rosa observes that "[t]he rhythm, speed, duration, and sequence of our activities and practices are almost never determined by us individuals but rather almost always prescribed by the collective temporal patterns and synchronisation requirements of society" (2013, 9). Urry, in turn, debates the validity of any patterns and synchronizations, and claims that, fundamentally relative, time is never relevant to its systems of measure (2010). A kind of consensus emerges from Tomlinson's principle of 'immediacy' that reflects on "ideas of a culture of instantaneity—a culture accustomed to rapid delivery, ubiquitous availability and the instant gratification of desires," based on "a new kind of vibrancy in everyday life" as enhanced by the rapid development and importance of modern media (2007, 74). Although focused on different aspects of modern temporalities, all these perspectives coalesce under a question: "[w]hat does it mean for society to accelerate?" (Rosa and Scheureman 2010, 1). Part of this question relates to the material dimension of time and literally asks about the role and condition of things in cultural acceleration. Whereas it is quite obvious that things are increasingly faster and more efficient these days (transportation, appliance, media), the nature of their contribution to the increase of the tempo of life is rather understated (and perhaps overlooked). It is more than apparent that the performance of things is an effect of human achievements: men make things and make them better (faster, smarter) as they themselves progress in technology and science. But the domination of man over things has radically reconfigured so that the obvious subjugation of objects to man is no longer the case. Our reliance on objects and their performance makes things take over our

Cultural Materialisms and Popular Processes of Late Modernity   37

lives and put them in the position of control. This is exactly what Schweizer means when he refers to Virilio's "light of speed":

> The light of speed is not the speed of light but rather the light that speed emits as, for example, when images flash across a screen. We don't wait for them. Laptops, Blackberries, cell phones, iPhones are to deliver information without making us wait. (2008, 6–7)

The impact of objects on our temporal schemes is manifested in the imposition of the manner of use on the user (i.e., in ways we respond to objects' functions and affordances). Programmed or designed to satisfy a certain operational manner, objects increasingly dictate the manner beyond human control. It is in many instances that we see how objects and their competences reorganize human performance. Acceleration is the process that perhaps best highlights the shift by clearly exposing the reversal of agency and control we have experienced in human–object relations on a constantly enlarging scale. Most of the objects with a direct impact on human velocities are an integral part of the popular practice. When it comes to speed, popular culture seems to operate by a developmental pace that shares the global tendency of fastness. "Take your time to go fast" says the 1980s slogan for the French high-speed train while at the same time defining the general intention of popular culture (Betts 2004, 39). Fastness 'ignites' the internal structures of popular culture (aesthetic temporalities) and its overall evolvement within cultural practice. Acceleration is therefore an inherently popular process, because, as Raymond F. Betts observes,

> Contemporary popular culture is all about movement, about seeing things, about buying and having, about being distracted and entertained. [...] The pace of life has changed dramatically, as has the space in which we now move. We also see more than did the people of previous cultures. Popular culture is about mass-produced images changing their form in seconds, popping up as advertisements on the computer screen, elegantly laid out in photographs in trendy niche publications. (2004, ix)

In the setting of popular culture, things attain certain vibrancy, which is characteristically popular. This vibrancy differs from other cultural vibrancies and confers on things a different temporal dynamic. The speed, spatiality, image or imagery of things in contemporary culture is therefore a matter of their aesthetic contextualization. As I have attempted to show, objects' affordances and qualities are shaped by and, to a large degree, depend on the environment that things actively create, overcoming their designed functionality. The experience of things in popular culture differs from the experience of things outside it. It is an effect of many processes that, often inherently popular, change the life of things. So do they change the lives of their users.

38 Anna Malinowska

References

Adorno, Theodor. 1970. *Ästhetische Theorie*. Frankfurt am Main: Suhrkamp Verlag.
Allen, Rob, and Thijs van den Berg. 2014. "Introduction." In *Serialization in popular Culture*, edited by Rob Allen and Thijs van den Berg, 1–7. London: Routledge.
Appadurai, Arjun. 2005. *Modernity at Large. Cultural Dimensions of Globalization.* Minneapolis: University of Minnesota Press.
Beck, Urlich. 1992. *Risk Society. Towards a New Modernity.* London: Sage.
Beck, Urlich, Anthony Giddens, and Scott Lash. 1994. *Reflexive Modernization. Politics, Tradition and Aesthetics in the Modern Social Order.* Stanford, CA: Stanford University Press.
Betts, Raymond F. 2004. *The History of Popular Culture. More of Everything, Faster, and Brighter.* London and New York: Routledge.
Bruke, Peter. 2009. *Cultural Hybridity.* Cambridge, England: Polity Press.
Debord, Guy. 1970. *Theory of the Spectacle.* Detroit, MI: Black and Red.
Espagne, Michael, and Michael Werner. 1985. "Deutsch-Französischer Kulturtransfer im 18. und 19. Jahrhundert. Zu einem neuen interdisziplinären Forschungsprogramm des C.N.R.S." *Francia* 13: 502–510.
Ferguson, Brian R. 1995. "Infrastructural Determinism." In *Science, Materialism and the Study of Culture*, edited by Martin F. Murphy and Maxine L. Margolis, 21–38. Gainesville: University Press of Florida.
Fiske, John. 1989. *Reading the Popular.* London and New York: Routledge.
Fornäs, Johan. 1995. *Cultural Theory and Late Modernity.* London: Sage.
———. 2014. "Mediatization of Popular Culture." In *Mediatization of Communication* (Handbooks of Communication Science 21), edited by Knut Lundby, 483–504. Berlin and Boston: De Gruyter Mounton.
Giddens, Anthony. 1991. *The Consequences of Modernity.* Cambridge, England: Polity Press.
Greenberg, Clement. 1961. *Art and Culture.* Boston: Beacon Press.
Greenblatt, Stephen. 2010. "Cultural Mobility: An Introduction." In *Cultural Mobility: A Manifesto*, edited by Stephen Greenblatt, 1–23. Cambridge: Cambridge University Press.
Harris, Marvin. 1979. *Cultural Materialism: The Struggle for a Science of Culture.* Walnut Creek, CA: Altamira Press.
———. 1999. *Theories of Culture in Postmodern Times.* Walnut Creek, CA: Altamira Press.
Hebdige, Dick. 1988. *Subculture. The Meaning of Style.* London: Routledge.
Illouz, Eve. 1997. *Consuming the Romantic Utopia. Love and the Cultural Contradictions of Capitalism.* Berkley: University of California Press.
Jameson, Frederic. 1984. "Postmodernism, or the Cultural Logic of Capital." *New Left Review* 146: 53–92.
———. 2005. "Reification and Utopia in Mass Culture." In *Popular Culture. A Reader*, edited by Raiford Guins and Omayra Zaragoza Cruz, 115–128. London: Sage.
Jenkins, Henry. 2006a. *Convergence Culture: Where Old and New Media Collide.* New York: New York University Press.
———. 2006b. *Fans, Bloggers and Gamers: Exploring Participatory Culture.* New York: New York University Press.
Kaplan, Abraham. 1966. "The Aesthetics of Popular Art." *Journal of Aesthetics and Art Criticism* 24: 351–364.

Cultural Materialisms and Popular Processes of Late Modernity   39

Katz, Linda S., ed. 1992. *Popular Culture and Acquisitions*. London and New York: Routledge.

Lindner, Christoph. 2014. "Foreword." In *Serialization in Popular Culture*, edited by Rob Allen and Thijs van den Berg, ix–xi. London: Routledge.

Lundby Knut. 2009. "Introduction: Media as Key." In *Mediatization. Concept, Changes, Consequences*, edited by Knut Lundby, 1–20. New York: Peter Lang.

MacDonald, Dwight. 1957. "A Theory of Mass Culture." In *Mass Culture: The Popular Arts in America*, edited by Bernard Rosenberg and David Manning White, 59–74. New York: Free Press.

Malinowska, Anna. 2014. "Cultural Transplantation and Problems of Transferability." *Word and Text. A Journal of Literary Studies and Linguistics* 6 (2): 24–36.

McRobbie, Angela. 1994. *Postmodernism and Popular Culture*. London: Routledge.

Miller, Daniel. 1998. "Why Some Things Matter." In *Material Cultures. Why Some Things Matter*, edited by Daniel Miller. London: UCL Press.

Moore, Kevin. 2000. *Museums and Popular Culture*. London: Cassell.

Morley, David, and Kevin Robins. 2002. *Spaces of Identity. Global Media, Electronic Landscapes and Cultural Boundaries*. London, New York: Routledge.

Rosa, Hartmut. 2013. *Social Acceleration: A New Theory of Modernity*. New York: Columbia University Press.

Rosa, Hartmut, and William E. Scheuerman. 2010. "Introduction." In *High Speed Society: Social Acceleration, Power, and Modernity*, edited by Hartmut Rosa and William E. Scheuerman, 1–32. University Park: Pennsylvania State University Press.

Sandvoss, Cornel. 2014. "The Death of the Reader? Literary Theory and the Study of Text in Popular Culture." In *The Fan Fiction Studies Reader*, edited by Karen Hellekson and Kristina Busse, 61–74. Iowa City: Iowa University Press.

Schaschek, Sarah. 2014. *Pornography and Seriality: The Culture of Producing Pleasure*. New York: Palgrave McMillan.

Schweizer, Harold. 2008. *On Waiting*. London and New York: Routledge.

Shusterman, Richard. 1992. *Pragmatist Aesthetics: Living Beauty, Rethinking Art*. Oxford: Blackwell.

Smith, Paul. 2005. "Tommy Hilfiger in the Age of Mass Customization." In *Popular Culture. A Reader*, edited by Raiford Guins and Omayra Zaragoza Cruz, 151–158. London: Sage.

Sontag, Susan. 2013. *Against Interpretation and Other Essays*. London: Penguin Books.

Stockhorst, Stephanie. 2010. "Introduction: Cultural Transfer through Translation." In *Cultural Transfer through Translation. The Circulation of Enlightened Thought in Europe by Means of Translation*, edited by Staphanie Stockhorst, 7–28. Amsterdam and New York: Editions Rodopi.

Storey, John. 2003. *Inventing Popular Culture. From Folklore to Globalization*. Oxford: Blackwell.

———. 2015. *Cultural Theory and Popular Culture. An Introduction*. London: Routledge.

Strinati, Dominic. 2014. *An Introduction to Theories of Popular Culture*. London: Routledge.

Tomlinson, John. 2007. *The Culture of Speed. The Coming of Immediacy*. London: Sage.

40 *Anna Malinowska*

Urry, John. 2010. "Speed Up, Speed Down." In *High Speed Society: Social Acceleration, Power, and Modernity*, edited by Hartmut Rosa and William E. Scheuerman, 179–200. University Park: Pennsylvania State University Press.

Virilio, Paul. 2005. *Negative Horizon: An Essay in Dromoscopy*. London: Continuum.

Williams, Raymond. 1983. *Keywords: A Vocabulary of Culture and Society*. New York: Fontana Press.

3 The Secret Life of Things
Speculative Realism and the Autonomous Object

Grzegorz Czemiel

> The object provokes thought without letting itself be thought; we are forced to think precisely because we have come across something that our thought cannot capture or identify, much less recognize.
>
> —Steven Shaviro (2014)

'The secret life of things' may seem a contradictory expression as we are not accustomed to the idea that things have lives. In a traditional view, matter is dead: it does not feel or think nor have any life whatsoever—let alone the secret one which happens beyond human awareness. A recent philosophical movement called Speculative Realism, however, challenges this view and claims that matter does live a full life of its own. In doing so, Speculative Realism revises the entire system of things, including ways we understand the structure of the world (ontology) and the powers of the entities that populate it (agency).

The interest of this chapter is in the animation of the world of things and, specifically, in how it became part of a philosophical movement that aspires to be called a realism. To explain that, the chapter problematizes the notion of realism with another realism-centered revolution—the one by James Joyce. His work can serve as a guide to the transition in the cultural thinking of matter marked by (1) the reworking of the notion of realism, and (2) the radical turn to matter as 'a field' fit for a serious inquiry. It shows how both these perspectives can be crucial for cultural studies, especially for the study of popular culture.

The Ithaca of Speculative Thought

In the penultimate chapter of *Ulysses*—"Ithaca"—James Joyce recasts Odysseus's return to his home island as the final stage of a peregrination that takes Leopold Bloom and Stephen Dedalus to the former's house late at night. They talk, sing, recite poetry, and debate all sorts of issues. Finally, they exit into the garden and contemplate "[t]he heaventree of stars hung with humid nightblue fruit" (Joyce 1998, 651). At that point, the more scientifically minded Bloom allows himself an imaginative flight of thought that combines creative daring with solid facts from natural history. In his

42   Grzegorz Czemiel

mind-bending train of thought all earthly issues are suddenly greatly diminished, while at the same time, Bloom is struck by our inability to grasp reality, which becomes in this light incomprehensible and oddly distant.

Significantly, Bloom realizes that the world we know may not be in fact tailored for us—it is not by design a home. In fact, the universe is rather a Utopia—a nonplace (οὐ-τόπος in Greek)—because it resists our efforts to domesticate it and turn it into a knowable 'place.' All such endeavors, in fact, are futile, because we delude ourselves that we are capable of transforming the unknown into the known. It would be vainglorious to assume that the structure of our knowledge perfectly conforms to the structure of reality.

Apart from intellectual musings, such cosmic spectacles also provoke aesthetic responses. Later in "Ithaca," we learn that, throughout history, the 'poetic' reactions to the said spectacle have oscillated between "the delirium of the frenzy of attachment" and "the abasement of rejection invoking ardent sympathetic constellations or the frigidity of the satellite of their planet" (654). From that perspective, humankind seems trapped in a radical dualism represented, on the one hand, by a firm anthropocentrism that comforts and reassures us of humankind's privileged position ("attachment"), and a repressed repulsion or horror at the thought of life finding little support in the cold cosmos ("frigidity"). Peter Mahon emphasizes the fact that this passage's criticism of "humancentric notions" is typical of *Ulysses* (Mahon 2009, 139–140). Nevertheless, the effort to "dislocate the centrality of the human" (140) is clearly visible in "Ithaca" due to its heavily depersonalized style, its focus on science, and its use of catalogues.

The inclusive technique of cataloguing finds frequent use in "Ithaca." According to Jeri Johnson, the chapter contains more factual information than any other part of the book. This is perhaps due to its "voracious" and "frantic" urge to catalogue phenomena and things (Joyce 1998, 958–959). As we go through the chapter, we get overwhelmed by lists of subjects of conversations, qualities of water, features of constellations, books from Bloom's library, items from a daily budget, and the full contents of two drawers. Things come to us in flocks as they are described collectively. The same technique is often employed in Speculative Realism; when presented en masse, objects seem more powerful and their agency more immediate than when they are seen in isolation. Long *enumeratio*, as a distinct tradition, has been an important element of rhetoric since ancient times. This device is often employed "where we do not know the boundaries of what we wish to portray" (Eco 2009, 15). In other words, we use enumeration to evoke the impression of infinity or at least a vastness inexhaustible by man. Catalogues remind us of our inherent limitations, be they scientific or literary. The list making in "Ithaca" "swerves into figurative trope" and makes "literature enter through the back door" (Joyce 1998, 959). No wonder it was Joyce's personal favorite: "the ugly duckling of the book" as he called it (quoted in Joyce 1998, 959).

The Secret Life of Things 43

The objects in Bloom's first drawer form a humble universe of ordinary content:

> A Vere Foster's handwriting copybook [...] 2 fading photographs of queen Alexandra of England and of Maud Branscombe, [...] a Yuletide card, bearing on it a pictorial representation of a parasitic plant, [...] a butt of red partly liquefied sealing wax, [...] a box containing the remainder of a gross of gilt «J» pennibs, [...] an old sandglass [...]. (673)

This democratic juxtaposition of items with Bloom's cosmic epiphanies allows for transcending the obscure plainness these objects ooze in everyday life. They become a source of puzzlement and wonder, no lesser than the stars and galaxies admired in the garden. After all, if we resolve to drop the "humancentric" bias, it may turn out that "a butt of red partly liquefied sealing wax" contains just as many secrets as Andromeda or Sirius. Painstaking catalogues of everyday objects that slumber crushed by our force of habit can emerge more fully as part of an entire army of things spilling out from the page.

Such an overflow serves to emphasize the overabundance of things that we encounter in everyday life, inviting us to reconsider their significance and influence. Catalogues like this seem open ended. The infinity they might indicate is related to the infinite regress of the things we think we know, but which nevertheless continue to slip from our grasp. Whenever we label something as 'known' and wish to deposit it safely in the knowledge vault—be it big as galaxies or small as bacteria—we seem to encounter a counterbalance that mocks our capacity for attaining absolute knowledge. This vanity was detected by Bloom, who proved able to recognize both 'attachment' and 'rejection' that affectively bind us to the world and unbind from it.

The resistance to the limits of essential 'thingness' that we humans impose on things with our notions of functionality has been a vital concern of philosophical discourse since the pre-Socratics like Empedocles and Heraclitus. In modernity, however, Hume and Kant in particular have invalidated such metaphysical speculation, privileging questions of epistemology. As a result, we now see little discussion of the unresolved problems that haunted those two philosophers. Hume rejected addressing reality beyond human cognitive habits, while Kant firmly shut us off from things-in-themselves, placing them beyond any possible reach. In order to consolidate their philosophical programs, the two thinkers ruled out any speculation about the actual structure of reality, focusing on human epistemology instead. Speculative Realism, on the other hand, attempts to restore a precritical mode of thought, which would favor attempts to at least acknowledge a fully autonomous reality without the tinge of human subjectivity.

Speculative Realism wishes to restore to human thought the spirit of discovery and the feeling of wonder inscribed in metaphysical speculation. This

44 *Grzegorz Czemiel*

is particularly visible in its criticism of the linguistic turn, which invites the poststructuralist idea that everything we know is necessarily of a textual character. However, the tide may be changing with a possible revival of the metaphysical tradition that acknowledges a fully autonomous reality and remains dedicated to considering it from a less anthropocentric point of view. Speculative Realism attempts to reorient thought toward a world independent of humanity. It turns to a reality that lies necessarily beyond our comprehension, thus engaging in the construction of an ontology that would account for both the world we know and the world that remains beyond our grasp, which can be reached only indirectly. However, it also discovers—with newly found awe—that it can just as well begin with the drawers in a desk. Thus, a speculatively inflected cultural studies could greatly contribute to a better understanding of material agency and the dynamics of ecologies formed by humans and nonhumans. This could be particularly productive in the field of popular culture studies, which often suffers from reductionist judgments.

By giving serious thought to *the popular*, Speculative Realism, like the "Ithaca" chapter of Joyce's *Ulysses*, has become an "ugly duckling" of the humanities, one that nonetheless seems capable of opening philosophy to new areas of study, ultimately establishing unbiased perspectives on *the material* and *the popular*. Speculative Realism (particularly its branch called Object-Oriented Ontology) has already confirmed its potential in reviving philosophical interest in the forms of popular culture, and as such—following the example of Joyce's text—it has proved that an ugly duckling can transform into a beautiful swan. After all, as Derek Attridge pointed out, Joyce both "introduced the trivial details of ordinary life into the realm of art" and "revealed the fruitful contradictions at the heart of the realist enterprise" (1990, 1). As this chapter aims to show, the same is possible for popular culture studies, especially for its interest in material artifacts.

The Speculative Life of Things

Speculative Realism emerged at a 2007 conference hosted by Goldsmiths College in London. Its participants have included Ray Brassier, Iain Hamilton Grant, Graham Harman, and Quentin Meillassoux. The movement, now also associated with Jane Bennett, Levi R. Bryant, Steven Shaviro, Ian Bogost, and Timothy Morton, is very diverse, the differences often sparking intense debate. As Louis Morelle puts it, speculative thought not only has become a fashionable reaction to poststructuralism, "crystallizing a Zeitgeist," but also "vociferously announces the end of correlationism and anthropocentrism [...] seeking to emphasize themes that have become relatively marginal in continental philosophy such as metaphysical speculation, the inorganic, or the absolute" (2012, 241–242). As the editors of the manifesto-like anthology titled *Speculative Turn* argue, "[t]hough it is too early to know what strange life forms might evolve from this mixture, it seems

The Secret Life of Things 45

clear enough that something important is happening" (Bryant, Srnicek, and Harman 2011, 1). Notably, those "strange life forms" now include works in areas frequently deemed as "ugly duckling[s]" of the humanities, previously often derogatorily deemed too 'popular' for serious critical taste: game and horror studies (Ian Bogost, Eugene Thacker) and investigations in the agency of matter and panpsychism (Jane Bennett, Steven Shaviro), as well as ground-breaking pursuits in radical ecology and geophilosophy (Timothy Morton, Ben Woodward).

The restoration of things as material fit for the humanities can be traced back to a landmark volume in sociology and cultural studies, *The Social Life of Things*. Its editor, Arjun Appadurai, remarks in the introduction that if we consider politics to be the force negotiating between the material circulation of objects and their value, then we are entitled to use "the conceit" that "commodities, like persons, have social lives" (1986, 3). Appadurai, however, clearly refuses to attribute any sort of *real* life (i.e., human-like agency) to objects. He remarks that "our own approach to objects is conditioned *necessarily* by the view that things *have no meanings apart from those that human transactions, attributions, and motivations endow them with*" (5, emphasis added). The only concession he makes in favor of the said "conceit" (also described as "fetishism") is that "following the things themselves" may be a suitable methodology allowing to "illuminate their human and social context" (5). Although Appadurai is willing to admit that the intense mobility of things may confirm their extensive influence (22), he retracts from analyzing them as beings that exist independently of human thought. They are invariably things-for-us and not things-in-themselves.

Appadurai's approach to things seems nevertheless strongly ambiguous: on the one hand, he is inclined to turn toward things, trying to discover their unique life stories, or "trajectories"; on the other, he remains firmly convinced that such an approach is guilty of commodity fetishism. After all, from his perspective things are hollow outside the social sphere. Objects have no meaning in themselves until they become entangled in the nets of man-made politics that produce value. Appadurai seems reluctant to assume the possibility that things enjoy a life *beyond* the boundaries set by anthropolitics. Perhaps beneath the question of "the politics of value" there lurks a deeper concern regarding the ontological status of humankind. Appadurai is right when he stresses the importance of politics in shaping exchange systems, especially in postindustrial economies of "capitalist realism." Still, his account of "the social life of things" is guilty of reducing them to mere tokens in the game played between elite powers that wish either to strategically suppress their circulation, or to propel their flow in order to facilitate power contests (57). Politics emerges from this account as invariably eliminativist or reductionist, with both options unabashedly upholding absolute anthropocentrism.

Following Appadurai's essay, in "The Cultural Biography of Things," Igor Kopytoff observes that the West has been culturally separating people from

46 *Grzegorz Czemiel*

things, ascribing the principles of individuation to people and of commodification to things. Crossing that boundary is considered ethically suspicious, with slavery quoted as a crucial case. This leads him to the conclusion that "societies *constrain* both these worlds [the world of people and the world of things] simultaneously and in the same way, constructing objects as they construct people" (90, emphasis added). This is a crucial point as it posits a "two-world theory" (i.e., the idea that there exist, distinctly, a world of objects and a world of subjects). Although Kopytoff admits that the relationship is reciprocal, it remains unresolved what degree of porousness would be admissible here. Certainly objects cannot become subjects in this account, nor can their mutual "constructing" allow for even a glimpse of a world that would be *unconstrained* by this correlation. Kopytoff remains firmly attached to the concept of necessary "constraining," or—to employ the term developed by Bruno Latour in *We Have Never Been Modern*—"purifying," which means dividing the world into strictly separated domains of nature and culture (1993). This entails, as Levi R. Bryant puts it in *The Democracy of Objects*, a "subtle transformation" that leads to a variant of reductionism: "the question of objects becomes the question of a particular relation between humans and objects" (2011, 16). In this sense, Appudarai and Kopytoff are not guilty of commodity fetishism, but rather of anthropocentric fetishism: they reduce objects to our access to them. They do try to broaden that access by somewhat refocusing on things, but in purely anthropocentric categories.

Mihaly Csikszentmihalyi seems to go further when he claims that to account for the world of objects properly it would be necessary to negotiate "a modus vivendi not only with the physical world [...] but also with the objects we are incessantly producing [...] [which] are like new species that reproduce themselves" (1993, 21). He expands the position of Appadurai and Kopytoff by raising issues that open a fissure in the anthropocentric prison: firstly, "the potentialities inherent in the objects themselves" (i.e., the surplus of existence in things that can surprise us) and, secondly—the "interdependence between our survival and that of the artifacts we produce" (i.e., the question of sustainability as something that indicates a broader coalition of humans and nonhumans) (21). In conclusion, however, Csikszentmihalyi comments that we surround ourselves with things "due to a paradoxical need to transform the precariousness of consciousness into the solidity of things. [...] We need objects to magnify our power, enhance our beauty, and extend our memory" (28). Therefore, the agency of objects would be strictly correlated with human goals and deprived of any inherent meaning beyond this correlation.

Such theoretical moves, despite their vague promise of emancipation of things, give absolute preference to human cognition as the foundation for all knowledge, and adopt human consciousness as the yardstick of all existence. These accounts simply project the structure of human biography onto the material world, therefore refusing to treat objects as something possibly more than man-made constructs. Although they animate things, the life they allow them is only a superficial, mechanical spectacle prepared with a human audience in mind. Things become material zombies whose existence cannot exceed the purely functional or sentimental dimension, as their being is invariably bound to social signification. The diplomatic task here would be to "resist that punchline" (Bennett 2004, 358) and endow objects with greater vibrancy.

Criticism of such a reductionist approach to things entails a radical break from the inherently anthropocentric "correlationism." The term correlationism was coined by Meillassoux in *After Finitude*, and it describes the view that "we only ever have access to the correlation between thinking and being, and never to either term considered apart from the other" (2009, 5). Correlationism is the effect of promulgating the Humean and Kantian view of the relation between subjectivity and reality. The so-called 'correlationist circle' becomes a trap when we realize that it forbids us to seriously consider anything "outside thought," effectively instituting a rigid division into that which is human or given to humans, and therefore knowable, and that which is nonhuman, and thus unknowable. Any autonomous reality becomes reduced in correlationist accounts to either a side product of human cognition, or a Kantian "Ding an sich"—that is, the inaccessible thing-in-itself.

According to Meillassoux, a direct challenge to this way of thinking is the "arche-fossil" that testifies to the existence of an "ancestral" reality independent of any correlation (i.e., not presenting itself to a sentient being). He shows that such material evidence of a nonhuman past poses a serious problem to correlationism, which is unable to fully account for a reality that has never been given to a thinking entity. In that sense, Meillassoux concludes, "[P]hilosophers have lost the *great outdoors*, the *absolute* outside of pre-critical thinkers: that outside which was not relative to us" (2009, 7; emphasis in the original). In his view, our efforts should be oriented toward restoring the concept of the absolute, conceived speculatively as the world-out-there, a glimpse of which can be sensed in the premonition of vastness experienced by Bloom and called "Utopia." In practical terms, this means acknowledging a previously unaccounted depth in even the most commonplace things, democratizing ontology, revising the scope of human and material agency, and reviving indirect forms of knowledge, especially metaphor.

The Latourian Connection

Speculative Realism takes its cue from Bruno Latour in an attempt to overcome the binaries that permeate correlationist logic: those of subject and object, of nature and culture, of the animate and the inanimate, as well as of the human and the nonhuman. Such endeavors are not meant to demean humanity, but rather to glimpse a necessarily 'weird' world beyond correlationism. This can only be achieved imaginatively, or 'speculatively,' by creating a metaphorical image of the world that would not be entirely reliant on human epistemological categories. "In the correlationist's view," Bogost explains, "humans and the world are inextricably tied together, the one never existing without the other" (2012, 4). Dismantling this royal intimacy entails the rejection of the idea that the world can be "paraphrased" or "immediately translated"; quite on the contrary, as Graham Harman argues, "Reality is weird because reality itself is incommensurable with any attempt to represent or measure it" (2011b, 51). In combating naïve, correlationist realism, he argues for acknowledging a vast, 'weird,' and fundamentally defamiliarized world beyond the strictly human, while at the same time attempting to reconfigure the political representation of things.

Latour's *We Have Never Been Modern* continues to apply anthropological methods to science and unveils the key paradox at the heart of the so-called "Modern Constitution": we take nature as transcendent (beyond our reach) and immanent (constructed in the laboratory) at the same time (1993, 32). In order to stabilize that system, it becomes something of a paramount importance to ceaselessly "purify" culture from nature, and vice versa. Though basically enmeshed, nature and culture are constantly separated, just as the subject is wrenched from the object, simultaneously repressing the work of translation to which we owe the assembling of real, "hybrid" networks that effectively mix nature and culture. The key question for Latour is "How can this terra incognita that is nevertheless so familiar to us be explored?" (77). The answer would be to acknowledge the ever proliferating existence of "quasi-objects" that are "[r]eal as Nature, narrated as Discourse, collective as Society, existential as Being" (77). Latour concludes that we should understand them much more broadly than before, which can be possible only when we overcome the said dualisms and "become once more what we have never ceased to be: amoderns" (90).

Graham Harman (2009) discusses the significance of this bold move in *Prince of Networks*: while Kant's "Copernican Revolution" in philosophy made humanity the center of the world and relegated the rest to a half-dark margin, Latour prescribes a "Counter-Revolution" (59). It would consist of an absolute democratization of all quasi-objects, now renamed as "actants"; without discriminating between them, we have to accept that "[a]ll that matters are actants and the networks that link them. To follow a quasi-object is to trace a network" (64). Those networks are flat, since no actant is *essentially* more privileged than any other, although they are all constantly put to various tests, or "trials of strength" in the process of becoming, each writing its own, unique "*curriculum vita*" and getting ready to "take off on lines of flight toward ever new adventures" (65). The actor-network theory (ANT) sketches a radically flat and democratic ontology, in which both animate and inanimate objects act upon, influence, and translate each other. In this paradigm, humanity loses its special footing and becomes unmoored from an illusionary position of ontological preference. Consequently, as

The Secret Life of Things 49

long as everything is a quasi-object, it is also a quasi-subject, since all of the 'modern' dualisms crumble under the sheer weight of intricate and complex webs of entanglements and makeshift alliances.

Latour claims that it is not enough to dismantle the subject–object dualism, and thus to redraw the ontological map that delineates the distribution of power; he insists on a general principle of "irreduction," which would guarantee that no entity can be reduced to another. Commenting on the "science wars" fought between philosophers of science and postmodernists, he observes that their *felix culpa* has been to assume that facts can be "objectively" or "socially" explained. This is, however, impossible due to "a general feature of *all* objects which is that they are so specific that they cannot be replaced by something else for which they are supposed to be a stand-in" (Latour 2000, 112). Anthropocentrism in the humanities and quantitative reductionism in science are both guilty of assuming that objects can be mastered. "On the contrary," Latour emphasizes, "they always resist and make a shambles of our pretensions to control" (116). As long as we keep reshaping reality in order to make it fit our cognitive schemas conveniently, we deprive all objects of their "objectity": their unique "ability to propel novel entities on the scene, to raise new questions in their own terms and to force the social and natural scientists to retool the whole of their intellectual equipment" (116).

In order to refocus philosophy on objects and create conceptual tools with which they can be approached, Harman draws on Latour's irreduction principle, but also uses Aristotle's theory of substance and Heidegger's analysis of tools. He argues that objects can be either small or large, empirically verifiable or purely imaginary, animate or inanimate. As Bogost wittily puts it, "all things equally exist, yet they do not exist equally" (2012, 11). No object can be elevated above any other object, and none serves as an absolute ground or container. All objects have distinct real qualities, which make them different from all other entities. Finally, objects are fully autonomous and their being cannot be exhausted by their relationships, including but not limited to their interaction with humans. The autonomy of objects depends on their withdrawal into subterranean existence, to which no other object can have access (Harman 2011a, 35–50). Again, Bogost offers a good metaphor by postulating a "black hole-like density of being," which entails that an "ontological equivalent of Big Bang rests within every object" (26). In this sense, the world of objects acquires more gravity and independence, dethroning man as the ultimate source of all meaning. Thus, Speculative Realism partakes in posthumanism insofar as it recomposes the notion of humanity, albeit not by dispensing with it, but rather by opening it up to the nonhuman. As Mark Fisher remarks on the Frieze Blog, object-oriented philosophy invites us to "consider object itself, alluring in its partial opacity," which leads to the conclusion that it is able to "attune us to the strangeness of objects once they are liberated from commonsense's somnambulant gaze" ("Clearing the Air").

Speculative Cultural Studies?

Cultural studies, Bryant argues, suffers from a "sharp divide between those forms of inquiry that focus on signification and those forms of inquiry that focus on *the material* in the form of technologies, media, and material conditions" (2011, 32). The areas of cultural studies focused on the anthropology of things are caught in a conceptual deadlock, which results from this divide. Speculative Realism brings a "theory class upgrade" by its encouragement to follow things themselves, offering a "weird, futuristic taste" of a world whose fullness has been restored instead of being reduced (Morton 2015). For thinkers like Morton and Bogost, the new framework redresses the balance between the human and the nonhuman, allowing the agency and gravity of both sides to be appreciated more accurately. Bogost wishes to "amplify the black noise of objects" (34) in order to at least attempt predicting what makes them tick, acknowledging a world that is not necessarily tailored for our perceptual apparatus or ideology. As the world becomes 'weird,' philosophy and cultural studies become more fictional and poetic, facilitating a reinvigoration of metaphor, albeit without eliminating those disciplines' credibility and descriptive potential. Therefore, studying popular culture from this new perspective would be an especially fruitful exercise in going "where everyone has gone before, but where few have bothered to linger" (Bogost 2012, 34). As the example of Joyce has shown, metaphysics can be rediscovered even inside one's drawer (i.e., in places that reveal the democratic, popular dimension of ontology).

Object-Oriented Ontology provides an intellectual framework for considering the richness of 'things themselves' without reducing them to correlates of language, social value, or other semiotic codes. Naturally, this does not mean that human agency is annulled—it is just put in a necessary perspective, setting the world free from the mighty grasp of Kantian seclusion, which can bring great relief. In this way, the poststructuralist fetishist guilt related to focusing on *either the material or* the medium is overcome. This move invests objects of all kinds—commodities, rocks, geysers, sputniks, cartoon characters, power plants, asteroids, or even Morton's sublime "hyperobjects" like global warming or ecosystems—with agency to establish their own relations.

Popular culture can only benefit from this investment because it obliterates hierarchies and can refocus scholarship on concrete alliances and networks of humans and nonhumans. Moreover, the de-anthropocentric tendency of the discussed philosophies allows overturning the absolute monarchy of humankind in culture. Assembling new "ecologies of things" entails acknowledging that "humans are always in composition with nonhumanity, never outside of a sticky web of connections" (Bennett 2004, 365). Adopting this perspective also leads to a rediscovery of humanity in all its fragility and actual dependence on *the material* and *the popular*. In one interview Timothy Morton even goes as far as to say that the

The Secret Life of Things 51

anxiety of being thing-like—that is, depersonalized, mute, and semiotically dependent—can be seen as crucial for constructing subjectivity. Speculative Realism invites us to see life beyond all flavors of vitalism and mechanism, to consider the idea that not all forms of meaningful existence are necessarily human. Meeting nonhumans can be stressful because—as Morton (2013) points out—it demonstrates to us the limitations of our assumptions regarding life and agency; paradoxically, "one of the people that I have to allow to exist is me, funnily enough, because I am also one of these nonhumans." Thus, a subjectless world in which humans are merely objects, equally existing among countless other things, may not be so scary after all. In such a world humans and nonhumans would coproduce each other, which means that *the popular*, material culture can as effectively produce subjectivity and meaning. Overturning hierarchies among objects also makes cultural studies focusing on *the material* and *the popular* particularly important, because they can show how deeply entangled we are in a myriad of lives that we often fail to properly acknowledge and whose agency we are disinclined to appreciate. Therefore, a speculative consideration of things may actually deliver us from the vagaries of an all-too-human perspective, inaugurating a new, democratic life among things that are more often than not also popular.

References

Appadurai, Arjun. 1986. "Introduction: Commodities and the Politics of Value." In *The Social Life of Things: Commodities in Cultural Perspective*, edited by Arjun Appadurai, 3–63. New York: Cambridge University Press.
Attridge, Derek. 1990. "Reading Joyce." In *The Cambridge Companion to James Joyce*, edited by Derek Attridge, 1–27. Cambridge: Cambridge University Press.
Bennett, Jane. 2004. "The Force of Things: Steps toward an Ecology of Matter." *Political Theory* 32 (3): 347–372.
Bogost, Ian. 2012. *Alien Phenomenology, or What It's Like to Be a Thing*. Minneapolis: University of Minnesota Press.
Bryant, Levi R. 2011. *The Democracy of Objects*. Ann Arbor: Open Humanities Press.
———. Graham Harman, and Nick Srnicek, eds. 2011. *The Speculative Turn: Continental Materialism and Realism*. Melbourne: re.press.
Csikszentmihalyi, Mihaly. 1993. "Why We Need Things." In *History From Things: Essays on Material Culture*, edited by Steven Lubar and W. David Kingery, 20–29. Washington, DC: Smithsonian Institution.
Eco, Umberto. 2009. *The Infinity of Lists: An Illustrated Essay*. New York: Rizzoli.
Fisher, Mark. 2008. "Clearing the Air." *Frieze Blog*, February 20. Available online at http://blog.frieze.com/clearing_the_air1.
Harman, Graham. 2009. *Prince of Networks: Bruno Latour and Metaphysics*. Melbourne: re.press.
Johnson, Jeri. 1998. "Introduction." In *Ulysses* by James Joyce, ix–xxxvii. Oxford: Oxford University Press.
———. 2011a. *The Quadruple Object*. Winchester, England: Zero Books.

52   Grzegorz Czemiel

———. 2011b. *Weird Realism: Lovecraft and Philosophy*. Winchester, England: Zero Books.

Joyce, James. 1998. *Ulysses*. Oxford: Oxford University Press.

Kopytoff, Igor. 1986. "The Cultural Biography of Things: Commoditization as Process." In *The Social Life of Things: Commodities in Cultural Perspective*, edited by Arjun Appadurai, 64–94. New York: Cambridge University Press.

Latour, Bruno. 1993. *We Have Never Been Modern*. Cambridge, MA.: Harvard University Press.

———. 2000. "When Things Strike Back: A Possible Contribution of 'Science Studies' to the Social Sciences." In *British Journal of Sociology* 51 (1): 107–123.

Mahon, Peter. 2009. *Joyce: A Guide for the Perplexed*. London: Continuum.

Meillassoux, Quentin. 2009. *After Finitude*. Translated by Ray Brassier. London: Continuum.

Morelle, Louis. 2012. "Speculative Realism. After Finitude and Beyond? A Vade Mecum." *Speculations* III: 241–272.

Morton, Timothy. 2013. "Timothy Morton with Greg Lindquist." *The Brooklyn Rail*, November 5. http://brooklynrail.org/2013/11/art_books/timothy-morton-with-greg-lindquist.

———. 2015. "Rock Your World (Or, Theory Class Needs an Upgrade)." *Los Angeles Review of Books*, July 28. Available online at https://lareviewofbook.org/essay/rock-your-world-or-theory-class0needs-an-reality-upgrade.

Shaviro, Steven. *The Universe of Things: On Speculative Realism*. Minneapolis: University of Minnesota Press, 2014.

Part II

From Material Media to Digital Materiality

4 The Representation of Book Culture in *It-Narratives*

Joanna Maciulewicz

An interesting aspect of the debate on literacy is the nature of the relationship between human ideas and the technology of writing. It is a part of a broader discussion about the relationship of human subjectivity and material objects that originated with the rise of consumer culture and that literature often thematized. Objects, as contemporary critics observe, do not necessarily remain in antithetical relations to humans but partake in their nature. Marshall McLuhan in his *Gutenberg Galaxy* points out that diverse technologies are nothing but the extensions of senses (1962, 4) while Julie Park demonstrates in *The Self and It* that the tools that people employ to increase their capacities become for them instruments of the expression of their selves (2010, xiii). Objects connected with writing and print technology are particularly well suited for this expressive function since their chief role is the preservation of human thoughts and ideas. As Deidre Shauna Lynch observes, the conflation of identity and writing is even manifest in the polysemy of the word 'character,' which signifies both human identity and a sign in the text (1998, 30). In his 1689 *Essay Concerning Human Understanding*, Locke points to this relation between personality, ideas, and typography by describing cognition as an act of inscribing or imprinting where mind is likened to paper and ideas to characters (Lynch 1998, 34). Human senses, thoughts, and cognition are thus associated with writing materials that partake in human consciousness.

The aim of this chapter is to analyze the way the relation between human self and writing instruments was represented in it-narrative, or object narrative—a genre of fiction that originated in the early eighteenth century, flourished in its latter half, and withered in the nineteenth century. Its defining convention was the use of an inanimate or an animal narrator that recounted its peregrinations among humans. The adoption of the unusual viewpoint to describe the circulation of objects makes the tale similar to the ancient genre of Mennipean satire, which conventionally used elements of fantasy to defamiliarize readers' perception of reality. The stories told by objects in it-narratives reflect the increasing fascination with things that circulated in the emerging consumer society. Yet, the fact that the objects caught in the perennial network of exchanges act in the capacity of authors also sheds light upon the circulation of writing in eighteenth century society.

56   Joanna Maciulewicz

It-narratives highlight objectification and commodification in the conditions of market economy and—by using inanimate narrators endowed with consciousness—explore the uneasy relationship between human and nonhuman aspects of human communication in literate societies. The analysis of the stories reveals the awareness of the impact of technology on communication demonstrated by eighteenth century popular writers and throws into relief the debates on the effects of our increasing reliance on digital media and on the nature of communication in our own times.

It-narratives were not the first texts to address the problem of the relationship between human subjectivity and writing. Plato had warned in his *Phaedrus* that words separated from the living presence of the speaker turned into lifeless, unresponsive, orphaned things. The association of writing with death recurred in the literate culture (Ong 2012, 81). There are, however, texts that portray writing and print as a way of preserving human thoughts and ideas rather than putting them to death. John Milton in *Areopagitica* (1664), a pamphlet written in protest against prepublication censorship, describes books as "the preserved essences of authors" (Rose 1993, 29). The expressions that Milton employs to describe the relation of writers and books emphasize the continuity between spoken words and their graphic representations. Writing does not kill them, but rather perpetuates their life. Books are thus repeatedly associated with the soul, spirit, and mind. They "contain a potency of life in them to be as active as that soul whose progeny they are" and "they preserve as in a vial the purest efficacy and extraction of that living intellect that bred them" (Milton 2005, 342). If books are the vessels of life, censorship can thus be legitimately likened to "homicide" and "martyrdom" (342). Given that print is capable of multiplication, censoring may assume the proportions of a horrifying act: "if it extends to the whole impression, [it becomes] a kind of massacre; whereof the execution ends not in the slaying of an elemental life, but strikes at that ethereal and fifth essence, the breath of reason itself, slays an immortality rather than a life" (342). It is the materiality of books that has the power of the immortalization of the immaterial aspects of human life: thoughts, ideas, and spirit.

When Milton writes about books' capacity of preserving "the precious life-blood of a master spirit, embalmed and treasured up on purpose to a life beyond life" (2005, 342), there is little doubt that he has good books in mind. The eighteenth century, when it-narratives originated and became popular, witnessed an uncontrolled proliferation of writing and printed matter, which was a direct consequence of the increase in literacy rates and of the lapse of the 1795 Licensing Act. It was no longer reasonable to expect that books would carry only outstanding ideas. It became apparent that print, writing, and paper, though tangible and seemingly more durable than a spoken word or an idea, would not guarantee the longevity of a text. The recurring motif of the stories that originated in the early stages of the literate world is the fear of perishing and longing for immortality. Jonathan Swift has his narrator say in the Epistle Dedicatory to His Royal Highness Prince Posterity, one of the paratexts of *A Tale of a Tub* (1697), that the majority of

The Representation of Book Culture in It-Narratives   57

writing is doomed to be destroyed by time, which is described as posterity's governor equipped with a "large and terrible *Scythe*" and "*Nails* and *Teeth*" notable for "the Length and Strength, the Sharpness and Hardness" (Swift 2010, 21). In Swift's text, writing and print are as perishable as spoken words. The newly written texts are described as "Unhappy Infants! [...] barbarously destroyed before they have so much as learnt their Mother-Tongue to beg for pity." Time is presented as a bloodthirsty monster that "stifles [some texts] in their Cradles, others he frights into Convulsions, whereof they suddenly die, Some he flays alive, others he tears Limb from Limb" (Swift 2010, 21–22). The images of destruction point to the fact that the embedment of words in the materiality of writing or print offers no guarantee for the longevity of words.

The descriptions of the variegated uses of manuscripts and printed paper that abound in eighteenth century literature seem to imply that immortal life is destined for very few books, while the majority of writing, produced for current and utilitarian uses, is doomed to swift extinction. The images of the variegated ways of paper destruction recurring in early modern texts reflect the fate of books in the period of the proliferation of writing and the popularization of print. Books are no longer seen as rare carriers of valuable ideas but rather as utilitarian and disposable scripts. Eighteenth century authors scrupulously compile the catalogues of the multiple kinds of demise books undergo. Swift says that they "like Men their Authors, have no more than one Way of coming into the World, but there are ten Thousand to go out of it, and return no more" (Swift 2010, 23). It "ill befits" the narrator to send "Prince Posterity" "for ocular Conviction to a *Jakes*, or an *Oven*; to the Windows of *Bawdy-house*, or to a sordid *Lanthorn*" (Swift 2010, 23), but these are the places that witness the reduction of books to the condition of mere paper. In the "Adventures of a Quire of Paper" (1779), the eponymous paper recounts that it was converted from "A Birthday Ode" into "a shroud to her dead kitten," from "an Elegy on a Much lamented Friend" into "a pattern for Master Wealthy's christening cap," from "a fast-prayer" into "the bottom of some mince pies," and as "a kind Warning to Christians, clapped under a pot of porter just taken from the fire, over which a chairman and a drayman were quarrelling, and damning each other with all their might" ("Adventures of a Quire of Paper," 451). *The Dunciad in Four Books* (Pope 2009), the last version of Alexander Pope's "epic of the printed word" (McLuhan 1962, 255), depicting the downfall of the civilized world brought about by "the invention of printing, a scourge for the sins of the learned," shows that authors were aware of the danger that threatened their texts. The unfortunate protagonist of *The Dunciad* is trying to burn his books in the attempt of sparing them "inglorious fates" (Sitter 1971, 19). They will not be given away for free or used as wrapping for oranges bought as pelting ammunition in playhouses or as tinder to "emblaze an Ale-house fire" (*The Dunciad in Four Books*, ll. 235). The writers seem to take delight in the enumeration of the trivial uses of paper as if they strove to ridicule the usual association of writing with greatness. The easiness of the reproduction

58 Joanna Maciulewicz

of texts stripped them of the air of rarity and uniqueness and, as a result, reduced them to the condition of disposable objects.

If books can be reduced to mere materiality so quickly, they can also regain their immaterial value. The motif of found manuscript, which was common in the early novelistic tradition, clearly reflects the fact that the vehicles of words and ideas preserve their immaterial qualities until they perish. Henry Mackenzie's *Man of Feeling* (1771), for one instance, is introduced by the editor as a story miraculously saved from the destructive hands of a curate who found it tedious as reading matter but appreciated its utility as "excellent wadding." "I always take it along with me a-shooting," he confessed. The editor in his turn admitted that he "had actually in [his] pocket great part of an edition of one of the German Illustrissimi, for the very same purpose." Since the curate took interest in the editor's manuscript equal to that the editor took in his, they reclaimed the manuscripts from their inglorious condition and restored them to their proper function of reading matter (Mackenzie 1958, 2). Sir Walter Scott, in the preface to his *Monastery* (1820), makes a jocular comment on the frequency of the redemption of books from their materiality:

> One walks on the sea-shore, and a wave casts on land a small cylindrical trunk or casket, containing a manuscript much damaged with sea-water, which is with difficulty deciphered, and so forth. Another steps into a chandler's shop, to purchase a pound of butter, and, behold! the waste-paper on which it is laid is the manuscript of a cabalist. A third is so fortunate as to obtain from a woman who lets lodgings, the curious contents of an antique bureau, the property of a deceased lodger.
>
> (Scott 1897, 42)

The fact that books can easily crisscross the boundary between matter and spirit, and nonhuman and human, invariably fascinates both scholars and writers. It-narratives not only share the fascination, but also reflect upon the ephemerality of the majority of texts. It-narratives can be thus read as "cognitive systems" (Lupton 2012, 52) considered to be stories narrated by objects that are usually "capable of cognizing but not of transcending their own fate" (51). It-narratives were never valued for their literary merits. Rather, they were regarded as products of "hackwork" (Blackwell 2007, 189), writing churned out for a market greedy for new reading matter. The object tales, particularly those narrated by writing instruments, describe the production of disposable writing and show longing for greatness, which would guarantee them immortality.

A good example of a tale aware of its teller's lowly status is "Adventures of a Pen" (1809). It begins with the pen's lamentation on the deterioration of biography caused by the popularization of writing. The narrator complains that the value of every successful publication decreases with the appearance of countless imitations, which deprive the genre of the air of

The Representation of Book Culture in It-Narratives   59

uniqueness: "[e]very insignificant emmet who crawls upon the face of the earth has thought proper to blot paper, and be the hero of a useless tale" (23).

Biography in the past was a celebration of outstanding individuals whose subject matter was "*such* actions as deserved regard and immortality" ("Adventures of a Pen," 24):

> [I]t was *formerly* a generous tribute which men of genius and curiosity paid to the names and reputation of their ancestors; it was a faithful register, in which was recorded the virtues and heroic achievements of such as had marked their lives with particular honours, and signalized themselves in the senate, on the ocean, or in the field: the magnanimity of the warrior, the loyalty of the patriot, and the wisdom of the counsellor, was equally applauded, and their examples recommended to our imitation.
>
> ("Adventures of a Pen," 23–24)

Modern biographers no longer describe heroic deeds, but rather the lives of common individuals who "have never distinguished themselves by any efforts either of manual, mental, or mechanic superiority" ("Adventures of a Pen," 24). The popularization of life writing contributed to the trivialization of its subject.

The account of the anthropomorhized pen that mediates the production of writing affords a fresh viewpoint on the uses of contemporary writing in the literate society. The biography of the pen will be no different from the modern life writing. The pen is aware that its narrative is of no great merit but it is encouraged to speak by the fact that other objects, a guinea and a halfpenny, have already described their experience. "[W]hy should not the Pen [...] communicate to the public the great events of an active and industrious existence?" ("Adventures of a Pen," 24), it rhetorically asks. The adventures of the talking pen testify to the triviality and utilitarianism of most contemporary writing. This, however, does not mean that the pen is satisfied with its mundane tasks. Its tale is suffused with the longing for the possibility of assisting in the creation of great works, which manifests itself in the way the pen describes its lineage. The narrator nostalgically writes that some of its ancestors assisted great writers: Virgil used one of them for "the composition of those elegant poetic lessons of piety and patriotism" (24), Shakespeare made avail of another to create the "*sublimest* pictures of human nature" (24). Many members of the pen's present family, though not all, as it honestly admits, also participate in the creation of history being "in the confidence of princes and statesmen" (24). The pen longs then for a similar chance to create works of great moment.

The endowment of the writing instruments with consciousness in it-narratives demonstrates their dependence on humans and creates a distancing effect necessary to assess the value of writing produced with their assistance. The genre shows its narrators as both identical and distinct from the humans who use them. The way the pen refers to his relatives suggests that quills are but extension of humans: "one of my uncles being a sort of hackney scrivener," "a distant relation bound apprentice to a political writer in the newspaper," while "my elder brother drew up the preliminary articles of peace" ("Adventures of a Pen," 24). The identification of the writing tools with their owners is not, however, total. Pens, quills, and paper preserve their own autonomous consciousness and the capability of reflecting on their relation to humans. The description of the act of writing from the point of view of the paper shows how limited a role writing materials play in the act of writing. "[The author] pulled eagerly one of my sheets from its concealment, cried vehemently 'I have it,' and instantly laying me prostrate before him, began to trace in black characters on my body, the ideas that laboured in his mind" ("Adventures of a Quire of Paper," 449). The way writing is described suggests violence, as if the human were overpowering the paper, which points to the powerlessness of the paper.

The fact that the writing tools conventionally preserve their own, autonomous consciousness while their bodies become enslaved makes it possible for them to pass judgments on the ways in which writers employ them (Festa 2015, 344). They assume the role of "a nonhuman witness of human passions" while their proximity to the owners creates the situation of "a sort of absolute espionage, unlimited by the extenuations and compunctions of a species looking obliquely at itself" (Lamb 2011, 205). In this way they can offer an objective perspective on the uses of literacy in the commercial society of eighteenth century England. The pen enumerates scrupulously the base deeds in which it has become complicit, which exposes the immoral uses of writing. Despite its lack of agency, it entirely identifies with its owner's actions. "I distracted *property, perplexed truth, unsettled jointures, conveyed away privileges,* and *sold birthrights, to unconnected relations,* or to friends of my own?" he says ("Adventures of a Pen," 188). The identification is, however, accompanied by a detached judgment. "I began to kindle with indignation at the *monster,* and even with *myself,* to reflect that I was instrumental to the seduction of innocence" ("Adventures of a Pen," 26). The pen stresses its own helplessness resulting from the condition of dependence upon the human. Its sentience gives it the capacity of forming a detached judgment but its actions are reliant upon human will.

In it-narratives, writing materials possess, nevertheless, some means of resistance. It is seen in the story of the pen when it assures the reader about the possibilities of thwarting the evil plans of its owner. For example, when trying to preclude a libertine from writing a seductive letter, it says, "I *twirled* myself around in his odious hand, and *endeavoured* to blot out those sentiments, that ought (for the sake of virtue, manhood, and society,) to be obliterated for ever" ("Adventures of a Pen," 26). The endeavors, however, come to no avail:

> and my refusal to mark the delusive expressions on paper (for indeed the ink had froze with horror to the nib) induced the barbarian to deepen the slit of my tongue; after which (not answering his purposes)

The Representation of Book Culture in It-Narratives   61

he dashed me with a malicious *force* against a corn bin on which he had been writing, and damning me for a good-for-nothing scoundrel, left me gaping, in the *agonies of ruin, on the ground.* (26)

On another occasion it "withered" when it was used to deprive a poor family of their humble possessions. Its compassion and indignation at the injustice in which it became an involuntary accomplice was so great that its "ink actually rose above the nib, and refused to flow, or mark a stroke upon the paper" ("Adventures of a Pen," 189). Despite the attempts at resistance, the pen has no power to prevent the acts of villainy committed with its assistance. Its role is thus to bear witness to the ignoble uses to which writing is put with the spread of literacy and to offer its testimony of downright baseness.

As demonstrated by it-narratives, the majority of writing produced in contemporaneous times is either despicable or trivial. In *The Genuine Memoirs and Most Surprising Adventures of A Very Unfortunate Goose-Quill*, the eponymous narrator offers an overview of different popular types of texts it contributed to create. The "exact and impartial Narrative of the Occurrences"—the actual adventures of the quill—clearly reveals the dependence of the quality of writing on the occupation, integrity, and intellect of the author. Petty minds, as the story demonstrates, cannot produce lasting compositions; the quill's successive owners write obsequious letters, prescriptions for monkeys, vindictive satires, and elegies for pets, all of which the quill inserts in its account. The writing that the quill produces is thus subordinated to the satisfaction of the contemptible desires of the patrons. It is ephemeral by its very nature—being either futile, and thus worthless when the immediate need has been satisfied, or dedicated to undeserving causes. It is produced by a wide spectrum of writers and for this reason it is natural that its greater part is transient. The most melancholy observation, however, is that in a society preoccupied with its trivial pursuits, there is little chance of creation of immortal literature.

It is not only amateur authors who use writing for trivial purposes but also those who live by the pen. Every it-narrative features an encounter with a hack showing the commodification of literature, which is a natural consequence of the logic of print. As Walter Ong argues, printing brought about the subjection of writing to the rules of the market (2012, 116). In the eighteenth century, the commodification of words entailed the reduction of authors to writing machines producing texts tailored to the tastes of the paying audience. In the conditions of book trade, as it-narratives make clear, the writers also lose their agency (Blackwell 2007, 189). They are doomed to produce ephemeral pieces to satisfy unrefined readers.

The sentient objects, however, dream of serving a better cause. "Adventures of a Quire of Paper," published in 1779 in *The London Magazine*—a tale about a series of metamorphoses of a thistle that, unsatisfied with its fate, eventually became paper—addresses the problem of this ambition. The eponymous paper recounts its adventures to a country curate who stepped

62   Joanna Maciulewicz

into a coffee house to read some pamphlets. In one of them he encounters a sermon written by a "*high* dignitary" much more prosperous than himself and is taken with envy. The paper upon which the sermon is printed comes to life; "its leaves fluttered as if ruffled by a sudden wind, and at length a low, yet articulate voice issued from amongst them" ("Adventures of a Quire of Paper," 355) to tell the curate its own story, which would cure him out of envy by showing him the vanity of worldly ambitions. The paper informs us that it was originally a thistle that "lived an easy, quiet, and secure life" ("Adventures of a Pen," 356), but it soon became envious of the fate of flax, which was the object of a farmer's admiration. Its wish to emerge from obscurity was granted; it shed its blossoms and turned into "a little heap of grain." The metamorphosis was accompanied by a message delivered by the voice of a "great and unknown monitor":

> You have your desire, and its consequence be on your head. Yet, remember this; that should misery, and repentance the offspring of misery, overtake you, you must never hope to be restored to your original condition, till you have undergone the changes incident to your present nature. Nay, you never *will* be restored to it again, should the pen of one of those fine but rare spirits, that dignify and adorn human nature, stamp immortality upon you, in a future transformation.
>
> ("Adventures of a Quire of Paper," 357)

The thistle experiences a number of painful transformations. Passing from hand to hand, it eventually changes into paper, which, however, is not a guarantee of its immortality. Preserved as a part of a book (Flint 2011, 173), it alters its physical form (becomes fragmented and scattered), and as paper is chosen "for printing a part of the Bishop of L—n's Translation and Exposition of Isaiah" ("Adventures of a Quire of Paper," 451). Although its immortality is hardly associated with the durability of paper, the narrator (the thistle) is happy to be a vehicle worthy of a sermon printed in a pamphlet. Books are seen as a prison for paper, while sermons printed in the pamphlet form are associated with the freedom of circulation (Lupton 2012, 63). The narrator, however, clearly associates this new form with the fulfillment of the condition of finding a pen that would "stamp immortality" on it. The immortality is not to be understood as a literal durability of the material form, but rather as the persistence of ideas. If sermons were ephemeral as literature (Flint 2011, 173), they could clearly instill ideas that could outlive the brief life of their material form. The narrator thus, in the shape of the sermon, declares that it expects to return to its original form. "I foresee my sufferings will shortly be ended [...]" ("Adventures of a Quire of Paper," 451). The story thus can be read as not only a celebration of the ephemerality and mobility of paper but also of the fact that it contributes to the spread of the ideas that it carries.

It-narratives are paradoxical in their nature. They belong to one of the ephemeral genres whose popularity quickly exhausted itself and yet, by

The *Representation of Book Culture in* It-Narratives   63

describing their own condition, they celebrate the immortality of literature. They highlight the materiality of writing and printing and remind the reader about the subservience of script and print to human spirit and thought, which they merely mediate. The employment of the inanimate but thinking and talking narrators provides an unusual perspective on the nature of writing and print in the literate world and diverse uses to which it is put.

The perceptions of the effect of the media of communication vary depending upon the historical context. Adrian Johns, in his *Nature of the Book. Print and Knowledge in the Making*, explains that print does not have any inherent qualities (1998, 2). The characteristics that it is believed to possess are nothing but discursive constructs. The title of Elizabeth Eisenstein's recent study on the history of printing, *Divine Art, Infernal Machine* (2011), renders a similar idea of inescapable differences in the conceptualization of printing and its qualities and effects on social life. Printers and publishers, for example, welcomed the invention with enthusiasm, while authors blamed it for the deterioration of culture (Eisenstein 2011, 98–99). According to Adrian Johns, the "cultural history of print [...] becomes a *result* of manifold representations, practices and conflicts, rather than just the monolithic *cause* with which we are often presented" (1998, 20). In this context, it-narratives are an interesting contribution to the history of the perception of writing and print.

Writing materials and their narratives expose the change in the use and conceptualization of the practice of writing and print at the times of the popularization of written communication. Words on paper as the materialization of language are no longer believed to be a guarantee of the permanence of words even if print is still, in our own times, credited with the capacity to stabilize text. This becomes particularly evident in the era of digital revolution when the "book dematerializes" (Grafton 2009, 288). As contemporary American novelist Jonathan Franzen said at the Hay Festival in Cartagena, Colombia, in 2012, a screen is "just not permanent enough" since it "always feels like we could delete that, change that, move it around." Print, in contrast, is more "reassuring"; "[e]verything else in your life is fluid, but here is this text that doesn't change" (quoted in Flood 2014). It-narratives show that texts on paper are fragile and perishable. In the period of common literacy and commodification of literature, writing and print no longer guarantee the durability of words since they serve common interests of common people. What perpetuates words is not their embedment in materiality, as object narratives seem to teach, but rather the greatness of the human mind and ideas by which they were created.

References

"Adventures of a Pen." 1806. In *European Magazine* July 1806: 23–26, Sept. 1806: 187–191, Oct. 1806: 277–282.
"Adventures of a Quire of Paper." 1779. In *London Magazine* Aug. 1779: 355–358, Sept. 1779: 358–398; Oct. 1779: 448–452.

64 *Joanna Maciulewicz*

Blackwell, Mark. 2007. "Hackwork: It-Narratives and Iteration." In *The Secret Life of Things. Animals, Objects, and It-Narratives in Eighteenth Century England*, edited by Mark Blackwell, 187–217. Lewisburg, PA: Bucknell University Press.

Eisenstein, Elizabeth L. 2011. *Divine Art, Infernal Machine. The Reception of Printing in the West from First Impressions to the Sense of an Ending*. Philadelphia and Oxford: Philadelphia University Press.

Festa, Lynn. 2015. "It-Narratives and Spy Novels." In *English and British Fiction 1750–1820*, vol. 2, edited by Peter Garside and Karen O'Brien, 335–352. Oxford: Oxford University Press.

Flint, Christopher. 2011. *The Appearance of Print in Eighteenth-Century Fiction*. Cambridge: Cambridge University Press.

Flood, Alison. 2012. "Jonathan Franzen Warns That Ebooks Are Corroding Values." Available at http://www.theguardian.com/books/2012/jan/30/jonathan-franzen-ebooks-values.

The Genuine Memoirs and Most Surprising Adventures of A Very Unfortunate Goose-Quill. 1751. ECCO Print Editions.

Grafton, Anthony. 2009. *Worlds Made By Words. Scholarship and the Community in the Modern West*. Cambridge, MA and London, England: Harvard University Press.

Johns, Adrian. 1998. *The Nature of the Book. Print and Knowledge in the Making*. Chicago and London: University of Chicago Press.

Lamb, Jonathan. 2011. *The Things Things Say*. Princeton, NJ: Princeton University Press.

Locke, John. 1689. *An Essay Concerning Human Understanding*. London: Penguin Books.

Lupton, Christina. 2012. *Knowing Books. The Consciousness of Mediation in Eighteenth-Century Britain*. Philadelphia: University of Pennsylvania Press.

Lynch, Deidre Shauna. 1998. *The Economy of Character. Novels, Market Culture, and the Business of Inner Meaning*. Chicago and London: University of Chicago Press.

Mackenzie, Henry. 1958. *The Man of Feeling*. New York: W. W. Norton and Company.

McLuhan, Marshall. 1962. *The Gutenberg Galaxy. The Making of Typographic Man*. London: Routledge and Kegan Paul.

Milton, John. 2005. "Areopagitica." In *Paradise Lost*, 382–391. New York and London: W. W. Norton and Company.

Ong, Walter. 2012. *Orality and Literacy. The Technologizing of the Word*. London and New York: Routledge.

Park, Julie. 2010. *The Self and It. Novel Objects in Eighteenth Century England*. Stanford, CA: Stanford University Press.

Pope, Alexander. 2009. *The Dunciad in Four Books*. London and New York: Routledge.

Rose, Mark. 1993. *Authors and Owners. The Invention of Copyright*. Cambridge, MA and London: Harvard University Press.

Scott, Walter. 1897. *The Monastery*. London: Adam and Charles Black.

Sitter, John E. 1971. *The Poetry of Pope's Dunciad*. Minneapolis: University of Minnesota Press.

Swift, Jonathan. 2010. *A Tale of a Tub and Other Works*. Cambridge: Cambridge University Press.

5 The Intimacy of Writing—Lost in a Digital Age?

Mayannah N. Dahlheim

> In a very literal sense, writing is technology.
>
> —Anne Mangen and Jean-Luc Velay

Cognition

This chapter germinated from an observation, anecdotal in nature yet thought-provoking in content. Teaching introductory Literary Studies courses for several terms allowed for a consistent exposure to young students fresh out of school, ready to tackle university. The first high hurdle in these Literary Studies courses was generally poetry. Poems from any time period perplexed the students, but not just because poetry is generally considered to be a 'tough subject.' There seemed to be a growing difficulty in connecting the signs, the words written, to the conceptual spaces available; there was a marked struggle in taking up the *signifiant-signifié* model and actually applying it to the texts at hand, greater than the usual first-term difficulties students worked to overcome.

The questions repeatedly asked in these courses regarding the connotations and associations available to the words written were astonishing. They showed that this was not the usual first term apprehension and bafflement, but an actual problem. Though anecdotal, the repetition of the questions and the similarity of the struggles suggested that this was not an isolated let alone individual case, but rather a continuous (and growing) difficulty across the board. Was there possibly something very definite taking place regarding entry-level students' abilities when it came to semantics and signs?

Conversations with colleagues from various universities showed that I was not the only one perceiving a change that was difficult to pin down with hard data. Even so, the question grew more urgent: were we experiencing new generations of young men and women, (all of whom were digital natives), whose cognitive skills were of a different nature from the skills of those raised in predominantly non-digital environments? It was an interesting question, and I was relieved to see that Literacy and Writing Studies were asking the same questions, as Anne Mangen and Jean-Luc Velay show in their widely quoted paper "Digitizing Literacy: Reflections on the

66 *Mayannah N. Dahlheim*

Haptics of Handwriting" (2010). In their introductory statements Mangen and Velay point out that

> [a] large body of research in neuroscience, biopsychology and evolutionary biology demonstrates that our use of hands for purposive manipulation of tools plays a constitutive role in learning and cognitive development, and may even be a significant building block in language development. (385)

This is noteworthy since handwriting and digital writing show completely different sets of 'manual use' and "manipulation of tools" (Mangen and Velay, 385). For example, in handwriting, "the writer has to graphomotorically form each letter," which means he or she has to "produce a graphic shape resembling as much as possible the standard shape of the specific letter" (386). This is quite different from typewriting, as Mangen and Velay name typing on any kind of keyboard, where

> during typewriting the visual attention is detached from the haptic input, namely the process of hitting the keys. Hence, typewriting is divided into two distinct, and spatiotemporally separated, spaces: the motor space (e.g., the keyboard) and the visual space (e.g., the screen). (385–386)

There are more differences, and they all show that the two kinds of writing require two kinds of "the skilful combination of technical/manual skill and intellectual/aesthetic aptitude." (Bolter, 2010, and Ong, 1982, in Mangen and Velay 2010, 387) Considering the fact that digital natives use typewriting far more than handwriting, how does this influence their cognitive abilities? And were I and my colleagues experiencing a consequence of the shift from handwriting to typewriting?[1]

Following the findings within "embodied cognition" which state that "perception and motor action are closely connected, and indeed, reciprocally dependent" (385), Mangen and Velay point to Gunther Kress's demand for "a new theory of meaning and meaning making that takes into account the materiality of the different semiotic modes (text, image, sound, etc.) and how they relate differently to bodily reception of meaning" (Kress, 2003, in Mangen and Velay 2010, 387), since there are definite cognitive repercussions regarding these modes and their digital changes, as Mangen and Velay's paper deftly shows.

Could this be an answer to what I was experiencing in my courses—that, due to a change in motor action, from handwriting to typewriting during key developmental stages, there also followed a change in the respective individuals' cognitive abilities? It seemed harsh to even consider this, but then Mangen and Velay's paper succinctly shows that during the act of handwriting "there is a strong relation between the cognitive processing

The Intimacy of Writing—Lost in a Digital Age? 67

and the sensorimotor interaction with the physical device." They add, too, that

> currently dominant paradigms in (new) literacy studies (e.g., semiotics and sociocultural theory) commonly fail to acknowledge the crucial ways in which different technologies and material interfaces afford, require and structure sensorimotor processes and how these in turn relate to, indeed, how they *shape* cognition. (397; italics in the original)

If this is so, and handwriting, as Mangen and Velay understand their findings, increases cognitive skill and ability, while we, in turn, are facing an inexorable increase in typewriting due to the ubiquitous use of digital devices, could my experiences in the introductory courses show that Mangen and Velay's following admonition is accurate?

> [M]edia and technology researchers, software developers and computer designers often seem more or less oblivious to the recent findings from philosophy, psychology and neuroscience, as indicated by Allen et al. (2004): "If new media are to support the development and use of our uniquely human capabilities, we must acknowledge that the most widely distributed human asset is the ability to learn in everyday situations through a tight coupling of action and perception" (p. 229). In the light of this perspective, the decoupling of motor input and haptic and visual output enforced by the computer keyboard as a writing device, then, is seriously ill-advised.
>
> (Allen, Otto, and Hoffman 2004, in
> Mangen and Velay 2010, 397)

I would, however, be cautious to come to the conclusion that typewriting is therefore the bane of cognitive development and ability. This is due to the other observation I made: when discussing the construction and style of a visual text, from the introductory scenes of a film adaptation of a Shakespeare play to the advertisement of a sports brand, the students were quickly able to identify the visual signifiers. They easily pointed out the way the music dramatized the plot, for example, and what intertextual references were being made via the visual images. They could read movie scenes and the sports advertisements with much greater alacrity than, say, a Robert Frost poem, secure in the codes as they were of the visual text. Their application of the *signifiant-signifié* model that the imagery used was oftentimes exemplary.

This surprised me, since most close readings with written texts, poems especially, failed to be this swift and forthcoming in points of analysis. It was, as I soon saw, not a matter of lacking skills. The cognitive mode had simply changed: from the written word to the visual text. The question then was how to cultivate the same speed and security when analyzing written texts that students already showed when it came to visual ones. And, most

68 Mayannah N. Dahlheim

of all, why was the difference so marked? Mangen and Velay's paper points to the interconnectedness of the haptic with the cognitive, yet there is little on the 'transferral' of skills, if you will, from one mode of perception—the alphabetic text—to another—the imagorial text.[2]

The Intimacy of Writing

It was hardly an effort to consider the fate of handwriting in our digital age after these observations. The peculiarity of digital communication is that the bulk of it necessitates writing: it requires an understanding of the alphabet, the language used, and its possible uses; yet, it also implements a kind of writing that requires no haptic skill save typing the words on a keyboard and, in the case of portable devices, often requires no more than the use of opposable thumbs.

The question of fluidity and motion, even of style, is no longer haptic in the digital sphere. It is confined solely to word choice and rhythm, rather than to the visual aspect of the words written. Although, with handwriting, an element of artistry is required when replicating the standardized form of the sign, this modicum of manual creativity and precision is nullified in typewriting. There is a very different hand-to-eye coordination when writing by hand than when typing, as Mangen and Velay aptly show,[3] whether with ten fingers or two thumbs (or even only one thumb). Considering that handwriting is already being termed an 'obsolete skill' online,[4] it does seem that a time-honored staple of human communication is being relegated to the backbenches in our increasingly digitalized world.[5]

Within the digital sphere, the haptic is something more observed than experienced, a virtual rather than physically present experience. Phenomenologically, the twice removed experience of haptic presences is very interesting, especially considering the centrality of the haptic in our lived experience all through time.[6] As shown previously, the haptic is coming into an increasing focus in debates about cognitive ability and communication, since we now live in a world where said haptic experience, at least as we have known it so far, is no longer necessary for communication to be possible.

What is interesting here is that, correspondingly, we have come to a point where handwriting and handwritten letters are heightened signifiers of intimacy, not just of the physical presence of the person writing, but also through the writing itself, by the fact that the individual penned their thoughts, experiences and feelings. For example, the 20,000 letters Voltaire wrote in his lifetime, especially his communications with the King of Prussia,[7] intimate who Voltaire and Friedrich II were, how they communicated in their day-to-day lives, and how they thought, felt, and came to conclusions.[8] Letters such as these, no matter the personality, are highly valuable windows to a time long past, windows that can still be accessed today once found, as can be seen in an incredible discovery in the Netherlands in 2015, where a seventeenth century postmaster's strongbox was shown to contain a treasure

The Intimacy of Writing—Lost in a Digital Age? 69

trove of undelivered and returned letters (Kennedy 2015). As Daniel Starza Smith, part of the collaborating team from several universities (Leiden, Oxford, MIT, and Yale) currently investigating the 2,600 letters, states:

> Something about these letters frozen in transit makes you feel like you've caught a moment in history off guard [...]. Many of the writers and intended recipients of these letters were people who travelled throughout Europe, such as wandering musicians and religious exiles. The trunk preserves letters from many social classes, and women as well as men. [...] Most documents that survive from this period record the activities of elites—aristocrats and their bureaucrats, or rich merchants—so these letters will tell us new things about an important section of society in 17th-century Europe. These are the kinds of people whose records frequently don't survive, so this is a fantastic opportunity to hear new historical voices.
>
> (Kennedy 2015)

What is handwritten is thus not simply inscribed. It is a document of time, allowing access to that very time, long after the period is firmly in the past. Due to its easy accessibility and lasting durability—if one leaves out fire, flooding, mold and blast charges—inscription has a highly beneficial recording strategy. In the case of handwriting, there is a different level of personal than digital communication, since it incorporates the very act of inscription. Not only the words written convey meaning, but also the way they are written—swiftly, carefully, sloppily or illegibly—imbue the words with an extra level of meaning, though one must be careful not to confuse forensic document examination with graphology.

The *presence* of handwriting—physical, mental, emotional—both in the writer and the reader is, I argue, the intimacy that gets lost in a digital exchange. The digital redefines this intimacy of communication by taking the haptic out of these concepts and experiences (meaning the direct bodily experience of the individual via hand and touch) into something that is—literally—not graspable. Consider the extent of the physical in handwriting as Abigail Williams (2011) shows in her recent analysis of Jonathan Swift's *Journals to Stella*. Swift not only writes onomatopoeic reenactments of past experiences with Esther Johnson, but also describes the physical dimensions of writing letters by hand. Williams points to the "explicit link [...] between the choice of linguistic form and the ideal of carving out emotional space within the form of the letter" (104). This can be seen in the following letter from Swift to Johnson:

Letter 14, 22 January 1710/1711:

> Starving, starving, Uth, uth, uth, uth.—Don't you remember I used to come into your chamber, and turn Stella out of her chair, and rake up the fire in a cold morning, and cry Uth, uth, uth? &c ([1:171–72] 105)

70   *Mayannah N. Dahlheim*

Together with Swift's "conflating of text and body," as Williams writes, thereby "substitut[ing] letter for body and body for letter" (105), the intimacy of the written word is all the more apparent, since Swift liked to write in bed, mornings as well as evenings:

> Letter 28:
>
> You are just here upon this little paper, and therefore I see and talk with you every evening constantly, and sometimes in the morning, but not always in the morning, because that is not so modest to young ladies. ([1:232] 105)

The sensuality and physicality of the exchange is permeated through the pen and paper—something that, in digital form, is hardly part of the exchange, despite the instantaneous replies possible, since the recipient can only ever touch the device 'holding' the pixilated words, rather than the actual paper held, written on, and folded up by the sender.

On a more contemporary note, there is the interesting case of American President Barack Obama's written apology to an art history professor, for seemingly disparaging the humanities, especially art history. Prof. Ann Collins Johns took exception to the president's remarks and wrote him a quietly critical letter. To her shock, the president answered with this note (Hoye 2014):

> Ann—
>
> Let me apologize for my off the cuff remarks. I was making a point about the jobs market, not the value of art history. As it so happens, art history was one of my favorite subjects in high school, and it has helped me take in a great deal of joy in my life that I might otherwise have missed. So please pass on my apology for the glib remark to the entire department, and understand that I was trying to encourage young people who may not be predisposed to a four year college experience to be open to technical training that can lead them to an honorable career.
>
> Sincerely,
Barack Obama

This quickly became part of the virtual news buzz when Prof. Johns posted President Obama's note on her Facebook page and a blogger in New York City picked it up—which is another interesting interface between the handwritten and the digital: Prof. Johns received an e-mail with a scan of the handwritten note, and the news of it was spread online. However, despite the digital gateposts, the handwritten note was given a kind of importance that is hard to reproduce in digital form—say, by an e-mail or a Tweet.

Additionally, the president of the United States gives numerous responses daily; however, it is this handwritten response that was a news item from the *New York Times* to the *Washington Post* and several other news outlets.[9] Additionally, if you consider the CNN footage, the president's note received

The Intimacy of Writing—Lost in a Digital Age? 71

awed responses because it was a personal, handwritten note—insofar that the president of the United States had personally taken time to answer Prof. Johns himself, rather than via an aide.[10]

The intimacy is signified, even present, in the very note. Just by existing as a handwritten note, it is clear that the president sat down, took a pen, and wrote out his apology. Finally, even once the White House sent the actual note after the e-mail to Prof. Johns, it created a haptic connection between an art history professor and the president of the United States of America. This is an intimacy that is not possible in a digital communication, never mind the actual use of the digital communications systems to send and receive the initial note, a disparity that is increasingly becoming a part of discourse about communication.

This shows that the actual haptic part of the written letter is part of the 'signifying practices' (Hall 1997; Higgins 2013) of our cultural signifiers of the intimate and the personal. So, are we losing something important with the increasing digitalization of our communication? Is the digital eating away at our means of the personal and intimate via virtually nonhaptic exchanges? Is this, in turn, leading to such a disconnect between the written signifier and the connotations and associations available via said signifier that younger generations are relying solely on visual imagery in their cognitive processes? Mangen and Velay seem to say so, yet, considering the fact that what is handwritten is still highly significant in our 'signifying practices' and that more and more people are aware of the disparity between the haptic and the digital, we are possibly witnessing the beginning of a process that may be reshaped to a less stilting and more diversified cultural practice.

Deceleration

Is it possibly simply a matter of speed? Writing a letter by hand, after all, takes time. Additionally, handwritten correspondence must be first sent and then read, before a reply can be thought of. One must rely on other human beings (e.g., the postal service) to deliver the message, rather than the impersonal, inorganic structure of satellites and fiberglass. The coordinates within which the letter must navigate are physical rather than virtual, unlike with instant messaging and texting.[11] Satellites and fiberglass have made written exchange much swifter, but also cancelled out the human component, which probably means fewer lost letters,[12] but also far less haptic, as in individual bodily contact. One may wonder if this is part of the anonymization of contemporary digitalized societies, but that is another subject altogether. One thing remains the case: the anticipation of waiting for a handwritten letter is of a different kind than that of waiting for a digital reply, which leads to a slowing of speeds, by the simple fact that one does have to wait for all the processes of sending and receiving to occur. Could it be, then, that what was done unconsciously in a predigital world now needs be done consciously: a deceleration of lived speeds, a slowing of processes via handwriting and other haptic practices in order to enable a full complex cognitive development? This seems to be the main thrust of the arguments made in a plethora of

72 Mayannah N. Dahlheim

recent articles concerned with education, perception, and cognitive development, all of which refer to Mangen and Velay's paper in some shape or form.

On a final note, after considering the previously mentioned debates regarding handwriting and haptic experiences, I began to wonder how far this binary digital/haptic is embedded in a cultural ideology of the digital, one that is seen as incompatible with the haptic experience of human lived experience and so regarded negatively. The fact remains that digital social and cultural practices have come to stay, and they are developing rapidly.[13] In light of this, is the apparent loss of the haptic as an ideological constraint, since the loss of personal, intimate spaces that are indeed 'of the body' is seen as an intrinsic part of the digital development? Humans are, after all, haptic beings, who can do little in lived experience without the use of their senses, not to mention the largest human organ, the epidermis. So, is this loss actual or simply perceived? Moreover, are there haptic signifying practices that are not being considered in this context?

One must also not forget that the question of handwriting versus typewriting is still largely a question in hypertechnological societies, where computers and digital media are readily available. For children living in the rural areas of developing countries, for example, the skill of handwriting, of putting a pen to paper and creating identifiable signifiers, is a major skill in order to achieve the necessary self-development to further themselves beyond the strictures they were born into. On the other hand, if one considers the skyrocketing success of *mpesa* payments in East Africa,[14] and the very high digital presence of people from all across the globe with the help of smartphones, we are not talking about an isolated phenomenon. It is part of a developing digital culture, global in scope, and highly layered in exertion, but so far I would refrain from saying that handwriting is doomed to extinction. It is, however, very important. As Collège de France psychologist Stanislas Dahaene states in a *New York Times* article concerned with handwriting, cognitive ability and education: "[w]hen we write, a unique neural circuit is automatically activated [...]. There is a core recognition of the gesture in the written word, a sort of recognition by mental simulation in your brain."[15] Thus, it is up to us as educators and researchers to not neglect this important skill for the sake of speed and convenience, but rather to incorporate it firmly into the signifying practices of a deeply digitalized world.

Notes

1. Especially if, for example, when writing by hand "the attentional focus of the writer is dedicated to the tip of the pen" in order to enable a replica of the standard form of the sign, yet when typewriting "the visual attention is detached from the haptic input, namely the process of hitting the keys," since the sign is already "readymade" in the word-processing systems used (Mangen and Velay 2010, 385–386).
2. I use these two terms since both texts are essentially visual in their cognition: one reads one and watches the other. The visual senses are needed for both types

The Intimacy of Writing—Lost in a Digital Age? 73

of text, though in the case of alphabetical texts, braille is also an option for the visually impaired. In the case of the imagorial texts, the only option available for the visually impaired is the spoken word, allowing the alphabetical text a greater scope of accessibility than the imagorial one.

3. As Mangen and Velay state: "Today, most of our writing is done with digital writing devices (the computer, the mobile phone, the PDA [i.e., personal digital assistant]), rather than writing by hand. The switch from pen and paper to mouse, keyboard, and screen entails major differences in the haptics* of writing, at several distinct but intersecting levels. Handwriting is by essence a unimanual activity, whereas typewriting is bimanual. Typically, handwriting is also a slower process than typewriting. Moreover, the visual attention of the writer is strongly concentrated during handwriting; the attentional focus of the writer is dedicated to the tip of the pen, while during typewriting the visual attention is detached from the haptic input—namely, the process of hitting the keys. Hence, typewriting is divided into two distinct, and spatiotemporally separated, spaces: the motor space (e.g., the keyboard), and the visual space (e.g., the screen). Another major difference pertains to the production of each character during the two writing modes. In handwriting, the writer has to graphomotorically form each letter—i.e. produce a graphic shape resembling as much as possible the standard shape of the specific letter. In typewriting, obviously, there is no graphomotor component involved, the letters are 'readymade' and the task of the writer is to spatially locate the specific letters on the keyboard. Finally, word processing software provides a number of features all of which might radically alter the process of writing for professional as well as for beginning writers." (2010, 385–386).

* Haptics is defined as a combination of tactile perception associated with active movements (i.e., voluntary movements generated by central motor commands that, in turn, induced proprioceptive feedback). Haptic perception is involved in exploratory hand movements and object manipulation.

4. A quick Google search shows plenty of questions regarding 'handwriting,' 'writing a letter,' and 'cursive writing,' together with instructions and discussion boards and forums on whether these skills are still needed today.

5. For an insightful article on how increasing digitalization influences higher education, consider María A. Pérez Alonso (2015). "Metacognition and Sensorimotor Components Underlying the Process of Handwriting and Keyboarding and Their Impact on Learning. An Analysis from the Perspective of Embodied Psychology."

6. See Simon J. Bronner (1998), "The Haptic Experience of Culture"; Manushag N. Powell and Rivka Swenson (2013), "Introduction: Subject Theory and the Sensational Subject"; Brian Rotman (2002), "Corporeal or Gesturo-haptic Writing"; Elizabeth J. Harvey, ed., (2005), *Sensible Flesh: On Touch in Early Modern Culture.*

7. See Nicholas Cronk, ed., (2009), *The Cambridge Companion to Voltaire.*

8. Or consider, on a more somber note, Anne Frank's diary, on display in the Anne Frank Museum in Amsterdam, documenting a young girl's experiences in Nazi-occupied Holland, helping generations after the Second World War understand better what happened during that awful time. I would argue that the fact that her diaries are handwritten, rather than typed, add to the intimacy of what she wrote about, since Anne Frank did take up a pen and put her words, her thoughts, and her observations to paper. (Writing is, after all, a fairly quiet action.) As the display cases of fragments of her diary show, the physical

presence of the written word, the ink inscribed on paper by the individual in question, inhabit a far more intimate position than what can be said of digital writing. One need only consider the fact that millions of human beings go to see the handwritten words of another human being who penned the circumstances of the historical time she was living in. Leaving aside the opportunity for commemoration of a courageous young woman that the Anne Frank Museum poses, the fact that the handwritten words are central to the museum is telling.

9. See, among others: Jennifer Schuessler (2014), "President Obama Writes Apology to Art Historian," and Julia Eilperin (2014), "Obama Apologizes to Art Historian for Public Quip."

10. As the CNN news report states: "Johns said she accepts the apology. 'I thought it was incredibly gracious and a lovely note. The poor man—he makes a glib remark," she joked. "He's trying to be funny. He's trying to be entertaining and everybody jumps on his case and so I was immensely pleased and the note was really, really lovely'" (Hoye 2014).

11. Though replies may take a while, the fact that with several widely used messaging services, one can see when the recipient not only received and read the message, but when he or she last used the messaging device, shows time and accessibility as radically different constituents to communication as they were when written messages were solely handwritten.

12. On the other hand, as seen in the recent Dutch discovery mentioned above, lost letters can be windows into worlds past, and so are in and of themselves very valuable, whether delivered or not. It is not clear if this can be said about digital exchanges, since what is a 'lost email' or a 'lost instant message'? The fact that digital messages can be deleted so easily is also a matter of anxiety for historiographers, since what will be left of a highly digital age in matters of physical objects and traceable socio-cultural habits and narratives?.

13. Just recently, for example, researchers at Karlsruhe Institute of Technology in Germany created a material that is invisible to touch. It will be interesting to see if and how this will influence digital interaction in the future. (KIT Press Release 086/2014, 2014).

14. See Ian Allison, "Bitcoin versus M-Pesa: Digital Payments Rumble in the Jungle." (Allison 2015).

15. Maria Konnikova (2014), "What's Lost as Handwriting Fades."

References

Allen, Brock S., Richard G. Otto, and Bob Hoffman. 2004. "Media as Lived Environments: The Ecological Psychology of Educational Technology." In *Handbook of Research on Educational Communications and Technology*, edited by D. H. Jonassen, 215–242. Mahwah, N J: Lawrence Erlbaum Associates.

Allison, Ian. 2015. "Bitcoin versus M-Pesa: Digital Payments Rumble in the Jungle." *The International Business Times*, December 1. Available online at http://www.ibtimes.co.uk/bitcoin-versus-m-pesa-digital-payments-rumble-jungle-1531208.

Alonso, María A. Pérez. 2015. "Metacognition and Sensorimotor Components Underlying the Process of Handwriting and Keyboarding and Their Impact on Learning. An Analysis from the Perspective of Embodied Psychology." *Procedia—Social and Behavioral Sciences* 176: 263–269.

The Intimacy of Writing—Lost in a Digital Age? 75

Bolter, Jay David. 2010. *Writing Space: Computers, Hypertext, and the Remediation of Print*. Mahwah, N J: Lawrence Erlbaum.

Bronner, Simon J. 1998. "The Haptic Experience of Culture." *Anthropos* 77 (2): 351–362.

Cronk, Nicholas, ed. 2009. *The Cambridge Companion to Voltaire*. Cambridge: Cambridge University Press.

Eilperin, Julia. 2014. "Obama Apologizes to Art Historian for Public uip." *The Washington Post*, February 18. Available online at https://www.washingtonpost.com/news/postpolitics/wp/2014/02/18/obama-apologizes-to-art-historian-for-public-quip/.

Hall, Stuart, ed. 1997. *Representation: Cultural Representation and Signifying Practices*. London: Sage.

Harvey, Elizabeth J., ed. 2005. *Sensible Flesh: On Touch in Early Modern Culture*. Philadelphia: University of Pennsylvania Press.

Higgins, John. 2013. *Raymond Williams: Literature, Marxism and Cultural Materialism*. London and New York: Routledge.

Hoye, Matthew. 2014. "Art History Professor Receives Handwritten Apology from Obama." CNN, February 19. Available online at http://www.politicalticker.blogs.cnn.com/2014/02/19/art-history-professor-receives-handwritten-apology-from-obama/.

Kennedy, Maev. 2015. "Undelivered Letters Shed Light on 17th-century Society." *The Guardian*, November 8. Available online at http://www.theguardian.com/world/2015/nov/08/undelivered-letters-17th-century-dutch-society.

KIT Press Release 086/2014. 2014. "KIT Researchers Protect the Princess from the Pea." *Karlsruhe Institute of Technology*, June 19. Available online at http://www.kit.edu/kit/english/pi_2014_15296.php.

Konnikova, Maria. 2014. "What Is Lost as Handwriting Fades." *New York Times*, June 2. Available online at http://www.nytimes.com/2014/06/03/science/whats-lost-as-handwriting-fades.html?_r=0.

Kress, Gunther. 2003. *Literacy in the New Media Age*. London and New York: Routledge.

Mangen, Anne, and Jean-Luc Velay. 2010. "Digitizing Literacy: Reflections on the Haptics of Handwriting." In *Advances in Haptics*, edited by Mehrdad Hosseini Zadeh, 385–402. Rijeka and Shanghai: InTech.

Ong, Walter J. 1982. *Orality and Literacy: The Technologizing of the World*. London and New York: Methuen.

Powell, Manushag N., and Rivka Swenson. 2013. "Introduction: Subject Theory and the Sensational Subject." *The Eighteenth Century* 54 (2): 147–151.

Rotman, Brian. 2002. "Corporeal or Gesturo-haptic Writing." *Configurations* 10 (3): 423–438.

Schuessler, Jennifer. 2014. "President Obama Writes Apology to Art Historian." *The New York Times*, February 18. Available online at http://artsbeat.blogs.nytimes.com/2014/02/18/president-obama-writes-apology-to-art-historian.

Williams, Abigail. 2011. "'I hope I write as bad as ever': Swift's Journal to Stella and the Intimacy of Correspondence." *Eighteenth-Century Life* 35 (1): 102–118.

6 Popular Digital Imaging
Photoshop as Middlebroware

Frédérik Lesage

> There is not only such a thing as being popular, there is also the process of becoming popular.
>
> —Bertolt Brecht

> My name is Donnie, and you suck at Photoshop. But don't worry. There's a place for people just like you—last place. Heh.
>
> —Troy Hitch and Matt Bledsoe

Adobe Photoshop celebrated its 25th birthday in 2015. Its long career has secured it a place within contemporary popular culture that is at once undeniable and problematic. Images created and edited with the help of Photoshop are abundant and the verb 'photoshop' (OED 2006) is now colloquially used to refer to any type of digital image alteration no matter the application software used to make such changes (Peck 2014, 1641). But the application software itself—Adobe Photoshop—remains an underexamined part of popular culture. On the one hand, it is a brand of creative tool used by skilled practitioners within diverse, highly specialized disciplines. On the other hand, it is a consumer product used in countless ways by millions of people, many of whom are amateur digital imaging enthusiasts. Drawing in part from a case study of the web series "You Suck at Photoshop," this chapter explores the seemingly irreconcilable meaning of application software as both ready-to-hand tools for the production of culture and as present-at-hand commodities of digital culture.

Popular Tools

A tool may be considered popular based on a positive assessment of its functionality by a group of people. How the group meaningfully articulates said functionality, however, is necessarily shaped by the politics of the technological imagination surrounding the tool's design and use. It is this imagination that, at times explicitly, at times implicitly, prescribes and orders the mode of conduct through which a person is considered to be properly applying said functionality. In this chapter, I set out to show how one might begin to study how Adobe Photoshop works as a mediating device for sorting and valuing culture.

A first step toward developing a framework for this type of study is to establish the contingency of object categories like 'tool' or 'commodity.' These categories are part of a thing's processual state of becoming (Kopytoff 1986). A good example is Jonathan Sterne's work on recorded music in which he usefully blurs the distinction between the categories of 'media' and 'instrument' for describing objects of musical creation and appreciation. He shows how complex things like audio editing suites shift between both categories depending on how they are used: "'reproduction device' and 'instrument' are really intermingled terms and practices. There is no reproduction without the artifice of an instrument, and all instruments in some way reproduce sound" (Sterne 2007, 14).

In line with Sterne's argument, Photoshop intermingles categories of medium and of tool: the former through practices of displaying and circulating an image and the latter through the practices of creating and altering said image.

The categorical intermingling I wish to focus on here is how Photoshop works as both tool and commodity. Having established the contingency of object categories, I wish to further refine my framework by introducing four additional claims. The first is that an object category like 'tool' is a relational property similar to how Susan Leigh Star and Karen Ruhleder (1996, 113) define infrastructure; it may be evident for one person that something is a tool while not for others depending on their relation to the thing. The second claim is that an object category is necessarily defined by its differentiation from other object categories, but that a thing can become more than one object category at the same time. How a person understands that something is a tool involves understanding how it is 'not a commodity' or vice versa, but this does not mean that the two categories are mutually exclusive. The third claim is that categorical differentiations must be materially and symbolically arranged through practices of sorting and valuing (Tsing 2013). Software is not in and of itself a tool and/or a commodity but rather must be sorted and valued in ways that make such intermingling categorizations possible. The shift from software to 'application software,' for example, requires a number of different sorting and valuing activities like designing, packaging, and marketing to establish its status as tool and commodity. These types of practices also take place once the thing is consumed and/or used. Lastly, how this type of categorical intermingling is sorted and valued through practices is embedded in relations of power. But before showing how I apply this framework to an example, I must first explain how power operates within this framework.

From Commodity Camaraderie to Middlebroware

In *Snap to Grid*, Peter Lunenfeld (2001) introduces the concept of 'commodity camaraderie' that he defines as "the primary cohesive force binding electronics artists, less a shared sense of artistic destiny than the common use of

78 Frédérik Lesage

similar tools" (see pp. 4 and 171). Lunenfeld uses the concept to argue that the exchange and circulation of information between producers and users in the development of digital media have created a new sense of community among digital media practitioners. The new social relationships of production enabled by these digital commodities are, according to Lunenfeld, a significant improvement over the kind of alienated labor that Karl Marx identified as the source of false consciousness:

> Technocultures are awash in tools. Generally considered the most important of the cybernetic tools, the computer is actually more of a workbench, or desktop, upon which one works with one's tools. The word processors, nonlinear digital video editing systems, database managers, Web server softwares, interactive multimedia programs, and even esoterica like virtual reality "world-building" kits are what constitute the tool commodities of the technoculture. These commodities are not simply consumed; instead, they produce new commodities and new work. It is, then, no longer a case of sellers and buyers, but of a relationship between hyphenates: between manufacturer-producers and consumer-producers.
>
> (Lunenfeld 2001, 5)

Lunenfeld points to one danger that risks undermining the commodity camaraderie. The sense of community between digital media practitioners requires the kinds of information feedback loops that maintain their sense of community through tools. Sacrificing this type of information exchange in order to produce greater economies of scale will, according to Lunenfeld, result in an increasing set of restrictions over the tool's ongoing development, thereby destroying the sense of community. He uses the example of Microsoft's "Windows Everywhere" strategy (2001, 6) as an example of a tool that has fallen prey to this problem and Apple Computer's "Mac Universe" (7) as an example of a set of tools that have been able to sustain commodity camaraderie. So while commodity camaraderie can supposedly expand the scope of cultural creation and circulation beyond elite or autonomous fields of production, it always risks overextending itself into an unmanageable and therefore alienating scale.

Lunenfeld's claim that increased economies of scale present a danger for commoditized digital tools raises a two-part problem. The first part of the problem consists of the type of process through which practitioners define 'common use' for commodity camaraderie. While the commodity camaraderie in some ways represents a welcome alternative to a restricted model of culture that idealizes pure autonomous production, it nevertheless relies on a calculation of proportional autonomy from commoditization. In other words, if the tool is too commoditized, the sense of community sustained by feedback loops that give it value weakens. (It would be interesting, for example, to know if Lunenfeld still considers Apple's "Mac Universe" an example of commodity camaraderie.) What is unclear here, however, is at what point the scale of commoditization tips the balance. The restriction in proportionality is likely due in part to his chosen example of information feedback loop. Lunenfeld emphasizes the 'demo' or demonstration—performing the tool's design and use "in real time in front of an audience" (2001, 13) as a significant mode of information exchange among digital media practitioners. He designates the "demo" as an "*intrinsic*" (19) part of all digital culture dating back to Douglas Englebart's early Stanford demonstrations in 1968 (17). In the era of the World Wide Web, this face-to-face definition of demonstration seems, rather, 'pre-electronic media.' As we will see in a case study later in the chapter, expanding what constitutes demonstration greatly complicates the politics of information exchange for digital tools.

The second part of this problem is the way in which Lunenfeld taxonomically defines 'tool.' As seen in the preceding quote, he places the computer at the level of the "workbench" and software applications at the level of "tools." But application software like Photoshop is itself a 'workbench' of features. In fact, documentation for the first Adobe-licensed version of Photoshop described its main interface as a toolbox containing discrete tools (features) for digital imaging (Adobe Systems Inc. 1990, 9). Part of Photoshop's early success was tied to a software cottage industry for creating third-party features by developing 'plugins' using a development kit (Pfiffner 2003, 122). Photoshop would also later be packaged as part of a 'Creative Suite' or, more recently, a 'Creative Cloud' of Adobe-branded applications. What constitutes a tool with respect to Photoshop extends into a kind of nesting doll structure that is problematic for any sense of collectivity if this sense depends on all practitioners using "similar tools."

My own previous research suggests that individual practitioners have different expectations of Photoshop depending on what discipline they work in (if they even see themselves as working from within a discipline) and how much practical experience they have with the application (Lesage 2015; Lesage and Smirnova 2015). I initially found it helpful to think of Photoshop and other similar media software (Manovich 2013) as a type of knowledge object (Knorr Cetina 1997). This is a type of object that has a "changing, unfolding character" and that lacks a "completeness of being" (Knorr Cetina 2001, 528) that in some ways makes it an ideal commodity (Zwick and Dholakia 2006). Conceptualizing Photoshop as a knowledge object partly addresses the issue of 'tool taxonomy' by acknowledging its continuously changing character. Other insightful researches for dealing with this expanded and dynamic definition of Photoshop are Robert Gehl's (2009) and David Beer's (2013) works on YouTube. Citing Geoffrey Bowker, Gehl shows how YouTube works as an archive for millions of video clips, becoming a "disaggregated classification awaiting reassembly into something new" (Gehl 2009, 46). The YouTube archive itself is not a manifestation of memory or commodity so much as "a *potential* cultural memory" or "*potential* new exchange-value" (Gehl 2009, 46). People who use the YouTube archive

80 Frédérik Lesage

effectively take on the role of 'curator.' While Photoshop does not afford the ability to sort and organize features in the same way that one can tag videos or create playlists on YouTube, it is possible to see a similarity between YouTube and Photoshop in that the latter is an 'archive' of features. Photoshop's extensive collection of features offers *potential* cultural creation as a tool or *potential* exchange value as a commodity. Also drawing from Geoffrey Bowker and Susan Leigh Star's work, Beer argues that archiving on YouTube is shaped by what he refers to as a "classificatory imagination" (Beer 2013, 60) that informs how people differentiate categories and how they organize its "infrastructures of participation."

My research into how people deal with Photoshop's continually changing character and ever expanding feature archive led me to define a new category of media software under the neologism 'middlebroware,' which I defined as "commoditized media software whose configuration of creativity and the technological [is] not bounded to a committed field of practice" (Lesage 2015, 108). Like Lunenfeld's commodity camaraderie, middlebroware recognizes a type of dialectical relationship between tool and commodity in media software but the circulation of power that shapes this relationship cannot be entirely captured by economic relations of production. Instead, the circulation of power also extends to the shared 'classificatory imaginations' for distinguishing and valuing what constitutes culture. The middlebroware imaginary speaks to a complex and at times contradictory classificatory imagination that intermingles discourses of creativity and technology, commodity and culture.

Before discussing a more detailed example of how this classificatory imagination informs sorting and valuing through Photoshop, let me first use two shorter examples. The first is based on Emma K. Frow's (2014) research on how scientific research journals deal with digital imaging. She shows how editors of scientific journals like the *Nature* family of journals have explicitly singled out Photoshop as the source of "temptation to 'beautify' (or in extreme cases to fabricate) images" (253) due to its "availability and ease of [use]" (253). These editors' reservations are not founded on the dangers of digital imaging per se; other applications are available for this type of digital imaging work. Instead, using Photoshop risks reducing the value of scientific practice by inappropriately altering the image. To avoid these risks, editors establish clear guidelines for people who submit images as part of their papers. Frow points to Photoshop's design and branding as commodity as part of the reason for editors' concerns. She claims Photoshop's branding as celebrating "creativity, imagination and artistic flair" makes it "orthogonal" to the kind of 'expert' technologies that scientific editors trust. Meanwhile, its "deceptively simple" interface means that its users have "little understanding of the mathematical transformations being applied" (259).

Other kinds of cautions about the proper way to use Photoshop as tool can be found elsewhere. Some people I interviewed who used Photoshop

Popular Digital Imaging 81

expressed real enjoyment in learning the application. But 'geeking out' on Photoshop also carried with it some risks. Interviewees explained how a certain amount of caution was required to avoid spending too much time and effort learning the application. One way in which this kind of self-discipline was articulated was through what I dubbed the 'Photoshop ratio,' which I defined as a "skewed proportion between the total amount of features available in the application compared to the amount of features one actually knew and/or used" (Lesage 2015, 101). For example:

> [H]onestly I use probably 5% of Photoshop's, probably less, of Photoshop's functionality, it's capability. Probably less. So, within my very narrow, but very deep use of it, um, my workflow has not been affected that much by [an upgrade to the latest version of Photoshop]. (Author's interview with Web designer and developer, Vancouver, January 2014)

While the exact numerical proportions varied widely, it soon became clear that practitioners applied the ratio as a sign of experience with Photoshop rather than as a gap in their knowledge of the application. The ratio demonstrated a certain level of self-awareness and self-control. Someone spending too much time and effort to know Photoshop ran the risk of being labeled a technician rather than a creative. In both of the preceding examples, we see how Photoshop as middlebroware is imagined as a slippery device whose complex, expansive, and expanding set of features represents at once a flexible potential for cultural creation but also a temptation or distraction. Part of the way in which this profligacy can be disciplined is through mediating instruments like those of Frow's scientific journal digital imaging standards or a personal axiom like the Photoshop ratio that locally sort and value Photoshop's differentiated entanglement between tool and commodity.

An Edge Case of Demonstrating Photoshop: "You Suck at Photoshop"

I mentioned before how Lunenfeld's definition of 'demos' as means of performing digital tools requires some updating to include non-face-to-face demonstrations. Photoshop video tutorials may at first seem incompatible with the kind of demos that Lunenfeld describes in large part because his demos are mostly of experimental technologies or prototypes. But if, as I have argued, software requires constant sorting and valuing as part of a classificatory imagination to establish its material and symbolic status as tool and commodity, then online video tutorials represent a seminal example of the demo.

A quick search online for Photoshop tutorials will easily produce an overwhelming number of choices. At the time of writing (November 2015), it is possible to access 'official' Adobe video tutorials for Photoshop via

82   *Frédérik Lesage*

help.adobe.com or tv.adobe.com. A keyword search on the Adobe-run Photoshop.com website for 'Photoshop' turns up 1,344 videos of 'tips and tutorials.' A search in Lynda.com, a commercial provider of instructional materials, brings up 21,119 different videos. A search using the term 'Photoshop tutorial' on YouTube's search engine generates about 1,100,000 results. Filtering the results of this YouTube search according to view count will indicate that some of these videos have been viewed millions of times. I list these haphazardly collected numbers to show how easy and accessible these videos are but also to wonder at the massive volume of offerings. The sheer glut of videos online would seem to complicate their status as purely pedagogical.

While future research should delve deeper into this genre, a systematic review and analysis of the genre is beyond the scope of this chapter. Instead, I will examine a rather odd example of the Photoshop video tutorial—the series "You Suck at Photoshop" (YSP) (Hitch and Bledsoe 2007)—to begin to map out some of the traits of Photoshop video tutorials as examples of demonstration. Troy Hitch and Matt Bledsoe originally created YSP in 2007. Both worked in marketing in Kentucky and were interested in experimenting with online viral marketing campaigns. The following discussion of YSP treats it as an 'edge case' of demonstrating Photoshop because it is not a typical case. YSP caricatures the tutorial genre (Hailey 2010, 29–30) for humorous ends, but in doing so highlights certain key aspects of demonstrating Photoshop through video tutorials that may otherwise go unnoticed. The following discussion highlights three examples of how demonstrating Photoshop involves sorting and valuing it in ways that intermingle tool and commodity.

Sorting the Subject: Angry Photoshop Guy

YSP's entire storyline is about a man who refers to himself as 'Donnie' (we later discover that his identity is somewhat more complicated), who uploads his own custom training videos for Photoshop while his personal life continues to fall apart. According to an interview with *Time* magazine, the creators of the series "had long nurtured an idea for a character they thought of as the Angry Photoshop Guy." The article quotes Bledsoe describing how they developed the stereotype based on their own experience working in the advertising business: He has horrible social skills and horrible things going on in his life, and the only thing he has going for him is that he can out-Photoshop the guy in the cube next to him (Quitner 2008).

Angry Photoshop Guy can usefully be contrasted to Lunenfeld's (2001, 18) 'demo gods.' On the one hand, Lunenfeld uses men like Steve Jobs of Apple to define a categorical archetype of men who heroically exert technical mastery over the tools they demonstrate on the mythical 'center stages' of digital culture. On the other hand, YSP's Angry Photoshop Guy operates in a caricature of the mundanely everyday. Although Donnie's nervous breakdown supposedly leads him to travel to all sorts of exotic locations, the backdrop

Popular Digital Imaging   83

of the series is almost entirely limited to his changing desktop images. His first words as he begins his first tutorial are

> My name is Donnie, and you suck at Photoshop.
> You do.
> You're awful, and that's why you're here.
> All right, let's get started.
> Tutorial one—distort, warp, and layer effects.
> This is basic to intermediate.
> But for you, I mean, this is going to be stupid hard, advanced, so just try
>   not to slow it down.
>
> (Hitch and Bledsoe 2007, volume 1)

These early sentences play off of the kind of sorting of viewers according to experience that usually takes place at the beginning of video tutorials. Tutorials not only establish the viewer's level of expertise but also confirm the demonstrator's status as someone who is knowledgeable about Photoshop. Part of the humor in the series is how Donnie repeatedly transgresses the unwritten rule that the demonstrator must keep himself in check—must project an air of calm and control as he takes us through the demonstration. How Donnie is cast into this white, middle-class, male, and socially awkward stereotype also speaks to a pejorative characterization of the 'Photoshop guy' as a kind of 'trainspotter' whose sociocultural status is limited by his extensive knowledge or even obsessive appreciation of minutia pertaining to his tools. The series also points to how another subject is sorted: Donnie's unrestrained pomposity throughout the 30 tutorials plays on expectations that the tutorial viewer is a keen and self-motivated learner, the kind of information worker who gets 'out-photoshopped' but aspires to more.

Sorting Knowledge and Skill

YSP is a work of fiction. The viewer watches the exploits of a fictitious character in a web series. The technical knowledge on display in the series, however, is 'real' in that Donnie's demonstrations of how to apply Photoshop features to achieve certain effects are consistent with best practices that are explicitly or implicitly prescribed in other Photoshop training materials. One example of these best practices is "nondestructive editing," which is defined as making "changes to an image without overwriting the original image data" (Adobe Systems Inc. 2015). In one YSP video, Donnie belittles his imagined pupil for trying to use the 'clone stamp tool' to modify an image that, depending on how it is used, would result in losing data from the original image:

> So here's our photo. And basically, what I want to do is get rid of the cat.
> The first thing I'm going to do is organize some layers. Let's start a new
>   layer group called new carpet, because what we're going to do is—I
>   know what you did.

84 *Frédérik Lesage*

Hey, I saw it. You went over to the clone stamp tool, didn't you?
Wrong.
Put it down.
We're going to go do it. That's Bush league, and we're going to do it
   this way. We're going to just go grab some carpet samples, and we're
   going to drop them in, and we're going to rebuild the carpet.
Everything's going to be all right.
Just settle down.

(Hitch and Bledsoe 2007, 1:22 to 1:54, volume 2)

The viewer is privy to a dramatized demonstration of good practice. Donnie
labels the clone stamp tool as the obvious "Bush league" choice of basic features. While it may afford the desired effect, the feature's improper use runs
roughshod over an established good practice for using Photoshop. Experienced Photoshoppers are rewarded with many of these kinds of 'inside
jokes' throughout YSP. Demonstration works differently in this video than
in Lunenfeld's demos because the technical feasibility of the performance is
not in question. However, Donnie's critique of the clone stamp tool signals
how demonstration is used to differentiate Photoshop features as commodity from features as tools for digital imaging. The clone stamp tool is not
only an inappropriate or inefficient feature but also an 'out-of-the-box' feature whose obviousness and accessibility belie the unthinking consumption
of commodities instead of the intentional use of tools.

Sorting the Image

To adequately discuss the aesthetics of digital imaging is beyond the scope
of this chapter (see Peck, 2014, for a good example of vernacular photoshopping), yet it is important not to exclude the image as a necessary component of demonstrating Photoshop. How someone describes an image
as 'photoshopped' can often carry pejorative connotations that decry the
conspicuousness of the digital intervention. In some cases, the intervention
may be so poorly executed that it is dubbed a 'Photoshop fail.' But images
are deployed differently in the context of demonstrations. The subject matter and aesthetics of images in video tutorials often seem incidental. The
formal properties of the images seem to be selected for their pedagogical
value over aesthetic value (see Lesage and Smirnova, 2015, for discussion
of other training materials). YSP makes use of the expected arbitrariness
of these types of images as a kind of double entendre. Donnie initially
presents his choice of image as a simple vehicle for demonstrating a particular set of digital imaging techniques, but the viewer soon discovers that
the image is connected to Donnie's ongoing 'psychological breakdown.'
   The double entendre here works to highlight Photoshop's "double articulation" (Lesage and Smirnova 2015, 226; see also Wajcman and Jones 2012)
as both content and technology. Nowhere is this doubling more evident than

Popular Digital Imaging 85

when examined through the lens of gender. Although the choice of images for tutorials is seemingly arbitrary, one cannot help but notice when navigating through countless video tutorials online that many of these images are of women. This choice extends all the way back to the original choice of image by one of Photoshop's designers, John Knoll, who used a scanned copy of a picture of his fiancée photographed from the back, reclining topless on a beach in Tahiti: "It was a good image to do demos with," Knoll recalls. "It was pleasing to look at and there were a whole bunch of things you could do with that image technically" (Comstock 2014).

The image became so recognizable that it was dubbed "Jennifer in Paradise" and a copy of the image was even included in early demo packages for potential clients. In this original image, as in the multiple images since, the woman's body is classified as both literal and figurative object of contemplation and modification. By minimizing the significance of the choice of image to purely formal considerations, the demonstrator excludes the more complex gendered politics involved in Photoshop's commoditization and its classification as digital imaging tool. Limiting our interpretation of the image to its pedagogical use-value for demonstrating Photoshop excludes or devalues its subjects in ways that reinforce implicit cultural power relations that cannot be captured in a straightforward sociotechnical or political economic analysis. In emphasizing Photoshop's double articulation we show how its symbolic and material configurations of meaning are not limited to its status as functioning technology but also as a commoditized and commoditizing medium.

Conclusion

The overarching narrative arc of the entire series of YSP videos plays out as a rather simplistic allegory about the dangers of using digital media as a means of escape from reality (which, apparently, only exists offline). When reinterpreted in light of the preceding discussion of demonstration, the accusation implied in YSP's title that "you, the viewer, suck at Photoshop" seems all the more harmless, even impotent. In this accusation lies the implicit claim on the part of the accuser that he has a greater understanding of the application. But as we have seen, such a greater understanding is in some ways fleeting and can even be perceived as an impediment to disciplinary skill. In the preceding edge case we see how Photoshop's demonstration simultaneously elevates and undercuts its cultural status—establishing a contingent 'middle' positionality between commodity and tool.

I have identified how YSP caricatures Photoshop's demonstration through video tutorials in ways that nevertheless point to key aspects of a classificatory imagination I refer to here as a middlebroware imaginary. How video tutorials sort and value Photoshop's subjects, its knowledge and skills, and its images requires further investigation, but I hope this chapter has gone some way toward establishing where such an investigation might start.

References

Adobe Systems Incorporated. 1990. "User Guide: Adobe Photoshop Macintosh Version." Available online at http://www.computerhistory.org/collections/catalog/102640940.

———. 2015. "Photoshop Help | Nondestructive Editing." Available online at https://helpx.adobe.com/photoshop/using/nondestructive-editing.html.

Beer, David. 2013. *Popular Culture and New Media: The Politics of Circulation*. Houndmills, Basingstoke, Hampshire: Palgrave Macmillan.

Comstock, Gordon. 2014. "Jennifer in Paradise: The Story of the First Photoshopped Image." *The Guardian*, June 13. Available online at http://www.theguardian.com/artanddesign/photography-blog/2014/jun/13/photoshop-first-image-jennifer-in-paradise-photography-artefact-knoll-dullaart.

Frow, Emma K. 2014. "In Images We Trust? Representation and Objectivity in the Digital Age." In *Representation in Scientific Practice Revisited*, edited by Catelijne Coopmans, Janet Vertesi, and Michael E. Lynch, 249–269. Cambridge, MA: MIT Press.

Gehl, Robert. 2009. "YouTube as Archive: Who Will Curate This Digital Wunderkammer?" *International Journal of Cultural Studies* 12 (1): 43–60.

Hailey, David. 2010. "Combining Rhetorical Theory with Usability Theory to Evaluate Quality of Writing in Web-Based Texts." In *Usability of Complex Information Systems*, edited by Michael J. Albers and Brian Still, 17–45. Boca Raton, London and New York: CRC Press.

Hitch, Troy, and Matt Bledsoe. 2007. "You Suck at Photoshop." Available online at http://www.mydamnchannel.com/channel/you_suck_at_photoshop_1906.

Knorr Cetina, Karin. 1997. "Sociality with Objects: Social Relations in Postsocial Knowledge Societies." *Theory, Culture & Society* 14 (4): 1–30.

———. 2001. "Postsocial Relations: Theorizing Sociality in a Postsocial Environment." In *Handbook of Social Theory*, edited by George Ritzer and Barry Smart, 520–537. London and Thousand Oaks, CA: Sage.

Kopytoff, Igor. 1986. "The Cultural Biography of Things: Commoditization as Process." In *The Social Life of Things: Commodities in cultural perspective*, edited by Arjun Appadurai, 64–91. Cambridge: Cambridge University Press.

Lesage, Frédérik. 2015. "Middlebroware." *The Fibreculture Journal* (25): 89–114.

Lesage, Frédérik, and Svetlana Smirnova. 2015. "'Keeping up' through Teaching and Learning Media Software: 'Introducing' Photoshop." *Canadian Journal of Communication* 40 (2): 223–241.

Lunenfeld, Peter. 2001. *Snap to Grid: A User's Guide to Digital Arts, Media, and Cultures*. Cambridge MA: MIT Press.

Manovich, Lev. 2013. *Software Takes Command*. New York: Bloomsbury Academic.

OED. 2006 "Photoshop v." *Oxford English Dictionary*. Oxford: Oxford University Press. http://www.oed.com/view/Entry/260649.

Peck, Andrew M. 2014. "A Laugh Riot: Photoshopping as Vernacular Discursive Practice." *International Journal of Communication*, 8: 1638–1662.

Pfiffner, Pamella. 2003. *Inside the Publishing Revolution: The Adobe Story*. Berkeley, CA: Peachpit Press.

Quittner, Josh. 2008. "Fun with Photoshop." *Time* 171 (19): 138–138.

Star, Susan L., and Karen Ruhleder. 1996. "Steps Towards an Ecology of Infrastructure: Design and Access for Large Information Spaces." *Information Systems Research* 7 (1): 111–134.

Sterne, Jonathan. 2007. "Media or Instruments? Yes." *OffScreen* 11 (8–9): 1–18.

Tsing, Anna. 2013. "Sorting out Commodities: How Capitalist Value Is Made through Gifts." *HAU: Journal of Ethnographic Theory* 3 (1): 21–43.

Wajcman, Judy, and Paul Jones. 2012. "Border Communication: Media Sociology and STS." *Media, Culture & Society* 34 (6): 673–690.

Zwick, Detlev, and Nikhilesh Dholakia. 2006. "The Epistemic Consumption Object and Postsocial Consumption: Expanding Consumer-Object Theory in Consumer Research." *Consumption Markets & Culture* 9 (1): 17–43.

7 When You Are Not What You Do Not Have

Some Remarks on Digital Inheritance

Marcin Sarnek

It was. It will never be again. Remember.

—Paul Auster

The question of this chapter is how the living imagine their postmortem identity to be reconstructed through digital assets. This entails examining how different approaches to digital inheritance, exhibited by different consumer types, help document shifts from the traditional understanding of ownership, personal property, privacy, and even identity. This will be done through a survey of behaviors of consumers of digital culture and of the emerging legal practices that regulate succession of digital assets. In effect, the chapter will show that the generational differences in attitudes to digital assets and to products of one's creativity make the Western perception of heritage and succession likely to undergo major changes in the near future.

The first of these generations is a consumer type classified as 'digitized consumers': people old enough to remember the protocols of consumption of analogue culture, who nonetheless eagerly accept 'native digital' media and tend to consume them enthusiastically. In result, they tend to perceive digital assets as if they were alienable. Their expectations about this consumption model call for a dramatic change in the field of succession law: an application of the logic of succession to nonmaterial digital assets, which would extend the Western definition of inheritable property.

The second consumer type, the so-called Generation Z, is younger consumers of digital culture with limited experiences of physical and tangible media. Just as they are more eager to accept the loss of intellectual property rights to the effects of their creativity and expression (like copyrights pertaining to their social media posts), they also embrace the potential ephemerality of their expression in social media. They do not necessarily panic when they learn the money spent on entertainment does not buy them alienable goods, but rather pays for online entertainment services (e-books, videogames, music), whose ownership is nontransferrable, and hence not inheritable.

Digital inheritance is related not only to succession law, but—indirectly— to the very definitions of privacy and identity. In fact, the Western definition

When You Are Not What You Do Not Have 89

of the right to privacy has undergone a similar conceptual shift as the one now observable in the case of digital property. Privacy was first established as a property right, then transformed into an immaterial right to extend one's active control over what information about oneself should be made public, and—finally—in the digital era it has again acquired material qualities (since privacy is now often seen as an alienable property) to complement its nonmaterial attributes. This chapter also discusses the relationship of the right to privacy and property to indicate that the current transition of concepts strictly related to 'property' is not an original or unique trend.

Digital Assets, Digitized Consumers, Millenials, and Generation Z

Digital assets remain increasingly difficult to define. Some definitions focus on the proprietary character of digital assets and the digital estate that is made of these assets. A digital asset is defined then as "content owned by an individual that is stored in digital form" (Romano 2011). Such a definition would see all e-books, sound files, photographs, videogames, text files, and any other content that might "have value" (Romano 2011) to fall into the digital estate that is potentially inheritable. Recent controversies around the right to access social media accounts of dead relatives make the lawyers pondering upon the scope of this definition also add to it the management of online accounts. Thus, a more "inclusive definition" reads: "a digital asset is digitally stored content or an online account owned by an individual" (Romano 2011). Conversely, other definitions focus on their nonproprietary characteristics and tend to see them mostly as content available through online services. In such definitions the category of 'use' becomes central: "[a] digital asset is any form of content and/or media that have been formatted into a binary source which include the right to use it" (van Niekerk 2006).

Neither of these definitions has been as yet established as a fixed element of legal reality in any jurisdiction, and lawyers all over the Western world struggle with nonconclusive definitions of digital assets and digital inheritance. These two conflicting types of definitions of digital assets coincide, though, with the emergence of two different digital consumer types: one sees digital assets as property; the other sees them as a service. Still, all of the digital assets are not tangible material objects.

Yet, those immaterial assets appear as material to many consumers who have had previous experiences with physical media. These individuals can be called "digitized consumers" (Colombani and Sanderson 2015), since—while they may prefer to use and consume digital media—their experience of physical media taught them the protocols of consumption of culture and trigger gut reactions to new distribution and consumption models. In result, hundreds of millions of Internet users and consumers of digital goods perceive online services as offers like any others on the physical markets. They also constitute a quickly maturing demographic; most of them have by now experienced a death of a parent, of a friend, of a colleague, or of an acquaintance. As they no longer feel immortal, they care about the issues of inheritance, both as a succession of property and the postmortem projection of identity or of memory. They attach special importance to the idea that they own the effects of their creativity and that these effects, too, are inheritable. These expectations are most strongly reinforced within the Western world by the notion of intellectual property. The ownership of consumers' expressions is prone, then, to become an intensely debated issue surrounding digital inheritance.

On the other hand, as documented by the success story of Snapchat,[1] the understanding of digital assets has been changing dramatically among younger consumers, who may no longer care that much about the ownership of content, since content itself becomes ephemeral. Two distinct younger generations of communications technology users, which can be called respectively 'digital natives' (the 20-to 30-year-olds, or the Millenials) and 'social natives' (Generation Z, born approximately after 1997), share a limited number of features, but one that stands out is the predilection to consume culture as an experience (a trend most characteristic for Millennials) (Walker 2014) and to shop for goods—including digital assets—online. A lifestyle study ordered by Eventbride (2014) reported that the preference of experience over ownership extends even to such traditionally significant institutions as home ownership:

> Although 71% of the respondents said they would like to own a home before 35, the same number said the prospect of paying for a mortgage was menacing, with a full 40% [...] admitting that they would defer buying a property in order to continue a lifestyle that offered experiences. 59% of the men questioned even said that enjoying experiences was more important to them than ever buying a home.

While both generations might actually remember the world in which physical media dominated as a preferred delivery technology for consumption of culture (although it is, obviously, the Millennials who can be expected to have frequent experiences with physical media), marketing and consumer behavior studies show Millennials and Gen Zs are more prone to predominantly consume media through online platforms. Generation Z, however, is famously the first generation to be born into the world of the Web and coming of age in the world of social media and mobile communication, which have become their natural environment for self-expression. They constitute a vast majority among Snapchat users: in 2015 the company reported that around 60% of their user base was aged 13–24. Privacy issues and other concerns that Snapchat sometimes raises aside, the Snapchat success story shows that these users may actually prefer the intangibility and transience of "native digital"[2] media over the physical media, which leave behind a trail of identity potentially reconstructed through a history of ownership.

When You Are Not What You Do Not Have 91

These young users also disregard the issues of heritage, mostly because they focus their energy on instantaneous communication rather than long-lasting effects of their expression. This is not to say that Gen Z users limit their online activities only to services that provide ephemeral experiences or that they universally do not care about property, their output, or perception by others. In fact, as a Sparks and Honey study showed, Gen Zs are significantly more 'into' property than the Millennials and are significantly more eager to spend on goods (2015). Also, their awareness of privacy issues is high, and when they trade privacy for the instantaneity of communication, they do it consciously. Research also shows that Snapchat users are aware that snaps sent over the application can be retrieved or stored regardless of the sender's intentions (Roesner, Gill, and Kohno 2014). The point remains, however, that Snapchat users for some reason accept privacy risks on the one hand and—on the other—accept or indeed expect the ephemerality of their expression.

Since digitized consumers, Millennials, and Gen Zs all prefer digital media platforms over their physical counterparts, it is easy to comprehend why the entertainment industry is now producing a very significant portion of the totality of its content for direct consumption via digital and mobile platforms. In one important example discussed in a 2015 Bain and Company study (Colombani and Sanderson 2015), the music industry now produces more content to be streamed or be otherwise directly available online than to be accessed through any other delivery technology. Young consumers—which the report dubs "Generation #hashtag", but which are the same group as iGens or Generation Z—tend to consume such digital native content first, sometimes even treating older delivery technologies with contempt (Colombani and Sanderson 2015, 2). Thus, the trend to observe in media that which relates to digital inheritance the most is the one picked up by the study, showing—among other findings—that "[e]ntertainment has passed a point of no return in its transition to native digital" (Colombani and Sanderson 2015).

Digitized Consumers Imagine Their Digital Property

Digitized consumers rarely consider the paradox inherent in their perception of what their behaviors as customers of online services: they would often proudly report that they had just bought a book from Amazon Kindle or a game from Steam, or a song from iTunes. One can never buy a Kindle book or buy a game from Steam, yet somehow many argue one can actually buy a song from iTunes. The dilemma (and the paradox) is embedded in the language of end-user license agreements (EULAs) that consumers (most often) accept without reading. Should the language of the EULA suggest the contract is purely a license agreement, American courts are likely to rule the license is violated when an attempt to pass access to a cultural product to a different 'owner' is made (what we traditionally understand as reselling).

92 Marcin Sarnek

If, alternatively, the language of the EULA suggests the contract creates a 'sale,' as is the case of the iTunes EULA, the music files bought from Apple might be resalable, and perhaps can also be subject to succession. In other words, every day, millions of consumers routinely enter contracts whose legal effects seem puzzling.

European consumers, however, have recently found themselves in a radically different legal reality; in 2012, in the case *UsedSoft v Oracle*, the European Court of Justice ruled that the sale of software, either in a physical store or through a download, constitutes a transfer of ownership in EU law. Thus, in Europe, purchases of software, even if done as direct downloads, seem to be fully protected by first-sale rights,[3] which should make software alienable, no matter what producers might choose to place in their EULAs.

Even though few consumers have actually managed to exercise these rights to resell digital assets,[4] these major variations between different jurisdictions seem odd. They apply to behaviors of a majority of members of a civilization (consumption of culture), yet those behaviors are not fully regulated on the level of a civilization, not even on a national level in any of the jurisdictions of the Western world. Courts all over the world have produced a variety of rulings to decide whether end users are only granted a license or ownership rights upon purchase in such cases. Although most of these cases involved software agreements, corporations have attempted to actually extend the 'license not sale' logic to music, films, and other products of culture.

First-Sale Rights and Inheritance

Until recently the right to resell the physical media on the secondhand market, which is promised by the first-sale doctrine, has not been challenged. This, in turn, illustrates the dual character of the cultural product: with each purchase, the ownership rights to the content stay with the copyright owner, yet the ownership rights of the physical medium move to new owners. In digital distribution there are no tangible media to speak of, hence first-sale rights are also immaterial. The logic applied here makes the digital purchase not a purchase at all, but rather a service, which EULAs state directly every time such transactions are made.

Thus, whether a book, a game, or a music track is stored on a physical medium or whether it uses digital distribution may be, in fact, irrelevant, yet it also makes all the difference, which lies in the largest trade-off of the new digital economy: the trading of the first-sale rights, which also secure succession rights, for the comfort provided by minimizing friction. After all, minimizing friction, which guarantees the smoothest possible consumer experience, makes digital markets so attractive, and hence consumers tend not to notice how a feature of the traditional physical medium market is replaced with nonmaterial comfort.

The physical medium market, even though it is likely to be targeted soon by the logic defining all cultural products as services (a process that already

When You Are Not What You Do Not Have   93

began with video games, for example), is still characterized by many qualities of markets that deal in physical goods. Among these qualities is scarcity. While it appears on the surface that a scarcity-oriented economy is giving way to a model in which prices no longer depend on the limited resources, the digital economy shows this is not really the case. Yet, the digital economy is definitely not a 'postscarcity' economy. In the traditional scarcity-oriented model, prices very roughly correspond to the amount and scarcity of resources that were used up in the process of production of an item. In a speculated postscarcity model, resources are not used up by production, hence the supply is potentially limitless.

This is partially true about the digital products (in which items are really digital copies), although this economy is also heavily resources dependent: for example, digital storage takes up space, consumes a significant amount of energy, and relies on a significant amount of human workload. Still, a single cultural product appears in its digital form as devoid of the quality of scarcity: making copies—after all—appears effortless. In fact, products of culture have for long belonged to an interesting class of products whose supply and—in result—price tags, have appeared to be partially regulated by scarcity, yet at the same time they have opened small windows into a different service-based economy. At least from the moment Western civilization began to regulate access to the products of culture through intellectual property rights, products of culture have acquired qualities of both material alienable objects (which are produced from resources, but also can be traded and inherited) and of services (consumers are only granted licenses to use content; even though they may 'own' the physical copy of the product of culture, they never can claim ownership to the actual content).

The dual character of the cultural product (treated as a physical artifact and as a service) is then best illustrated by how two distinct cultural markets operate. The first of these markets—the street price market—regulates the price of cultural content not in relation to the scarcity of content or of resources, but by the general policies of the publishers (vastly simplifying: all CDs or all books cost more or less the same amount of money, no matter what the actual production costs are). In this sense the scarcity of the original product is simultaneously illusory (because, if needs arise, all demand is satisfied by producers) and very real (because these artifacts have price tags reflecting a complex structure of expenses reflecting the scarcity of resources and markups). The street prices reflect, then, a compromise between the value of the service and the value that scarcity of the resources entails.

The prices in the other type of the cultural market—the secondhand market—are motivated nearly purely by the scarcity of the physical medium. Secondhand prices of sought-after first editions testify to that. The significance of the scarcity-based secondhand market is often exploited by these publishers, who intentionally build their reputation on artificial scarcity of their products: releases from cult publishers make them collectible items from the get-go.

Collecting and Digital Inheritance

Collections, as well as the practice of collecting, help us understand the basic differences between physical scarcity and artificial scarcity. Most valuable collections communicate their value to others on an intimate level, helping people define themselves (and helping them to be defined by others) through the stuff they own. However, this is often emotionally consuming, for example, when it comes to taking stock of inherited collections that belonged to one's kin. Yet, collections also have an economic dimension: they are properties, which are subject to appreciation, trade, and inheritance. In fact, inheritance of valuable collections is understood in Western civilization as an integral property right. Since the scarcity of collectible items is simultaneously intrinsically linked to the economic power an individual exercises and—by extension—to his or her identity, inherited collections tell very intricate stories of past lives. This is also precisely why studying collections and collecting—in particular, digital collections—may be crucial for further research on digital heritage and digital inheritance.

Collecting digital assets appears to be a suspect concept. Without the scarcity of physical collectible media, the digital assets may fail to generate enough emotional vitality to be 'collectible.' Their greatest shortcoming in this respect is the lack of economic value since they cannot be resold. Digital distribution platforms are experimenting, however, with artificial scarcity—for example, through time-limited offers, promotions, special sale coupons, etc. These practices attempt to recreate the dynamics of scarcity-driven collectible markets. In 2013 Valve, the owners of the Steam platform, introduced exchangeable collectible virtual cards. Unlike the equipment useful in combat in MMORPGs (massively multiplayer online role-playing games), these cards, which can be earned by Steam users in the games they play, have no practical purpose, but only create the incentive to play more often. They cost real (if little) money on the collectible market, can be traded for other cards, and could be mistaken for physical objects that can make up an identity of a Steam user. Yet, so far, they cannot be inherited.

Regulating Digital Inheritance

The scope of the current legal regulations concerning digital inheritance does not meet the public expectations voiced by media. The problems of digital inheritance are introduced first as a problem of regulating property (the succession rights to digital assets such as music files, games, e-books, etc.) and only second as regulating access to products of human expression (access to social media accounts). For example, an article at MarketWatch.Com asked on August 18, 2012: "Who Inherits Your iTunes Library?" "What Happens to All That Digital Goodness You Have Purchased after You Die?" asks another story at TechDirt.com in 2012. "Who Owns Your iTunes Library after Death?" asks yet another at *Slate Magazine* on August 22, 2014, etc.

In a wider perspective, however, the complex issues of digital inheritance have not attracted a lot of media attention. Also, it seems that consumers and companies alike have so far failed to recognize the significance of digital inheritance, although it can be speculated that as the generations of Internet users get older, new trends will be established among other signs of maturing of the Internet. For example, around 11% out of 2,000 polled Britons include account passwords in their wills. The financial value of digital assets is also significant: the same poll estimated that the combined value of digital assets stored by Britons online amounts to approximately £2.3 billion (Yardley 2015). Although no similar studies were undertaken in America, we can only expect the data to be even more intriguing. It is in America, too, that the significance of digital inheritance began to be recognized by the authorities and businesses.

In August 2014 Delaware became the first U.S. state to introduce a law that allows family members or other fiduciaries to access digital assets of the deceased. Delaware has become, then, the first state to create a uniform legal infrastructure to begin the process of settling the issues of digital inheritance. Until this infrastructure is reached, no estate attorney can suggest a surefire procedure that would secure the survivors' access to 'the digital estate' left behind by their loved ones, although many do attempt to do so, as 'digital undertaking' and digital estate management are becoming viable sources of business for a growing number of legal firms all over the world. Securing digital inheritance has been described as problematic not only because it is still unclear in many jurisdictions who actually 'owns' the digital goods stored online, but also because particular provisions of terms of use of a vast majority of online services would, until very recently, literally specify that user accounts are nontransferrable and are either to be frozen or deleted in case of a user's death. By now, a total of nine states have adopted some form of digital inheritance laws, are currently working on them, or plan to enforce them in the near future. Most of these regulations have originated in less than three years.

As groundbreaking as the Delaware regulations now seem, the most crucial event in the brief history of the concept of digital inheritance came in February 2015, when Facebook announced it now recognizes users' rights to appoint their digital fiduciaries to manage the accounts upon death. For nearly a decade, Facebook responded to notifications that account holders were deceased by verifying the death and freezing the account so no changes could be made. In 2015 the company changed this policy: "[w]e heard from family members who wanted to post funeral information or download and preserve photos," said Facebook product manager Vanessa Callison-Burch, as quoted by a *Telegraph* article on February 12, 2015. "We realized there was more we could do," she continued. This policy completely misses the point of what digital inheritance might be—for example, it fails to mention what happens to the effects of user expression and who owns and controls them after user's death.[5]

96   *Marcin Sarnek*

All these legal and corporate regulations may affect our perception of privacy and property in ways difficult to predict. For example, it seems logical to expect that the provisions of digital inheritance laws will attempt to create some system of privacy securities for the individuals involved in communications with the deceased. An indiscriminate access to one's online accounts would reveal, after all, a plethora of private information concerning not only the deceased, but also his or her whole social network. Hence, Facebook now blocks access to these private messages after a user's death. This regulation is strikingly different from more traditional inheritance laws, which do not discriminate between private and nonprivate assets. When individuals inherit private letters, rarely are their rights to read them questioned, although this correspondence is authored by people who never granted any such access. The potential access to often intimate instant messages or to the volumes of e-mail communications dramatically call for balanced digital media regulations. Users may build seemingly excluding identities through different online interactions, which may contain traces of historical indiscretions or ongoing transgressions of trust, and thus digital inheritance affects not only the memory and the postmortem identity of the dead, but also the future of relations between the living. If digital inheritance laws are to include blanket permissions for the surviving family members to access all information, all this is likely to change our understanding of online privacy.

So perhaps a discriminatory and controlled access is the model that should be sought after—one that would require from the conscious 'netizens' incessant proactive management of all their digital assets. The necessity of a detailed plan of what within our digital heritage is supposed to be 'forgotten' and what is supposed to be passed on may suddenly turn our online existence into a more tedious experience. If we begin to think that these future regulations may actually apply not only to the emotional load the inherited digital assets are prone to bring, but also to digital collections possibly worth significant amounts of money, we may experience a major headache just trying to figure out how to systematize access to different forms of our digital heritage.

Privacy and the Projection of the Self

The regulation of digital inheritance partially extends from three important products of the digital era—the trading of first-sale rights for the lack of friction, the shifts in contemporary understanding of intellectual property, and the monetization of identity (the most important commodity in the digital market)—which in turn develop because of the redefining of the relationships between individuals and corporations in terms of control. For example, numerous digital rights that originate from the more traditional rights to privacy have been defined in terms of exercising dynamic control over the dissemination of information about ourselves to the outside world and a personal dynamic management of information. This is a major shift from more static definitions of privacy, which saw protection of privacy rather in terms of setting up passive systems of defenses provided by the legal framework. In other words, individuals cannot expect their privacy to be protected only by passive access-control devices such as paddle locks or cryptographic technologies, but they are expected to actively control the dissemination of knowledge about them. Thus, the projection of a private self to the outside world is now often seen as a product of one's autonomous decisions pertaining to one's own perception of oneself, or to the image of oneself that one wishes to imprint in others. The users are supposed to decide what to share and—as the recent history of the 'right to be forgotten' shows—they may have some say in what information about them stays public and what can be withdrawn. While this may sound like an interesting proposition, such definitions of privacy relieve the social media services of the responsibilities to provide automatic traditional protections and to replace them with a system of 'privacy settings,' which, when used ineffectively, create problems the users (and not the businesses) have to cope with. The history of this process overlaps with the history of property, including digital property.

Privacy rights originate in part from material property rights, also from a hotly contested form of property that we call today intellectual property. In eighteenth century England, the right to privacy was legally protected solely by similar mechanisms as property. For example, in 1741 the British poet Alexander Pope found himself involved in a legal case against a bookseller who obtained and published without consent letters exchanged between Pope and Jonathan Swift. The privacy of Pope's letters was upheld in court on the grounds that the writer of a letter has a property right in his expression (Deazley 2004, 71–74). Moreover, Lord Hardwicke famously commented upon the case in his decision, establishing the duality of cultural products in the English-speaking world:

> I am of opinion that it is only a special property in the receiver, possibly the property of the paper may belong to him; but this does not give a license to any person whatsoever to publish them to the world, for at most the receiver has only a joint property with the writer.
> (quoted in Deazley 2004, 71)

The proprietary dimension of privacy dominated the legal discourse until the actual right to privacy was invented by the future Supreme Court Justice Louis Brandeis and his friend Samuel Warren.

The movement toward a more dynamic understanding of privacy coincided with the birth of serious legal interest in privacy issues in the U.S. Louis Brandeis and Samuel Warren set this in motion in their 1890 *Harvard Law Review* article, calling for a stricter protection of individuals against the curiosity of sensation-greedy journalists. In the article, Brandeis and Warren, enraged by the prying of the press into Warren's private affairs, summed up most of the privacy issues the Supreme Court would be occupied with in

98   *Marcin Sarnek*

the years to come. This diagnosis, one might notice, sounds eerily accurate today:

> The press is overstepping in every direction the obvious bounds of propriety and of decency. Gossip is no longer the resource of the idle and of the vicious, but has become a trade, which is pursued with industry as well as effrontery. To satisfy a prurient taste the details of sexual relations are spread broadcast in the columns of the daily papers. To occupy the indolent, column upon column is filled with idle gossip, which can only be procured by intrusion upon the domestic circle. The intensity and complexity of life, attendant upon advancing civilization, have rendered necessary some retreat from the world, and man, under the refining influence of culture, has become more sensitive to publicity, so that solitude and privacy have become more essential to the individual; but modern enterprise and invention have, through invasions upon his privacy, subjected him to mental pain and distress, far greater than could be inflicted by mere bodily injury.
>
> (Warren and Brandeis 1890)

The real significance of the article, although it brought no swift legal revolutions, lies in further voicing of the changing sensitivity to the notion of privacy, as it separates it for good from the notion of property: "[the] principle which protects personal writings and all other personal productions, not against theft and physical appropriation, but against publication in any form, is in reality not the principle of private property, but that of an inviolate personality" (Warren and Brandeis 1890).

Recent decades have shown, nonetheless, that a new dynamic approach to privacy is necessary, since privacy extends to all aspects of identity and is not limited to physical protection against invasion of the boundaries of identity defined as a material self, residing in matter occupying some physical space. Traditional and static definitions of privacy defined the concept as, for example, secrecy, anonymity, and solitude. An often quoted definition by Ruth Gavison makes privacy a limitation of others' access to an individual through information, attention, or physical proximity (1980, 433–447). Other definitions saw it as intimacy: as "the voluntary and temporary withdrawal of a person from the general society through physical or psychological means, either in a state of solitude or small-group intimacy or, when among larger groups, in a condition of anonymity or reserve" (Westin 1970, 7). All of these only hint at the active role of the individual in securing privacy, by suggesting a conscious character of decisions pertaining to this 'withdrawal.' All these definitions see privacy as a kind of asset (although residing in the physical spaces as well as in the psyche) to be protected by voluntary action calling for secrecy, anonymity, intimacy, etc., thus describing the whole 'right to privacy' rather as the right to protect oneself than the right to be protected.

When You Are Not What You Do Not Have 99

The new dynamic definition explains the shift from seeking privacy in physical spaces to trying to assure it in virtual spaces where sensitive personal information is particularly open to abuse. As identity dynamically extends via communication from within the physical space (after all, people occupy physical spaces), all these extensions through media have to be included in the very definition of privacy: the new definition is not to protect premises (physical spaces), but rather the information about individuals that they themselves choose to project. Thus, as the shift gained momentum with the development of communication technologies of the late twentieth century, this also highlighted the need for defining and protecting 'informational privacy.'

The notion of informational privacy is based on a definition of privacy put forward by Alan Westin, who defined it as the "claim of individuals, groups or institutions to determine for themselves when, how, and to what extent information about them is communicated to others" (Westin 1970, 7). Importantly, it is closely related to the concept of 'financial privacy'—the rights of individuals to control the collection, storing, use, and dissemination of information concerning their personal financial affairs by their financial institutions and third parties. In short, it extends the definition of the right to privacy to the control of personal information.

The projection of the self to the outside world and the interaction with others cocreate the self that needs to be protected by a complex negotiation of boundaries of private space, yet that nevertheless may be projected onto the public sphere. This illustrates how privacy came to be understood as a right protecting the dynamic metaphorical space rather than proprietary physical and psychological aspects to the self. This definition also explains why people want to control personal information: "control over personal information is control over an aspect of the identity one projects to the world, and the right to privacy is the freedom from unreasonable constraints on the construction of one's identity" (Agre 2001, 7). The right to privacy is then not a right to shut down physical access to the self, but a right not to be limited in one's active constructing of the self. Finally, such a definition explains how the privacy debates can be viewed as the forum for a discussion of human rights—once we count privacy among the factors safeguarding and modeling identity, it may appear clear that intrusion of privacy is inevitably violence—not against the objective (and objectified) secret, but rather against subjectivity, which by such intrusions becomes objectified. This explains in the end why these intrusions are felt to be humiliating, downgrading, and sacrilegious.

This more positive definition of privacy as projection of self cannot make us forget how crucial property is to establishing private relationships and—by extension—to establishing identity. In general, recent developments in technologies have forged a set of perceptions of privacy in numerous places resembling the historical proprietary approaches, and then in others breeding original trends. These trends are at least partially modeled by the inflating objectification of the individual perceived as a collection of assets, among which individual privacy has been reduced to a transferable commodity, which had been made possible by the emergence of a digital market.

The most important example of such processes comes from a massive redefinition of the contemporary understanding of intellectual property regulations, which have been successfully shifting from models providing incentive for creativity into ones that focus on control over the effects of creativity. And—again—copyrights and how we treat them today illustrate how easy it is to link the seemingly ungraspable aspects of human identity and privacy with ownership, and hence with property, which has been in fact the root of all privacy regulations in the Western world. The great turn-around that the notion of privacy seems to have completed—from being defined as property, then as a dynamic projection of self, and then again as an asset—also helps define more precisely the problems our civilization has with digital inheritance. In a sense, digital inheritance rights address the most sensitive aspects of human privacy and, paradoxically, these are exactly the ones that have suffered from this redefinition. Digital inheritance—as with the right to privacy—is understood more in terms of property than in terms of control over one's projection to the world.

In the end, we are left with potentially excluding logics of digital inheritance: one is focused on the effects of human creativity, another on a peculiar type of property that in some way just evaporates the moment we stop breathing. Yet, there seems to be also another logic that perhaps regulates the attitudes of the youngest digital consumers, who will soon—as they continue to mature—create their own, more conscious understanding of property, privacy, and—by extension—inheritance. This new understanding can be perhaps summed up quite briefly, too: digital property? We don't really care.

Notes

1. On January 11, 2016, *Bloomberg Business* in the article "Snapchat's Daily Mobile Video Views Said to Rival Facebook's" reported that by the end of 2015 the number of daily video views nearly matched Facebook's at approx. six billion views a day. In a matter of a month the updated user statistics published by Snapchat estimated this number to have grown by another billion. Note that these videos were sent among about 100 million active users, which looks both bleak and spectacular once it is compared to Facebook's eight billion daily views shared by over one billion users. Snapchat videos are supposed to be permanently deleted from servers once they are seen by the user to whom they were sent.
2. Native digital media are media whose primary delivery technology is digital and online.
3. The first-sale doctrine limits certain rights of copyrights holders, in that once the "first sale" is made it allows individuals who legally acquired copyrighted goods to resell the goods or otherwise manage them in whatever manner they like. First-sale rights include, then, the individual's right to resell, lend, give away, throw away, destroy, etc. physical media.

When You Are Not What You Do Not Have   101

4. For example, since the *UsedSoft v Oracle* ruling German courts refused twice the claims of consumer rights activists that Steam-purchased games should be alienable (resalable).
5. It should be noted that in 2013 Google did the same, becoming the first of the new media giants to recognize the social sensitivity to the complexities of digital inheritance. The difference between Google's and Facebook's gestures is a major one, though. Facebook did succumb to pressure from a number of its users to drop its policy of freezing an account after a user's death, hence generating significant media attention. Google's proactive decision, on the other hand, failed to generate any major discussion on the issue.

References

Agre, Philip. 2001. "Introduction." In *Technology and Privacy: The New Landscape*, edited by Philip Agre and Marc Rotenberg, 1–28. Cambridge, MA: MIT Press.

Colombani, Laurent, and David Sanderson. 2015. "Generation #Hashtag Ascendant: Think Native Digital First." Bain and Company Study. Available online at http://www.bain.com/Images/BAIN_BRIEF_Generation_hashtag_ascendent.pdf.

Deazley, Ronan. 2004. *On the Origin of the Right to Copy: Charting the Movement of Copyright Law in Eighteenth Century Britain (1695–1775)*. Oxford and Portland, OR: Hart Publishing.

Eventbride. 2014. "UK Study Reveals Millennials Want Experiences, Not Possessions." Available online at http://www.pressat.co.uk/releases/uk-study-reveals-millennials-want-experiences-not-possessions-1f90ece0f2f8747abe7bf057dbcc443d/.

Gavison, Ruth. 1980. "Privacy and the Limits of Law." *Yale Law Journal* 89 (3): 421–471. Retrieved from http://www.jstor.org/stable/795891.

Roesner, Franziska, Brian T. Gill, and Tadayoshi Kohno. 2014. "Sex, Lies, or Kittens? Investigating the Use of Snapchat's Self-Destructing Messages." Financial Cryptography and Data Security Conference, 2014.

Romano, John. 2011. "A Working Definition of Digital Assets." *The Digital Beyond*. September 1. Available online at http://www.thedigitalbeyond.com/2011/09/a-working-definition-of-digital-assets/comment-page-1/.

Sparks and Honey. 2015. "Gen Z 2025. The Final Generation." Available online at https://reports.sparksandhoney.com/campaign/generation-z-2025-the-final-generation.

The Telegraph. 2015. "Facebook Will: Users Can Now Appoint 'Heir' to Manage Account When They Die." Available online at http://www.telegraph.co.uk/news/uknews/11408898/The-Facebook-will-users-can-now-appoint-heir-to-manage-account-when-they-die.html.

van Niekerk, A. J. 2006. "The Strategic Management of Media Assets; a Methodological Approach." Available online at http://www.widen.com/the-dam-basics/what-is-a-digital-asset/.

Walker, Mark. 2014. "Study: Millennials Want Experiences More Than Anything." Eventbride study. Available online at http://www.eventbrite.co.uk/blog/millennials-want-experiences/.

Warren, Samuel D., and Louis D. Brandeis. 1890. "The Right to Privacy." *Harvard Law Review* 6 (5). Retrieved from http://groups.csail.mit.edu/mac/classes/6.805/articles/privacy/Privacy_brand_warr2.html.

Westin, Alan F. 1970. *Privacy and Freedom*. Oxford: Bodley Head.

Yardley, Christina. 2015. "Digital Inheritance of Digital Assets." Available online at http://www.actons.co.uk/latest/2015/04/digital-inheritance-digital-assets.

Part III

The Agency of Things and the Negotiation of Meaning

8 I See Faces

Popular Pareidolia and the Proliferation of Meaning

Joanne Lee

In recent times it has been hard to avoid the contemporary fascination for 'pareidolia'—that curious act of facial recognition performed upon everyday things and places—when variously smiling, perplexed, or grimacing faces are identified in such unlikely objects as cheese graters, parking meters, or coat hooks. Such instances are often shared online via specific sites, blogs, and social networks using an #iseefaces hashtag; British comedian Dave Gorman has an amusing Flickr pool devoted to the matter, and photographer Francois Robert produced a best-selling calendar featuring pictures of the 'faces' he discerned among mops, sockets, and hinges. That the phenomenon also appeared in the 2013 Venice Biennale—when examples from surrealist Roger Callois's collection of 'pictorial stones' were exhibited, including among their number an agate wherein emerges the form of a ghostly little creature to which had been assigned the name Le Petit Fantôme—demonstrates something of its enduring interest to artists and scholars of aesthetics, alongside those who find such stuff merely diverting.

Pareidolia—the term originates from the Greek 'para' (παρά—beside or beyond) and 'eidōlon' (εἴδωλον—form or image)—occurs when we perceive 'meaning' in random source material as a result of the human visual system's tendency to extract patterns from 'noise.' It is not just faces we see—we spot animals in the shapes of billowing clouds, letter forms in stones, and the outline of familiar countries or islands in mere marks on the wall. The tendency is not only visual but also occurs in sound: Leonardo da Vinci described hearing names and words conjured in the sound of bells, and when John C. Lilly recorded the word 'cogitate,' looped it, and played it back repeatedly, his several hundred listeners identified over 2,000 different words and phrases amidst the resulting audio. Having come to remark the sheer number of posts devoted to the subject within contemporary popular culture online, I found myself thinking about the human desire to read into things, and about the way such interpretations are subsequently treated. As an artist-researcher working with the everyday, I have realized that I am committed to a project to *enlarge* what can be generated from the ordinary objects and materials that surround us, rather than coming to definitive interpretations, as might 'normally' be the case in other disciplines. I have become interested therefore in the propriety of what it is possible to think and in what happens if these 'possible thoughts' are pursued creatively and critically.

106 *Joanne Lee*

My desire for enabling a richer panoply of interpretive routes takes up Michel Foucault's assertion that as academics we are suffering from "channels that are too narrow, skimpy, quasi-monopolistic, insufficient" and his suggestion that "we must multiply the paths and the possibility of comings and goings" (Foucault 1996, 305). It also responds to Gerald Raunig's more recent criticism of research in the current university regime through which "wild and transversal writing" is tamed by being fed into the "creativity-destroying apparatuses of disciplining institutions" wherein researchers are subjected to the 'fetish of method' and required "to squeeze the last vestiges of their powers of invention into the straitjacket of the essay industry" (Raunig 2013, 35).

My own attempt to multiply possibilities and to wriggle free from the institutional straitjacket is made through an independent serial publication, the Pam Flett Press,[1] Issue #5 of which, "I See Faces," specifically considers pareidolia as a kind of process and metaphor for the generation of meaning and interpretation, a method that opens up routes for critical and creative work. While I came to know of the term pareidolia through the proliferation of online sites devoted to recording and sharing the phenomenon, I realize that my first encounter took place long before this, thanks to the patterned Anaglypta wallpaper of my childhood bedroom: in those twilight minutes before I slept, I would see devilish or comic faces emerge as I gazed absently at the pattern of raised swirls. Years later, I was still preoccupied by such things: having stripped the paper from a house during renovations, I found myself drawn to the strange faces formed out of scuffed and stained plaster, and rather than having attended, as I ought, to the necessary redecoration, instead I spent hours with a pen, recording their variety in a series of drawings.

The propensity for pareidolia seems to go back a very long way in human history. There is, for example, the Makapansgat pebble, a river-worn stone whose naturally formed contours resemble crude eyes and a mouth; it was found associated with an australopithecine burial in South Africa, many miles away from what would have been its original source. While it is impossible to know how this stone was viewed or interpreted at the time, as well as what the perceptive and cognitive capabilities of such beings were, thanks to its apparently purposeful relocation, archaeologists have hypothesized that it may well have been recognized as a face, and that this seemed to have some significance for the hominids concerned (Dart 1974).

The ability and desire to perceive 'meaning' in random source material has been a regular human occurrence. It can be discerned via the countless references in literature and art. Take, for example, the act of seeking and finding shapes in cloud forms—nephelococcygia—that is recorded in Aristophanes' play *The Birds*, when its characters erect a perfect imaginative city (so-called cloud cuckoo land), or how Shakespeare has Hamlet toy with Polonius as he points out a cloud he at first claims might resemble a camel, then a weasel, and finally a whale. (*The Simpsons* surely riffs on this with a scene in "The Telltale Head," in which clouds "start looking like stuff"—variously a cherry bomb, a guy with a switchblade stuck in his back, a school bus going over a cliff in flames with kids inside screaming, and the statue of Springfield founder Jebediah Springfield—without the head, of course) (*The Simpsons* 1990). Dario Gamboni's *Potential Images* offers a compendium of artists and thinkers inspired by sky gazing: he lists Piero di Cosimo looking at the sky for pictorial inspiration, Novalis writing of figures forming therein, Denis Diderot desirous of leaving the imagination free "like children seeing shapes in clouds," and Odilon Redon's reminiscence of his father's instruction to see in the changing shapes "apparitions of strange, fantastical and marvelous beings" (Gamboni 2002, 69).

Gamboni notes how such tendencies have long been used by artists as triggers for creative work. One eleventh century treatise by Chinese painter Sung Ti suggests that the artist use an old tumbledown wall spread with piece of thin white silk:

> [G]aze at it until at length you can see the ruins through the silk, its prominences, its levels, its zig-zags and its cleavages, storing them up in your mind and fixing them in your eyes. Soon you will see men, birds, plants and trees, flying and moving among them. You may then ply your brush according to your fancy.
>
> (Gamboni 2002, 24)

Leonardo da Vinci's *Treatise on Painting* famously recommended artists look at rock formations, walls, and stained surfaces, as well ashes, clouds, mud, and other seemingly unlikely sources in order to inspire landscapes, scenes, men and animals, devils and monsters:

> If you have to invent some scene, you can see there resemblances to a number of landscapes, adorned in various ways with mountains, rivers, rocks, trees, great plains, valleys and hills. Moreover, you can see various battles, and rapid actions of figures, strange expressions on faces, costumes, and an infinite number of things, which you can reduce to good, integrated form.
>
> (Da Vinci 1956, i, 50–51; 35v, para 76)

During the Renaissance, actual 'pictorial stones' seeming to depict strange cities and landscapes were collected and enjoyed as works in themselves; in some cases they were further developed by an artist, worked up with additional overpainting, as in Johann König's 1632 *The Last Judgement* and *Crossing of the Red Sea*, paintings in which the agate itself variously makes up the cloud formations or the tumultuous sea from which painted figures emerge.

Alexander Cozens's 1785 *A New Method of Assisting the Invention in Drawing Original Compositions of Landscape* suggested the artist: "[p]ossess your mind strongly with a subject" and "with the swiftest hand make all possible variety of shapes and strokes upon your paper" in such a way that was unpremeditated, unguided, and unconscious (Oppé 1952, 173). The painter should then study the shapes until some "proper meaning such as the blot suggest" has been produced, "taking care not to add anything not suggested by it, and leave out what appears to be unnatural" (173). Cozens relates how he had stumbled across his idea upon pulling out a dirty piece of paper upon which to demonstrate something to a student, where he had found the preexisting marks thereon to help him to crystallize an idea.

By the early twentieth century, with representational orders called into question, artists were interested once more in potential images, ambiguity, and interpretability: as a child Paul Klee was obsessed with the grotesque creatures he saw in the marble tabletops at his uncle's restaurant, and Salvador Dali gazed at the stained ceiling of his school where he found detailed images he imbued with personality. While the art historian H. W. Janson resolved artistic approaches as definitively falling either into *mimesis*—artists' 'discovering' what nature put there—or *fantasia*—as when artists actively read into or interpret vague forms, perhaps in clouds or flames—Marina Warner considers this too stark a binary categorization given that mimesis "depends on a language of signs that is rooted in the world of the imagination with analogy, metaphor, and associations" (Warner 2006, 108). She describes how, in the effort to figure the unseen, when artists thought they were looking empirically at hidden forms they were in fact being led by their fantasia, which in turn was shaped by "diverse, buried codes of cognition and communication" (108).

Pareidolia is not just of interest to artists: it continues to recur in religion. Following a 1992 apparition experienced by Anita Contreras, the image of Our Lady of Guadalupe was 'seen' in the bark of an oak tree in a park in Watsonville, California (Carroll 2015). Years later Contreras's cousin, Elvira Mendoza de Vidales, continued to maintain the shrine each day, pointing out the shape to visitors with the aid of a tilted mirror; she said she had come to see other sacred images in trees and on the ground. In Chicago, Obdulia Delgado told friends she had seen the Virgin Mary in the salt stains that had appeared on the wall of a concrete viaduct; by the following day a group of faithful had gathered at the site, which turned in time into a small shrine with flowers and votive candles (Zorn 2006). Muslims too have claimed to see the name of Allah spelled out in Arabic in a host of unprepossessing locations and objects—the brown and white pattern of a lamb's coat, within the seedy interior of an aubergine, the scales of a fish. ...

These days, many people enjoy poking fun at the devout—whatever their creed—who believe themselves to have seen signs of their faith in some everyday object or surface. The web post *50 Objects That Look a Little like Jesus* is typical of this in the way it sneers at the possibility of seeing the savior's face in unlikely places: its extensive list includes a glass of chocolate milk, the patterns on a small turtle's shell, the brown patches of a

I See Faces 109

discolored grape or the skin of a bruised banana, in grease on a burger grill, and the burnt residue on the bottom of an iron, as well as in stains on the floor, swirls of paint on a wall, and the knots in timber doors and planks (Burns 2011). For the most part such found forms and imagery are these days considered mere curiosities or a momentary amusement, their significance often restricted to the potential of an object to generate media coverage or financial reward. Myrtle Young of Fort Wayne, Indiana, became famous via her appearances on the Johnny Carson and David Letterman shows for the collection of potato crisps in which she had distinguished the faces and shapes of a host of creatures, famous people, and cartoon characters—there were horses' heads, dogs, and ducks;, a sleeping bird; Mr Magoo, Yogi Bear, and Mickey Mouse; Bob Hope and George Bush (these last rather dating their discoverer to a particular era of television viewing). People have claimed to see the likeness of Kate Middleton in a jellybean, Elvis in a piece of toast, and Mother Teresa in a cinnamon bun. This last, the 'miracle nun bun' as Nashville coffee shop owner Bob Bernstein termed it, spawned printed mugs and a range of other products until Mother Teresa's lawyers told him he did not have permission to use her image for commercial purposes and he withdrew them from the market (Bernstein 2004). More recently, one sports fan thought he spotted Rory McIlroy's face in a Danish pastry: as a result, Rob Price bet on the golfer's performance in the 2014 U.S. Masters tournament and, though McIlroy did indeed have a hugely successful year (scooping two major titles), unfortunately the Masters was not among his wins (Fearon 2014). Perhaps Price should have had a little more patience and waited a while for his payoff: he could have followed the example of Florida's Diane Duyser, who, upon 'recognizing' an image of the Virgin Mary in her grilled cheese sandwich, kept her culinary-religious treasure in a Tupperware container for some ten years before deciding to auction it on eBay; it went on to make her $28,000, having been bought by Internet casino GoldenPalace.com, which planned to tour it internationally (BBC News 2004).

Some are concerned to disavow the misperceptions of what they consider to be such gullible types. As its name indicates, Phil Plait's *Bad Astronomy* website normally specializes in debunking myths and misconceptions about astronomy, but his skeptical blog post occasioned by 'discovering' Lenin's face in stains on his shower curtain causes him to reflect upon the long history (and enduring contemporary fascination for) humans seeing faces and creatures in inanimate objects (Plait 2003). He reminds us that the astronomical constellations were named for the mythological figures they were said to resemble and goes on to remark how, when photographs of the Eagle nebulae were released, many rushed to say they had discerned the face of Jesus in its cloudy masses. While he admits that, if you stand back and squint, it vaguely resembles the way Jesus is represented in Western art, he is quick to counter: "[o]f course, it's not Jesus, it's just a random swirl of gas in a cloud 7,000 light years away." With our human ability to see patterns

110 *Joanne Lee*

in random material, he says that, if he scrutinized the Hubble pictures, he could also spot a Scottish terrier sitting up and begging, as well as a couple of cats, a buffalo, a bird, and several more faces.

Of course, all interpretations are culturally particular and depend a great deal upon the society in which we live, the artifacts within our knowledge or experience (a person would not see a ship in a cloud if the person had no knowledge of what a ship is or looks like), and how we have learned to see and think via the representational traditions of our society (when Americans look at the moon they tend to see the face of a man, while East Indians see a rabbit, Samoans a woman weaving, and the Chinese a monkey). As Marina Warner points out in her own reference to the varying patterns found by different cultures in the random scattering of stars, people have tended to begin with the same salient constellations, but to interpret them in diverse ways: Babylonian and Egyptian traditions were adopted by European astronomers and became the dominant way of naming groups of stars, but the Amerindian peoples saw alternative stories and characters—for the Barasana people the zodiac includes such evocatively named combinations as the Old Adze, Poisonous Snake, Caterpillar Jaguar, Scorpion, Big Otter, Fish Smoking Rack, Foam Egret, Large Umari Fruit Fence, Headless One, Armadillo, the Small Otters, and the Corpse Bundle (Warner 2006, 108).

Although familiar stellar groupings seem so fixed in Western astronomy, during the Early Modern period a veritable 'constellation mania' saw astronomers 'discovering' a host of star figures that they then named for patrons and famous people of the time, motivated apparently by political or financial ambition: in 1679 one Augustin Royer proposed a group of stars in the form of a scepter and hand in honor of Louis XIV, and in 1684 Gottfried Kirch spotted the crossed swords of the Electors of Saxony and named the constellation for Leopold I. Later, around the 1800s, stargazers saw manifestations in the form of contemporary technological developments—a hot air balloon, an electric generator, a printing office, and Herschel's large telescope number among those spotted. None of these survived the International Astronomical Union's designation of eighty-eight key formations: at this point over one hundred star 'patterns' were 'eradicated.' For artist Julia Christensen, via whose project I encountered these examples, this shows that such patterns "are nothing more than manifestations of the imagination, constructs we dream up to help us navigate the vast cosmos in which we dwell" rather than some type of fact to be discovered and verified (Christensen 2014, 45).

That Gaston Bachelard rather neatly described the constellations as "the Rorschach test of infant humanity" brings me to remark, too, on the famous test mobilized in psychiatric medicine, when patients responded to apparently abstract information contained in a collection of ink stains, with their response interpreted in turn by a trained clinician, working to a sanctioned method (Bachelard 1943, 202). In Rorschach the psychologist becomes "the rational interpreter of irrational interpretations" but is also practicing an art, investigating a phenomenon situated at the uncertain boundaries "where the actual shape of the self and the shape the world presents to it are hard to distinguish" (Starobinski 1958, 190). The technique's origins in the parlor game of 'klecksography,' when players took turns to drip ink and fold paper in order to see what figures emerged, reveals the conjunction of play and imagination at work with interpretation. This is surely there too in pediatrician and psychoanalyst D. W. Winnicott's 'squiggle game,' where a series of additive drawings, accompanied by dialogue about their potential meanings, would allow Winnicott to converse through drawing with those young patients who found it hard to put into words the difficulties they were feeling (Berger 1980).

This relationship of psychiatry and psychoanalysis to the interpretation of abstract data continues in those forms of mental illness in which sufferers find meaningful patterns in ways that are not sanctioned. In such cases, contrary to certain popular conceptions of what it is for someone to be 'mad,' it is not that things do not make sense, but rather that they start to make too much of it: things *mean* to excess. Such sensations were recognized by Klaus Conrad as marking the onset of delusional thinking in psychosis when sufferers begin to "repetitively and monotonously experience abnormal meanings in their experiential field" (Mishara 2010, 10). He characterized this as *apophänie*, inventing the neologism 'apophany' (from the Greek apo [away from] + phaenein [to show]) to describe how some psychotics initially experience delusion as revelation, but the insights they have as a result are only self-referential, solipsistic, and paranoid. August Strindberg's *Inferno* gives a sense of this:

> There on the ground I found two dry twigs, broken off by the wind. They were shaped like the Greek letter[s] for "P" and "y." I picked them up and it struck me that these two letters P-y must be an abbreviation of the name Popoffsky. Now I was sure it was he who was persecuting me, and that the Powers wanted to open my eyes to my danger.
> (Strindberg 1962, 68–69)

If seeing patterns in sticks is a sign of paranoia in some, for certain others—paranormal researchers, for instance—it may designate a way of tracking the mysterious 'Bigfoot': in Lisa Shiel's *Backyard Bigfoot: The True Story of Stick Signs, UFOs and the Sasquatch*, she notes sticks arranged in meaningful and distinctly unnatural displays, which she considers the vehicle for their nonverbal communication (Shiel 2006). I am in no position to comment on the legitimacy or sanity of Shiel's work, but I am interested to think how skilled hunters also read into the disposition of sticks and other debris on a forest floor in order to determine the passage or presence of animals of various sorts, and I wonder if matters here relate to a question of what it is proper and acceptable to look for at a given cultural moment.

112 *Joanne Lee*

Neuropsychologist Peter Brugger draws upon Strindberg's experiences in a paper about the role of the brain in the 'pattern recognition' of creative people, scientists, people with paranormal beliefs, and those suffering psychotic episodes. Brugger delineates a continuum, which has *detection* of real patterns at one end, and the 'hypercreative' *interpretation* of patterns in 'noise' at the other. Brugger notes that "[t]he ability to associate, and especially the tendency to prefer 'remote' over 'close' associations, is at the heart of creative, paranormal and delusional thinking" (2001, 196) and notes that the readiness to see connections between unrelated objects or ideas is what "most closely links psychosis to creativity" (205). Like Conrad, he suggests that a key symptom of psychotic experience is "a heightened awareness of the meaningfulness and personal relevance of any event together with the absolute conviction that no two things in the world are devoid of meaningful connections" (204). He quotes the testimony of two people who had encountered such sensations in their own psychotic breakdowns. For the first: "[e]very single thing 'means' something. This kind of symbolic thinking is exhaustive. I have a sense that everything is more vivid and important; the incoming stimuli are almost more than I can bear. There is a connection to everything that happens—no coincidences. I feel tremendously creative" (Brundage 1983, 584). And for the second: "[m]y trouble is that I have too many thoughts. You might think about something, let's say that ashtray and just think 'Oh! yes, that's for putting my cigarettes in,' but I would think of a dozen different things connected with it at the same time" (McGhie and Chapman 1961, 108).

For Brugger, the ability to see patterns and make connections is a hallmark of the creative mind in any field, but he distinguishes between the practices of art and science, suggesting that the arts can acknowledge and take advantage of the "purely subjective aspect of perceiving," while, by contrast, "scientific creativity requires not only the ability to detect patterns, but also the *interpretation* of their underlying cause" (205). He goes on to describe the potential errors to which the human mind is liable: "[i]ncorrectly assuming the presence of a pattern where, in fact, none exists, is labeled in the language of statistics a Type 1 error. In contrast, a Type 2 error refers to the incorrect conclusion that the data reflect 'noise' when a pattern is actually present" (205). In his thinking through the relativity of creativity—which runs, he says, from the correct detection of existing patterns to discovering pattern where none exists—he wonders why the genetic aspect of a predisposition to psychosis persists despite what he considers are the disadvantages it presents the species, and concludes that "[t]he price for a protection against committing Type 2 errors is a susceptibility to commit Type 1 errors" (210). Brugger asserts: "[a]s puzzling as it may read, a proper understanding of the world sometimes requires the successful *inhibition* of associations" (207). While Brugger repeatedly denigrates the projective imagination of psychoanalytic techniques, considering that they stray well beyond the 'proper' boundaries of interpretation, Marina Warner

I See Faces 113

notes how diagnostic tools relying on such techniques lie at the heart of so many nineteenth and twentieth century attempts to interrogate the psyche/self, including such disciplines as clinical psychology, psychoanalysis, and the activities of literary and artistic Surrealism. Warner saw graphology, lie detection, Rorschach testing, psychometrics, and the like as akin to those earlier Platonist traditions in which God's messages were thought to be concealed in text, when a gifted 'scryer' could reveal the secret significance of cryptic material; she notes how both Freud and Jung had something of a divinatory practice in their discovery of unconscious symbols in dream imagery and art. As a result, she writes,

> When the name of Allah is found inscribed in the heart of an aubergine, or Jesus' face in a burned tortilla, or pyramids on Mars, or the Virgin Mary in a tomato, or any such items beloved of organs such as the *National Inquirer*, and the world-wide web, we are not straying very far afield from rather more respected methods of interpretation, surprising as it may seem. (2006, 106–107)

Warner makes the case that from the nineteenth and twentieth centuries, "rather than discerning the activity of occult powers or revealing the hidden workings of divine providence, now the process tends to hold a mirror to the psyche of the subject" (2006, 107). She goes on, "When we see what we think we see, this can tell us something about who we are." At which point I find myself doing just that, using my fascination with the faces seen in stained walls, or in cheese graters and other such quotidian objects—as a means to figure and reflect on my own role and methodology as an artist-researcher, and the potential 'knowledge' generated as a result.

In my own thinking through practice—essaying the everyday in writing, photography, print, and audio—I want to credit the creative propensity, noted by Brugger, for making sense of data in ways usually considered improper in a serious inquiry. At art school I learned to make connections between seemingly disparate aspects, between high and low, *the popular* and abstruse, the overly familiar and the overlooked; to accommodate contradiction; and to read material in such a way that I could make new and mobile meanings from what is encountered. Museum director Christopher Woodward once suggested that while archaeologists see artifacts and sites as clues to a puzzle of which only one answer is correct, for artists, "any answer which is imaginative is correct" (2001, 30). I am curious therefore, in the work I do, to test the effects of such an approach within the academy.

I have come to think about the criticality of contradiction itself. Hans Magnus Enzensberger, whose "willingness to embrace contradictions [...] always marked his approach," according to David Blackbourn, took the essay as his favored form, and he mocked those academics who "with an air of triumph accused the essayist of contradictions, just imagine—contradictions!"

114 *Joanne Lee*

(Blackbourn 2010, 15). For the Hungarian writer Miklós Szentkuthy, the need for contradiction was explicit:

> For me the most incomprehensible secret is how someone can keep writing or building on a subject in one style to the very end. To achieve that degree of consistency I would need to freeze into some sort of intellectual tetanus as I am in a constantly changing relationship to my subject, and that is the most fundamental reality. (Szentkuthy 1995 translated and quoted in Tompa 2013, 289)

In terms of a constantly changing relationship to one's subject matter, I saw how this desire has been echoed by others in recent thinking on interdisciplinary research: Paul Carter characterized such research as being like "the shuttle ducking and weaving across the warp" of a loom, recalling the "physical sense of running hither and thither" evoked by the word 'discourse'; for him the aim of this process is "to *materialise discourse itself*" (2004, 9). For Irit Rogoff, art itself is an interlocutor: "it's the entity that chases me around and forces me to think differently" (2000, 10). She is clear that she is "trying to avoid the work being hijacked by some academic paradigm which would dictate a relation between objects and knowledge" (8).

The shifting exploration is evoked, too, by the 'semionaut'—that figure whom Nicolas Bourriaud identified as someone who invents paths through culture and signs. He claims that DJs, Web surfers, and certain types of contemporary artists project new, possible scripts endlessly onto culture, and he describes how "[w]hen we start a search engine in pursuit of a name or a subject, a mass of information issued from a labyrinth of data-banks is inscribed on the screen. The 'semionaut' imagines the links, the likely relations between disparate sites" (Bourriaud 2005, 19). Bourriaud's identification of a concern for "relations between disparate sites" finally draws me back to one of the specific historical examples of pareidolia I mentioned earlier: the identification and naming of the constellations. I want to use this as a means to figure an alternative to the linear academic thesis. I remembered how these imaginative manifestations had been mobilized by no lesser figure than Walter Benjamin in a powerful image for the historical work in which he was engaged. His metaphorical conception of the 'constellation' first appears in the prologue to his *Origin of German Tragic Drama* (1925), where he writes that "ideas are timeless constellations, and by virtue of the elements being seen as points in such constellations, phenomena are subdivided and at the same time redeemed" (Benjamin 2009, 34). In Benjamin, critical work is done in the connection between fragments and between different objects, registers, and discourses. Norm Friesen connects Benjamin's constellationary thinking with that of Siegfried Giedion and Marshall McLuhan, identifying "[j]uxtaposition and ironic counterposition across time and space [as] obviously modernist tropes" (Friesen, 2013, under *Conclusion: Redemption or Ricorso?*). He considers such thought in relation to Mieke Bal's idea of the 'traveling concept,' which is elastic ideas or metaphors, offering "sites of debate, awareness of difference and tentative exchange" (Bal 2002, 13).

So, while those online postings about faces seen in satchels, chairs, mops, foodstuffs, and culinary utensils alerted me to a phenomenon that seemed at first merely humorous and diverting, the contemporary fascination revealed a longer human history of pareidolia and its role in creativity, religion, mythmaking, science, psychoanalysis, and psychiatry. I came to understand that, as Howard Margolis' classic work makes clear, "the brain has a bias favouring seeing something rather than nothing, so that it tends to jump to a pattern that makes sense of a situation" (Margolis 1987, 38–39) and, indeed, that there may be evolutionary advantages to humans via such a propensity (Brugger 2001, 210). But while Brugger suggests that this leads too frequently to erroneous conclusions, the continuum of interpretative responses to 'data' of various sorts is creatively and critically of interest to me. Artists, academics, paranormal researchers, psychoanalysts, and the psychotic all have their differing take on what they think they see, and what they know as a result: I want to hold these perspectives in productive relation, rather than hierarchizing or definitively categorizing these according to their propriety.

Seen perhaps in terms of an immaterial illusion, pareidolia allows for richer, stranger readings of the everyday material we encounter. It in fact is a method with a long history that alters our perception and changes an approach to pattern recognition, interpretation, and the generation and proliferation of meaning. Artistic research can make knowledge in the form of possibilities, but it is thanks to the very objects and their place in popular culture that my project and practice were rethought and reenvisaged. By drawing together a critical constellation of references, responses, and reinterpretations, I refigure what kind of knowledge I make and what this can in turn make of me. Responding to Foucault's recognition of academic skimpy insufficiency, and to Raunig's desire for transversal, inventive writing within the university institution, I think of this work as the popular life of things creating their own complex agenda; the things think me. As a result I echo the aspiration of novelist William Gass: "you hope that the amount of meaning that you can pack into the book will always be more than you are capable of consciously understanding. Otherwise, the book is likely to be as thin as you are" (Gass, quoted in Colter Walls 2013, 22).

Note

1. The Pam Flett Press—its name plays on the idea of the pamphlet and evokes those historical or contemporary connotations of political, religious, or poetic pamphleteering—takes up the assertion credited to Andre Breton and widely circulated among independent-minded makers that "one publishes to find comrades" (quoted in Branwyn 1997, 52). The serial publication explores such phenomena as graffiti on urban walls, vacant lots that perforate the urban fabric, the ubiquitous plastic bag, the scatter of gum on city pavements, the pareidolic

116   *Joanne Lee*

desire to see faces in ordinary objects, and through the activity of *making* (publications) becomes both a making-one's-way-into-understanding the everyday *and* an increasingly metacritical project in which the everyday as material in turn rethinks my academic and artistic work. It pursues an interest in the creative and critical possibilities of the essay form—recalling that the etymological 'essay' comes from ideas of trial, test, and experiment (French speakers will know that 'essayer' is 'to try.') That an essay can be made from diverse material suits both the attention to disparate everyday subject matter and my own training in conceptual art when an appropriate form or material is sought for ideas rather than having a particular medium in mind in the first instance. An essay might certainly be written, but it could also be intended as audio, as in pieces for radio or Internet podcasts; it could be visual, using photographic, film/video, animation, or sequential images; it might be a physical exhibition, where ideas can be disposed and unfold in physical space and time or an interactive site online. My work with the Press was also motivated by Foucault's call for "a new age of curiosity," where one takes care "for what exists and could exist" and there is "a readiness to find strange and singular what surrounds us; a certain relentlessness to break up our familiarities and to regard otherwise the same things; a fervor to grasp what is happening and what passes; a casualness in regard to the traditional hierarchies of the important and the essential" and a need for "differentiation and simultaneity of different networks" (Foucault 1997, 305). It draws upon the insights and experiences of those within the academy that deliberately tarry in the vague terrains of practice, emerging from the apparently marginal grounds of scholarship where knowledge and knowing are themselves problematized, and multiple interpretations remain simultaneously and intentionally possible. (See Lee 2011a, 2011b, 2013, 2015).

References

Bachelard, Gaston. 1943. *L'Air et les Songes*. Paris: Corti.

Bal, Mieke. 2002. *Travelling Concepts in the Humanities: A Rough Guide*. Toronto: University of Toronto Press.

BBCNews. 2004. "Virgin Mary Toast Fetches $28,000." Available online at http://news.bbc.co.uk/1/hi/4034787.stm.

Benjamin, W. 2009. *The Origin of German Tragic Drama*. London: Verso.

Berger, Lawrence R. 1980. "The Winnicott Squiggle Game: A Vehicle for Communicating with the School-Aged Child." *Pediatrics* 66 (6): 921–924.

Bernstein, Bob. 2004. "The Nun Bun[TM]."*Skeptic Report*. Available online at http://www.skepticreport.com/sr/?p=432.

Blackbourn, David. 2010. "In the Opposite Direction." *London Review of Books* 32 (6): 15–18.

Bourriaud, Nicolas. 2005. *Postproduction: Culture as Screenplay: How Art Reprograms the World*. Berlin: Lukas & Sternberg.

Branwyn, Gareth. 1997. *Jamming the Media: A Citizen's Guide Reclaiming the Tools of Communication*. Vancouver: Chronicle Books.

Brugger, Peter. 2001. "From Haunted Brain to Haunted Science: A Cognitive Neuroscience View of Paranormal and Pseudoscientific Thought." In *Hauntings and Poltergeists: Multidisciplinary Perspectives*, edited by James Houran and Rense Lange, 195–223. Jefferson, NC: McFarland.

I See Faces   117

Brundage, B. E. 1983. "First Person Account: What I Wanted to Know but Was Afraid to Ask." *Schizophrenia Bulletin* 9 (4): 583–585.

Burns, Ashley. 2011. "50 Objects That Look a Little like Jesus." *Uproxx*. Available online at http://uproxx.com/webculture/2011/06/50-objects-that-look-a-little-like-jesus.

Carroll, Robert T. 2015. "Our Lady of Watsonville." *The Skeptic's Dictionary*. Available online at http://skepdic.com/watsonville.html.

Carter, Paul. 2004. *Material Thinking: The Theory and Practice of Creative Research*. Melbourne: Melbourne University Press.

Christensen, Julia. 2014. "Artist Project/Burnout." *Cabinet* 53: 44–49.

Dart, Raymond. 1974. "The Waterworn Australopithecine Pebble of Many Faces from Makapansgat." *South African Journal of Science* 70 (June): 167–169.

DaVinci, Leonardo. 1956. *Treatise on Painting*. Translated and edited by Philip McMahon. Princeton, NJ: Princeton University Press.

Fearon, Alana. 2014. "Golf Fanatic Bets £10K on Rory McIlroy to Win the Masters after Seeing Golfer's Face in a Danish Pastry." *The Mirror*. Available online at http://www.mirror.co.uk/news/uk-news/masters-2014-golf-fanatic-bets-3392438.

Foucault, Michel. 1996. "The Masked Philosopher." In *Foucault Live (Interviews, 1961–1984)*, edited by Sylvère Lotringer, 302–307. New York: Semiotext(e).

———. 1997. *Ethics. Subjectivity and Truth*. New York: The New Press.

Friesen, Norm. 2013. "Wandering Star: The Image of the Constellation in Benjamin, Giedion and McLuhan." Available online at http://learningspaces.org/wordpress/wp-content/uploads/2013/06/Wandering-Star-BenjaminGiedionMcLuhan21.pdf.

Gamboni, Dario, *Potential Images: Ambiguity and Indeterminacy in Modern Art*. London: Reaktion.

Gass, William. 1975. Quoted in Seth Colter Walls. 2013. "Something Unsafe about Books." *London Review of Books* 22: 22–23.

Lee, Joanne. 2011a. *Call Yourself a Bloody Professional*. Sheffield/Brighton: Pam Flett Press.

———. 2011b. *Lord Biro and the Writing on the Wall*. Sheffield/Brighton: Pam Flett Press.

———. 2013. *Gumming Up the Works*. Sheffield/Brighton: Pam Flett Press.

———. 2015. *Vague Terrain*. Sheffield/Brighton: Pam Flett Press.

Margolis, Howard. 1987. *Patterns, Thinking, and Cognition: A Theory of Judgment*. Chicago: University of Chicago Press.

McGhie, Andrew, and James Chapman. 1961. "Disorders of Attention and Perception in Early Schizophrenia." *British Journal of Medical Psychology* 34: 103–116.

Mishara, Aaron L. 2010. "Klaus Conrad (1905–1961): Delusional Mood, Psychosis, and Beginning Schizophrenia." *Schizophrenia Bulletin* 36 (1): 9–13.

Oppé, Adolph P. 1952. *Alexander and John Robert Cozens*. London: A & C Black.

Plait, Phil. 2003. "Just Another Face in the Crowd." *Bad Astronomy*. Available online at http://www.badastronomy.com/bad/misc/lenin.html.

Raunig, Gerald. 2013. *Factories of Knowledge, Industries of Creativity*. Los Angeles: Semiotext(e).

Rogoff, Irit. 2000. *Terra Infirma: Geography's Visual Culture*. London: Routledge.

The Simpsons. 1990. "The Telltale Head." Twentieth Century Fox Home Entertainment [distributor]. Film.

Shiel, Lisa. 2006. *Backyard Bigfoot: The True Story of Stick Signs, UFOs & the Sasquatch*. Lake Linden, MI: Slipdown Mountain Press, LLC.

Starobinski, Jean. 1958. "Des Taches et des Masques" *Critique* 135 (36): 792–804.

118 *Joanne Lee*

Strindberg, August. 1962. *Inferno*. London: Hutchinson.

Szentkuthy, Miklós. 1995. Translated by and quoted in Tompa, Maria. 2013. "Backdrops to the Ultimate Questions: Szentkuthy's Diary Life." *Hyperion: On the Future of Aesthetics* 8 (2): 282–318.

Warner, Marina. 2006. *Phantasmagoria: Spirit Visions, Metaphors, and Media into the Twenty-first Century*. Oxford: Oxford University Press.

Woodward, Christopher. 2001. *In Ruins*. London: Vintage.

Zorn, Eric. 2006. "Our Lady of the Underpass, One Year Later." *Chicago Tribune*. Available online at http://blogs.chicagotribune.com/news_columnists_ezorn/2006/04/our_lady_of_the.html.

9 From Piss-Communication to GraffARTi

Hegemony, Popular Culture, and the Bastard Art

David Walton

The (Un)popular Thing Called Graffiti

Joe Austin (2010) has made the point that 'graffiti art' is neither just graffiti nor art, but rather a new form of visual "cultural production" that "exceeds both categories" (33). Graffiti art differs from movements like Neo-Dada and Pop Art (mainly manifested on canvas and hung on gallery walls), because it is materialized on walls beyond the galleries in the public sphere. To take account of this kind of cultural production, analyses have drawn on both art history and urban studies (Goldman and Papson 1996; Morley 2003; Taylor 2008; Shannon 2009; Mirzoeff 2012) to investigate the practices that Austin has called the "more mundane experiences of urban walls and streets" (33). It is these 'more mundane' (but not insignificant) phenomena within the visual urban studies that will be explored in this chapter. According to Jeff Ferrrell (1996), graffiti can help to "investigate the social construction of everyday life" (xi) while illuminating a vital part of contemporary urban culture (3). Investigating graffiti also crosses over into the subcultural life that produces it (Macdonald 2001; Miller 2002; Kaltenhäuser 2007). This chapter will combine these approaches but, in the spirit of innovation and pushing the debates further, will merge them with other critical possibilities concerned with popular culture, hegemony, and practices of marking and pollution.

Graffiti is understood here as the product of a set of social practices that will be discussed in two main ways. Firstly, I will analyze what might be loosely called *uninvited forms of inscription*[1] associated with unlawful things from scratching, stencils, posters, throwups, plaques, photos, tags (even stick-on tiles and sculpture) to anything done with marker pens, paintbrushes, or spray cans. These are traditionally taken for delinquent individual acts often (but not necessarily) linked to subcultures. Secondly, I shall reflect upon manifestations that are the products of the same kinds of processes but that are considered legitimate and legal (even if they began, like some of Banksy's 'works,' as manifestations of the first category). I am treating graffiti as a thing—a visible set of objects that cannot be reduced to a simple definition.[2] The 'thing' of this chapter is, therefore, to discuss whatever comes out of the set of social practices designated as 'sign wars' (Goldman and Papson 1996)

120   *David Walton*

that make graffiti a complex form of struggle. This struggle complicates the meaning of *the popular*, which in cultural studies is a notoriously ambivalent term. As Raymond Williams points out, *the popular* could be anything from that which is well liked by many people to inferior kinds of work or cultural products; it is culture made specifically to win favor with the people, or actually made by the people for the people's use (1976, 237).

Apart from Williams's all-binding principle, one of the chief ways of defining *the popular* within cultural studies has been with relation to Adorno's notion of the culture industry where it is merely an extension of the capitalist machine that generates trivial, dehumanizing, and depoliticizing entertainment for profit (Adorno 1991, 143). Graffiti, however, does not fit this definition very easily, although it might be noted that the culture industries have certainly appropriated many of its styles (in music videos, games, ads, film, etc.). Another dominant way of discussing the term draws on Stuart Hall's deconstructive idea that *the popular* is actually structured against notions of 'high culture' (the great works of literature, philosophy, music, painting, and so on), which serve to maintain *the popular* as inferior (Hall 2009, 448).

From a contemporary point of view, the notion of *the popular*, although extremely complex, can be articulated with relation to hegemony theory, especially as used by the Birmingham School. This insists on seeing popular culture with reference to "forms and activities which have their roots in the social and material conditions of particular classes" and are "embodied in popular traditions and practices" (Hall 2009, 449). Since popular culture cannot be reduced to class relations, it is analyzed with relation to the ways it is in tension with the dominant culture (449). This requires consciousness of what pertains to the "central domain of elite or dominant culture" and the culture of the 'periphery.' This opposition, present at different moments in cultural history, configures the domain of culture into the 'popular' and the 'nonpopular,' the official or nonofficial (448–449). Therefore, popular culture is seen in political terms as a Gramscian site of struggle over its meaning and status and asks important questions about the social site of cultural exclusion and how ordinary people (or those excluded from power) express resistance against the "culture of the powerful" (453).

It may seem incongruous that I insist on discussing graffiti in terms of the discourses of popular culture, especially when one considers that it is not associated with the culture industries' requirement to manufacture popular entertainment for financial gain. However, as indicated before, notions of *the popular* transcend this narrow definition—John Fiske defining it not only as a consequence of an industrial system but also 'of the people' where, to be successful, industrially produced products must be able to appeal to the specific tastes and interests of the people. Popular culture is not just unthinking consumption but "an active process of generating and circulating meanings and pleasures" (1998, 23). Graffiti is made by sectors of the people but whether or not it is popular (in the terms described before) is a moot point. It is practically omnipresent but its 'consumption' is guaranteed because it can hardly be ignored and, rather than be popular because it is

From Piss-Communication to GraffARTi 121

"well-liked by many people" (Williams 1983, 237), may only be 'appreciated' by minorities. This opens up the idea that its popular life as a cultural 'thing' may entail its very opposite (or is profoundly ambiguous): it is always on the border of being (un)popular. As will be evident later in this chapter, as a material practice, it is often about taking liberties rather than exercising those freely given.

Piss-Communication, Excretion, and Other Territorial Appropriations

Graffiti goes back to at least the world of antiquity where, in 3,000 years or more of history, all kinds of people have created what Keegan calls "non-official texts and images" (2014, xii) for anyone who cares to engage with them. What characterizes graffiti from all over the world is the freedom it confers on people to release them from "everyday restraints," promoting "uninhibited reign" to thoughts (Peden in Keegan 2014, 1). Owing to its countercultural nature, graffiti has often been depicted as a kind of subcultural 'plague' (see the 1983 film *Style Wars*) that represents, for Michel Serres, a practice of appropriation akin to all living things (2008, x). We do that by marking them and, at the same time, polluting them in a variety of ways. These marking practices take different forms and range from twittering and howling to spitting, 'snotting,' urinating, or defecating. They all are manifestations of the human arrogation of land—whether that be the simple plot for personal use or the town, city, or entire geographical regions in the name of the nation (Serres 2008, 1–12)—associated with the possibilities of (de)(re)territorialization, whose social potential has been theorized within cultural materialism.[3] For Serres, however, these excretory marking rituals (which carry a primitive message of territorial ownership) are first and foremost the practices of writing: inscriptions to express certain cultural ownership and identity. My pun, 'piss-communication,' is a symbolic expression of the act of marking (and all its affiliate rituals), which, as signifying practices, plot, blot out another's smell, stake a claim, and therefore engage in struggles for control and sovereignty. As a form of artistic discharge, graffiti is absorbed into the history of marking and appropriation as a kind of subcultural 'piss' (Figure 9.1).

Serres also connects the act of squatting (to urinate, to defecate, to give birth) to its modern-day meaning of to occupy and possess (4f.) and graffiti is also one of the chief ways that the squatter stakes a claim and domesticates uninhabited spaces. In this way 'the squat' serves as a compelling symbol not only of law-breaking appropriations but also of the whole of 'civilization' itself: it is fabricated on habits of marking and annexation. Accordingly, when squatters commandeer a vacant building, they are, employing Serres's way of conceiving the conduct of all species, acting out an indispensable and primary survival ritual, which does not inevitably have to be connected to property rights. Nonetheless, the behavior of squatters can be understood as a radical form of interrogating ideas and practices of ownership and property rights, combined, as they are, with the imperatives of Serresian survival

122 *David Walton*

tactics. Yet this is, moreover, habitually merged with the practice of graffiti (see Figure 9.2), which (in a double appropriation) also contests ownership rights—in this instance, of visible space.

The Bastard Art of the Ill-Famed Streets

In this section I want to address the question of graffiti as a form of counter-hegemonic practice and how the Art establishment has attempted to appropriate it. Since the 1960s, the increasing proliferation of wild style and other forms of graffiti, manifested on anything from cars and walls to trains, has given greater visibility to these largely uninvited (un)popular visual experiences, which generally ride roughshod over the general desires of not only public institutions but also the public itself. However, advertising, serving the ends of commerce, is generally authorized and officially endorsed, whereas graffiti is generally represented as antisocial and the consequence of individual or collective responses and interests. However, the fate of the life of this (un)popular form has meant that selected aspects of it, while drawing on the kudos of it as marginalized, unofficial, chaotic, and illegal, have been transmogrified as officially sanctioned 'Street Art.' However, this is not just a process of appropriation by galleries and other art institutions.

Here defiant inscribers are involved in processes of counter-hegemony, pitting themselves against the general imperatives of sectors of the power bloc (and other people or groups with relatively little power, like neighbors). It is not that all inscriptions are illegal per se but rather that, within capitalism, some forms will be privileged over others. For example, while the rebellious tagger is "sometimes dragged into the courtroom against the advertising executive," it is possible to ask by what right advertising executives are allowed to pollute with their 'dirt' (Serres 2008, 56). Taggers can be seen to criticize this form of filth by imitating it.[4] This kind of reading facilitates possibilities of interpreting graffiti of all kinds in a way analogous to de Certeau's method in *The Practice of Everyday Life* (1988), where all forms of graffiti (from the discreditable racist slur to declarations of love and the political slogan) can be seen as a knock against the establishment. Here graffiti (like squatting) is a material practice that generally refuses the property rights and ownership installed as pivots of the capitalist system but it is, at the same time, 'dirt'—a part of the greater whole of territorialization and pollution of all kinds (whether chemical gas, radiation, or signs) that increasingly threaten the environment. If graffiti is thought of in terms of popular culture, this would fit in with Fiske's argument that popular culture "always has progressive potential" but that the politics of popular culture are 'full of contradictions' and may even be reactionary (1998, 177).

The gradual assimilation of illegal street interventions (or works indebted to their particular aesthetic styles) into the art establishment is, perhaps, best summed up by the Banksy phenomenon, where 'works' placed illegally in different urban sites have now been transformed into objects of Art worthy

From Piss-Communication to GraffARTi   123

of both economic and aesthetic value. This has been the fate of many graffiti practitioners from the 'aerosol kingdom' (Miller 2002) and beyond (those working with instruments other than spray cans, like stencils, posters, etc.). The (un)popular life of graffiti styles has meant that the style has now taken on an autonomy of its own, where the financial gains of the gallery begin to upstage the street itself. This is exemplified by practitioners like Thierry Guetta (AKA Mr. Brainwash) who, having absorbed the styles of his favorites (Banksy, Invader, Shepard Fairey, Poster Boy Seizer, Cyclops, Azil Borf, and Sweet Toof, among others) and, in the minds of some practitioners and gallery owners, without doing a proper apprenticeship, created his 'Barely Legal' exhibition in Hollywood in 2008, which was an enormous success.[5]

This absorption of the everyday[6] into the art establishment, of course, is nothing new. At least since Duchamp's urinals and bicycle wheels to Pop Art's Campbell's soup tins, giant comic strips, Typhoo Tea packets, and Brillo Pad boxes, the lives of popular things have been transformed. No matter whether these things once existed in the supermarket or were designed to assault, scandalize, or reject the notion of 'Art,' they can be commodified by it (Baudrillard 1998, 115). As Marcuse insisted, capitalist forces can commodify anything (even the avant garde) and assimilate it into its all-encompassing one dimensionality (1986, 61f.). However, graffiti (or Street Art), like Pop Art, takes objects from one domain (the supermarket, the factory, the street, etc.) and transfers them into another field (the aesthetic), while conferring on them an economic value far in excess of their original worth.

Yet, in the world of Pop Art there is a tension between the objects' humble origins as simple consumer objects and the new lofty status conferred upon them. Their lowly value functions as the extreme opposite of what they have become. In the case of graffiti styles in the gallery, the objects are taken from the street (this argument does not refer to works created in the studio to resemble the kinds of phenomena created by 'delinquents' in the streets) and, like Pop Art, they are legitimated by high-art institutions; however, they are commodified in such a way that commercial value is given where *none* existed before their assimilation. Furthermore, graffiti 'Art' (incorporated by markets and galleries alike) can draw on the objects' (un)popular prelife because this confers a value on it that is absent in the case of objects drawn into the avant garde or Pop traditions. Yet, I want to suggest that art institutions can never wholly absorb graffiti's more unruly, disorderly, and politically questionable characteristics. Nonetheless, the graffiti practitioner (while developing distinct calligraphic styles and adapting images taken from advertising, comics, video games, and so on) may draw on the immense reserves of canonical art traditions. One consequence is that, as Kramer (2010) has suggested, to practice graffiti is not necessarily to be an outsider: it is perfectly possible to be a member of a graffiti crew while embracing wholly conformist values.

The opening up of public spaces for graffiti is becoming increasingly common. For example, in front of the Merced campus of the University of Murcia (Spain) there are a number of graffiti murals, officially authorized by the city

124   *David Walton*

council. One of them features Mother Teresa and another Kofi Annan, and they are very much inspired by the graffiti muralist Conor Harrington's style along with the traditional painting styles found in art galleries all over the world (see Figure 9.3a and b.). Here it is possible to see how things, which have often been considered a 'plague' (by the authorities), have been assimilated and contained by the power bloc that attempts to control public space.

However, these works by what might be called the "Michaelangelos of graffiti" (Dorment 2008) have been defaced. The mural of Mother Teresa became the site where illegal, uninvited inscribers hit back by painting a goatee beard on her chin in bright red and inscribing the word 'puta' (whore) beside her face. The Kofi Annan mural did not fare better because mucus was made to look as if it were hanging out of his nose and the word 'nigger' was scratched onto his face. Officially sanctioned graffiti-mural Art is made of something that had its provenance in the street, it is incorporated into it, and yet, through the uninvited inscription, it is reincorporated into the chaotic, unpredictable, and uncontrolled world of the insistent everyday, illegal inscriber. The inscriptions on the murals are returned to what the French photographer and essayist Brassai called "l'art batard des rues mal famées"—"the bastard art of the ill-famed streets" (quoted in Stahl 2009, 7), where inscribers give themselves the liberty to express anything—in this case the politically incorrect messages of misogyny, racism, and antireligiosity. This is the excluded 'other' that gives 'Street Art' something of its kudos but which cannot be fully contained by it. In this sense the street will not shut up (as the title of a Mexican documentary on graffiti announced: *La Calle No Calla* [*The Street No Street*] 2007).

Much graffiti, official or unofficial, may appear identical in formal and aesthetic terms but I coin the term 'graffARTi' for all examples of graffiti (whether 'rescued' from the street or deliberately fashioned in the studio for the gallery) that is associated with the values, interests, and (harmless) preferences of the dominant hegemonic forces that govern official cultural production. Here, while the exhibited piece is an inscription drawing on practices associated with the street, it will not provide a space for *completely uninhibited* inscriptions. This is not to romanticize unconstrained/uninvited inscriptions: these are as liable to be offensive as they are challenging. However, when the styles of graffiti are appropriated into the terms of official culture, this will not necessarily involve the filtering out of politically motivated or potentially disturbing or shocking messages (graffiti 'Art' is often highly critical of orthodox styles of Art and the establishment) but it will de-emphasize the inappropriateness (the sexism, misogyny, racism, sexism, homophobia, etc.) of the unruly street message.

GraffARTi, then, describes the cultural tensions of drawing graffiti into the official space of the gallery and is manifested in two corresponding singularities. One is expressed by the New York detective Bernie Jacobs who, in the documentary *Style Wars* (mentioned earlier), stated that by the early 1980s tagging and bombing practices were obviously not 'Art' but rather 'crime' (reflecting the processes of criminalization that would spread through the U.S. and other countries in the following decades). The other

From Piss-Communication to GraffARTi   125

is illustrated by how, by the end of the 1970s, opportunities were given to practitioners of graffiti to exhibit and sell their work in galleries (in 1979 Fab 5 Freddy and Lee Quinones were invited to exhibit their work in Rome).

This about-turn can be seen as part of processes that began to legitimize but also contain what were once uninvited inscriptions and images. However, the miscreant's art was slow to be digested by the official organs and, by the turn of the twentieth century, the artist associated with delinquent acts was still only cautiously invited into the fashionable and consecrated cultural spaces reserved for art specialists and dealers. (Of course, my way of referring to the gallery here reflects Walter Benjamin's notion of how Art is contemplated [1992, 211f].) This cultural transition has repeatedly been termed 'the Banksy effect,'[7] yet Banksy himself did not start to get incorporated until around the turn of the century.[8] The vigorous debate about the cultural worth and legitimacy of graffiti mirrors, as intimated before, analogous debates about Pop Art (figures like Basquiat and Keith Haring offering links between the two cultural spheres) and further addresses themes pertinent to questions of cultural hegemony.[9]

The hesitant espousal of graffiti (or whatever challenges the status quo) by the dealers and galleries is not, of course, uncharacteristic of the institutions governing the legitimatization of Art; in fact, it is rule: all major movements tend to pose challenges to preceding canons and customs. This is parallel to the processes I described earlier with regard to Pop Art. That is, graffiti 'Art,' like Pop Art, introduces the everyday into the sphere of 'high Art' (creating what Fredric Jameson termed the "postmodern" forms, which defied the 'high/low' distinctions, lowered the tone of High Modernism. and commodified artistic practice [1991]). In this way the scratching, stencil, throwup, tag, icon, plaque, symbol, sculpture, and so on are reinscribed from street into the gallery and manifest themselves both internally and externally. These styles may exist both on the inside and the outside of walls. (An example is the 'Street Art' exhibition held in the Tate Modern in 2008.)

In this it is possible to see how hegemonic struggles *within* the academy lead to the reevaluation of things once deemed to be beyond the artistic pale. This debate has been extremely vigorous in both the media and on blog pages. "Banksy: the Michelangelo of graffiti?" (Dormant 2008) sums up the positions well, as does "Banksyyy—Best of British now an American Arts Hero?" (*Art Knowledge News* n.d.), where it is OK to like Banksy's work "so long as you don't kid yourself that this is 'art.'" Bansky is seen as "a background artist" and, like all graffiti, is little more than "an accompaniment to other activities," whereas the reason "to admire Damien Hirst is that he makes art as if art mattered. In Banksy, the philistines are getting their revenge."

Yet the hegemonic struggles move in the other direction because these arguments about the prestige and worth of graffiti styles are also very much a part of those who practice graffiti outside the academies. The so-called delinquents also challenge the old order and make special claims that would elevate what happens in the street to the status of legitimate 'Art.' This aspect of inquiry affiliates my particular analysis with the politics of *the popular* within cultural studies, where confrontations are seen with relation to hegemonic

126   David Walton

struggles over the value and meaning of cultural forms but where the interests of ordinary people (outside the cultural institutions) are taken into account in terms of what Hall (2009) and others like Fiske (1998) call cultural hegemony. Sifting through books, blogs, and other websites dedicated to illegal graffiti, it is possible to find numerous claims by graffiti 'criminals' and their followers that unauthorized graffiti (in the street, on the sides of trains, etc.) is 'Art.'

These claims mount to a powerful critique of official art institutions and represent a counter-hegemonic challenge to those who govern the art world and the institutions that proscribe uninvited acts of graffiti. This is what has been called an "outsider aesthetics of rebellion" (a term I borrow from Sarah Schulman, in Benjamin Shepard 2009). Robert Kaltenhäuser's book, *Art Inconsequence: Advanced Vandalism* (2007), offers a potent example of this counter-hegemonic position. Kaltenhäuser acknowledges that these unsolicited interventions are forms of vandalism but insists that they traverse the "boundaries between art and criminality" (2007, 17). In stating this, Kaltenhäuser exploits the ambiguities where street interventions that were previously maligned (like a number of Banksy's stencils) are, at a later stage (after official appreciation and acknowledgment), reevaluated and endorsed (21). Here practitioners of 'nonart' graffiti stake *their own counter-hegemonic claims* to be practicing 'Art.' Again, the street answers back.

The ambiguity of official discourses is exploited to the point where 'advanced vandalism' can be asserted as 'Art,' which can then be legitimated within the avant garde discourses of Modernism. Kaltenhäuser sees "advanced vandalism" as an "interventionist strategy" (no matter whether it is comprehended as painting up slogans, putting up posters, or situationist street action), which involves seeing any illicit street intervention as "a concerted effort to break away from the moneyed and politically corrupt museum establishment" (25). This counter-hegemonic position comprises the notion that graffiti 'vandalism' (or the Thoreau-like obligation of 'civil disobedience') not only questions the art establishment and has enduring effects on legal and social structures but also challenges capitalist values: it refuses to recognize property rights and values and recoups the 'visual landscape' (25–33). This is a message that is reminiscent of some of the ideas outlined earlier in Serres's work and that is reflected in the work of Joe Austin, who claims that Street Art "defaces the commonsensical, recognized, expected authority lodged in the property ownerships of classical (and neo-) liberalism, public or private, effecting a detraction of pleasure and security in some viewers" (2010, 44). Austin goes even further, providing a further ground for counter-hegemonic struggle: he views graffiti art as a "site of aesthetic pedagogy" (which is persuasive in terms of the instances he offers for analysis). However, he (like Serres) tends to detach some aspects of unlawful urban interventions from others; my argument does not contradict this but insists that the examples he privileges do not include the marginalized and excluded: the full extent of 'bastard art' of the street (see my earlier analysis of the Mother Teresa and Kofi Annan murals). Here the GraffARTi (while excluding the full extent of the chaotic, unruly side of graffiti) stakes its own claims to cultural legitimacy and, while actually pushing in the same direction as the representatives of what is seen as the affluent and politically debased museum establishment, mounts its own attack on those who only *seem* like allies. In this way, counter-hegemonic forces are involved in complex processes that challenge cultural orthodoxies but fold back upon one another in mutual struggles to exercise cultural power, legitimacy, and authority.

Figure 9.1 Graffiti as marking territory, Cieza, Murcia. (Photo by Margarita Navarro Pérez.)

Figure 9.2 Squat and double appropriation in Madrid. (Photo by Ana Rull.)

128 *David Walton*

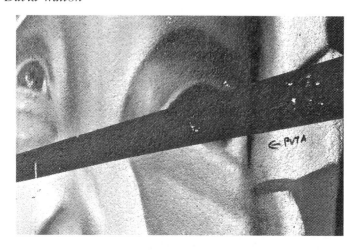

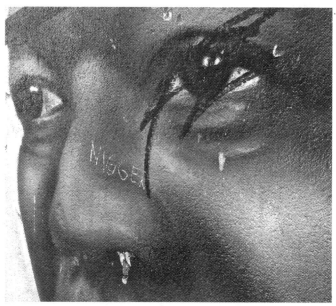

Figure 9.3(a) and (b) The street answers back. Details: Mother Teresa and Kofi Annan. (Photos by David Walton.)

Notes

1. I suggested this idea in Walton (2013, 26). In this chapter I develop a number of ideas I first explored in that chapter. This chapter was written with the aid of a Seneca Foundation grant (15397/PHCS/10).
2. Although contemporary graffiti styles have now become globalized in very self-conscious ways (Austin 2010, 35), they cannot be understood without reference to the way these styles are manifested within particular cultural contexts (Nguyen and Mackenzie 2010, 80)—inspired by the locality of practices, policies, and everyday life.

From Piss-Communication to GraffARTi   129

3. I am, of course, referring to the tradition of theorizing space that has been inspired by Deleuze and Guattari's *A Thousand Plateaus* (1987). For graffiti and subculture, see Macdonald (2003).
4. It might be noted here that some contemporary graffiti is actually involved in *cleaning up* pollution (Moorstedt 2011, 48–49).
5. The Banksy documentary *Exit through the Gift Shop* gives an overview of how Guetta put the show together, how he was helped by key figures in the street art world, and how others in the 'business' were skeptical of his achievements. However, there have been rumors that the whole thing was a hoax perpetrated by Banksy and possibly Shepard Fairey (Shone 2010; Walker 2010). That he has not been a flash in the graffiti pan is shown by his success in designing album covers (clients included Michael Jackson, Madonna, the Red Hot Chilli Peppers) and the fact that he has made films and put on seven exhibitions since "Life Is Beautiful."
6. I use this word to suggest anything that stands outside or is opposed to the official organs of culture. Recently, John Storey (2014) has helped to clarify its multiple and often contradictory meanings.
7. 'The Banksy effect' is a phrase used by Max Frasier in December 2006 on CNN and then repeated thereafter in the media. See Frasier (2006).
8. Banksy's initial, and mostly disregarded, exhibition at the Severnshed restaurant in Bristol was not until February of 2000 and his first (unofficial) London exhibition took place in 2001; it was not until 2002 that he officially exhibited in Los Angeles (See Joseph, 2008, for a useful summary.) This was the same year that a group of international graffiti practitioners were exhibited alongside Dubuffet in Brescia, Italy. The "Dubuffet e l'arte dei graffiti" exhibition was shown at the Palazzo Martinengo between May and September in 2002—an exhibition that helped to show the connections between Dubuffet's aesthetic and that of those practicing graffiti styles. See http://www.domusweb.it/en/art/dubuffet-and-the-art-of-graffiti/.
9. Not all critics, however, see Haring and Basquiat as bona fide representatives of 'graffiti art.' See Austin (2001, 40).

References

Adorno, Theodor. 1991. *The Culture Industry: Selected Essays on Mass Culture.* London: Routledge.

Art Knowledge News. n.d. "Banksyyy—Best of British now an American Arts Hero?" Available online at http://www.artknowledgenews.com/banksyamerica nartsherohtml.html.

Austin, Joe. 2001. *Taking the Train: How Graffiti Art Became an Urban Crisis in New York City, 1970–1990.* New York: Columbia University Press.

———. 2010. "More to see than a canvas in a white cube. For an art in the streets." *City* 14:1–2.

Baudrillard, Jean. 1998. *The Consumer Society: Myths and Structures.* London: Sage.

Benjamin, Walter. 1992. *Illuminations.* London: Fontana.

de Certeau, Michel. 1988. *The Practice of Everyday Life.* Berkeley: University of California Press.

Deleuze, Gilles, and Félix Guattarri. 1987. *A Thousand Plateaus: Capitalism and Schizophrenia.* Minneapolis: University of Minnesota Press.

130 David Walton

Dorment, Richard. 2008. "Banksy: The Michelangelo of Graffiti?" *The Telegraph*, May 8. Available online at http://www.telegraph.co.uk/culture/art/3673172/Banksy-the-Michelangelo-of-graffiti.html.

Ferrell, Jeff. 1996. *Crimes of Style: Urban Graffiti and the Politics of Criminality*. Boston: Northeastern University Press.

Fiske, John. 1998. *Understanding Popular Culture*. London: Routledge.

Frasier, Max. 2006. "White House Plays Host to Powerful Shiite Leader; British Police Head to Moscow to Look for Leads in Former Russian Spy's Death; Disaster in the Philippines." CNN, December 4. Available online at http://transcripts.cnn.com/TRANSCRIPTS/0612/04/ywt.01.html.

Goldman, Robert, and Papson, Stephen. 1996. *Sign Wars: The Cluttered Landscape of Advertising*. New York: Guilford Press.

Hall, Stuart. 2009. "Notes on Deconstructing 'The Popular.'" In *Cultural Theory and Popular Culture: A Reader*, edited by John Storey, 508–518. Essex, England: Pearson.

Jameson, Fredric. 1991. *Postmodernism, or, the Cultural Logic of Late Capitalism*. London: Verso.

Joseph, Claudia. 2008. "Graffiti Artist Banksy Unmasked ... as a Former Public Schoolboy from Middle-Class Suburbia." *Mail Online*, July 12. Available online at http://www.dailymail.co.uk/femail/article-1034538/Graffiti-artist-Banksy-unmasked---public-schoolboy-middle-class-suburbia.html.

Kaltenhäuser, Robert. 2007. *Art Inconsequence: Advanced Vandalism*. Mainaschaff, Germany: Publikat.

Keegan, Peter. 2014. *Graffiti in Antiquity*. New York: Routlege.

Kramer, Ronald. 2010. "Painting with Permission: Legal Graffiti in New York City." *Ethnography* 11 (2): 235–253.

La Calle No Calla. Arte Urbano en Mexico [*The Street No Stree. Urban Art in Mexico*]. 2007. Produced by Aiwey Films. Mexico D. F.

Macdonald, Nancy. 2003. *The Graffiti Subculture: Youth, Masculinity and Identity in London and New York*. New York: Palgrave.

Marcuse, Herbert. 1986. *One-dimensional Man: Studies in the Ideology of Advanced Industrial Society*. London: Ark.

Miller, Ivor. 2002. *Aerosol Kingdom: Subway Painters of New York City*. Jackson: University of Mississippi Press.

Mirzoeff, Nicolas. 2012. *The Visual Culture Reader*. London: Routledge.

Moorstedt, Tobias. 2011. "Graffiti Inverso: Convertir lo Viejo en Nuevo." *The Mini International* 34: 48–49.

Morley, Simon. 2007. *Writing on the Wall: Word and Image in Modern Art*. London: Thames and Hudson.

Nguyen, Patrick, and Stuart Mackenzie, eds. 2010. *Beyond the Street: The 100 Leading Figures in Urban Art*. Berlin: Gestalten.

Serres, Michel. 2008. *Malfeasance: Appropriation through Pollution?* Stanford, CA: Stanford University Press.

Shannon, Joshua. 2009. *The Disappearance of Objects: New York and the Rise of the Postmodern City*. New Haven, CT: Yale University Press.

Shepard, Benjamin. 2010. *Queer Political Performance: Play, Pleasure and Social Movement*. London: Routledge.

Shone, Tom. 2010. "Is Banksy's *Exit through the Gift Shop* a Hoax Too Far?" *The Times*, Feb 27. Available online at http://www.thetimes.co.uk/tto/arts/film/article2432593.ece.

From Piss-Communication to GraffARTi   131

Stahl, Joannes. 2009. *Street Art*. Köln, Germany: Ullmann.
Style Wars. Directed by Tony Silver. 1983. Public Art Films. 2003. DVD.
Storey, John. 2014. *From Popular Culture to Everyday Life*. London: Routledge.
Strinati, Dominic. 2004. *An Introduction to Popular Culture*. London: Routledge.
Taylor, Brandon. 2008. *Urban Walls: A Generation of Collage in Europe and America*. New York: Hudson and Ellis.
Walker, Alissa. 2010. "Here's Why the Banksy Movie Is a Banksy Prank." *Fast Company*. Wed April 14.
Walton, David. 2013. "The 'Inglorious Basterds' of Graffiti: Pollution, Urban Space, Cultural Hegemony and the Popular." In *Popular Culture: A Reader*, edited by Otto von Feigenblatt and Beatriz Peña Acuña, 26–45. Newcastle upon Tyne: Cambridge Scholars Press.
Williams, Raymond. 1976. *Keywords*. London: Collins.
———. 1983. *Keywords: A Vocabulary of Culture and Society*. London: Fontana.

10 From Performance to Objects and Back

London's *InterAction*

Lucia Vodanovic

The 2013–2014 exhibition *Re-staging Revolutions*—part of Susan Croft and Jessica Higgs's project "Unfinished Histories"—about alternative theater practices in the boroughs on Camden and Lambeth, included a small portion of ephemera about the work of the InterAction group in Kentish Town. The exhibition covered the period of 1968–1988, which saw the formation of over 700 companies of street theater, community arts, political theater, gay, lesbian, black, Asian, disabled, and women's companies, with evocative names such as Hesitate and Demonstrate, The Phantom Captain, Sadista Sisters, Recreation Ground, and several others. Part of this landscape was InterAction—an umbrella organization for a number of arts projects that went beyond a high artistic agenda and produced a framework for community engagement that can be considered 'intangible heritage' (Smith 2006) in the area.

InterAction's practices aimed at creative interventions into everyday life. Like every form of 'intangible heritage,' they provided field for artistic experiences of a direct and measured value for social development. The group's main preoccupation was the use of communal spaces—mostly adaptations of unexploited 'urban forms' (buildings, grounds, streets, institutions)—that the group members turned into flexible environments open to random interaction with a variety of users. A known manifestation of InterAction's creed was the InterAction Centre[1] in Kentish Town working as the group's headquarters and a local culture center. Its mutable structure and a provisional character catered to the ever changing expectations of local artistic and nonartistic communities. It also encouraged social interactions in flexible settings, inviting people to reexperience the rigid routines of the mundane.

This chapter examines social and cultural dimensions of InterAction's architectural thinking from the perspective of the formation of 'intangible heritage' through uses of popular space. It brings together archive material from the period during which the group was active in Kentish Town (from its origins in 1968 to the mid-1980s),[2] and some contemporary outputs, covering both information specific to InterAction itself and material related to its legacy—for instance, the Kentish Town City Farm. It also draws on a series of interviews with several key members of the group, conducted at different points during 2014. This interdisciplinary approach allows for a better exploration of the group's legacy, especially in relation to its experiential learning that, free of the constrains of usability, concentrated on the possibilities of the flexible material.

The Unbearable Lightness of Form: Transforming Routines into Fun

InterAction was formed in 1968 by American activist and playwright Ed Berman, with the view of bringing arts closer to community.[3] The group was motivated by skepticism toward the effects of fixed structural formations and by a belief that "theatre is a structure which can intercede in reality" (Berman in Itzin 1980, 54). Structural interventions practiced by InterAction relied on contesting established patterns and daily routines. Common practices included: lunchtime theater (as opposed to evening performances), 'almost free tickets' (a challenge to the economic system of the entertainment business), or street shows for average passers-by (that promoted cohabitation with art and cultural living). The most memorable intervention of this kind was arguably *Fun Art Bus*: a London double-decker that hosted theater performances and cinema screenings.[4] It had a picnic scene painted on the roof so that people in offices and high buildings could be tempted to divert from their work schedules. The conductor offered tickets with poems in praise of escapes from daily routines that alluded to delays, commuting, life, love, and boredom.

Disrupted quotidian rhythms prepossesed InterAction also through their engagement with Berman's dramatic writing. The plays he selected for *Fun Arts Bus* reconstructed the metaphor of moving through time and space—the actual bus materialized in real life. The *Bus* was InterAction's main drive to "upset the formal" (Berman and Wintle 1973, 29). According to Berman and Wintle, "as a real environment the Bus provide[d] a form or set of forms, which passengers [could] immediately recognize as a distant aspect of their everyday experience [...]" (1973, 29). Through that, audiences revisited their daily routines and reconceptualized mundane settings. These settings—"distorted in terms of sight, sound and people" (1973, 29)—provided escapist entertainment that opened life's taken-for-grantedness to new interpretations and new readings.

Entertaining appropriations of physical environments became central to InterAction activism in 1973, when Berman looked for a permanent operational space. At that time, together with the architect Cedric Price, he started a 'process' or a 'journey' (Powell in discussion with the author, November 2014) to develop what would later become a multipurpose community center built alongside the railway viaduct at Kentish Town rail station: "part theatre, part commune, part school, and part creative-play place" (Mathews 2007, 187). The aim was to create an interactive and socially oriented space that would both foster a sense of identity in the area and embody the ideals of fluidity, freedom, and agency that were central for Price's architectural vision.

The main concept of Price's architecture was 'temporal limitedness' (1996, 2003a, 2003b). Constructions, he believed, should be ephemeral in structure and so built from cheap materials and easily dismantled parts; therefore, plasticity, rearrangeability, and the incorporation of change were

134 *Lucia Vodanovic*

revealed as main constructional qualities. This was possible due to flexible components such as moving walls and removable floors that enabled size changes as well as constant alterations of living/working spaces and their usability. Some of Price's designs also included elements of antisolidity (optical barriers or warm air curtains) or prefabricated kits (as in his project about a collapsible and transportable holiday house consisting of a central unit and four additional elements that could be expanded or retracted). They added to the effect of impermanence and, in this vein, freed buildings of heavyweight tradition and promises of future glory.

Price's interest in flexibility was reflected in several urban projects, such as *Zoo Aviary* (1961) or *Potteries Thinkbelt* (1964). *Zoo Aviary* is an actual construction in the London Zoo, presenting an aluminum frame, gently wrapped in a weightless net, floating like a bird and "changing its form as the wind loading varies over time" (Obrist 2009, 11). The project, designed in collaboration with photographer Lord Snowdon, was planned as a long, tent-like structure able to accommodate the natural flight patterns of birds; it was intended as a challenge to the limitations of fixed structures with flexible systems. The technical know-how for this radical and unconventional construction relied on principles of discontinued compression and was provided by the engineer Frank Newby. *Potteries Thinkbelt* was an uncompleted construction of mobile learning facilities designed with an intention to transform the disused infrastructure of North Staffordshire Potteries into a university site. That project envisioned mobile, rail-mounted classrooms moving constantly along the refurbished railway lines, and units for student housing that could be removed or reconfigured to individual demand. The *Potteries Thinkbelt* rejected the elitist view on education and did not see it as a marker of social nobility or status but rather as a marker of technological innovations fueled by a constantly evolving knowledge-based economy.

Similar concerns were evident in *The Fun Palace* (initially conceived and commissioned in 1961)—Price's best known project, often referred to as the most famous of his many "un-built buildings" (Hatherley 2012, 120). *The Fun Palace* brought together a variety of emerging culture and design discourses: cybernetics, information technology, game theory, and situationism, "to produce a new kind of improvisational architecture to negotiate the constantly shifting cultural landscape of the post-war years" (Mathews 2005, 73). It intended to offer a new life balance that would change the dynamics between work, education, and leisure, in favor of the latter. Like *Potteries Thinkbelt*, it responded to the changing British cultural landscape, marked by deindustrialization, the growing importance of popular culture, and the demands for new skills that would make leisure a productive aspect of life. *The Fun Palace* was not meant as a building in a conventional sense; rather, it was intended as a place for social interaction: an assemblage of pedagogical and leisure environments that would familiarize audiences with industrial space (through the use of cranes and prefabricated modules) and that would develop new models of personal and social

From *Performance to Objects and Back*   135

development. Work on this project began in 1962 through the collaboration between Price and the theater producer Johan Littlewood. Littlewood's theatrical background directed Price's concept toward interactive, performative architecture, which in turn encouraged a more active and engaged contribution of audiences to the creative process. Described as a "kit of parts, not a building" (Matthews 2005, 80) and a "laboratory of fun" (Bell 2004), *The Fun Palace* was planned as a dynamic form of architecture for common citizens to invite the multitude of indeterminate uses.[5] As Stanley Mathews argues, *The Fun Palace* "was about potential use, rather than dedicated purpose [...]; the difficulty was in not knowing in advance exactly what people might be doing there" (2007, 175).

Randomness, Unstructure, Mobility, and Game

Although *The Fun Palace* failed to draw funding, the project itself has helped to perpetuate Price's cult status. He became known as an artist determined to "free the human within the structure" (Obrist 2009, 11). Stanley Matthews, who has written extensively about Price's work in a series of publications (2005, 2006, 2007), underlines Price's engagement in reconceptualizing the idea of form and structural perpetuation reflected in his advocacy for constructional finitude. As Price has described, the InterAction Center "was always unfinished—it could always change: adding other structures and reducing some, throughout its life" (in Obrist 2009, 87). Matthews, one of the few authors who has acknowledged the importance of this building in the architect's work, details some firsthand impressions of it:

> I visited the centre in 1988, hordes of people of all ages, from the neighborhood, were swarming over the building. Activities were taking place in various areas. A dance group was rehearsing, children were learning to read, a volunteer lawyer was helping to explain the intricacies of the English legal system to immigrants, someone else was learning digital imagining, a gay and lesbian neighborhood association were conducting a meeting while elsewhere an amateur signing group was recording their own rap CD. As with the Fun Palace, groups could use pre-fabricated panel systems to assemble their own offices, studios, and workshop. When interest in one activity waned, the space was dismantle[d] and used by another group.
>
> (Matthews 2007, 191)

InterAction's program and its modus operandi expressed a strong concern about material fluidity. The group's commitment to both structure and indeterminacy has been reflected in two major constructional qualities: randomness and mobility. Their primary interest was to explore how a mobile system of entertainment and education would expand the audience's cognitive skills. Both randomness and mobility were best manifested in *Fun Art*

136 *Lucia Vodanovic*

Bus—a project described in the previous section—and also in *Animobile*: a set of activities focused on bringing farm animals to school children in Kentish Town. *Animobile* combined with InterAction's theatrical projects and contributed to their educational frame. It also became a part of the peculiar history of Kentish Town City Farm (founded in 1972)—the first of its kind in Britain, particularly through *The Last Straw*, one of InterAction's plays about a group of farmers so angry at motorways running through their lands that they decide to bulldoze a farm in the middle of the city. A stage for this play was a real city farm. As Berman explains, "We couldn't see the difference between building an environmental farm inside a building or a real farm outside one: you need the same materials and the same structure—the animals, buildings, fences, a financial structure, care of animals, an educational programme, an audience" (1973, 56).

Practices of improvisation and appropriation of materials that reinforce this notion of fluid materiality are still present in the DIY aesthetic and mode of production of the contemporary Kentish Town City Farm, whose very existence constantly appears as precarious and under threat; therefore, it is required to constantly reinvent itself (Cooper 1997). A feasibility study carried out by the Farm in the run-up for an application for funding as part of a number of initiatives at the turn of the millennium, for instance, emphasizes that this is not a zoo for domestic animals or a museum, separating it from those leisure spaces that have been traditionally associated with a passive and contemplative visitor experience. The public is encouraged to participate and therefore to create the farm, as the Fun Palace also proposes. In the same document, a description of the premises illustrates the make-it-along-the-way aesthetic of the actual site: "[t]he buildings vary in age with early Victorian stables, a turn-of-the-century house, a 50's railway office building, a prefabricated 'modern' stable bloc and a collection of semi derelict shed[s] built with DIY technology" (Kentish Town City Farm 2000). While stressing the precariousness of the material fabric of the farm, the text celebrates its "random building techniques" and the need to "preserve" that productive tension between randomness and structure, as illustrated by this passage:

> The defects in the fabric are being continually repaired on an ad hoc basis and the repairs cannot deal with the fundamental problems. There is however a quality of the kind of "random" building techniques and styles that is worth preserving and any future radical refurbishment should take this into consideration.
>
> (Kentish Town City Farm 2000)

Another key example of InterAction's preoccupation with fluid materiality was a training technique the group deployed in workshops called the InterAction Games Method. Based on children's games, it was designed to encourage participants to work together creatively and provided the basis

From Performance to Objects and Back 137

for their approach to community and arts creation, as well as its experimental theater performances. This had been initially developed by Berman when he was working in Notting Hill. He always thought of the method as something easily taught to others and worth spreading to encourage people to create their own companies: "I think there is no better proof of the uses of this approach than those companies we have encouraged to set up. We simply provide a structural framework and a season to cut their teeth on" (Berman in Itzin 1980, 54). As he contends,

> I used the Inter-Action creative game method with anybody, whether they were psychiatrists in training to kids with disabilities, adults with disabilities. I would run 3 or 4 sessions a week myself and then as I trained other people they would run 2, 3 or 4 sessions a week, so I went into remand homes and disabled clubs, really anybody, because this method can be used with anybody 'cause it taps into games that we learn in childhood from peek-a-boo onwards to hide and seek and so on.
>
> (Berman 2010)

The unpublished handbook of a summer school by David and Harriett Powell (1983), two of the original members of the group, details some of the games at the core of the method (about 200 different games were used according to David Powell, who defines it as a "cultural characteristic" of InterAction). They are based on patterns that allow interaction to take place, ranging from the simplest ones (people forming a circle, numbering themselves and then adopting a role for the time of the game, which was undefined) to jazz performances. A section of the handbook entitled "Copying and Creativity" develops the notion of framework, which consists in at least two components—what they call the "Rules for Action" and the "Content":

> Either or both of these may be varied to open or close, loosen or tighten the framework. In "Two claps, two spaces do or say [...]" (rules for action) can become "In two claps, three, or four or as many spaces as you need do or say." "Your name" (content) can become a "sound with a gesture that says how you feel now, the next words in the story about [...] told in the style of [...]"
>
> You need to know the rules in order to change them. That is why there is value to stating the rules. In this way you give yourself and the group the opportunity to vary the rules, to increase their opportunities for choice and creativity. (Gorvey and Powell 1983, 9)

The handbook explicitly mentions that the group wanted to teach people "how things can happen" before establishing what they want to do, which otherwise "becomes a fixed idea" (Gorvey and Powell 1983, 9). It is a

138   *Lucia Vodanovic*

'grammar,' Powell states, taken from children's games, or a 'structure' that, in his view, mirrors InterAction's organization of space before and after it took its most definitive form in the shape of Price's center: "[y]ou got the structure and then something happens in the middle [...]. The game was a virtual form or a metaphor for the Centre" (Powell in discussion with the author, November 2014).

Powell (personal communication, 2014) declares that all his professional work in the area of community engagement after InterAction is informed by the method. Carry Gorvey, another original member of the group, also acknowledges the importance of the method in her work in other areas of London and stresses how it was very much an attempt to create a structure that would engage even the most challenging people. According to her, the game formed a 'code' or 'language,' a tool to work without the need to fully resolve the tension between randomness and structure (Gorvey in discussion with the author, December 2014). She sees everything that InterAction did in its different incarnations as starting from that core and, as a result, it is this form of experiential learning framed in that code that is preserved in the various projects of the organization around Kentish Town and beyond.

Indeed, this structural fluidity is also reflected in InterAction's legacy and their desire to reach other similar groups through training, consultancy, and their published handbooks.[6] In 1972 they started to provide advisory services for new groups on an impressive scale (1,200 groups per year), yet this legacy was never prescriptive. According to Powell, they were interested in creating a minimal yet flexible frame that could be adapted and transferred to a different context. Berman (2010) refers to this way of working as the 'Lone Ranger' technique: InterAction would bring in adults to learn to do similar things with their own children to what the organization was doing, so that they could then run their own play schemes in other areas of London and even away from the city, adapting the initial structure as they went along.

Inherited Practices

The former discussion suggests that InterAction is an example of 'intangible heritage,' a form of legacy that Laurajane Smith defines as an "experience" and as a "cultural and social process, which engages with acts of remembering that work to create ways to understand and engage with the present" (2006, 2). Smith's work is placed among the growing interdisciplinary body of writing that challenges traditional frameworks in heritage studies and brings notions of identity, dissonance, intangibility, loss, and others to the discussion. Her writings and those of other authors, such as Akagawa and Smith (2009), focus on heritage as a process rather than as a 'thing,' which avoids, as Harvey (2001) would put it, the consideration of heritage as 'a given.'

Without negating or devaluing the material form of heritage artifacts, Smith's key premise is that all heritage is 'intangible'—in other words, that these artifacts are meaningful because of the cultural processes and activities

From Performance to Objects and Back   139

that take place around them. (She uses the example of Stonehenge: without the meanings attributed to the site, and the cultural practices that take place in and celebrate it, it could be simply described as a group of rocks arranged in a particular disposition; the practices that take place in the site are then the key dimension of it.) Additionally, heritage institutions do not simply 'find' a site that merits being protected and conserved; "[...] heritage is heritage *because* it is subjected to the management and preservation/conservation process, not simply because it *is*" (Smith 2006, 3). This is a "constitutive cultural process that identifies those things and places that can be given meaning and value as 'heritage,' reflecting contemporary cultural and social values, debates and aspirations" (Smith 2006, 3), and gives rise to the understanding that heritage can be mapped, managed, listed (Hafstein 2009). Smith's argument is that heritage cannot be just defined as grand, monumental, and aesthetically pleasant sites and buildings that would be 'passed on' to the future but rather as an 'experience' (2006, 2) and a "set of values and meanings" constructed and regulated by cultural practices (2006, 11).

It is important to note that Smith's argument distances itself from UNESCO's definition of 'intangible' heritage—another essential framework for discussions within heritage studies since the 2003 *Convention for the Safeguarding of the Intangible Cultural Heritage*, which looks after the "means the practices, representations, expressions, knowledge, skills—as well as the instruments, objects, artifacts and cultural spaces associated therewith—that communities, groups and, in some cases, individuals recognize as part of their cultural heritage" (UNESCO 2003, 2). Intangible heritage includes, for instance, oral traditions and expressions (including language), rituals and festivals, traditional craftsmanship and other forms of cultural and social practice. The difference is that, according to Smith, all heritage is intangible (not just a portion of it) and therefore intangible heritage is not the 'other' of mainstream heritage, which in the case of UNESCO would be the 1972 *Convention Concerning the Protection of the World Cultural and Natural Heritage* concerning monuments and groups of buildings and sites, because all heritage is defined as such by a number of cultural and social values that are intangible. If anything, the discussions generated by the 2003 *Convention for the Safeguarding of the Intangible Cultural Heritage* have made more apparent that the values that frame an artifact or practice as 'heritage' are not universal (Blake 2009) and therefore that the "*idea* of intangible heritage forces a recognition of the inherent dissonant nature of heritage because of the immediacy of its production and consumption" (Akagawa and Smith 2009, 5). This understanding of heritage as cultural practice resonates with, for instance, Harvey's, who argues that heritage should not be identified with a noun but rather with "a *process*, or a verb, related to human action and agency" (2001, 327), emphasizing that heritage has to do with practices of 'making' and therefore that is constantly produced and consumed. Similarly, Smith and Waterton (2009, 292) suggest that heritage should not be determined by its materiality or nonmateriality,

140 *Lucia Vodanovic*

"but rather by what is done with it." Indeed, the intangible is not less 'real' or 'material' than the tangible (Smith and Waterton 2009, 292).

It could be argued that InterAction's heritage in the area could be framed within this legacy as practices of making intangible processes, which are material themselves (in spite of this intangibility) and also take different forms in physical spaces, such as the City Farm, in experiential activities such as those initiated by the Game Method and in the reproductions of those initiatives in and beyond the zones in which the organization operated. Original Inter-Action members founded, for instance, WAC Arts, a college that still provides alternative education in arts and media for young people aged between 14 and 19; there is also the Talacre Sports Center, built in the same area as the old InterAction center as a community space for leisure and the work of the Talacre Action Group right behind this new building, providing affordable childcare and support for children at social risk.

Beyond this specific area, the Fun Palaces initiative, active since 2014, makes direct reference to Price's desire for his own fun palace.[7] Luxuriously grand and noneconomical in terms of its aspirations, the original Fun Palace would have been dismantled after two decades of preparation but only a decade of functioning, but through the work of InterAction it has, to a small extent, existed—now and then—as a horizon or desire about being and making differently, a drive that has preserved itself as an experience that continues to be appropriated.

Conclusion

Following Laurajane Smith's and other authors' discussion of the notion of 'intangible heritage,' this chapter has argued that the work of the community art group InterAction in the area of Kentish Town (London) and beyond could be considered as a form of experiential legacy, which has been materialized in specific forms (i.e., the Kentish Town City Farm) and practices (e.g., the work that some of its original members have continued to do with the principles of InterAction's game method), characterized by a productive dynamic between structure and randomness. This dynamic is mirrored in the fluid materiality of InterAction's building, a frame that housed a number of planned and unplanned activities. As a result, the discussion allows for a rethinking of the notion and uses of preservation, which, in this case, is not attached to a monument or a predefined building or form.

Notes

1. The building was demolished in 2003 to allow the construction of the Talacre Sports Center.
2. After that period, the organization then gradually dissolved into other enterprises.
3. Berman was also a founder of other initiatives, including a publishing branch (In-Print), film company (In-Film), and a counseling, advisory, and training service in art, IT, and communication.

From Performance to Objects and Back   141

4. The bus has been recreated in the contemporary short film *Omnibus* by Unfinished Histories.
5. Several authors, like Banham (1977), Bell (2004), and Mathews (2005), have acknowledged the importance of *The Fun Palace* for other innovative buildings such as the Centre Pompidou in Paris, even though the potential for interactivity and fluidity of the latter is much more restricted.
6. An example of such published handbooks is the book, *Which Software? Which Hardware?* (Berman and Dewhurst 1987), which aimed to train other similar groups in computer skills, given that Inter-Action members were early adopters of technology. The tone of this particular text (as with others) is hard to replicate: it is both an art book and a practical handbook, with drawings of a humorous nature combined with specific tips about using computers and certain software in a community project, from Excel spreadsheets to payroll. Another important handbook published by the organization is *Where to Find City Farms in Britain* (1980), an essential text for the history and ethics of city farms in the country.
7. *The Fun Palace* initiative was set up by Stella Duffy as a celebration of Joan Littlewood's centenary without making it into 'another revival.' It is now celebrated every year and encourages people to create their own fun palace anywhere they are, either in a real space or virtually. The fun palaces website provides information, a toolkit, posters to be downloaded, and other sources of help for those interested. The experiential aspect of the project and its links with the 'making' heritage of the original fun palace is expressed in some of Duffy's statements, such as "About making a Fun Palace. Having a Fun palace. Being a Fun Palace. Somewhere we live and make and play and people (public) can come in and see and join in and listen and watch and engage or view as suits them" (Duffy 2013).

References

Akagawa, Natsuko, and Laurajane Smith, eds. 2009. *Intangible Heritage*. New York: Routledge.
Banham, Reyner. 1977. "Centre Pompidou." *Architectural Review* 161: 270–294.
Bell, Jonathan. 2004. "The Enclosure Business. Cedric Price." *Frieze Magazine* 82. Available online at http://www.frieze.com/issue/article/the_enclosure_business.
Berman, Ed. 2010. Interview by Susan Croft. DVD-Rom discs. December 2010 and February 2011. British Library, London.
Berman, Ed, and Leslie Dewhurst. 1987. *Which Software? Which Hardware? For Effective Voluntary Agencies, Charities and Youth and Community Education Groups*. London: Cassell.
Berman, Ed, and Justin Wintle. 1973. *Fun Art Bus*. London: Eyre Methuen.
Blake, Janet. 2009. "UNESCO's 2003 Convention on Intangible Cultural Heritage. The Implications of Community Involvement in 'Safeguarding.'" In *Intangible Heritage*, edited by Natsuko Akagawa and Laurajane Smith, 45–73. New York: Routledge.
City Farm Groups. 1980. *Where to Find City Farms in Britain*. London: Inter-Action Trust.
Cooper, Pam. 1997. "25th Anniversary: The Land That Became the City Farm." Photocopied brochure.
Duffy, Stella. 2013. "Joan Littlewood's Centenary, October 2014: A Thing." *Devoted and Disgruntled*. Available online at http://www.devotedanddisgruntled.com/events/devoted-and-disgruntled-8/reports/joan-littlewoods-centenary-october-2014-a-thing/.

142 *Lucia Vodanovic*

Gorvey, Carry, and David Powell. 1983. "Handbook Notes Summer School 1983." Typewritten manuscript.

Hafstein, Valdimar. 2009. "Intangible Heritage as a List: From Masterpieces to Representation." In *Intangible Heritage,* edited by Natsuko Akagawa and Laurajane Smith, 93–111. New York: Routledge.

Harvey, D. C. 2001. "Heritage Pasts and Heritage Presents: Temporality, Meaning and the Scope of Heritage Studies." *International Journal of Heritage Studies* 7 (4): 319–338.

Hatherley, Owen. 2012. *A New Kind of Bleak: Journey through Urban Britain.* London: Verso.

Itzin, Catherine. 1980. *Stages in the Revolution: Political Theatre in Britain since 1968.* London: Methuen.

Kentish Town City Farm. 2000. "Kentish Town City Farm—The Next 25 Years." Printed manuscript.

Kentish Town Memories: 40 Years of Kentish Town City Farm. "KTCF 2012 Heritage Documentary." Kentish Town City Farm. Available online at http://40years. ktcityfarm.org.uk/the-first-40-years/.

Mathews, Stanley. 2005. "The Fun Palace: Cedric Price's Experiment in Architecture and Technology." *Technoetic Arts: A Journal of Speculative Research* 3 (2): 73–91.

———. 2006. "The Fun Palace as Virtual Architecture: Cedric Price and the Practices of Indeterminacy." *Journal of Architectural Education* 59 (3): 39–48.

———. 2007. *From Agit-Prop to Free-Space: The Architecture of Cedric Price.* London: Black Dog Publishing.

Obrist, Hans Ulrich. 2009. *Cedric Price.* Cologne, Germany: Walter König.

Price, Cedric. 1996. "Anticipatory Architecture: Cedric Price Special Issue." *Architect's Journal* 204 (8): 20–41.

———. 2003a. *Re: CP,* edited by Hans Ulrich Obrist. Basel, Germany: Birkhäuser.

———. 2003b. *The Square Book.* Chichester, England: Wiley-Academy.

Smith, Laurajane. 2006. *Uses of Heritage.* London and New York: Routledge.

Smith, Laurajane, and Waterton, Emma. 2009. "'The Envy of the World?' Intangible Heritage in England." In *Intangible Heritage,* edited by Natsuko Akagawa and Laurajane Smith, 289–302. London and New York: Routledge.

UNESCO. 2003. *Convention for the Safeguarding of the Intangible Cultural Heritage.* Paris: UNESCO.

11 Bohemian Bourgeoisie and Subversive Commodities

Bartosz Stopel

The general aim of this chapter is to analyze the actions, products, and consumer behavior related to the social groups often referred to as 'bohemian bourgeoisie' or 'creative class' in the context of research on material culture. Thus particular attention will be paid to specific products and items associated with the lifestyle of the creative class, which can be seen as attributes of their status and social position as well as the broader socioeconomic consequences of their consumer behavior. The first part of the chapter will focus on forging a proper definition for the social groups in question along with tracing their historical roots. The second part will explore the consumer behavior of the creative class and interpret it through Bourdieu's (1984) and Veblen's (2007) theories of distinction and conspicuous consumption. Even though the lifestyle and consumer patterns of the creative class are often regarded as desirable and beneficial to society as a whole (most notably by Richard Florida, who coined the term), they do, in fact, reinforce and deform the existing relations of production and consumption, aggrandizing social conflicts and inequalities and reproducing relations of hierarchy, division of property, and inefficient, expensive methods of productions.

Merging Bourgeois and Bohemian Values

Throughout this chapter, I will use the terms 'creative class' or 'bohemian bourgeoisie' ('bobos'), which both relate to post-1960s influential social groups with very particular lifestyles and modes of consumption. I will use these terms interchangeably, though they are not necessarily equivalent. Despite differences, both groups share an extensive body of features (specifically, those of vital interest to my argument) and hence my decision to conflate both concepts. 'Bohemian bourgeoisie' is a concept whose origin is linked to David Brooks's *Bobos in Paradise* (2000), a book exploring the cultural transformations of the post-war U.S., with particular emphasis on the changes in what constitutes cultural elites and in consumer patterns. The term is largely self-explanatory, since for Brooks it denotes a contemporary social group that finally merges the historical and apparent polar opposites of urban culture (43). In an American context, this merging is associated with the collapse of the dominant role of white Anglo-Saxon Protestant industrialist elites and the rise of counterculture. Regardless of differences between Brooks's and Florida's (2012) discussions, they hold the same opinions about the nature of precountercultural American capitalism and social order, whose key features included reliance on mass production, inherited wealth, and family ties and the dominance of the sedentary bourgeoisie. Moreover, they agree about the broad economic and cultural changes correlated with the emergence of bohemian bourgeoisie (Brooks 2000, 18–53) and (or) creative class (Florida 2012, 1–12).

Perhaps until the 1960s, the American class system was clearly dominated by traditional bourgeois values of "material wealth, productive work, social stability and respectability" (Heath and Potter 2004, 194). These values in turn largely imitated the aristocracy with wealth replacing land as the chief determiner of class identity. Within the bourgeois social order, typical status markers of a given occupation were strictly tied to "the importance of the task performed, the authority inherent in the job, the knowledge and the brains required, the dignity of the tasks performed, and the financial rewards" (200–201). This entailed that the most valued jobs included judges, physicians, bankers, business executives, ministers, and college professors (202). The list consists of highly paternalistic professions associated with a great deal of social power and influence. In other words, representatives of these professions were members of the elite that regulated and controlled the social order whose success was based, apart from wealth and the work ethic these professions entailed, on the network of family and school ties along with other in-class connections and acquaintances.

The latter point has some bearing on the essential features of the pre-1960s economy and consumer patterns. Despite the popular view on the close connection between the celebration of the free-spirited individualistic entrepreneur and protestant-capitalist work ethic, it would be more apt to say that the cultural and financial elites that defined American postwar capitalism represented an ideology that was more collectivist than individualist. This can be seen in the list of most desirable occupations mentioned in the preceding paragraph, which reflects commitment to maintaining and reproducing stable bourgeois social order. It celebrates social elites responsible for the community's well-being and not individualist free-spirits. Moreover, the very nature of one's social position, when aspiring or belonging to the dominant class, was chiefly dependent on the 'starting position'—that is, on inherited wealth or family and school ties, none of which have much to do with individual effort and the self-made man myth. Finally, the dominant mode of production of that time was highly collectivist and uniform, as it was the era of mass-produced homogeneity.

If one recognizes that individual success is only possible owing to contributions of other members of one's environment (chiefly family and friends), there is little space for display of uniqueness, as one's identity is defined as being part of the group, rather than as autonomous self-made individual. This is clearly mirrored in consumer products typically associated with

Bohemian Bourgeoisie and Subversive Commodities   145

American capitalism up to the 1960s—the era of standardized mass production symbolized by the Ford Model T, which tended to value uniformity and homogeneity in terms of consumer patterns and automatized modes of production. Apart from automobiles, famous examples would include dress code, involving uniforms or plain suits, coats, and hats; fast food chains; Coca-Cola; Wonder Bread; and shopping malls, as well as the Levittown suburb, which contributed to the development of standardized, mass-produced housing.

If the preceding outline could serve as a general description of the values, consumer patterns, and organization of the early twentieth century bourgeoisie, its binary opposition—its antithesis, in terms of social groups—would be the bohemians with their commitment to art and aesthetics, pleasure, creativity, rebelliousness, individuality, romanticism, and Dionysian spirit against bourgeois celebration of wealth, work, ethics, duty, conformity, social order, collectivism, classicism, and Apollonian spirit.

In the context of postwar America, the distinction was famously framed into hip versus square by Norman Mailer in 1950s, where the former corresponds to the bohemians and the latter to the bourgeoisie. According to Mailer, being hip entailed being black, nihilistic, self-oriented, anarchistic, and sinful, as well as displaying preference for the body over (square) mind and, regarding commodity choices, marijuana over (square) alcohol. Conversely, squares were white, authoritarian, social, and pious (Mailer 1959, 339).

Both Brooks and Florida agree that the rise of counterculture created certain social groups that apparently have successfully merged both sets of values, thus significantly altering American (and, consequently, Western) culture and economy. Both authors are, somehow contrary to Heath and Potter, highly optimistic about the groups' potential and success in transforming capitalism.

Brooks sees bobos as the new cultural elite whose emergence is directly traced to the postwar growth of universities and the unprecedented increase in the number of college graduates. In his view, the fact that large numbers of baby boomers entered the job market with college degrees was a major factor responsible for kick-starting the information era and, thus, for a substantial transformation in the American economy, where social position and personal achievement were becoming less dependent on inherited wealth and ties and more dependent on education and merit. This is clearly reflected in the emergence of the new occupations in the information era that Brooks lists: "creativity officer, chief knowledge officer, team spirit coordinator [...], Web page designer, patent agent, continuity writer, foundation program officer, talk show booker" (37). Though he considers the nature of these professions surprising for previous generations, probably some further, more contemporary examples would be equally surprising for Brooks from the time he wrote the book. It is indisputable, however, that such a transition has taken place; as illustrated in the famous examples of achievement and the rise to cultural prominence: "in this era [...] oddballs like Oliver Stone become multimillionaire moguls and slouchy dropouts like Bill Gates get to run the world" (37).

146   *Bartosz Stopel*

The affluence of the new, educated elites, as Brooks consistently calls them, is tightly connected with their merit, due to the fact that they are rewarded for skills through salary rather than simply inheriting amassed wealth. The economic changes correlated with the emergence of educated elites and with the overthrowing of the old bourgeois order did not result in a dialectical shift with WASP culture's antithesis taking over. On the contrary, as Brooks notes, the educated and rebellious (and thus bohemian) new elites managed to merge and reconcile the opposites in "a way of living that lets you be an affluent success and at the same time a free-spirit rebel" (42). In this interpretation of historical events, there was nothing that resembled class conflict, as the border between both groups simply blurred in a way where it was impossible to tell whether one of the two dominated and absorbed the other: "in the resolution between the culture and the counterculture, it is impossible to tell who co-opted whom, because in reality the bohemians and the bourgeois co-opted each other" (43). There are some objections to Brooks' highly enthusiastic perception of the bobo phenomenon, but they will be voiced later in this chapter.

Bobos could be seen as part of what Richard Florida calls "creative class," a broader phenomenon which he, contra Brooks, sees as primarily economic rather than just cultural (xxii–xxv). According to Florida, the chief driving force of postindustrial capitalism is creativity and, if one traditional myth regarding economic growth is the ability to attract business to a given area, nowadays, it is the ability to attract creative people whom companies follow (rather than the other way around). Florida found that most innovative companies, particularly those associated with high-tech industries, have a tendency to grow or relocate in areas with relatively high concentration of gay people,[1] writers, artists, performers, etc. Thus, economic development "was occurring in places that were tolerant, diverse and open to creativity" (xxiii).

Florida defines creative class according to occupations that "create meaningful new forms" and further divides it into supercreative core and creative professionals. The former includes "scientists and engineers, university professors, poets and novelists, artists, entertainers, actors, designers, and architects [...] nonfiction writers, editors, cultural figures, think-tank researchers, analysts, and other opinion makers" (38), a group that he aptly calls "thought leadership" (38) of society. The outer crust of creative class includes other "knowledge-intensive industries" such as "high-tech, financial services, the legal and health care professions, and business management" (39).

Florida's aims outreach those of modest description as his analysis smoothly goes to present its underlying normativity. If creative class is the driving force of contemporary economy, then in order to grow, cities must introduce policies that would attract the creatives. This has already happened in business, which for decades has been continuously tuning in to the ideas of horizontal organization, mobility, flexibility, designing creative spaces, or promoting casual dress codes. As Heath and Potter (2004) comment, creative work space needs to be open and have "lots of funky art on

Bohemian Bourgeoisie and Subversive Commodities   147

the wall" (202). The premises should have a socializing area where one can "throw a Frisbee, play video games, work out or brew up an espresso shot" (202). Instead of mere salary, the creative class wants "free tickets to the game, free massages and prepared dinners they can take home with them" (202). Likewise, it is no longer enough for cities to ensure there is a well-developed system of public transportation, low crime rate, and the basic social services, but they also must cater to the needs of the creatives' lifestyle, offering, among other things, "large-scale recycling program, plenty of funky cafes, vegetarian restaurants and specialty stores selling a full array of organic products" (203). Moreover, in accordance with Florida's observations, the city needs a diverse and tolerant population with prominent ethnic and sexual minorities, as well as "thriving club and music scene, [...] and easy access to areas of mountain-biking, rock-climbing and sea-kayaking" (203). Although some of Heath and Potter's claims are exaggerated, they give a general sense of direction cities should be heading, turning away from a sedentary bourgeoisie lifestyle and embracing bobo values, being cool, and consequently prospering.

Subversive Commodities

One key feature of countercultural rebellion that shaped bobo mentality is the emphatic shift from the collective, the mass, the social toward individuality. This is, in fact, the very core of the bohemian opposition against the allegedly totalitarian, controlling, and soul-destroying capitalist society of the earlier bourgeoisie. If what defined such a society and those who participated in it were the modes of production and the patterns of consumption, then the natural way of opposing it would be to reject them altogether. This drive toward 'alternative community' in the spirit of Herbert Marcuse surely gained some ground within the vast and heterogeneous countercultural movement. It has, however, produced little change in capitalist economy as we see it nowadays. The conciliatory bobo approach, as indicated earlier, means using the rebel spirit to subvert and transform capitalism from inside; starting with individual transformation and liberation from the oppressive society, it is supposed to lead to broader socioeconomic changes. This logic implies that you can only fight the alleged evil of mass society by awakening and supporting the individual free spirit. It can hardly go unnoticed in a variety of contemporary commercial and popular slogans (one of them being Apple's famous "Think different") that if you want to change the world, you should start with changing yourself. These slogans stress the idea of personal development and promote a search for one's true identity and freedom of expression. They also emphasize the necessity to take individual action and its socially transformative value (as in the motto "think globally, act locally").

Overall, it might be said that if the earlier, 'mass production type' of consumerism was mostly motivated by generating an abundance of goods

148 *Bartosz Stopel*

in order to satisfy the basic and practical needs of the general populace, thus minimizing conspicuous and competitive consumption, bobo consumer patterns are the opposite as they emphasize *coolhunting* and the need to subvert and change the social order. Heath and Potter's compelling discussion concludes that the elusive 'cool' label that bobos look for is derived from a bohemian value system and is equivalent to being fresh, subversive, and rebellious (2004, 205), expressing the consumer's individuality and uniqueness. This itself should allegedly pose a threat to the homogenous mass economy, but it also smoothly proceeds to a conviction that those consumer patterns that oppose global, corporate capitalism and mass production will eventually create a better society.

One famous and historically significant illustration of the bobo consumer attitude is the 1984 Apple TV commercial alluding to Orwell's work. It presents a young athlete furiously storming into an auditorium and throwing a hammer at the screen where Big Brother delivers his speech to a gray, homogenous and undifferentiated mass of people. The contrasting colorful hair and clothes along with a lively behavior indicate a rebellious, free-spirited individual. The off-screen narration suggesting that the introduction of the Macintosh computer in 1984 would guarantee reality in no way resembles Orwell's vision. Clearly, what is communicated is that if consumers buy products associated with individuality and coolness, the world will literally become a better place. It is surely ironic that Apple has managed to retain its cool image, even though the company relies on cheap Asian labor and contributed immensely to the overwhelming presence of technology along with control and surveillance of client data.

The consumer attitude sketched here has recently been brilliantly parodied in the celebrated TV show *Silicon Valley*, which depicts the struggle of aspiring start-up geeks with powerful IT corporations. One comical strategy applied there is to contrast the high, unrealistic ambitions of IT culture with the blatant insignificance of the products and services offered. One member of the start-up develops an application called "nip alert," designed to give users the location of women with erect nipples. The creative space in the biggest IT company, Hooli (an explicit reference to Google), serves at some point as a test lab for potato canons. But the most biting satire comes from the Hooli commercial presented in the show, where its CEO talks about developing a ground-breaking data compression algorithm that can, again, make the world a better place, confidently saying, "If we can make your audio and video files smaller, we can make cancer smaller. And hunger. And ... AIDS" (wikiquote).

Perhaps bobo consumer behavior could be considered a form of commodity fetishism, where special, almost magical qualities are ascribed to commodities whose acquisition and consumption are supposed to fundamentally alter the socioeconomic reality. The same consumer patterns appear across a variety of products and, in each case, the grandiosity of the belief in their transformative value starkly contrasts with the actual effects.

Bohemian Bourgeoisie and Subversive Commodities 149

Heath and Potter (2004) devote substantial space to discussing this problem, so I will only enumerate the most illustrative examples. One obvious case of transition from mere utilitarian commodity value toward subversive consumerism concerns clothing and related accessories. No longer are consumers forced into standardized, plain clothes of the pre-1960s; rather, they presently can (or so it seems) choose the type of apparel that suits their individuality best. As with other examples of bobo consumerism, this could be considered naïve, as clothing brands are one of the clearest markers of social status, rather than expressions of creative individuality (161–188).

Likewise, Heath and Potter discuss bobos' aversion to (square) cars and their preference for bikes. Even though there is no denying that car overpopulation is a serious problem for city policies worldwide, it should not be overlooked that the bicycle market has spontaneously delivered a variety of commodities producing similar effects to those in the fashion industry. It generated a diversity of bike brands, whose central role is to serve as class markers and fuel bobo conspicuous consumption. Heath and Potter recall their participation in a Critical Mass anticonsumerist protest where a large number of bikes cost more than the used cars they owned (2004, 288).

Overall, the paradoxical anti-capitalist overproduction of consumer goods, associated with conspicuous consumption, is less harmful than the effects bobo lifestyle has on some basic products (e.g., food). Heath and Potter cite two stories taken from lifestyle magazines that are in accordance with bobo principles of anticonsumerism, ecology, slow life, and slow food. In one telling example of the slow-food approach, where the main idea is the consumption of organic and locally produced foods from small-scale farmers, a Canadian national decided to move her slow-food business from her home country to Southern France, due to longer vegetation growing cycles and a greater variety of accessible fruits and vegetables (2004, 306–307). In other words, bringing about social change by adhering to slow-food principles is, in this case, only possible if one is rich enough to move to Southern France. The other anticonsumerist story concerns a woman who moved from Vermont to Hawaii, where she bought some land with the intention of cultivating a small garden, growing tea and sandalwood (hiring a full-time employee to take care of it while she was away), and then selling organic products locally (156–158).

What both stories demonstrate is that anticonsumerist tendencies of bobos promote inefficient, labor- and time-consuming methods of production and manufacturing and promote expensive products, all of which results in pushing cheap, mass-produced food out of the market and reducing its availability for the poor. In reality, thus, the anticonsumer attitude toward food can lead to potentially disastrous consequences, driving wealth inequality to the point where the rich and the poor eat radically differently in terms of food quality. It seems, then, that slow food and slow life amount to little more than pursuing pastimes of "the rich and bored" (Heath and Potter, 2004, 305–306), leading to harmful social change.

150 *Bartosz Stopel*

In spite of the anticonsumer and anticapitalist ideology, bobo consumer patterns seem to be different when explained with concepts such as Bourdieu's *distinction* or Veblen's *conspicuous consumption*. The fact that the former is associated primarily with aesthetic taste, rather than with mere consumerism, is even more to the point here when taking into consideration bobo bohemian aspirations, which mark a drive toward the aesthetization of commodities such as food or clothes. Another prominent feature of *distinction* is marking one's status owing to the acquisition of considerable amounts of cultural capital and thus differentiating from common, ordinary tastes. This is perfectly illustrated both by the bobo emphasis on socially aware, transformative consumerism and by their attempt at rejecting mass-produced commodities in favor of fresh, cool, custom or exclusive, difficult-to-access goods. 'Coolness' is, in fact, a never-ending and ever-changing mark of distinction that requires a constant accumulation of cultural capital to stay in touch with what currently marks the social status.

Veblen's analysis of conspicuous consumption is a perfect complement to considerations about the detrimental and unintended effects bobo consumerism has on the economy, although, again, it might not seem so at first. The analysis originally referred to the unnecessary display of wealth by engaging in leisure activities or consumerism by an aristocratic leisure class and by those who tried to imitate their lifestyle. Even though rhetorically bobos oppose traditional class distinctions and markers, their actions seem not to confirm this. They do indulge in the display of wealth by means of lavish expenditure on exclusive and expensive cool and subversive products. If it is not the goods themselves that go to waste, it is definitely the extensive time and effort necessary for their production and consumption.

To sum up the relation between bobos and commodities, it is only through particular material objects that bobo lifestyle can be manifested. These objects, in turn, are of special importance to contemporary Western urban culture and include highly specific subgroups of objects of everyday use. The feature that is shared across all categories, or rather the one that is attributed to them by their users, is the belief in their subversive qualities that lead to personal and socioeconomic change. In order to provide a more detailed overview of some typical examples of objects involved in the creation of bobo lifestyle, I will use Henry Alford's "How I Became a Hipster" (2013), which describes the journalist's attempt at becoming a Brooklynite bobo. All the examples listed here come from his article.

One broad category of bobo-oriented products includes artisanal, custommade, or locally produced commodities, which stand in opposition to mass-produced goods. The most obvious example of artisanal products includes food and drink: products from artisanal cheese shops, bakeries, or even an "all-artisanal mayonnaise store" along with "espresso soda" or "hibiscus soda syrup" seem to be cornerstones of bobo meals. When it comes to desserts, Alford mentions a company selling artisanal chocolate whose production is entirely under their control, wind-sailing cocoa beans from the Dominican to Brooklyn, then hand-sorting them and letting the chocolate rest 30 days before sale. The artisanal mode of production should generate better quality goods or so the movement believes, though this clearly remains debatable, but some indisputable features include lesser accessibility, a wider range of products, and high prices, all of which drive conspicuous consumption and offer more opportunities for defining one's identity through commodities.

Another important feature of bobo lifestyle is the aesthetization of everyday objects and elevation of a subversive, alternative style that covers food, clothing, body, modes of transport, etc. Alford mentions a hip Brooklyn pizzeria whose entrance presents "barbed wire leading to heavily graffitied concrete cinder blocks: gulag in da hood." His description of bobo Brooklynites' apparel, which he often summarizes as "19th century farmer" or "Abraham Lincoln," constantly refer to simplistic and natural products such as "plaid flannel shirts," "vintage work boots," "lumpy wool cardigans," "corduroy vests," etc. One example of body aesthetization includes visiting barbers where one can be treated with "eucalyptus-scented towels" and "delicate razor strokes" as well as "use some moustache counseling." Perhaps the most extreme form of the ecological and anticonsumer lifestyle is the tendency to be a self-sufficient producer, somehow personifying the nineteenth century farmer Alford alluded to. Again, food production seems to be the most essential area, both because of biological necessities and because the production is extremely removed from consumers. Consequently, activities such as butchering, "chickeneering," rooftop gardening, cardboard furniture making, and other small-scale modes of production are very popular among bobos.

Overall, the objects produced in artisanal and other alternative modes of production are all attributed high, though perhaps varying, degrees of uniqueness, aesthetic value, high-quality, status markers, subversiveness, coolness, ecological value, and socioeconomic justice. Interestingly enough, owing to the aesthetization or care for quality and uniqueness that drives bobo consumerism, they cannot be said to be entirely antiaristocratic. This somehow resonates with Sontag's (2009) idea of aristocracy of taste discussed in note 1 and marks the fact that even the bohemian bourgeoisie cannot entirely escape imitating aristocracy.

It should come as no surprise that "cool" American cities that attracted significant numbers of bobos as if following Florida's suggestions struggle with problems generated by the bobo lifestyle. The most striking one is the rise in wealth inequality and urban poverty in places restructured with bobo gentrification. The arrival of the rich and the creative has altered living standards, increasing housing prices and changing the market structure in a way so that, whatever wealth trickles down thanks to the presence of the creative class, it does not compensate the losses of the poor. According to official data, Washington, DC, and San Francisco, typically listed as 'cool cities,' "also have among the highest percentages of poverty of any

152 Bartosz Stopel

major urban center—roughly 20 percent—once cost of living is figured in" (Kotkin 2013). Instead of being revitalized, the urban landscapes become full of stark contrasts, where artisan cheese shops and bakeries selling exclusive and expensive products (against, say, mass-produced cheap white bread) are surrounded by a poor majority. Studies have found that, in gentrifying Brooklyn, 25 percent of the population lives below the poverty line and receives food stamps (Kotkin 2013).

Another objection against implementing bobo-friendly policies is that they require substantial resources while being relatively small in numbers and highly specific concerning their lifestyle needs. Moreover, despite their proclaimed diversity, bobos are predominantly white, single, and in their twenties, and their presence actually reduces ethnic and cultural diversity, pushing (by economic means) poorer residents (often ethnic minorities) out of the cities and areas they select as cool. This reduction of diversity includes commodities and services, too, as the bobo consumer choices are quite uniform and tend to replace traditional local products. Quoting some studies on gentrification in New Orleans, one author has bitterly remarked that "the creatives replace the local culture with the increasingly predictable [...] offering beet-filled ravioli instead of fried okra" (Kotkin 2013); regarding the rather paradoxical uniformity of bobo consumerism, the author stated that "the 'unique' amenities you find now, even in New Orleans, [...] are much what you'd expect in any other hipster paradise, be it Portland; Seattle; Burlington, Vermont; or Williamsburg" (Kotkin 2013).

Conclusion

Brooks's bobos as the cutting edge of Florida's creative class are the epitome of postcountercultural revolution that embraced Western economy, culture, and lifestyle. The economic transformations connected with the rise of the number of college graduates, development of IT and services, and decline of industry go hand in hand with significant changes in consumer behavior. Bobos oppose the sedentary collectivist lifestyle of the old bourgeoisie, as well as homogenous, mass-produced goods. Instead, they want the type of commodities that would emphasize their individuality and subvert the totalizing corporate economic order, leading to social change. This implies that everyday consumer products gain an aura of both coolness and salvation, but it appears that the former is largely congruent with such concepts as distinction or conspicuous consumption, whereas the latter produces adverse economic effects. As a result, consumption of products in terms of "coolhunting," rather than promoting individuality and subversion of mass consumption, leads to consolidation of the phenomena that it was supposed to undermine.

The bobo approach to commodities is clearly another example of capitalism absorbing those who want to oppose it and ultimately making them conform, as, apart from individual consumer satisfaction (which is entirely in tune with capitalist ideology), there are hardly any serious advantages of subversive commodities hunting. Quite the opposite, it merely illustrates the malleability of capitalism and its ability to adapt and adjust. But even this does not appear to be a compromise on the side of economic reality. Whereas the old bourgeoisie had a tendency to imitate aristocracy, rely on family ties, and promote mass production and communitarian ethics, bobo free-spirited individualism, mobility, and volatility seem to express the nature of capitalism more adequately and, hence, be even more conformist in relation to the dominant economic ideology. The conformity is striking when one places bobo consumerism and Florida's vision of urban policy in the broader framework of a neoliberal agenda. His ideas are a perfect match for neoliberal policies since both encourage moving away from traditional industry and manufacturing and cutting down the functions of the state, which should no longer actively participate in the market but only create proper conditions (usually by simply rolling back) for the development of the free market. The fiasco of implementing Florida's policies is yet another illustration of the overall fiasco of a neoliberal agenda, as broad social problems cannot be solved by simple reduction of the state's regulatory role and reliance on individual, rather than system-scale, actions.

Note

1. Even though Florida does not elaborate on the relation between homosexuality and the creative class, merely including LGBT as a subgroup of largely childless bobos, the peculiar relation between homosexuality, art, and creativity has long been noted in cultural studies. Susan Sontag famously claimed that Camp taste is partly snob taste and contemporary representatives of this snobbism include to a large extent homosexuals who are "aristocrats of taste" (Sontag 2009, 290). Likewise, Jack Babuscio (1993, 19) defines gay sensibility as "creative energy reflecting consciousness that is different from the mainstream."

References

Alford, Henry. 2013. "How I Became a Hipster." *The New York Times*. Available online at http://www.nytimes.com/2013/05/02/fashion/williamsburg.html?_r=0.
Babuscio, Jack. 1993. "Camp and Gay Sensibility." In *Camp Grounds. Style and Homosexuality*, edited by David Bergman, 19–38. Amherst: University of Massachusetts Press.
Bourdieu, Pierre. 1984. *Distinction. A Social Critique of the Judgment of Taste*. Cambridge, MA: Harvard University Press.
Brooks, David. 2000. *Bobos in Paradise: The New Upper Class and How They Got There*. New York: Simon and Schuster Paperbacks.
Florida, Richard. 2012. *The Rise of the Creative Class*. New York: Basic Books.
Heath, Joseph, and Andrew Potter. 2004. *Nation of Rebels. Why Counterculture Became Consumer Culture*. New York: HarperBusiness.

154 *Bartosz Stopel*

Kotkin, Joel. 2013. "Richard Florida Concedes the Limits of the Creative Class." *The Daily Beast.* Available online at http://www.thedailybeast.com/articles/2013/03/20/richard-florida-concedes-the-limits-of-the-creative-class.html.

Mailer, Norman. 1959. Advertisements for Myself. New York: Putnam.

Wikiquote. "Silicon Valley." Last modified October 27, 2015. Available online at https://en.wikiquote.org/wiki/Silicon_Valley_%28TV_series%29#Articles_of_Incorporation_.5B1.03.5D.

Sontag, Susan. 2009. *Against Interpretation and Other Essays.* London: Penguin.

Veblen, Thorstein. 2007. *Theory of the Leisure Class.* Oxford: Oxford University Press.

Part IV
Popular Narratives and Material Culture

12 Objects Don't Lie. The Truth and Things in Detective Stories[1]

Joanna Soćko

Detective fiction has undergone many formal and thematic transformations but its core remains unchanged: it seeks to assert the truth. Roland Barthes regards this literary genre as the most typical example of what he calls "hermeneutic code" in fiction ("Voice of Truth")—a narrative that constructs an enigma, introduces suspense, and finally discloses the secret (1990, 47). It is not a coincidence that detective fiction grew in popularity in the second half of the nineteenth century when the common understanding of truth was largely influenced by two phenomena: a massive production of fictitious narratives and the development of historical disciplines such as evolutionary biology, archaeology, and cosmology. The first phenomenon may relate to the long-lasting process of secularization and its defiance against scripture as a narrative that explains the world. Since the sacred 'master plot' was no longer reliable (Brooks 1992, 6), narratives that helped to organize and reformulate individual and social life gained a new sense of urgency. The second phenomenon concerns the conviction that the truth about some fundamental aspects of the world (the origin of the solar system, the provenance of man, etc.) can be asserted by the analysis of empirical data. A variety of developments contributed to the interest in empirical evidence. They involved Charles Darwin's analyses of animals and plants that laid the foundation for his theory of evolution; archaeological research of historical layers of Hissarlik, believed to be a historical site of Homer's Troy; and the paleontological study of fossils, which enabled the determination of the historical development of living organisms. In this way, secularization and science brought about the rise of detective fiction and helped maintain its popularity as a literary genre that continues to provide, in the words of Lawrence Frank, a "narrative model for arriving at the truth of the moment" (2003, 29).

The aim of this chapter is to explore the role of things in the epistemic structures embedded in detective fiction. It examines the ways in which objects stand as substitutes for the authoritative, sacred 'master plot' in order to reveal the workings of literary discourse, which transforms common things into evidence for social mysteries and stories behind violent acts. It also analyzes how inanimate things, in terms of their abilities to hide and uncover secrets, contribute first to the construction of the narrative enigma and then to the ultimate revelation of the truth. As such, it attempts to prove that objects actively participate in the narrative and that they

158 *Joanna Soćko*

possess a discursive potential. For that purpose, the chapter investigates the genre's conventional narrative pattern by reading classical detective stories (E. A. Poe's "Tales of Rationalization," and A. C. Doyle's and A. Christie's fiction) and, to a lesser degree, some contemporary crime dramas.

Objects Are Important

In the opening scene of the Danish/Swedish TV crime drama *Bron/Broen* [*The Bridge*], we see a car stop on the bridge between Denmark and Sweden. It is late night and as the driver gets out and walks down the empty road, the lights on the bridge go out. So do the monitoring cameras. When the light reappears, there is a body lying right in the middle of the bridge, partially covering the borderline between the countries. The police arrive at the crime scene and the traffic is stopped for two detectives to examine the evidence. With lights flashing and sirens screaming, an ambulance threatens to intrude on the investigation area. A woman comes out of the vehicle and pleads with the detectives for permission to transport her dying husband for an emergency heart surgery on the other side of the bridge. But rigidly following the crime scene protocol, the Swedish detective Saga Norén refuses to allow the ambulance to pass. The protocol states: "[o]ne of the most important aspects of securing the crime scene is to preserve the scene with minimal contamination and disturbance of physical evidence" (Technical Working Group on Crime Scene Investigation 2013, 1). For Saga, the procedure is clear: by no means can the material evidence be disturbed.

The reason why the physical qualities of the crime scene are given priority over the patient's life is that the truth they may reveal reaches far beyond the problem of an individual death. If the main ethical concern of detective fiction were to do justice to the individual (that is, in this case the person who was murdered), risking another human life would be unthinkable, and the ambulance would be given passage. But here the life of the whole society is at stake. The disturbance of physical evidence therefore means the disturbance of the social order and poses a threat to every member of the community. The blackout in the opening scene of *Bron/Broen* is a metaphor of the failure of surveillance and policing: for one moment society loses control over its own established order. Consequently, the secret occurrence of the crime transforms into a real *mysterium tremendum,* the utterly ineffable event whereby the ripples of the unreachable past spread across contemporary social life. Since the immediate access to the past is denied, the only way to solve the enigma of the crime—to reconstruct its motive and execution—is to examine the physical evidence left behind. The mystery of the unreachable event must be solved to create the illusion that order has been restored and that prevention is possible.

Reading Matter

Attention to the significance of physical traces has been a central trope in detective fiction. Drawing on authentic investigation procedures, literary

Objects Don't Lie. 159

discourse uses a crime scene and the corpse's whereabouts as areas of the semiotic transformation of objects where they gain hidden meanings and, consequently, acquire narrative potential. The police barrier tape, for example, separates objects from their common contexts, turning them into signs in the order of crime. The structure of these signs is based on reversal of what Roland Barthes called "language-object" relation (1991, 114). It is not words that refer to things but rather objects that refer to words—that is, they allude to stories behind them. Since the barrier type detaches objects from their common functions, things connected with crime produce a mythical mode of signification as defined by Barthes. In a crime context, the material signs operate like signifiers, which acquire another *signifié* and denote a new meaning. As a result, physical qualities of things become (meta)physical connotations to be deciphered in the course of interpretative procedures.

These procedures emerged from the overlap of the historical disciplines of the nineteenth century (philology, archaeology, evolutionary biology, etc.), and, according to Lawrence Frank (2003), they most significantly influenced the development of detective fiction. The convergence of empirical data of sciences with the language units of philology makes the crime scene a signifying texture of objects—a text made of matter. The corpse of the murdered person is the most important element of this text. The body, like every object found on a crime scene, is being empowered with additional meaning: it not only refers to the fact that someone lost his or her life, but also indicates that some mysterious happenings have occurred. It becomes, then, a sign whose meaning is—to use a spatial metaphor—an empty place. This empty place is complete with the help of other things in a crime scene, which results in a complex system of references that defers the ultimate arrival of meaning.

The fact that detective fiction doubts the veracity of testimonies and potential witness accounts, and bestows confidence on objects, results from apparent distrust toward narratives as such. Unlike reliable empirical data, narratives are fictitious and cannot be verified by means of methodological analyses. Agatha Christie's most famous detective, Hercules Poirot, rehearses this belief in *The Murder of Roger Ackroyd*: "You will find, M. le docteur, if you have much to do with cases of this kind, that they all resemble each other in one thing [...]. Everyone concerned in them has something to hide" (Christie 2011, 84). Also, Dr. House, one of the contemporary incarnations of Sherlock Holmes, repeats this conviction with emphatic skepticism: "Everybody lies." In the pilot to *MD House*, a patient loses her ability to speak, which symbolically shows that the words of patients are useless. What brings doctors to the solution of medical enigmas are physical symptoms and patients' living environments. This means that in detective narratives the unveiling of the truth still relies on a hermeneutical process of reading signs, but language is replaced by the physical qualities of material reality.

If the tapestry of things reads like a text, then the detective is a hermeneutist who provides the ultimate interpretation. As Bill Brown observes, "Whereas Heidegger believed that the right kind of attentive passivity

160   *Joanna Soćko*

would enable us to hear things [...], it turns out that things 'talk' differently to different interlocutors" (2006, 119). Detectives certainly are those who hear more of the objects' murmurs: "[t]o me they speak sometimes—chairs, tables—they have their message!" says Hercules Poirot (Christie 2011, 91). Masters of analysis, detectives learn to know things by examining surfaces, material clues and traces. In *A Study in Scarlet*, Sherlock Holmes shows his expertise in things relying on his knowledge of chemistry, anatomy, botany, and geology (Doyle 2001, 12), which all contribute to the art of material exegesis he so often performs on the crime scenes, as in the following passage:

> As he [Sherlock Holmes] spoke, he whipped a tape measure and a large round magnifying glass from his pocket. With these two implements he trotted noiselessly about the room, sometimes stopping, occasionally kneeling, and once lying flat upon his face. So engrossed was he with his occupation that he appeared to have forgotten our presence, for he chattered away to himself under his breath the whole time, keeping up a running fire of exclamations, groans, whistles, and little cries suggestive of encouragement and of hope.
>
> (Doyle 2001, 27)

Hercules Poirot examines the area of objects' signifying texture with similar proficiency:

> We went up together to the room of the tragedy. Poirot locked the door on the inside, and proceeded to a minute inspection of the room. He darted from one object to the other with the agility of a grasshopper. I remained by the door, fearing to obliterate any clues.
>
> (Christie 2015, 21)

The Plot Pattern of Detective Narrative

The plot pattern characteristic of detective narratives depends on the diegetic potential of materiality. In other words, detective plots dramatize matter to allow for new narrative possibilities of the mystery. These possibilities are reflected in the double-ness of this type of a narrative scheme. As John G. Cawelti observes, in detective stories the plot is double because it relates the story twice: first, when it "is narrated as it appears to the bewildered bystanders who observe the crime [...] but who cannot arrive at its solution," second, when detectives read clues and interpret traces that eventually lead them to the solution of the crime (1997, 10). The first plotting formulates an enigma and holds it in suspense; the other explains how the truth has been retrieved from objects featured in the narration.

In *The Poetics of Prose* (1977), Tzvetan Todorov introduces a typology of detective by distinguishing two phases of the plot: "the story of investigation" ("how we come to know about it") and "the story of crime" ("what

Objects Don't Lie. 161

really happened") (45). These two stories relate to the concepts of *fabula* and *sjužet* formulated by Russian Formalists (45). *Fabula* is "the original story," the sequence of events the narrative intends to recount. *Sjužet*, in turn, is the way in which the narrative organizes the events and puts them into discourse chosen for rendering a given plot. Thus, "the story of crime" refers to *fabula* ("what really happened") and it represents "real" events: the truth. "The investigation story," on the other hand, is how the *fabula* is being presented in the course of the narrative.

It is worth noting that although "the story of crime" chronologically precedes "the story of investigation," it is not revealed until after the detective explains the meaning of clues and reconstructs the past events in his revelatory monologue. In *The Murders in the Rue Morgue* (Poe 2014), for example, the reader is informed about the crime when C. Auguste Dupin and his friend, who narrates the story, read about it in a local newspaper. Thus, the reader is immediately introduced into the story of investigation, which begins when the detective character is informed about the murder and starts reading the material clues in order to guess what has happened. This 'what has happened' is 'the story of crime,' which, apparently, has occurred before "the story of investigation" begins. But the reader does not has access into the past events and he or she usually learns how and why the murders were committed at the end of the whole story, when the detective reveals secrets of these happenings and thereby represents "the story of crime." In this way, the chronological order of the crime and investigation is reverted, which, as we shall see, is of great importance for the narrative epistemological pattern established by detective fiction.

The Poetics of Things

When analyzed from the perspective of the ancient distinction between *mimesis* (which imitates and shows rather than relates) and *diegesis* (which tells the story rather than represents it), "the investigation story" parallels the mimetic mode and "the story of crime" the diegetic. As a result, objects contributing to detective narrative assume different roles. In the mimetic "story of investigation," things trigger the plot by denoting the mystery. For example, in Poe's *Murders in Rue Morgue*, objects map the crime scene:

> The apartment was in the wildest disorder—the furniture broken and thrown about in all directions. There was only one bedstead; and from this the bed had been removed, and thrown into the middle of the floor. On a chair lay a razor, besmeared with blood [...].
>
> (Poe 2014, 11)

Here, disorder and chaos are the traces of mystery narrated through the arrangement of objects. The objects denote that some mysterious events have (just) happened. Bodies work in the same way: they become the material

162 Joanna Soćko

core of the enigma; their physical qualities serve as mysterious clues to open different possibilities for the development of the plot:

> The body was quite warm. Upon examining it, many excoriations were perceived, no doubt occasioned by the violence with which it had been thrust up and disengaged. Upon the face were many severe scratches, and, upon the throat, dark bruises, and deep indentations of finger nails, as if the deceased had been throttled to death.
>
> (Poe 2014, 12)

In the course of "the investigation story," things play hide and seek. On the one hand, they guide the detective toward the truth; on the other hand, they complicate the plot by leading the main protagonist astray as they turn out to be "false clues." These false clues are simply objects that denote some pieces of information that, nevertheless, remain irrelevant to the solution of the crime. Moreover, things, as we said earlier after Brown, "talk differently to different interlocutors," and they often force the characters to take actions that are mysterious for the others. This makes the plot more dynamic and becomes the source of tension for the detectives' systematic analysis and the narrative itself:

> I turned to Lawrence, to suggest that I had better leave them now [...] but the words were frozen on my lips. Never had I seen such a ghastly look on any man's face [...] his eyes, petrified with terror, or some such kindred emotion, stared fixedly over my head at a point on the further wall. [...] I instinctively followed the direction of his eyes but I could see nothing unusual. The still feebly flickering ashes in the grate, and the row of prim ornaments on the mantelpiece, were surely harmless enough.
>
> (Christie 2015, 15)

What, for Hercules Poirot's friend remains an innocent object, is in fact a material actor of mystery that affects other characters and makes them act suspiciously or incomprehensibly until the secret function of this object is revealed. In the passage from *The Mysterious Affair At Styles* I quoted before, the same mantelpiece becomes a catalyst for different types of emotions:

> Poirot had walked over to the mantelpiece. He was outwardly calm, but I noticed his hands, which from long force of habit were mechanically straightening the spill vases on the mantelpiece, were shaking violently. "See here, it was like this," he said at last. "There was [...] some piece of evidence, slight in itself, perhaps, but still enough of a clue to connect the murderer with the crime."
>
> (Christie 2015, 41)

The "piece of evidence" mentioned here by Hercules Poirot is a fragment of a letter in which the murderer owns up to the plotting of the crime.

Objects Don't Lie. 163

The detective realizes that the letter has been either hidden or destroyed, which makes him angry, and his agitation is shown by the nervous movements of hands "mechanically straightening the spill vases on the mantelpiece." The narrator pays special attention to the relation between Poirot and objects. We learn that it is the "long force of habit" that pushes the detective to put things in a correct order. Poirot's systematic approach to objects leads to the discovery of the evidence of crime: the lost pieces of the murderer's letter left in the spill vases on the mantelpiece become discovered. The connection between the detective and material evidence leads him to final solution of the crime. During his explanatory narrative about how the murder was committed and the evidence hidden, Poirot addresses his friend as follows:

> Do you remember telling me that my hand shook as I was straightening the ornaments on the mantelpiece? [...] I remembered that earlier in the morning, when we had been there together, I had straightened all the objects on the mantelpiece. And, if they were already straightened, there would be no need to straighten them again, unless, in the meantime, someone else had touched them.
>
> (Christie 2015, 110)

In the diegetic 'crime story' finally reconstructed by the detective, things that appear in the course of the mimetic narrative become arguments in favor of the exegete's interpretation. The detective's hypothesis about "what really happened" is usually formulated on the basis of different circumstantial pieces of evidence. Even though those pieces of evidence are sometimes not material things, they must be aligned with physical objects to confirm their validity. Only when conformed with the mimetic description of physical evidence does the hypothetical explanation become a valid reconstruction of the *fabula*. By comparison, in *The Murders in the Rue Morgue*, signs of incomprehensible violence are encoded in the arrangement of the objects and suggest that the murderer could not have been human. This hypothesis must be confirmed by the physical traces left on the body: the impressions of the strange bruisings upon Madam L'Espanaye's throat do not fit the form of human fingers. This is revealed when Dupin asks his friend to try to repeat the deadly embrace: "[t]his—I said—is the mark of no human hand!" (Poe 2014, 33).

The impression that the story behind a crime is gradually being revealed in the process of investigation is only the effect of 'mimetic illusion' generated by the narrative discourse. This mimetic illusion leads the reader to imaginatively hold *fabula* chronologically precedent to *sjuzet* by the force of the storytelling. According to John G. Cawelti, the plot in crime stories is not only double but also duplicitous because "the story of investigation" purposely blears the *fabula* so that it stays secret until the final revelation of what actually happened. Cawelti observes that "the writer tries to tantalize

164　*Joanna Soćko*

and deceive the reader while, at the same time, inconspicuously planting the clues that will eventually make the detective's solution plausible" (1997, 11). The first tentative attempt at guessing what happened is, therefore, always purposely vague and misleading. Thus, the detective's final interpretation is construed in such a way as to give the impression of revealing what has been previously hidden by the perpetrator. But the equation of "the investigation story" with *sjužet* and "the story of crime" with *fabula* enables us to claim that a different process is at work: the narratological approach proves that *fabula* is not being revealed but constructed by *sjužet*. As Brooks (1992) observes:

> The apparent priority of *fabula* to *sjužet* is in the nature of a mimetic illusion, in that the *fabula*—"what really happened"—is in fact a mental construction that the reader derives from the *sjužet*, which is all that he ever directly knows. (13)

The structure of the plot keeps the reader away from the *fabula*, and all that the reader knows is what the writer chooses to reveal. From this perspective, "the story of crime" reconstructed by the detective does not discover what has been hidden throughout the narrative; rather it formulates what has been constructed in the mimetic "story of investigation." As a consequence, the objects do not hide or reveal the truth, but rather create what in the final account appears to be the truth of the whole story.

The manifold references to objects in crime stories contribute to the ultimate shape of the *fabula* and make them active agents in the construction and constitution of truth. In his essay on the Berlin key, Bruno Latour rephrases J. L. Austin's influential concept of how to do things with words into "How to Do Words with Things" (1991), suggesting that a similar performative act can be done with objects. This rhetorical reversal casts objects in a new conceptual framework whereby they are bestowed with active roles in creation of social relations. As Latour contends on the example of the Berlin key, objects participate in "a bitter struggle for control and access" (1991, 18), and therefore they may be perceived as mediators between human agents. This performative affordance of things, however, can only be noticed if we recognize them as equal participants of the social sphere. For Latour, objects involved in the process of signification do not merely convey meanings, but rather reshape these meanings by activating significations that have so far remained unrecognized: "the meaning is no longer simply transported by the medium but in part constituted, moved, recreated, modified, in short expressed and betrayed" (1991, 19). Similarly, in detective fiction the represented objects do not merely signal the *fabula*; on the contrary, the *fabula* must come into line with things represented in the course of narration. Viewed in this way, the discourse of detective fiction, guided by objects it refers to, constitutes the truth of the story and makes things both create and assert its legibility.

Conclusion

In the nineteenth century, when the epiphanic character of scripture is put into doubt by Western societies, detective fiction emerges in response to this epistemological shift. The plurality of possible narratives in the conveyance of truth undermines the power of texts as carriers of revelation. In response to this crisis, there emerges confidence in science and the scientific method, which also transfers to literary fiction. This establishes a modern pattern of storytelling and searching for the truth. In detective fiction the truth ("what really happened") assumes the role of a socially significant mystery, which is to be solved in a procedure that resembles scientific investigation characteristic for the nineteenth century. Additionally, this investigation is presented in a discursive form typical for historical disciplines. So, on the one hand, the physical evidence is examined by an expert (science); on the other, the story that the evidence reveals is a reconstruction of the past (history). A narratological analysis shows, however, that the resemblance to science is superficial and that literature, in fact, inverts the scientific scheme as it uses physical evidence—not in order to reveal but rather to create the truth of the story (*fabula*). In this way, objects exhibit their discursive potential and shape the narrative to render the truth.

The narrative potential of common things is not limited to literary texts. In his *Defence of Detective Stories*, G. K. Chesterton claims that detective fiction provides the poetics of modern life—a discourse that makes the social reality meaningful. According to Chesterton, the reality that we live in nowadays appears as "a chaos of conscious forms" that, thanks to popular literature, is being organized and transformed into a signifying texture:

> The lights of the city begin to glow like innumerable goblin eyes, since they are the guardians of some secret, however crude, which the writer knows and the reader does not. Every twist of the road is like a finger pointing to it; every fantastic skyline of chimney-pots seems wildly and derisively signaling the meaning of the mystery.
>
> (Chesterton 1976, 4)

Chesterton observes that the "poetics of objects" developed in crime fiction shapes readers' perception of the surrounding world. Crime fiction represents materiality full of hints, messages, and histories and it uses common objects as custodians of reliable narratives that may elucidate some aspects of social life. This marriage of words and things restores the credibility of a literary text and equips physical reality with (meta)physical potential.

Note

1. This chapter is the result of research conducted in the framework of research project no 2013/11/N/HS2/03523 financed by the Polish National Science Center.

166 *Joanna Soćko*

References

Barthes, Roland. 1990. *S/Z*. Oxford: Basil Blackwell.
———. 1991. *Mythologies*. New York: The Noonday Press.
Brooks, Peter. 1992. *Reading for the Plot. Design and Intention in Narrative.* Cambridge, MA and London: Harvard University Press.
Brown, Bill. 2006. "Murmuring Matter." *Metascience* 15 (1): 117–121.
Cawelti, John G. 1997. "Canonization, Modern Literature, and the Detective Story." In *Theory and Practice of Classic Detective Fiction*, edited by Jerome H. Delamater and Ruth Prigozy, 5–15. London: Greenwood Press.
Chesterton, C. K. 1976. "A Defense of Detective Stories." In *The Art of the Mystery Story: A Collection of Critical Essays*, edited by Howard Haycraft, 3–6. New York: Biblo and Tannen.
Christie, Agatha. 2011. *The Murder of Roger Ackroyd*. New York: HarperCollins.
———. 2015. *The Mysterious Affair at Styles*. New York: Clue Publishing.
Doyle, Arthur Conan. 2001. *Study in Scarlet*. London: Penguin Classics.
Frank, Lawrence. 2003. *Victorian Detective Fiction and the Nature of Evidence. The Scientific Investigations of Poe, Dickens, and Doyle*. New York: Palgrave Macmillan.
Latour, Bruno. 1991. "The Berlin Key or How to Do Words with Things." In *Matter, Materiality and Modern Culture*, edited by Paul Graves-Brown, 10–21. London: Routledge.
Poe, Edgar Allan. 2014. *The Murders in the Rue Morgue*. CreateSpace Independent Publishing Platform.
Technical Working Group on Crime Scene Investigation. 2013. *Crime Scene Investigation. A Guide for Law Enforcement*. Largo, FL: US National Forensic Science Technology Center.
Todorov, Tzvetan. 1977. *The Poetics of Prose*. Utica, NY: Cornell University Press.

13 Emotional Territories

An Exploration of Wes Anderson's *Cinemaps*

Nicolás Llano Linares

Maps, Cinema, and Emotions

Maps are broad cultural texts that exist in various political, cultural, and social dimensions and promote a graphic visualization of our relationship with the environment. The history of maps has been traced in parallel with two larger modern processes: industrial developments and the birth of the nation-state (Wood 2010). Before the development of the contemporary technogeographical tools that have changed contemporary cartography, the industrial progress made in printmaking, engraving techniques, photographic reproduction, and the papermaking industries contributed to the cartographic transition from unique hand-made elements to mass popular cultural objects. This proves the map to be a peculiar thing: a "synthesis of signs and a sign itself" (Wood and Fels 1986, 54); the map conceals its makers' agenda under the mask of factuality and objectivity but at the same time asserts and conveys its ideological validity.

The 'mapping impulse' that has flourished as part of the well-known 'spatial turn' in social sciences and the humanities is a clear indication of potential connections between maps (no longer understood as an objective image of the world), cartography and mapping processes, and several academic fields. These fields may include art (Watson 2009), literature (Rossetto 2014), and film studies (Hallam and Roberts 2014). In addition, the mapping impulse invites the exploration of the spatial metanarratives and metaphorical dimensions of cultural texts and objects (Caquard 2011).

Maps are common features of a number of societal and cultural spheres: official institutions, touristic industries, scientific fields, and popular culture productions. Maps are also recurrent objects in films. Although their historical formation is radically divergent, both cartography and cinema rely on the "same resources and virtues of the languages that inform their creation" (Conley 2007, 1). Maps appear in films as decorative artifacts, as metaphorical extensions of narrative themes, and as means of location. From this perspective, mapping, as well as filmmaking, incorporates a series of processes that expand from cognitive operations regarding the structuration of spatial knowledge to the analysis of the discursive cacophony surrounding a particular ontological and visual regime (Castro 2009).

168 Nicolás Llano Linares

For Les Roberts, academic works that involve the 'cinematic cartography' concept can be organized in five thematic frames: "(1) maps and mapping in films, (2) mapping film production and consumption, (3) movie mapping and place marketing, (4) cognitive and emotional mapping, and (5) film as spatial critique" (2012, 201). The aim of this chapter is to explore the *cinemaps* in Wes Anderson's films—"maps in motion developed specifically in cinema for narrative purposes" (Caquard 2009, 46)—by drawing on theoretical contributions from two of those categories: maps and mapping in films. This offers a focus on maps depicted within the narrative spaces of the film texts and the cognitive and emotional mapping category (Conley 2007; Bruno 2007; Caquard 2009) that conceptualize maps and mapping processes as sites of critical analysis on the nature of the cinematic medium and the subjective (e)motional processes embedded in visual culture.

Maps' natures are inherently narrative; they tell stories about what they depict—where we are, how the territory is organized—and also about what they conceal. A map lies by omission; this is a part of its selective and political nature. The map tells stories about the world, but when used as an analytical device, it also allows for the exploration of different dimensions of cinematic narratives (Caquard and Naud 2014). The work of Tom Conley (2007) and Giuliana Bruno (2007) are remarkable examples of the numerous possibilities of interpreting maps and mapping processes when dealing with the symbolic, cognitive, architectural, emotional, and affective dimensions of the filmic language.

During the last two decades, Wes Anderson's films have been critically acclaimed and gained cult status for their aesthetic sensibility and visual expressiveness. In his cinematic universe, singular characters share the stage with custom-made sets and objects, from paintings and books to trains and ships, creating detailed yet comprehensive worlds. Among these objects, maps appear as recurrent elements in all of his eight major films.

Wes Anderson's style of filmmaking has been associated with the "smart" film movement (Sconce 2002), the 'quirk' (MacDowell 2012; Bose 2008), and classified within the 'new sincerity' camp (Olsen 1999) and the 'American New Wave' (Hill 2008). He is recognized for his use of God's-eye-view shots that date back to his directorial debut, *Bottle Rocket* (1996) as well as for other "stylistic tics" (Seitz 2013a, 2013b), such as 90-degree whip pan, slow-motion sequences, centered framing and symmetrical compositions, snap-zooms, music in montage, and slow-motion sequence color palettes (Boschi and McNelis 2012).

For Jason David Scott (2014), fictional or semifictional locations·like the New Penzance Island in *Moonrise Kingdom*, the Ping Islands in *The Life Aquatic with Steve Zissou,* and the Tenenbaums' home on "Archer Avenue" in *The Royal Tenenbaums* can easily be translated into real-life equivalencies by the viewer: Coastal New England, the Mediterranean Sea, New York's Upper West Side. These are familiar yet fictionalized spaces that maintain the hermetic lid of Anderson's elaborated fictional creation. The spatial

Emotional Territories   169

ambiguity is also informed by the way the references made to on-screen objects, popular culture, and artistic texts (mostly books and works of art) are carried on by the director. By presenting elements of conflicting eras, the films produce an anachronistic illusion that makes it hard for the viewer to pinpoint the stories to a particular place and time (Scott 2014).

The same link between fictional and familiar can be identified in the characters that populate Anderson's movies. For all the idiosyncratic (highly elaborated moral codes of behavior) and somewhat artificial (ironic sincerity) traits of the "deadbeat dads, tough mothers, lost souls, precocious children, charismatic schemers, impractical dreamers" (Kunze 2014, 4–5), they often amplify relatable human pursuits such as recognition, romantic love, and family acceptance that are easy for the viewer to empathize with (Hill 2008).

I argue that the *cinemaps* in three of Anderson's films (*The Life Aquatic with Steve Zissou, The Darjeeling Limited*, and *Moonrise Kingdom*) can be interpreted as metaphorical extensions of the characters' personal journeys that tell stories not only about the spatial settings of the narratives, but also evoke the life stages the characters find themselves in, thus creating an intersection of affective cartographies that extend the larger themes raised in the films.

Wes Anderson's *Cinemaps*

Wes Anderson's films are distinctively *andersonian* to the limit. The majority of his films are filled with ornate elements that create particular worlds that define the tone of the story, the visual and material dimensions of his sets, and the particularities of the characters. For all the detailed elements found in his movies, the on-screen appearance and abundance of objects is not gratuitous: "when things are shown they have significance. They are not merely background objects there to 'fill out' space, but carefully chosen elements that resonate with meaning for viewers even on a subconscious level" (Scott 2014, 84). The intricate level of material details put into the luxurious *The Grand Budapest Hotel*, the eclectic decoration of the Tenenbaums' home, the unusual rooms and compartments of *The Life Aquatic*'s Belafonte boat, the visual distinctiveness of Max Fischer's school clubs in Rushmore suggest that, much more than other directors, Anderson focuses on objects, whether real or custom made, as much as on character development or dialogue in order to convey the full visual expectable of his cinematic artifice (Chabon 2013).

In Anderson's films, different objects and popular cultural references convey information about narrative and character particularities (Kunze 2014). They materialize psychological content, concerns, tensions, and relations (Gooch 2007; Chabon 2013)—for example, the Oedipal tensions between paternal narratives and object-desires (e.g., the books and records Suzy carries with her in *Moonrise Kingdom*, which suggest a longing for a broader symbolic connection to outside members of her family; see Gooch 2014); the

170 Nicolás Llano Linares

acuteness of grieving (as in the dispute about the Whitmans' late father's belt and glasses in *The Darjeeling Limited*); the deferral of objects of desire (in *The Royal Tenenbaums*, Margot plays Richie's records as a way of acknowledging the impossibility of their romantic passion; see Gooch 2014); and the structure of the patriarchal family as embodied in the Tenenbaums' home and the organization of train compartments in *The Darjeling Limited* (see Baschiera 2012).

In general terms, maps have a double function in Anderson's cinematic worlds: as material objects, they contribute to the creation of material ambience; as territorial representations, they help validate Anderson's elaborate cinematic worlds. Anderson uses different types of maps for a variety of purposes—*to each film its map* (Conley 2007, 5). The great majority of those maps are physical and fixed (screen maps are only present in *The Life Aquatic's* navigation monitors while animated maps appear exclusively in *Moonrise Kingdom*). Maps in Anderson's films are predominantly reference maps (topographical and nautical) that break down in fictional or semifictional (e.g., the physical maps that Max uses and hangs on his tent in *Moonrise Kingdom* and the modified Ping Island topographic maps in *The Life Aquatic with Steve Zissou*) and real geographies, which are the maps of individual countries, continents, or nautical diagrams usually displayed on walls, as in *The Life Aquatic's* Belafonte boat. Another example is the continental maps that serve as the background for Max Fischer's participation in the Model United Nations Club. More real geographies in the form of decorative maps are used in the home and office of Dr. Raleigh St. Clair, along with Richie's terrestrial globe/lamp, his marked continental map on top of his bed, and the atlas he is reading as a child.

In relation to the intradiegetic maps found in Anderson's work (Joliveau, Caquard, and Mazagol 2010), there are two main purposes of use that are directly linked to the film genre frames in which Anderson works—a mixture of comedy and adventure-driven narratives: to navigate through the spatial settings of the film's location (*The Darjeeling Limited, Moonrise Kingdom, The Life Aquatic with Steve Zissou, Fantastic Mr. Fox, The Grand Budapest Hotel*) and to plan different types of future actions (*Bottle Rocket, Fantastic Mr. Fox, Moonrise Kingdom*).

Maps in Motion

Three of Anderson's movies (*The Life Aquatic with Steve Zissou, The Darjeeling Limited*, and *Moonrise Kingdom*) have explicit references to maps in their storylines. I argue that these references can be interpreted as metaphorical extensions that evoke the affective itineraries of the characters. These evocations stress the key themes of most of Anderson's films: death and grief, the need to reconnect with family, and the absent father figure. In these three films, there is an interplay between the narrative spatial translocation, the film-genre classic tropes, and the individual (e)motional

Emotional Territories 171

voyages that expresses their mediation between their life's transitional periods: from denial to acceptance, from pretending to confronting, from controlling to letting go.

The notion of "evocative objects" formulated by Sherry Turkle (2011) can assist understanding of the metaphorical extensions I argue are embedded in the *cinemaps* that appear in the aforementioned three films. Turkle's characterization of our relationship with objects is based on the symbolic possibilities that arise during specific moments—moments denoting transitional (Winnicott 1969) and ritualistic stages of personal transformation (Turner 1987). In Anderson's films, maps do not assist rites of passage, nor do they amplify the transformation of characters (unlike with music, which serves this function; see Hrycaj 2014). The evocative potential in his films is realized through characters' direct references to maps at moments of change or transformation.

In all three films, maps do not produce any causal narrative developments; instead they reveal some of the motivations behind the character's actions as well as evoke their own personal emotional journeys. Moreover, a similar role of maps in the three films results from Anderson's dedication to road movies and adventure motifs, in which "deep contemplation and inner reflection" are more important than the excitement of the open road (Duarte 2015, 9).

Maps appear when the (social) situation calls for it (Wood 1993), which is true for all three films. The road-driven narratives—"desperate journeys" in the words of Tom Conley—entail the need for location devices, meaning that maps emerge because the characters are lost (*The Darjeeling Limited*) or when a character feels the need to point to an actual position or future destination (*Moonrise Kingdom* and *The Life Aquatic with Steve Zissou*).

In terms of the material dynamic between the characters and the on-screen maps in both *The Life Aquatic with Steve Zissou* and *Moonrise Kingdom*, the main characters deal with the map-objects several times. With the exclusion of *The Darjeeling Limited* sequence in which the map is not handled by any of the Whitman brothers, the main characters perform with the map-objects as they establish a dialogue with other characters. In the case of *Moonrise Kingdom*, Sam and Suzy's careful examination of the map is expressive of preadolescent innocence (symbolized by Suzy's flower arrangement). Each one grabs a corner of the map in order to allow Sam to explain to Suzy their following route. In contrast to the seemingly delicate treatment of the object by the young kids, Steve Zissou's treatment of the map seems rather hostile.

Three Maps and Their Films

The Darjeeling Limited

The Darjeeling Limited (2007) is part road movie, part spiritual voyage, and part self-discovery journey. Three American brothers reunite after their father's death for a train trip across India organized by Francis, the eldest, who has secretly planned the journey to renew their family bonds and

172 Nicolás Llano Linares

confront their reclusive mother. Filled with the technical cinematic tropes and attention to detail characteristic of Wes Anderson's movies, it is a story about the impossibility of planning and controlling every aspect of life, finding one's place in the world, and the importance of family trust in turbulent times. Several maps are seen throughout the film; however, a direct reference to a map is made in a scene in which the three brothers—Francis (Owen Wilson), Peter (Adrien Brody), and Jack (Jason Schwartzman)—get out of the train in their pajamas to see why the train has stopped abruptly. Gathered around several maps, various train employees and Francis's assistant, Brendan, seem to be trying to find their position while three mechanics work on fixing the train's engine. The following exchange takes place with the Indian desert as the backdrop:

FRANCIS: What's going on, Brendan?
BRENDAN: I don't know. I guess the train's lost.
JACK (to Peter): What'd he say?
PETER: He says the train's lost.
JACK: How can a train be lost? It's on rails.
BRENDAN: Apparently, we took a wrong turn at some point last night.
FRANCIS: That's crazy.
JACK: How far off course are we?
BRENDAN (shrugs): Nobody knows. We haven't located us yet.
FRANCIS (immediately): Say that again.
BRENDAN (hesitating): What?
FRANCIS: Repeat what you just said.
BRENDAN: We haven't located us yet.
FRANCIS (loudly): Ho! Ha! Is that symbolic?
      (Brendan looks confused. Francis turns to Peter and Jack and says energetically): We. Haven't located. Us. Yet!

"We haven't located us yet"; Francis's sentence directly references the metaphorical association between the paradoxical occurrence and the emotional tribulations the characters are going through: Francis dealing with the aftershock of a near-death experience, Jack processing his troubled romantic relationship, and Peter trying to come to terms with the fact that he is going to have a baby with a woman he always thought he would divorce from.

The fact that Francis is the one who translates the meaning of the improbable yet 'real' event of a train lost on its own tracks and the failure of locating their position on the map into their current personal lives is directly connected to the purpose of each of the three brothers. For Francis, the main objective of the journey is to achieve an individual and communal spiritual revelation that would lead to rebuilding the trust between the three siblings after their father's death; as for the other two brothers, the trip represents a momentary break from having to accept personal failures and the consequences of unexpected events.

Even though the map's appearance does not constitute a pivotal moment in the film's story (it does not holds the same importance as posterior sequences do), the whole scene is built around the suggestion of the changing nature of the topography (feelings, decisions, relationships) within the map's projected territory (their projected lives). The direct reference made by Francis and the map's on-screen materialization reveal the transitional aspects of their lives, at least in Francis's case, by evoking the realization that something went wrong in terms of the paths their lives were supposed to follow.

The Life Aquatic with Steve Zissou

The tale of Steve Zissou concerns an egocentric middle-aged oceanographer and documentary director trying to find the professional success and respect he once possessed. Played by Bill Murray, Zissou sets out on his last adventure to avenge—and film—the death of his long-time collaborator Esteban, who was eaten by an almost mythological jaguar shark during the filming of his latest cinematic flop. The adventure-driven journey is a nautical exploration of Anderson's recurrent themes: death, grief, middle-age crisis, fatherhood, failed relationships, and acceptance (Past 2009). After trespassing on private property and finding the shark's location using equipment belonging to Alistair Hennessey (Zissou's 'nemesis'), an unhappy and worried script girl, Anne-Marie Sakowitz, confronts Zissou while holding a map in her hand:

ANNE-MARIE SAKOWITZ: Steve!
STEVE ZISSOU: Aha.
ANNE-MARIE SAKOWITZ: Do you know that you just charted us on a course through unprotected waters?
STEVE ZISSOU: Yeah. We're taking the shortcut.
ANNE-MARIE SAKOWITZ: But it's outside I.M.U. jurisdiction. There isn't any protection.
STEVE ZISSOU: I know, honey. Look at the map. We go your way, that's about four inches (measures with his fingers). We go my way it's an inch and a half. You want to pay for the extra gas?

At this juncture of the movie, Zissou is still in denial of many aspects of his life: the psychological aftershock of his best friend's death; the appearance of his supposed son, Ned Plimpton; the fact that his marriage is falling apart; the fading aura of his cultural relevance; and, most importantly, his failed role as a friend and a family member. In this case, contrary to the scene in *The Darjeeling Limited* in which Francis acknowledges the metaphorical core of the object being referenced, the evocative proprieties of Zissou's cartographic "shortcut"—a term suggestive of his unwillingness to face the reality of his personal and professional life (the "unprotected waters")—are not obvious either to the character or the viewer.

174 *Nicolás Llano Linares*

The journey's resolution is developed in two subsequent scenes. The first one begins after they have gone to one of the Ping Islands, where pirates are supposedly holding Bill, a kidnapped "bond company stooge." After falling down the stairs, Zissou lets his guard down and breaks out of his public character in order to express his true feelings.

Moments after he reads the draft of the article that a magazine reporter (Jane Winslett-Richardson, played by Cate Blanchett) has written about him and acknowledges the reality of his words and actions, the original score composer of the documentary team tells Zissou they have detected the signal of the jaguar shark. In the following scene Zissou and his whole crew appear underwater inside the team's submarine. After the sudden appearance of the enormous and elusive jaguar shark—a figure that encapsulates his most profound fears, Zissou enters into a revelatory and reflective mood.

It is at the moment when the shark interacts with the submarine that Zissou recognizes the real motivation behind the shark's chase (a 'deeper search,' as the name of the submarine suggests): to confront the death of his friend Esteban, accept the decline of his cinematographic career, and embrace the consequences of his past actions. The whole sequence stands out as the inevitable resolution of coming to terms with his emotional 'uncharted waters.' In that sense, the different phases that Zissou's affective cartography goes through are interwoven with the tone and pace of the narrative unfolding, thus transforming the revenge-driven adventure into a self-discovery voyage.

Moonrise Kingdom

The film tells the story of Khaki Scout Sam Shakusky and the temperamental bookworm Suzy Bishop, a couple of twelve-year-olds who fall in love and decide to run away from their homes and adult authority in New Penzance Island to pursue their love and adolescence on their own terms. In the case of *Moonrise Kingdom* (2012), maps are used not only by the main characters on their journey across New Penzance Island, but also as visual resources Anderson employs to construct the narrative's contours.

At the start of the film an animated map of the island appears accompanied by the voice of the film's narrator (Bob Balaban). In this case the roles of maps and the narrator are complementary in the structure of the film; the narrator's voice enriches the spatial characterization of the story. While the maps are used to promote a sense of "fallacious authenticity" (Conley 2007, 4) and enrich the spatial and narrative dimensions of the film, the narrator details the territory, providing information about wind patterns, distances, land extensions, and general topographical elements of the island that serve as the backdrop for the film's main narrative events.

There is a marked difference between the function of maps in this movie and the one in the other two films. While the characters in the other two movies must come to terms with uncertainty and the evocative function

Emotional Territories 175

of the map points to their current transitional periods, Sam and Suzy find comfort in the ability to map their own path. After finding Suzy at their designated encounter point, Sam says:

SAM: Can you read a map?
SUZY: Uh-huh.
SAM: I do cartography. (Sam points to one of the patches on his sash. It has a protractor embroidered on it. He unfolds the map.): I feel we should go halfway today and halfway tomorrow, since you're a less experienced hiker, and you're wearing Sunday-school shoes.
SUZY: OK.
SAM: (pointing on the map): Here's where we are right now. I'd like to pitch camp here by sixteen-hundred, which means four o'clock. How does that sound?
SUZY: Fine.

Sam's "I do cartography" works as verbal reassurance to Suzy: a way to let her know that he is certain about how to trace the best plan for their future, it shows in familiarity with the territory (the future's possibilities) and the ability to map it with her. Even though mapping and map interpretation are technical cartographic skills, the confidence of his speech and the precise information he gives during the dialogue can be interpreted as a symbolic commitment to the love he and Suzy have articulated.

In this film, the amorous cartography of Suzy and Sam's lives is open for further development, a completion that will be performed by selecting elements from the numerous possibilities their journey as a couple can provide: "Maps, records of learning, after all, follow experience. They come into existence after the path has been traveled (Bruno 2007, 5). The map (Suzy and Sam story) is still at an early stage of completion; thus, mapping (selecting and projecting) becomes an important tool to plan the territory that lies ahead for the two characters, a long-term project that represents the desires placed on the passing from childhood to adolescence.

Conclusion

I have argued that Wes Anderson's *cinemaps* can be read as metaphorical devices that evoke the emotional fabric of the personal journeys of the characters of three of his films. The films' direct references to maps illuminate the dialogue between the characters' emotional states and the narratives by rearranging and updating the relationships between the signs that constitute the totality of the map (their lives) and the environment's reality. The characters' experiences and personal realizations are drafted in parallel, a two-sided itinerary in which emotions are translated as physical movements.

The metaphorical relation between the direct reference and its affective meanings only makes sense after we have seen the end result of the

176 Nicolás Llano Linares

characters' transformations. It is only then that the map is partially completed, by redirecting the characters' subjective transits through their own emotional cartographies. By turning Denis Wood's understanding of maps as arguments about the nature of the world (2007) and our relationship with the territory we occupy (1994) into an emotional and experiential dimension, the maps depicted in the three films can be interpreted as arguments that inform not only the nature of the spatial setting of the story but also the characters' positions within their own projected personal cartography.

Maps are neither central nor defining object-features of Anderson's cinematic productions; in contrast to other types of popular objects that frequently appear in his films (books; music, and music players), maps do not stand for lost objects' desire on the parts of the characters. Nonetheless, maps are, along with many other objects that populate Wes Anderson's mise-en-scène, not only particular rich in affective and symbolic meanings for the viewers, but also constitutive aesthetic and diegetic elements that form the basis of his particular cinematic worlds.

References

Baschiera, Stefano. 2012. "Nostalgically Man Dwells on This Earth: Objects and Domestic Space in *The Royal Tenenbaums* and *The Darjeeling Ltd*." *New Review of Film and Television Studies* 10 (1): 118–131.

Boschi, Elena, and Tim McNelis. 2012. "'Same Old Song': On Audio-Visual Style in the Films of Wes Anderson." *New Review of Film and Television Studies* 10 (1): 28–45.

Bose, Nandana. 2008. "*The Darjeeling Limited*: Critiquing Orientalism on the Train to Nowhere." *Mediascape: UCLA's Journal of Cinema and Media Studies*. Available online at http://www.tft.ucla.edu/mediascape/Spring08_DarjeelingLimited.html.

Bottle Rocket. Directed by Wes Anderson. Criterion Collection, 2008. DVD.

Bruno, Giuliana. 2007. *Atlas of Emotion: Journeys in Art, Architecture, and Films*. London: Verso.

Caquard, Sébastien. 2009. "Foreshadowing Contemporary Digital Cartography: A Historical Review of Cinematic Maps in Films." *Cartographic Journal* 46 (1): 46–55.

———. 2011. "Cartography I: Mapping Narrative Cartography." *Progress in Human Geography* 37 (1): 135–144.

Caquard, Sébastien, and Daniel Naud. 2014. "A Spatial Typology of Cinematographic Narratives." In *Developments in the Theory and Practice of Cybercartography: Applications in Indigenous Mapping* (2nd ed.), edited by D. R. Fraser Taylor, associate editor Tracey P. Lauriault, 161–174. Oxford: Elsevier.

Castro, Teresa. 2009. "Cinema's Mapping Impulse: Questioning Visual Culture" *Geographic Journal* 46 (1): 9–15.

Chabon, Michael. 2013. "Wes Anderson's Worlds." Available online at http://www.nybooks.com/daily/2013/01/31/wes-anderson-worlds/.

Conley, Tom. 2009. "Locations in Film Noir" *Cartographic Journal* 46 (1): 16–23.

The Darjeeling Limited. Directed by Wes Anderson. 2007.Century City, Los Angeles: 20th Century Fox Home Entertainment, 2008. DVD.

Duarte, José. 2015. "The Importance of Being 'On the Road': A Reading of the Journey in *The Darjeeling Limited* (2007) by Wes Anderson." *ELOPE: English Language Overseas Perspectives and Enquiries* 12 (1): 77–89.

Fantastic Mr. Fox. Directed by Wes Anderson. Twentieth Century Fox Film Corp. 2010. DVD.

Gooch, Joshua. 2007. "Making a Go of It: Paternity and Prohibition in the Films of Wes Anderson." *Cinema Journal* 47 (1): 26–48.

———. 2014. "Objects/Desire/Oedipus: Wes Anderson as Late-Capitalist Auteur." In *The Films of Wes Anderson: Critical Essays on an Indiewood Icon*, edited by Peter C. Kunze, 181–198. New York: Palgrave Macmillan.

Hallam, Julia, and Roberts, Les. 2014. "Mapping the City in Film." In *Toward Spatial Humanities: Historical GIS & Spatial History*, edited by Ian N. Gregory, Alistair Geddes, and David J. Bodenhamer, 143–171. Bloomington: Indiana University Press.

Hill, Derek. 2008. *Charlie Kaufman and Hollywood's Merry Band of Pranksters, Fabulists and Dreamers: An Excursion into the American New Wave*. Harpenden, UK: Oldcastle Books.

Hrycaj, Laura. 2014. "Life on Mars or Life on the Sea: Seu Jorge, David Bowie, and the Musical World in Wes Anderson's *The Life Aquatic*." In The *Films of Wes Anderson: Critical Essays on an Indiewood Icon*, edited by Peter C. Kunze. 139–152. New York: Palgrave Macmillan.

Joliveau, Thierry, Pierre-Olivier Mazagol, and Sébastien Caquard. 2010. "Cinemaps, Typologies and Functions of Maps in Movies." Conference Presentation: Cartography & Narratives. ETH Zürich, 2012. Available online at https://www.researchgate.net/publication/235410971_Cinemaps_Typologies_and_Functions_of_Maps_in_Movies.

Kunze, Peter C. 2014. "Introduction: The Wonderful Worlds of Wes Anderson." In *The Films of Wes Anderson: Critical Essays on an Indiewood Icon*, edited by Peter C. Kunze, 1–12. New York: Palgrave Macmillan.

The Life Aquatic with Steve Zissou. Directed by Wes Anderson. 2004. Burbank, California: Touchstone Home Entertainment. 2005. DVD.

MacDowell, James. 2012. "Wes Anderson, Tone and the Quirky Sensibility." *New Review of Film and Television Studies* 10 (1): 6–27.

Moonrise Kingdom. Directed by Wes Anderson. 2012. Indian Paintbrush, 2012. DVD.

Olsen, Mark. 1999. "If I Can Dream: The Everlasting Boyhoods of Wes Anderson." *Film Comment* 35 (1): 12–17.

Past, Elena. 2009. "Lives Aquatic: Mediterranean Cinema and an Ethics of Underwater Existence." *Cinema Journal* 48 (3): 52–65.

Roberts, Les. 2012. *Film, Mobility and Urban Space: A Cinematic Geography of Liverpool*. Liverpool: Liverpool University Press.

Rossetto, Tania. 2014. "Theorizing Maps with Literature." *Progress in Human Geography* 38 (4): 513–530.

Rushmore. Directed by Wes Anderson. 1999. Burbank, California: Touchstone Home Video, 1998. Film.

Sconce, Jeffrey. 2002. "Irony, Nihilism and the New American 'Smart.'" *Film Screen* 43 (4): 349–369.

Scott, Jason David. 2014. "'American Empirical' Time and Space: The (In) Visibility of Popular Culture in the Films of Wes Anderson." *The Films of Wes Anderson: Critical Essays on an Indiewood Icon*, edited by Peter C. Kunze, 77–88. New York: Palgrave Macmillan.

178 *Nicolás Llano Linares*

Turkle, Sherry. 2011. *Evocative Objects: Things We Think With*. Cambridge, MA: MIT Press.

Turner, Victor. 1987. "Betwixt and Between: The Liminal Period in Rites of Passage." In *Betwixt and Between: Patterns of Masculine and Feminine Initiation*, edited by Louise C. Mahdi, Steven Foster, and Meredith Little, 3–19. La Salle, IL: Open Court.

Seitz, Matt Zoller. 2013a. "*The Darjeeling Limited*. Video Essay." Adapted from the book *The Wes Anderson Collection* by Matt Zoller Seitz, chap. 5. Available online at https://vimeo.com/77556248.

———. 2013b. *The Wes Anderson Collection*. New York: Abrams.

Watson, Ruth. 2009. "Mapping and Contemporary Art." *Cartographic Journal* 46 (4): 293–307.

Winnicott, Donald Woods. 1969. "The Use of an Object and Relating through Identifications." *International Journal of Psychoanalysis* 50 (7): 711–716.

Wood, Denis. 1993. "Maps and Mapmaking." *Cartographica* 30 (1): 1–9.

———. 1994. "Memory, Love, Distortion, Power: What Is a Map?" *Onion* (13): 24–33.

———. 2007. "A Maps Is an Image Proclaiming Its Objective Neutrality." *Cartographic Perspective* 56: 4–16.

———. 2010. *Rethinking the Power of Maps*. New York: Guilford Press.

Wood, Denis, and John Fels. 1986. "Designs on Signs/Myth and Meaning in Maps." *Cartographica* 23 (3): 54–103.

14 The Poetics of Objects in *True Detective*

Karolina Lebek

This chapter is concerned with the creative use of objects in the processes of complex televisual storytelling and world-building on the example of the first season (eight episodes) of *True Detective* (2014), an HBO crime drama TV series written by Nic Pizzolatto and directed by Cary Joji Fukunaga. *True Detective* (henceforth *TD*) assumes an anthology format, which means that each season of the series tells a complete story with its own set of characters. The season has garnered considerable critical acclaim (in contrast to the second season aired in 2015)[1]—most importantly, for its use of intertextuality and remediation (Demaria 2014), whereby it utilizes genres, narrative conventions, and visual techniques developed in other media forms (short and serial pulp fiction, novels, the cinema).[2]

Apart from this generic and stylistic hybridity, the communication of *TD*'s fictional story exemplifies complex television as defined by Jason Mittell (2015). Its two most distinctive features are a complication of the formal means of conveying the fictional story (that is, the chronological story time) through manipulations of narrative discourse, and a structural and narrative balancing of "the competing demands and pleasures of episodic and serial norms" (Mittell 2015, 19) in connection to allotted screen time. Nevertheless, the show has been praised for its persistent focus and intense coherence of the story, which can only be further confirmed by the nature of the program's fan fiction. As Cristina Demaria observes, *TD* does not easily allow retellings or extensions, but rather inspires texts that are "[...] more like a gloss, an annotation, the adding of a thin background that *remains in the background*" (2014, 21, emphasis original).

As cultural hybrid using formal complication to produce a coherent televisual text, *TD* is an exemplary case of aesthetic popular processes described by Anna Malinowska in this volume (Chapter 2). It also affords an ideal case study for a demonstration of how *the popular* appropriates *the material* through what I provisionally call 'poetic artifaction,' which can be defined as appropriation of social objects (Harré 2002) for the purposes of media-dependent craft, whereby objects acquire a poetic function. Such appropriation turns objects into tools of storytelling and world-building, and then into tools of comprehension by the viewers. This must be premised on the figurative ties of such objects to the social context of crafting and the

180 *Karolina Lebek*

social context of reception, the latter of which may involve cultural transfer. The claim of this chapter is that a skilled employment of poetic artifacts is in part responsible for *TD*'s narrative and visual coherence.

The Theory of Poetic Artifaction

In the essay "Material Objects in Social Worlds," Rom Harré (2002) assumes that a thing may only become a social object if it is included in a narrative through which it performs social work. Social objects connote individual or group identities and express one's subjective identity. Ian Woodward comments on this capacity of objects by underlining their cohesive properties: "[o]bjects [...] can assist in forming or negating interpersonal and group attachments, mediating the formation of self-identity and esteem, and integrating and differentiating social groups, classes or tribes" (2007, 135). With respect to personal identity, Woodward stresses the performative potential of things, whereby "objects *assist the credible, effective performance* of an identity" (137, emphasis original).

The performative functions of social objects depend on the specific material dispositions of things and on discursive intentions of social narratives that engage them. They regulate the actual scope of roles afforded to things (and their material attributes) in given social and cultural contexts. These roles are understood as affordances of social objects. A lot of potential narratives may engage a thing so that "social objects [...] have multiple context-bound affordances" (Harre 2002, 27). Hence, a thing can become multiple social objects, performing multiple social functions for different individuals or groups, without losing its material integrity. For example, a Lone Star beer can at the same time participates in practical order (drinking) and in expressive order (making a metaphorical statement about the drinker). Harré limits object expressiveness to "social hierarchy, honor and status" (2002, 32), but it can be extended onto the range of meanings encompassed by Sherry Turkle's notion of evocation, whereby objects participate in the (cognitive) processes of feeling and thinking (2011).

Storyworlds are second-order social narratives that depend on (primary) social narratives for comprehensibility: this necessarily involves objects. Even in creation and reception of highly speculative and fantastic narratives, their point of reference is our actual reality. This relation between reality and storyworlds has already been theorized in a number of critical works, whose conclusions have been gathered and extended by Mark J. P. Wolf (2012). Wolf observes that storytelling and world-building may have conflicting aims in storyworlds: while storytelling advances the narrative, world-building mainly relies on digressive exposition and description (textual or visual). Yet, "[w]orlds can exist without stories, but stories cannot exist without a world" (29).

A successful storyworld may depend on a mutual reinforcement of story and world. This happens when a story is anchored in a world that projects depth of construction: an illusion that it stretches beyond the fragment

The Poetics of Objects in True Detective 181

immediately available to the audience. Objects may participate in both storytelling and world-building and, therefore, the measure of their respective significance within a storyworld may lie in such double participation. The ring of power in Tolkien's *Lord of the Rings* provides an example: it shapes the story and embodies world-building elements (politics, history, geography, genealogy, and technology).

The contribution of objects to the construction of characters and the construction of events is what connects storytelling to world-building. The association of objects with characters suggests availability of such objects in the world. The construction of events advances the progress of the plot. In character-building, objects are tools of what Mittell calls character elaboration (2015, 136) by communicating social and subjective identities, as well as interpersonal relations. To paraphrase Ian Woodward (2007, 137), in storyworlds, objects assist the narrative performance of identity. This performance is responsible for the viewer's engagement with characters through alignment strategies employed by a text or show.

In televisual narratives, those strategies involve following characters' experiences (attachment) and affording access to "subjective interior emotions, thought processes and morality" (Mittell 2015, 129). Objects may become access-granting devices as material "exterior markers" (134) of character psychology, supporting direct windows of access like confessional voiceovers, dialoguing, or behavior. The conflicting messages of material markers and, for example, explicit confessions may offer further tools for complication and play. Objects also anchor feelings and morality with simultaneous references to the intrinsic storyworld norms and to the extrinsic social norms. Affording feats of narrative economy, materiality reveals disproportions or outright conflicts between the two sources of norms and so assist the production of heroes, antiheroes, or straightforward villains.

With respect to events, objects may trigger, facilitate, hinder, or choreograph them; they may help construct direct narrative statements or, more importantly, generate unexplained narrative enigmas or offer their resolutions. When objects form a core of such mysterious events, then we might call them material enigmas, which serve to motivate further action in the story. In crime dramas, for example, narrative progress often hinges on access to material evidence (remains, traces, clues).

In a storyworld, objects or object-bundles may carry different poetic importance. Following Seymour Chatman's vocabulary, to speak about events, Mittell introduces a distinction between kernels and satellites, which may be adopted to describe materiality. Kernels are occurrences "that clearly change the narrative," whereas satellites do not affect the plot and could be removed without damage (2015, 24). Similarly, material kernels remain indispensable for the construction of narrative elements, whereas material satellites are glosses carrying aesthetic modality and rehearsing meanings communicated through other tools. Although material satellites form narrative accessories, they are important for the concretization of the storyworld

182   Karolina Lebek

through world-building, as in the case of the rows of doughnuts in the Twin Peaks Police Station. Similarly to events, things introduced as material satellites may later turn out material kernels and surprise the audience in the production of narrative special effects (2015, 43).

The convergence of storytelling and world-building also manifests in the use of objects as markers in the manipulation of story time through discourse time. This often takes place in complex television when a show employs advanced narrative strategies through fractured temporalities. Objects then may help viewers (and characters) put the pieces of a temporal puzzle together: they may anticipate events, suggest transitions in chronology, or provide anchors in flashbacks or flash-forwards. Such techniques expose the operational aesthetics of a given show by bringing the viewer's attention to the formal poetics of a particular narrative effect (Mittell 2015, 42). Operational reflexivity of complex television is thereby set in motion: viewers engage with the story and, at the same time, find pleasure in noting the formal tools of its presentation (46).

In this theoretical context, poetic artifaction relies on the establishment of double semiotic affordance of social objects: an internal figurative capacity (in the storyworld) and an external figurative capacity (between the storyworld and social reality). Even when the role of objects seems purely decorative, things in narratives always assume this double persuasive function, rhetorically aligned with the discursive aims of the storyworld. The internal capacity relies on two signifying trajectories. One of them refers to the establishment of an indexical relationship through objects with the fictional beyond of the immediately represented piece of the storyworld. The second trajectory denotes the contribution of objects to the narrative elements within the accessible fragment of the storyworld.

The external figurative capacity of objects is mimesis. Even in fantastic settings, to afford comprehension, objects work as metaphors of the actual world, often with the aim of evoking emotional and aesthetic responses. This happens even in fictional incorporations of specific objects: in a storyworld, the Empire State Building is and is not the real Empire State Building because, for example, King Kong is climbing it. Keir Elam called such cases "iconic identity" with reference to theater, whereby an object is represented by itself (2002, 20). The external figuration can also involve the narrative capacity of objects to refer to historical uses of things in other cultural narratives. This may happen through direct material quotation, intertextual allusions, or whole transplantations of use, which help establish a storyworld's generic identity and conventional allegiance. Such a mode of material presence builds viewer procedural literacy, "a recognition on the part of consumers that any mode of expression follows particular [formal] protocols" (Mittell 2015, 53). This cultural skill is pertinent for viewer engagement and pleasure in following a narrative. Procedural literacy is formed, then, by popular culture's capacity to reproduce itself in the dialectics of repetition and difference (originality) in the production of popular materialities.

The Poetics of Objects in True Detective   183

Poetic Artifaction in *True Detective* (TD)

TD's narrative structure employs strategies of complex television to complicate a focused and linear plotline. Set in South Louisiana, the story spans seventeen years (1995–2012) and follows two homicide detectives, Rustin Cohle (Matthew McConaughey) and Martin Hart (Woody Harrelson), who trace a prolific serial killer, Errol Childress (Glenn Fleshler)—first a victim and then an agent of a ritual cult around Carcosa, a place of worship and sacrifice.

This story is communicated through several devices. First, *TD* employs flashbacks in discourse time: it opens in 2012 as Marty and Rust (no longer on the force) are interviewed by two detectives about their 1995 case and the events of 2002, when Rust leaves Louisiana for eight years. In 2012 a body has been discovered with signatures specific to those found on murder victim Dora Lange in 1995. Rust and Marty are believed to have caught and shot Dora's killer, but the recently discovered body reopens the case. Second, the show creates dissonances between knowledge gained through subjective retellings and objective visual exposition. Third, it uses different subjective points of focalization (mainly Rust and Marty, but also Maggie, Marty's ex-wife, and Errol) to reveal different facets of the story. The parallelism of two personal narratives expands the puzzle further, because the viewer needs to negotiate between three sets of verbal information: what Rust says, what Marty says, and what they both agree on (which is usually when they lie). Fourth, it carefully designs episodic resolutions with the aim to advance the serial arch. This last strategy shapes the flow of affective expectation and encourages viewer speculation. Keeping in mind that the 2012 interview functions as a narrative mortar, episodes 1–5 cover the events of 1995, while episodes 5 and 6 cover those in 2002. With the conclusion of episode 6, the remaining discourse time (episodes 7 and 8) merges with the story time, culminating in the showdown in Carcosa.

The show's coherence in turn hinges on two narrative tropes: discovery and conflict, the latter played out during the development of the former. What helps build this coherence is poetic artifaction, which is revealed in the patterns of material culture distribution. This requires a discussion—not of how the fictional story unfolds in discourse time, but rather how its elements are designed to connect with a very specific conclusion in mind. The material topography of conflict and discovery in *TD*, then, should reveal the cohesive logic behind the use of objects.[3]

The season's narrative spiral of discovery is aimed at revealing Carcosa—Errol's workshop and the heart of ritual abuse and murders. The place itself is a maze-like structure of old brick tunnels and multiple chambers, partially in ruin and overgrown by vegetation. Those tunnels are laden with stacks of driftwood, scattered heaps of old clothes, bundles of children's shoes, and, occasionally, bodies wrapped in cloth. Its central domed chamber contains the figure of the Yellow King (a skeletal sculpture of wood and bone, with multiple branchings for arms) and a sacrificial stone in front of it.[4]

184 *Karolina Lebek*

In the season's showdown, Carcosa is revealed, metaphorically speaking, as a center of spiritual gravity, a black hole of horror. The existence of this place—the acts it affords—creates disturbances in the surrounding world. Outside its walls, this disturbance can be registered (in the police archives, for example) as two kinds of imbalance in the economy of things: lack (absence) or excess (presence). Lack is generated by disappearances of (socially and economically underprivileged) women and children. This haunts their families and, when noted, creates a puzzle for the state (represented by the police force): the body politic is missing its members and should react. This may provide an explanatory context for Rust's quoting from Corinthians when asked why he wanted to join the Homicide Department, "'The body is not one member, but many. Now are they many, but of one body.' I was just trying to stay a part of the body" (episode 2). Disturbing excess is produced by material splinters of Carcosa's grind: dead bodies in ritual garb (like Dora Lange and the unnamed victim of 2012), which at the same time materialize lack, and devil's nests (i.e., twig sculptures, smaller scale echoes of driftwood constructions found in Carcosa's corridors). These sculptures are found at crime scenes, places associated with the missing people (Marie Fontenot), and, most significantly, in one of the disused Tuttle schools, where Rust discovers a whole classroom of them in 2002. They seem to be symbols of material substitution (for a person) and transformation of living matter into dead matter. In episode 8, Errol speaks about "leaving his mark" and infernal "ascension," while Rust witnesses a maelstrom cloud spiral of cosmic matter with its eye directly over the dome of the Yellow King.

Two types of material imbalance establish two kinds of connection to Carcosa. One is metonymic material evidence: bodies and ritual objects (mapping excess). The second is metaphoric material evidence: stories, notes and sketches, testimonies, reports, pictures (mapping lack). Carcosa has produced the metonimic evidence that forms a relationship of material contiguity with the place; the metaphoric evidence describes it and relates its workings—tools for understanding its methods and scope. The key to finding Carcosa and its agent (Errol) is to link these two types of evidence in a single narrative that will lead to its actual location and exposition. Rust dedicates years of his life to collecting and reading evidence in order to build a persuasive story and account for all the material traces, coordinating metonymy and metaphor.

The progress of discovery, when looked at from the perspective of material affordances (revelation) can be divided into three stages: the first in 1995, the second spanning over ten years from 2002 to 2012, and the third in 2012. The first stage develops three tributaries of material that flow into one stream of evidence, leading the detectives to Reggie Ledoux, Errol's acolyte and lover. The first tributary goes from the body of Dora Lange (through the testimony of her ex-husband and friends) to her diary and then through a leaflet in the diary to the burnt remains of the First Revival Church, where Rust and Marty find murals corresponding with Dora's crime

The Poetics of Objects in True Detective   185

scene. Finally, it runs to the congregation itself, now gathering in a tent, where the detectives learn about her meeting with a giant man with burn scars on his jaw. The second tributary encompasses the disappearance of a 10-year-old girl, Mary Fontenot, in 1990 (they find a twig sculpture in her playground), who attended a religious school, one of a network of schools run by a Wellsprings foundation, sponsored by a powerful Louisiana family, the Tuttles. This context also provides a tangential piece of evidence: a memory sketch of "a [green-eared] spaghetti monster" (episode 1), reportedly chasing a different little girl in the woods. The third tributary involves the body of Rianne Olivier, whose case Rust ferrets out from the archives, convinced that Dora was not the first victim. Olivier's death is classified as drowning, but Rust manages to find signatures that were also left on Dora (wound types and their pattern, crystal meth in the blood, a spiral tattoo on the neck). Through Olivier's grandfather, Marty and Rust get access to her things (a yearbook of another Wellsprings school) and learn about her boyfriend, Reggie Ledoux.

The three tributaries join on the level of metonymy, by the sculptures and tattoos, and on the level of metaphor: both Marie and Rianne went to a Wellspring school; Dora's ex-husband showed her pictures to his cell mate, Ledoux, the latter trading a story of Carcosa and the Yellow King, both mentioned in Dora's diary: "[h]e said that there's this place down South where all these rich men go to devil worship [...]. They sacrifice [...] [w]omen and children all got murdered there and [...] [s]ome place called Carcosa and the Yellow King. He said there's all these old stones out in the woods" (episode 4). The case is then presumed closed with the showdown at Ledoux's hidden compound, where he and his cousin cook meth. The compound's décor prefigures Errol's house in arrangement and material condition of things. It also echoes Carcosa, being its spiritual offshoot, in its labyrinthine architecture, the presence of twig sculptures, and the inclusion of a place of torture, where they keep abused children. The production designer thought out the compound as a stitched out deformity, consisting of a found trailer, a shipping container, a deer blind, wrecked cars, and a cube from a cube truck (Martin 2014b). This architectural monstrosity materializes and reverberates the monstrosity of its users.

The second stage of the investigation begins in 2002, when Rust learns that Carcosa still operates and that its major agent has not been eliminated: a third man with the Ledoux cousins, the worst of them all, a giant with a scarred face (as Rust learns from the surviving victim). Neither his bosses nor Marty wants to hear about reopening the case, so Rust investigates on his own and eventually gets suspended. He builds a map of missing persons along the coast, interviews families, and uncovers traces of child abuse at the Wellspring schools (gathering more metaphoric evidence). He revisits the original crime scene and finds a spiral circle of twigs; in the abandoned school attended by Olivier, he finds murals similar in style to those found in the burnt church as well as a classroom filled cluttered with devil nests

186   *Karolina Lebek*

(metonymy). DiGerlando describes the making of this scene: "[w]e sculpted the desks to make a maze for Rust to walk through, leading him to the reveal of the devil nest sculptures. We wanted them to feel like they were sitting there, as if they were students in the classroom" (DiGerlando in Martin 2014b). This clearly shows the logic of material substitution: the place of victims (the missing children) is filled by Errol's artwork.

The poetics of evidence, built from the crossing of the metonymic and metaphoric axes, comes sharply into focus in episode 7 (2012). The things collected and exhibited in Rust's storage unit serve a formal purposes of exposition, summary, evocation, and argument. The display of these objects (hanging on walls and accumulating on desks and shelves), all created by the show's prop master, Lynda Reiss, and her team (Martin 2014b), follows a certain key: looking from the entrance in, the space on the left carries objects related to Carcosa's rituals and the material symbols it produces. The space on the right shows documentations and maps related to missing persons (probable victims) and the sprawl of the case. The space in the middle gathers all the information about Dora, Rianne, and Marie, with the spaghetti monster sketch, antlers attached over the likeness in the center. The material representations in the middle concretize the mechanisms revealed by the other two sectors of evidence in that they show how the hidden ritual appropriated the members of society (the social body) and produces dead bodies. This spatial arrangement is also a projection of the temporal progression of the narrative and represents a map of the episodes, with a suggestion that Rust's work (implied in the fictional story) has not all been represented through discourse time (the viewers were not shown all of his activities). The evocative function of the objects focuses on the externalization of Rust's thought process: how he thinks with things and how much imagination and intellect he has invested in the case. As DiGerando says, the container has an area "where he experiments with the construction of how he might make a devil's nest" (DiGerlando in Martin 2014b). Directly, persuasive function is to solicit Marty's help—indirectly, to build a case for the viewers and convincingly link all the evidence scattered throughout the show in one feat of disclosure, hinting at the creative mastery behind *TD*. The argument that Rust launches is meticulously organized to fulfill the demands of suspense, ignoring the more logical efficiency of a direct demonstration of the most convincing evidence first: as such, it self-reflexively alludes to its artifaction as part of a TV show.

Rust's argument has to connect the collected evidence with one place (Carcosa) and one man (Errol, the giant), protected by (and perhaps working for) some powerful men of Louisiana's society, particularly with the Tuttles. First, he shows that the disappearances happened in the areas where Wellsprings schools operated (which were also the sites of child abuse by men in animal masks), at the same time connecting Marie Fontenot to one of those schools. Then he links the spaghetti monster with the Lange case's scarred giant (spaghetti as childlike metaphor). Then, he links the Tuttle

The Poetics of Objects in True Detective   187

family with Erath, the place of the first crime scene and of a primitive winter Mardi Gras festival, celebrated "heavy on the Saturnalia." The pictures of this festival show men in animal masks around a central figure of a bound and blindfolded girl. What finally recruits Marty is a videotape with a recording of Marie Fontenot in Carcosa, stolen by Rust from a safe in one of Billy Lee Tuttle's homes. The actual production of the tape precedes a narrative theft (with a visual flashback), further postponing the tape's revelations: Marie, dressed up for the ritual, surrounded by masked men, is being led toward an altar. The show's viewer, however, is denied the conclusion, which is replaced by a close-up of Marty's facial reactions and then his scream of pain and rage, while Rust turns his back on the image.

The videotape is the single most important poetic artifact in *TD* due to its representational potential and the actual placement in the flow of narrative. Thus, the most gruesome object affords, if we may risk it, one of the show's narratively most satisfying moments. As an object of possession, the tape surfaces from Tuttle's safe, which symbolizes its (hidden) valence in his private life, implicating his family in the workings of Carcosa. Metonymically, it belongs to Carcosa's physical splinters (it was used on site); metaphorically, it is the most faithful recording of how Carcosa works. The temporality imprinted on its matter spans the whole case because it goes back to 1990, building an arch over the different pieces of evidence.

The design of its appearance in the narrative discourse underscores its formal function with reference to the expository mechanics: its message can make sense to the viewers only after they've learned about the story from other pieces of the puzzle. The tape also serves as a tool for a double interlinked narrative climax: one, in the narrower discursive design of the logic of Rust's exposition to convince Marty, and the second in the broader context of the whole case, spanning the previous episodes. The master rhetorical use of the tape by the creators, nevertheless, leaves the very core of Carcosa's black hole invisible (we do not see what actually is done to Marie). Carcosa's terror disseminates through the reactions it causes (Marty's and then the Iberia sheriff's): the screams of horror of tough men, who have seen and lived through things spared the great majority of society.

The tape's convincing material opens the third stage in the process of discovery, when Marty and Rust join forces and use Marty's official access to federal and state databases. They identify Errol's family as an illegitimate Tuttle offshoot and learn about the Childress and Son Maintenance company. Then they associate its working itinerary with the locations of the schools, which already coincide with the areas of high missing-person rates along the coast. They also confirm that a tall man with burn scars on his jaws was part of the team. This allows them to locate Errol's house and find the nearby Carcosa. Despite Rust's long dedication to the case, Marty takes the crown of this stretch of investigation by displaying database dexterity and then by linking two vital pieces of evidence together (the green-eared giant with a 1995 picture of a then freshly painted green house). Rust so far has

188 *Karolina Lebek*

remained blind to those connections and is ready to move the investigation away from this context. This narrative solution in the progress of discovery also makes sense considering the show's design of the dynamic conflict.

Material culture in the show's domestic spaces assists the articulation of conflict between Marty and Rust, as well as between them both and Errol. The home affords the expression of "the individual/ society dialectics" (Woodward 2007, 156), so interiors reveal social norms and, as spaces of privacy, reflect the psychological makeup of their inhabitants.[5] The show establishes the integrity of the family home (with women and children at the heart of it) as something most vulnerable and thus most requiring protection. At the same time, the men that set out to protect this integrity either use it to their own emotional ends (Marty) or outright reject participating in its construction (Rust).

Episode 1 establishes Marty's middle-class house as the embodiment of traditional American values with the family at its core, which he takes for a moral benchmark to negotiate his drives, obsessions, and anxieties. The first glimpses of his home come when we see him return at night from the Dora Lange crime scene. The camera offers a close-up of a door frame with markings of his daughters' growth over time; then we see the sleeping girls (while Marty ponders them with tired concern). The morning reveals a living room in a state of cozy disarray, with scattered toys and cushions—traces of play and lax atmosphere. For Marty, the validity of social rules and boundaries must not be undermined because "a man without a family can be a bad thing." Although a man may break the rules, which Marty does by having affairs, a sense of guilt will afford correction. On the one hand, then, Marty objectifies and idealizes the sphere of the home and the people in it as things to protect or to use for moral guidance. On the other, he uses this very sphere for the consumption of comfort (watching TV and enjoying mealtimes), with his wife and children to help him cope with the job and to meet his (material and emotional) needs.

This makes him blind to signs of dissonance and dissent as he puts his personal crisis first: the death of his father and the stress at work cast as problems, alcohol abuse and his affair cast as solutions. As he says, the latter serves him "[to] smooth out the other parts of my life" (episode 4). But this blindness is untenable and the corrupting influences Marty wishes to keep off (not realizing that his behavior is the strongest factor of dysfunction) resurface in the least expected context: after a heated argument with Maggie, Marty discovers his small daughters staging a Barbie gang rape scene, which the camera shows in close-up; later in the show, the older daughter, Audrey, has trouble at school because she drew sketches of an explicit sexual nature, encouraged by her girlfriends (which Marty trivializes).

Marty's home also alludes to his social connection as it showcases pieces related to Marty's favorite pastime: fly fishing. The very first close-up of the home space consists of Marty's tools for tying artificial flies for fishing, later elaborated on by the objects found in his studio. They all connect to fly fishing, yet communicate different aspects of life: the kit for tying affords

The Poetics of Objects in True Detective   189

craftsmanship, a collection of fish artwork (taxidermy, replicas, sculpture, sketches, and paintings) affords aesthetic appreciation and photographs of catches afford contemplation and memory; finally, a considerable display of trophies suggests skill and social recognition. Fly fishing has importance in a broader context of *TD*'s world of masculine hierarchies, with allusions to the ubiquity of this activity and its milieu scattered throughout the season: for example, both in 1995 and 2002 we find taxidermied fish and photographs of catches in the major's office; in 2012 a fishing expedition organized by Marty serves as a successful ploy against the Iberia sheriff, who provides knowledge about Marie Fontenot's case in 1990. This casts fly fishing as the social mortar of male bonding, which corresponds to the respect and friendliness Marty enjoys at work. He takes up the role of a mediator between Rust and their police social context, where Marty poses as a leader in the partnership, whereas, considering the real police work, the place should go to Rust.

Contrasting with Marty's house, the Spartan décor of Rust's apartment also corresponds with multiple aspects of the character. The space he inhabits holds neither furniture nor ornaments (souvenirs, pictures, or paintings), except for a mattress on the floor, a camp chair, a table (added in 2002), a wooden crucifix hanging over the mattress, and a coin-size mirror on the wall. The only objects he keeps from his traumatic past (the loss of a daughter, a divorce, an extensive time as deep undercover narco junkie) are work related and resurface as props in an off-book stretch of the investigation that leads them to Ledoux (a biker jacket with bullet holes, an AK rifle, hand grenades, empty sling bags, a hip flask, a bottle of whiskey). Rust maintains life but refuses the cultivation of the self (the mirror) and social bonding. His lifestyle reflects his ideas on society as mass illusion, and on personhood (implying the importance of the individual) as only an "accretion of sensory experience and feeling" (episode 1), which serves for biological survival. Although Rust is an atheist, he keeps the crucifix to channel the need for contemplation on the nature of sacrifice (which will resonate in the final scenes of the season) and the thought that his only remaining purpose in life (which he still self-critically recognizes as biological programming) is to bear witness to human degeneration.

Rust's flat also epitomizes his skill of "negative capability" (episode 3), which makes him a master at coaxing confessions during interrogations. He can easily sense suspects' need for absolution and tells them what they want to hear. By extension, he serves as an empty site for people's projections, be they hope or fear, as his uncompromising mode of being throws their own images back at them. Accordingly, Rust exposes Marty's denial and hypocrisy, which in turn explains Marty's discomfort about Rust's presence in his family's house. In episode 2 Marty throws a show of anger and anxiety at Rust, when he finds him chatting with Maggie over tea, and learns that Rust has mown their lawn. It seems that Marty reads Rust's actions as accusations of negligence (the lawn "needed mowing"), as cause for jealousy, and as a direct threat to the idyllic image of the home found in Rust's opinions.

190 *Karolina Lebek*

The most important function Rust's apartment performs is to materialize his obsession with the case and the season-long investigation (Martin 2014a). He keeps stacks of books on serial killers, forensic science, and investigation procedures, as well as cardboard boxes of notebooks and a growing number of case-related material. This spread of reading matter traces the rhythms of the investigation, taking over wall space as well. In 2012 this obsession with the case is reinforced by a further reduction of the living space (represented only verbally in episode 2—"I live in a little room out in the country, behind a bar") and by the transfer of Rust's spatial alignment onto the storage unit. In this sense, the show uses Rust's space as a tool to materialize his thought process, repeatedly showing him in contemplative interaction with case materials. His ledger constitutes a logical extension of this space, which he carries around for noting observations, sketching, and mapping the thread of evidence. His pronouncements then about bearing witness find support in the way Rust uses objects and places for keeping records and building narratives. He lives in the world of representations of Errol's work and influence, becoming the killer's photographic negative: his shade is the reverse (he does not kill), but he is perceived by society as carrying a similar imprint.

Located near Carcosa, Errol's house stands in direct opposition to Rust's apartment, yet it echoes its break with social normativity. The house is also an obscene version of Marty's ideals of domesticity, so consequently it builds a paradoxical bridge between Rust and Marty across their differences. There are evident reverberations between the three places ascribed to the three characters, but Errol's home constitutes a visual argument for the viewer why Rust and Marty must unite against its obscene secret existence. The disturbing material aura of the place is achieved by formal means (unusual arrangement and distribution) and the condition of things (age, dilapidation, dirt, decay). This affects furniture (stacks of chairs and lamps)—some of it antique—utensils (kitchenware, dirty towels, used plastic bags), and material media (newspapers, books, video tapes), as well as ornaments, artwork, and toys (rows of colored glass bottles, paintings, rows of dolls). Objects spill around the house in patches and batches, which often suggests they are not used according to the intended function (except for the video tapes, perhaps). The dirt and decay reign in the upstairs bedrooms as well, where the disgusted Marty finds a stained mattress, an old metal bathtub (bundles of car fresheners swaying over it from the ceiling), several old stained duvets, and towels on the floor. The interior walls and windows are overgrown with things, as they are overgrown with vegetation from the outside. This makes the kitchen and the living room bathed in semidarkness.

Individual objects notwithstanding, the house as a whole is a site of abject aesthetics, retentive hoarding, and exaggerated multiplication of the same category of objects, as if matter were proliferous. The creators were careful, nevertheless, to suggest a pattern of incestuous domestic life, at the same time making the very thought of its possibility repulsive. The horror of the family life is enhanced by the gruesome shed where Errol keeps his father's tortured

The Poetics of Objects in True Detective   191

corpse. The viewer, however, will recognize some common motives connecting Errol's house with the general picture of decay, negligence, and poverty in the show's South Louisiana.[6] The work of the camera communicates the social invisibility of the house and its spatial isolation: after the opening sequences of the episode in which the interior of the house is exposed, the camera withdraws outside and shows the neglected state of the façade and, then, in receding cuts, the country road and the asphalt road along the Creole Nature Trail. Then it rises to embrace an arial view of the surrounding swamps.

If conceptualized in terms of binary opposition in material inhabitation, the axis of antagonism stretches between Rust and Errol and intensifies in the progress of discovery. This may also serve to explain why Rust needs Marty's assistance and why it is Marty who makes the final leap in the investigation. Rust's self-inflicted asceticism reverberates with his radical nonconformism, which gradually detaches him from the police force (insubordination, suspension, resignation). Errol's acts and his material aura signal an overindulgence of the self in his transgressions of social boundaries. Rust's and Errol's radically opposing modes of existence seem, however, to be similar in the degree of intensity and disregard for social norms. This makes Rust suspect in the eyes of the state, so the two CID police detectives in 2012 accuse him of committing the murders and tampering with the evidence. Also, a weird spiritual connection is established between the two characters through Carcosa, as if they could feel the other's presence and intent. Just before his death, Reggie whispers to Rust: "[y]ou are in Carcosa now with me. He sees you" (episode 5). This spiritual link notwithstanding, Rust is blind to traces of Errol in his ordinary social capacity as maintenance man: they meet in front of Rianne's disused school at the end of episode 3. Marty mediates between those two extreme modes of intensity and breaks Rust's detective's curse, opening a pathway for the final agon.

The poetic artifaction in *TD* contributes to the centripetal pull of the story's focus by working against the centrifugal forces of narrative discourse. Material culture then performs two formal functions in the show's design: first, props and set pieces mediate between the needs of world-building and storytelling; second, in terms of storytelling alone, through patterns of distribution, they symbolically express the relational dynamic of conflict (concerned with character elaboration) as well as dramatize the progress of discovery. The season also rehearses some popular material motives for the purpose of original repetition like the exposition of female dead bodies, the poetics of the investigation board, or the transgressive interiority of serial killer homes.

Notes

1. See, for example Yuhas (2014); for *TD*'s second season's failure see Marche (2015).
2. For TD's use of cultural references, see Taveira (2014) and Colon (2015).
3. Two articles based on interviews with Alex DiGerlando, *TD*'s production designer, offer behind-the-scenes insights on some of the props, set pieces, and original artwork created by artist Joshua Walsh (Martin 2014a, 2014b).

192 *Karolina Lebek*

4. For details of design and location, see Martin (2014b).
5. The books that also contributed to my thinking about domesticity in *TD*, although I do not quote them directly, are Bachelard (1958) and Miller (2001).
6. On *TD* as dystopia with an extensive treatment of the image of its location, see Demaria (2014).

References

Bachelard, Gaston. 1958. *The Poetics of Space*. Boston: Beacon Press.

Colon, Gilbert. 2015. "True Detective: Pulp, Crime, and the Weird Tale of Nic Pizzolatto." Available online at http://www.tor.com/2015/06/19/true-detective-pulp-crime-and-the-weird-tales-of-nic-pizzolatto/.

Demaria, Cristina. 2014. "True Detective Stories: Media Textuality and the Anthology Format between Remediation and Transmedia Narratives." *Between* 4 (8): 1–25. Available online at http//www.Between-journal.it/.

Elam, Keir. 2002. *The Semiotics of Theatre and Drama*. London and New York: Routledge.

Harré, Rom. 2002. "Material Objects in Social Worlds." *Theory, Culture and Society* 19 (5/6): 23–33.

Marche, Stephen. 2015. "Why True Detective Season 2 Failed." Available online at http://www.esquire.com/entertainment/tv/a37065/true-detective-season-2-review-failed-murder-mystery/.

Martin, Denise. 2014a. "Devil's Nests and Beer-Can Men: The Origins of 13 True Detective Set Pieces." Available online at http://www.vulture.com/2014/03/true-detective-alex-digerlando-set-design-props-interview.html.

———. 2014b. "True Detective's Production Designer on the Finale's Mazelike Fort." Available online at http://www.vulture.com/2014/03/true-detective-finale-production-designer-fort-maze.html.

Miller, Daniel, ed. 2001. *Home Possessions: Material Culture behind Closed Doors*. Oxford: Berg.

Mittell, Jason. 2015. *Complex TV. The Poetics of Contemporary Television Storytelling*. New York and London: New York University Press.

Taveira, Rodney. 2014. "True Detective Lassos the Yellow King in Hollywood South." Available online at https://theconversation.com/true-detective-lassos-the-yellow-king-in-hollywood-south-24113.

Turkle, Sherry. 2011. *Evocative Objects. Things We Think With*. Cambridge, MA, and London: MIT Press.

Wolf, Mark J. P. 2012. *Building Imaginary Worlds: The Theory and History of Sub-creation*. New York: Routledge/Taylor & Francis.

Woodward, Ian. 2007. *Understanding Material Culture*. Los Angeles, London, New Dehli, Singapore: Sage Publications.

Yuhas, Alan. 2014. "HBO's True Detective Is Bizzare, Entertaining and Really Worth Your Time." Available at http://www.theguardian.com/tv-and-radio/tvandradioblog/2014/feb/12/hbo-true-detective-bizarre-entertaining-harrelson-mcconaughey.

15 Mapping the Daytime Landscape
World-Building on U.S. Soap Operas

C. Lee Harrington and Byron Miller

Introduction

In his recent landmark book, Mark J. P. Wolf (2012) explores the imaginary worlds introduced through books, videogames, television, and other pop culture forms, arguing that the worlds themselves, not just the narratives, set within them or the media in which they appear, hold rich potential for media scholars. The term 'world,' as Wolf uses it, is both geographic and experiential, referring to fictional terrain that "invit[es] us to enter and tempt[s] us to stay, as alive in our thoughts as our own memories of lived experience" (2012, 2). Anyone who has yearned to visit the intricate landscapes of Westeros (*Game of Thrones*),[1] Middle-earth (*Lord of the Rings*),[2] or the Tommy Westphall Universe (reader: please Google this) identifies immediately with Wolf's claim, and the disappearance or deep freeze of such worlds—through network cancellation, a creator's death, or an author's decision to end a book series—can have devastating consequences for fans. Some imaginary worlds leave a material legacy in that books can be reread and movies rewatched, while others are ephemeral. When the virtual space of EA-Land (formerly The Sims Online) shut down at precisely 4:35 a.m. Pacific Standard Time on August 1, 2008, its world was "forever deleted not with a bang, but an error message" (Lowood 2009, 121).

Given the allure of imaginary worlds, a core activity of modern participatory culture is the combined efforts of fans and creators to help map the boundaries of fictional terrain. Imaginary worlds can be enormous: difficult to grasp in their totality and resistant to analysis in that they are often transmedial, transnarrative, and transauthorial (Wolf 2012, 3). For example, Lucas film has recently announced that the expanded universe of the *Star Wars* franchise—"essentially, all of the stories told in ancillary material outside of the six core movies and Clone Wars television stories"—was no longer part of the larger continuity of the 30-year-old narrative. Fan reactions ranged from "the resigned to the excited," with one fan admitting that between "the comic strip series, the novels, the kids [*sic*] books, the junior novels, the role playing and computer games, etc., there's just no way to make it all 'fit'" (McMillan 2014). These complex worlds are experienced via different media windows or portals and "only an aggregate view combining a variety of [them] can give a complete sense of what the world is

194   *C. Lee Harrington and Byron Miller*

like and what has occurred there" (Wolf 2012, 2). Synthesizing disparate strands of media and cultural studies—including those focusing on media franchises, entertainment supersystems, database narratives, and transmedia storytelling—Wolf advocates for the study of imaginary worlds as its own subdiscipline within media studies.

This chapter focuses on imaginary worlds introduced via television—specifically, U.S. daytime soap operas—and the window into those worlds offered by soap fan magazines. In television, serialized narratives such as soap operas are uniquely structured to encourage world-building in that the intimacy offered by the medium as a whole is exaggerated on soaps: they air five days per week in the U.S., are populated by the same actors/characters for decades at a time, and cultivate a devoted fan base. Imaginary TV worlds typically emerge in the form of *towns* (Wolf 2012, 124), such as Harmony (the fictional setting of NBC's *Passions*) or Springfield (the fictional setting of CBS's *Guiding Light*). While elements of the towns are revealed on-screen, the entire towns are not, thus generating off-screen world-building efforts to animate the towns' geographic maps. In this project we explore how fan magazines serve a world-building function for U.S. soap operas.

The World(s) of Daytime Soap Operas

The emergence of modern imaginary worlds dates back to the late nineteenth century in the U.S. and Europe amid the growing legitimization of imagination itself (Saler 2012). As part of a broader fictionalist turn in Western culture, we gradually became more "adept at accepting difference, contingency, and pluralism: at envisioning life not in essentialist, 'just so' terms but rather in provisional 'as if' perspectives" (Saler 2012, 7).[3] The emergence of episodic broadcast media in the 1920s extended this cultural turn, and radio dramas and comedies used ongoing characters to thread narratives and landscapes together. The shift from radio to television was no doubt jarring, as consumers could now see fictional worlds and their inhabitants rather than merely hear them, and many programs did not survive the transition. Indeed, radio producers occasionally protested attempts to adapt serials to other formats on the grounds that the imaginary world would be damaged. For example, Paramount's mid-1930s effort to make a film version of the radio drama *One Man's Family* was blocked with the claim that "any drastic alterations would conflict with the conception created in the minds of listeners and [...] the program, voted second most popular by radio editors, would be injured by a typical motion-picture version" (Churchill 1937).

Guiding Light, which launched on radio in 1937 and was successfully adapted to television (CBS) in 1952, endured to become the longest running soap opera and longest running imaginary world in twentieth century broadcast history.

The imaginary landscapes of soaps are typically introduced via program bibles: the original outlines of a program's characters, communities, and foci. The bible written for *As the Earth Turns* (retitled *As the World*

Mapping the Daytime Landscape 195

Turns and airing from 1956 to 2010 on CBS) introduces the setting of the narrative—the fictional town of Oakdale, Illinois—as follows:

> Let us for the moment walk down a street of an ordinary suburban family. It is more than obvious that many of the homes were designed by the same architect. Yes, there is somewhat of a sameness in design, construction, and if you walked up to the steps, and could without being seen open the doors to many of these homes, you would find that they all housed families. This is not only true of the homes on Oakdale Avenue, this is true of every community the world over.[4]

This cozy suburban setting echoes the small-town origins of most U.S. soap operas. Indeed, a central pleasure of the genre since its beginning has been the deliberate temporal and geographic congruities between characters' and viewers' inhabited spaces—soaps' "implicit claim to portray a parallel life" (Porter 1977, 783)—such that Christmas is Christmas both on- and off-screen, and the fictional community of Bay City, Illinois (the setting of NBC's *Another World*), is presented to viewers as a mere car ride away, albeit sadly inaccessible via that mode of transport. Over time and due to storytelling imperatives (the creative demands of filling 130 to 260 hours of airtime each year), the simplicity and real-world familiarity of soaps' early settings evolved into sophisticated, diverse, and somewhat improbable landscapes:

> Where else but daytime can a landlocked suburban hamlet contain a beach, a lake, a river, a rock quarry, a mountain with an underground city inside it, high-rise buildings, a multibillion-dollar oil corporation *and* an oil reserve, a high-fashion magazine, two hot nightclubs and a Latino quarter, all with Philadelphia around the corner?
>
> (Flynn and Owens 2008, 80; emphasis in the original)

Welcome to Llanview, Pennsylvania, the fictional setting for ABC's *One Life to Live* (1968–2013). When it debuted in 1968 the soap centered on domestic encounters between a small handful of families from diverse backgrounds; as the preceding quote attests, the town (the world) has grown dramatically since then.

Our interest, as noted earlier, is how fan magazines facilitate world-building by expanding viewers' geographic and experiential knowledge of soap opera communities. Our data set is a collection of print issues of two prominent U.S. weekly magazines—*Soap Opera Digest* (1975–present) and *Soap Opera Weekly* (1989–2012)—totaling 952 issues from 1999 to 2010.[5] The soaps and their settings covered in this time period include:

All My Children: fictional town of Pine Valley, Pennsylvania (ABC, 1970–2011)
Another World: fictional town of Bay City, Illinois (NBC, 1964–1999)
As the World Turns: fictional town of Oakdale, Illinois (CBS, 1956–2010)

196   *C. Lee Harrington and Byron Miller*

The Bold and the Beautiful: real city of Los Angeles, California (CBS, 1987–present)

Days of Our Lives: fictional town of Salem, state unspecified (NBC, 1965–present)

General Hospital: fictional town of Port Charles, New York (ABC, 1963–present)

General Hospital: Night Shift: fictional town of Port Charles, New York (2007–2008)

Guiding Light: fictional town of Springfield,[6] state unspecified (CBS, 1937–2009)

One Life to Live: fictional town of Llanview, Pennsylvania (ABC, 1968–2013)

Passions: fictional town of Harmony, New England (NBC, 1999–2007)

Port Charles: fictional town of Port Charles, New York (ABC, 1997–2003)

Sunset Beach: real town of Sunset Beach, California (NBC, 1997–1999)

The Young and the Restless: real town of Genoa City, Wisconsin (1973–present)

While several of these exist in the real world, they are also imagined on-screen (and in fan magazines) through the naming and location of restaurants, gym clubs, hotels, residences, employment settings, and local landmarks. As such, for the purposes of this chapter we consider *all* of these to be imaginary communities.

In the remainder of this chapter, we explore three themes related to world-building on U.S. daytime soap operas: *inventing* worlds, *living in* worlds, and *ending* worlds. We conclude with a discussion of the types of imaginary worlds that most soap operas represent and the changing role of soap magazines in fans' access to those worlds.

Inventing Soap Worlds

Inventing daytime worlds begins with the sets and props that present those worlds to viewers. Unlike the realist serials more common in the UK, Australia, and elsewhere, U.S. daytime soap operas are decidedly *interior*, with action unfolding in specially constructed sets: living rooms, hospital lounges, restaurants, corporate offices, and so on. Outdoor spaces such as parks and waterfronts are also typically constructed indoors—these sets' unnaturalness is obvious to viewers but an accepted feature of the genre. There are exceptions, of course, ranging from on-location shoots to the construction of a (truly) outdoor shopping mall (on NBC's *Days of Our Lives*), but in general soap narratives unfold indoors. Fans then use their secondary imagination[7] to help construct the larger landscapes introduced on-screen. Soap magazines aid in this process by including stories describing set design and interior decoration with titles such as "Backstage Pass"

(*Soap Opera Weekly*, May 22, 2001, 27–49), "Ready, Set, Go!" (*Soap Opera Digest*, March 11, 2008, 46–49), and "Space Junkies" (*Soap Opera Digest*, July 31, 2007, 72–81). Viewers (readers) learn about room layout, where a door or staircase *really* leads (often to nowhere), and details of prop selection. World-building is augmented when interior spaces reflect the personalities of a show's characters and actors. For example, *One Life to Live* (ABC) production designer Roger Mooney explains how the set of Rae's (played by actress Linda Dano) home was constructed: "This set is really very tailored, elegant, eclectic and strong like Linda [...]. [The] 19th century Chinese Chippendale is the centerpiece of the living room, but the temple lion statue costs $60,000" (*Soap Opera Weekly*, March 6, 2001, 30).

Similarly, *All My Children* (ABC) production designer Boyd Dumrose describes the living room of legendary soap character Erica Kane: "The French furniture is something that [actress] Susan [Lucci] likes. And she likes crystal, so there was no reason why Erica wouldn't like the same thing" (*Soap Opera Digest*, October 3, 2000, 97).

Feature articles such as "Backstage Pass" also depict actors taking photos with fans, reading scripts, getting dolled up by makeup artists, working with producers, and set blocking[8] (*Soap Opera Weekly* May 22, 2001, 39). For Juliet Mills (Tabitha on NBC's *Passions*), blocking is helpful because

> it gives you a first chance to walk around the set and work with props that you might not have seen [...]. Also, it's a chance to come up with any of your own ideas such as moves that the director can then implement into his or her camera blocking. (49)

Soap fans pride themselves on knowing minutiae about their favorite imaginary worlds, but magazine readers are privy to the intricacies of sets that are not shown on-air or might be missed when viewing. For example, *Soap Opera Weekly* has a regular feature titled "Set Tight: What You Can't See Unless the Camera Zooms In!" that provides readers a close look at specific items. Darin Brooks (Max on NBC's *Days of our Lives*) gave the magazine a tour of the set of Max's Garage which includes fancy tires with chrome wheels, a gas analyzer, donuts, and a set of lockers he describes as "the infamous 'whore' lockers, where Chelsea wrote something very mean to Stephanie. They came from the Salem High School set. I opened them up one day and there was a textbook inside" (*Soap Opera Weekly*, January 16, 2007, 29).

Similarly, during a tour of his character's office at the fashion firm Forrester Creations, actor John McCook (Eric Forrester on CBS's *The Bold and the Beautiful*) mentions that the office props were pilfered from the set of the canceled soap opera *Capitol* (CBS, 1982–1987). He goes on to discuss the paintings displayed on the walls, an urn holding the ashes of Eric's mother-in-law, sketches of dresses he pretends to draw (Eric is a fashion designer), and a small box that "looks like it has something really important

198   *C. Lee Harrington and Byron Miller*

in it, but it has breath mints in it because it's a soap opera box, not a Forrester box" (*Soap Opera Weekly*, November 2, 2003, 30). An interview with Robert S. Woods (police commissioner Bo Buchanan on ABC's *One Life to Live*) on-set at his character's office at the police station demonstrates how magazines give soap fans additional insight into character background: "In addition to the police badges, wanted posters, and RJ water cooler, [Woods] points out a "memorial wall for all the cops that are killed in the line of duty, and that's why Drew (Bo's son) is up" (35).

Some soap opera scenes are so dramatic or action packed that details about staging are reported. Describing the stunts behind a character falling through the ice (*Soap Opera Digest*, March 11, 2003, 66–67) or two antagonists' physical confrontation at a christening party (*Soap Opera Digest*, November 19, 2002, 24–25), an ongoing feature titled "Behind the Scenes" explains how particular scenes are staged and filmed. For instance, actress Martha Byrne (Rose on CBS's *As the World Turns*) enjoyed being seven months' pregnant while filming a boat scene, remarking that "the whole studio was just the boat and handheld cameras. It's the *Jaws* boat" (*Soap Opera Digest*, September 2, 2002, 56–57). Another "Behind the Scenes" describes the challenges of a rare live-on-air episode of *One Life to Live* (*Soap Opera Digest*, June 18, 2002, 48–49), and yet another asks if fans "wondered what goes into getting just the right photograph for a *Digest* story?" as it documents a photo shoot for Paul Leyden (Simon) and Terri Colombo (Katie) from *As the World Turns* (CBS) (*Soap Opera Digest*, April 16, 2002, 58–59). "Behind the Scenes" features give readers temporally and/or spatially relevant insight into the daily taping of a soap opera.

Nothing makes imaginary soap worlds more 'real' for fans than scenes shot in actual real-world locations. From seeing Ross and Tea (played by Shawn Christian and Florencia Lozano on ABC's *One Life to Live*) leave fictional Llanview, Pennsylvania, only to *really* become stranded in Hawaii, and Gwen (played by Jennifer Landon on CBS's *As the World Turns*) leave fictional Oakdale, Illinois, only to be tied to the *real* tracks along the Branson Scenic Railway in Missouri (*Soap Opera Weekly*, July 17, 2007, 24–25), staging imaginary worlds in real settings offers enhanced world-building opportunities. Says one lucky fan, who landed a small part on *As the World Turns* (CBS), shot on location in Pittsburgh, Pennsylvania, "[t]here was a buzz around town. It's a big deal when stuff happens here!" (*Soap Opera Digest*, December 8, 2009, 84–85). This collision of *real* and *reel* spaces helps bring soap worlds to life. It also contributes to the long-standing reputation of soap fans as unable to tell the difference between fiction and reality (Harrington and Bielby 1995), such as when fans hail "Massimo! Massimo!" to actor Joseph Mascolo (Massimo Marone on *The Bold and the Beautiful* [CBS]) as he walks down the streets of Portofino, Italy, during a special taping of the show. According to co-star Bobbie Eakes (Macy), the "whole town was going crazy" (*Soap Opera Weekly*, December 24, 2002, 16–17). Viewers' knowledge of how soap worlds are invented is even given reliability

Mapping the Daytime Landscape 199

checks through magazine articles such as "Setting Pretty" that challenge readers to "guess where [their] favorite characters are" in a variety of different scenes from different soap operas (*Soap Opera Digest*, November 10, 2009, 84–85). Since only viewers with a comprehensive understanding of soap landscapes can accurately determine the location of the scenes, these tests confirm the cultural capital that operates within fandoms.

Living in Soap Worlds

Once soap landscapes are invented or created, how do magazines help viewers "live" in those worlds? Both *Soap Opera Digest* and *Soap Opera Weekly* run features that introduce soap towns to readers. These include chamber-of-commerce-style "welcome to our town" pieces, guided tours of the town, histories of the town, and articles on specific town landmarks. One article on CBS soaps ("Eye-ball Your Favorite Locales On ..." (*Soap Opera Digest*, October 10, 2000, 46–59) welcomes readers to the imaginary world of *The Young and the Restless* (CBS): "Welcome to Genoa City. Pay a visit to Genoa City and you're likely to stay. It offers fantastic career choices, wonderful homes and great dining. If you're looking for romance, opportunities abound" (58).

The article goes on to describe the Chancellor mansion, the restaurant Gina's Place (with a shout-out to the house specialty, spaghetti), the local coffeehouse Crimson Lights (where readers are warned to "steer clear of the newest server, Carter. He has a secret agenda," 59) and the legendary Newman Ranch:

> You probably caught sight of this sprawling ranch on your drive into Genoa City. For years, townspeople quietly speculated that Nikki Newman suffered from agoraphobia because she never left the main house [...]. Pay special attention to the "No Trespassing" signs. The property is littered with booby traps. [...] And watch out for the cobweb-covered fallout shelter that no one seems to know about. (59)

Actors are sometimes recruited by magazines to offer a guided tour of their (character's) town. One feature, titled "Grand Tours" (*Soap Opera Digest*, July 29, 2008, 74–83), includes Aiden Turner (Aidan on ABC's *All My Children*) describing Pine Valley's favorite bar: "A rowdy bar with a lot of biker chicks and biker guys. It's not too far from the Yacht Club, but the road leading up to it is quite dark and dangerous. It's where you go when your hair's not done" (81).

A tongue-in-cheek fan letter published in *Soap Opera Weekly* suggests new slogans for the "Welcome" signs leading into soap towns, modeled after real-life signs common across small-town U.S. Based on specific plot points, suggested slogans include one for Llanview (*One Life to Live*, ABC) reading "Population 2,987 (not counting alternate personalities)" and one for Salem

(*Days of Our Lives*, NBC) reading "Welcome to Salem. (Five miles later.) In case you have developed amnesia in the last five miles, Welcome to Salem" ("Public Opinion," *Soap Opera Weekly*, October 4, 2005, 36).

Magazines often move beyond a purely geographic focus in their discussion of soap landscapes by acknowledging the relevance of narrative to soap worlds. As Wolf notes, while "the experience of a *world* is different and distinct from that of merely a *narrative* [...] the narratives have much to do with the worlds in which they occur, and are usually the means by which the worlds are experienced" (2012, 11; emphases in original). For example, a feature on ABC soap settings includes lengthy descriptions of the historical interest surrounding local landmarks (i.e., what past and current storylines were centered on the landmarks; "Special ABC Section," *Soap Opera Digest*, July 4, 2000, 40–48). Magazines also acknowledge the imaginariness of the towns. For example, *Soap Opera Digest* asks actors, "Which of your show's places of business would you patronize if it really existed?" ("Roundup," August 29, 2006, 56–57). Finally, magazines offer "real" tours of "fake" places—the even-more-fictional landscapes *within* landscapes that are part of soap worlds:

> When making your travel plans this summer, may we suggest exotic locales as the majestic snow-capped alps of Mendorra, the lush jungle gardens of Puerto Vista or San Cristobel's stately palaces? Oops. Those places only exist on soaps. We've provided the following travelog [*sic*] anyway so you can see what you're missing and even provided a 1–5 star rating (5 being the best). Bon Voyage!
> ("Tripping Out," *Soap Opera Digest*, July 11, 2006, 74–83)

Why would soap writers invent imaginary "exotic locales" to send characters to, rather than send them to Switzerland or Japan or Venezuela? It is not for purposes of fictional congruence (i.e., a fake domestic town necessitating a fake foreign destination), but rather for both narrative and industry convenience—to circumvent viewers' real-world knowledge of how legal systems work or how royal lineage operates, to stash characters in faraway places while an actor waits out a contract dispute, or to script a plot-suitable political revolution when one is, inconveniently, not taking place in real life (for example, see "Tripping Out," *Soap Opera Digest*, July 11, 2006, 74–83). But soap creators sometimes remind fans that the lines between imaginary and fictional worlds are blurred by having celebrities like pop-culture icon Bob Barker (long-time host of the CBS game show *The Price is Right*) appear as himself on *The Bold and the Beautiful* (CBS) (*Soap Opera Digest*, April 30, 2002).

One of the biggest production challenges in preserving the integrity of soap worlds is the occasional need to sync them geographically and/or temporally, whether due to character crossovers (when a character from one soap town visits another) or to multiple versions of the world unfolding simultaneously (a common issue in some pop culture realms such as comics but rare

Mapping the Daytime Landscape 201

in television). Crossovers are a treat for fans who watch multiple soaps, but from a production perspective, they are ultimately about ratings. Explains Dona Cooper, senior vice president of programming at ABC Daytime:

> If we can interest viewers [of one soap] in a character from another show, then they might follow that character back to his usual show. They'll either try out the new show for the first time, or in the case of lapsed viewers, pick it up again.
>
> (Kelley 1999, 44)[9]

An early 1990s crossover from CBS's *The Bold and the Beautiful* to its sister show, *The Young and the Restless*, is considered the industry gold standard:

> Take a popular nutcase [a character named Sheila] with ready-made story, then slowly integrate her into the second show while simultaneously continuing her plot on the first. "It's all a function of interweaving" [explains a supervising producer]. "Both shows have to be kept up-to-date about what's happening on the other. So in Sheila's case, the characters on [*Young and Restless*] spoke about her disappearance."
>
> (Kelley 1999, 44)

One of the trickiest crossovers occurred on ABC in the late 1990s, when actress Linda Dano's character traveled to three different network soap towns: Pine Valley, Llanview, and Port Charles. The network hired someone whose primary job was tracking the "on-screen quantum physics" of Dano's comings and goings, "all the physical realities of the character, making sure [she] doesn't get on a plane in Llanview in one outfit and get off in Port Charles wearing something else" (vice president Cooper quoted in Kelley 1999, 46).

In contrast, the two-season production of ABC's *General Hospital: Night Shift* (a primetime spin-off of *General Hospital*) offered a "what not to do" lesson in geographic, temporal, and narrative continuity. When announcing the spin-off, ABC executives emphasized that *Night Shift* would represent a completely separate version of the town of Port Charles, with *GH* focusing on the town as a whole and *GH:NS* focusing on its hospital scene. Despite many central characters slated to appear on both shows, network execs promised that viewers would be able to follow each program without having to watch both. However, production proceeded with much less separation than expected; story points from one program spilled over into the other and characters displayed confusingly different "selves" on each show. Viewers were frustrated:

> Is there anyone who is as confused as I am with the GH/NIGHT SHIFT sequence? Jason sits in maximum security prison on GH and on NIGHT SHIFT, he is taking Spinelli to the ER. Jason can't be in jail and running around the hospital at the same time.
>
> ("Mail Bag," *Soap Opera Digest*, August 14 2007, 110)

202   C. Lee Harrington and Byron Miller

Producers had planned to integrate the two story canons by the end of *Night Shift*'s second season but numerous contradictions in character and plot development made this impossible; for example, major story points were resolved on one narrative canvas but remained unaddressed on the other. While *Night Shift* was a bold experiment in a time of declining ratings, the strategy may have permanently damaged ABC's relationship with long-term viewers (Gonzales 2010).[10]

These viewer frustrations point to a final way that fan magazines impact the "lived worlds" of soap opera—by assessing just how well (or poorly) those worlds are being imagined. As noted earlier, U.S. soap operas were historically designed to unfold in real time, thus preserving the authorial conceit that the fictional towns portrayed on-screen might neighbor the viewer's own. Published commentary from both viewers and professional critics routinely points out discontinuities of time, weather, and geography:

> If timing is everything, General Hospital really missed the boat—er, plane—when Jason trekked all the way to Italy to "rescue" Carly. One minute Jason was in his Port Charles penthouse, talking to Michael. The next, he was in an Italian jail with Carly and company. How the heck did he get there? A leftover Concorde? ("Hit or Miss," *Soap Opera Weekly*, July 13, 2004, 38)

> AMC's [writers] must've had too much eggnog! Swimming outside in Pine Valley, PA, in the winter? Come on! ("Mail Bag," *Soap Opera Digest*, January 29, 2008, 111)

> DAY's Max was recently loading cargo onto a ship traveling from Salem to Ethiopia. This is highly improbable and geographically ridiculous. Salem has historically been known as a Midwestern [U.S.] city and Ethiopia is a landlocked country in Africa! ("Mail Bag," *Soap Opera Digest*, May 13, 2008, p. 110)

These quotes remind us that *imaginary* worlds are also *negotiated* ones. Over the course of the twentieth century soap viewers gradually became used to temporal distortions[11]—rapid aging of child characters, (on-screen) days that last (real-world) weeks, stories unfolding in unexpected flashbacks to the 1800s, and so on—but over the past 20 years "soap opera time" has elasticized even further to allow for more story possibilities in a dwindling marketplace. The head writer for *One Life to Live* (ABC) laughingly explains, "We have real time; we have airtime; we have Llanview time" (Flores 2000, 74). Other industry insiders agree, arguing that viewers have "gotten used to it" while acknowledging that they still "can't get away with flagrant inconsistencies" (2000, 75). In short, soap time is flexible ... to a point.

Ending Worlds

Our final theme is the ending or disappearance of soap worlds. As with all well-crafted, imaginary worlds, soap landscapes become vividly alive to viewers over time. A separate project conducted by the first author of this chapter included a survey question asking fans: "If you could visit Oakdale [the fictional setting of CBS's *As the World Turns*] for a day, where would you go, who would you visit, and what would you do?" Responses were heartfelt and humorous:

> Breakfast at Al's would be nice [...] followed by a tour of the TV studio with Kim and Brad as guides. [I'd like a] tour of the Snyder farm to see if it is really big enough to accommodate all the people that have stayed there recently. I'd try to get in a quick shopping trip at Lisa's boutique [...]. Dinner at Lucinda's mansion would be a real treat [and] Doctor Bob can drive me home—it would be about a 6 hours' round trip! (female viewer, age 70, watched for 50+ years)

> I'd have a girls' lunch with Lisa, Barbara, Lucinda, Emma, Nancy and Kim. After that I'd stroll around Emma's farm and visit the Snyder Pond [...] I'd end my day with martinis and dinner at the Lakeview [and] then I'd try to get out of town before I was shot, kidnapped, held for ransom, or became a victim of a psychopath (female viewer, age 60, watched for 40+ years)

U.S. daytime soaps (like those in the UK, Australia, and elsewhere) are crafted with an open-ended narrative structure—designed to *never* end—and are marked instead by an "indefinitely expandable middle" (Porter 1977, 783). This contributes to soaps' more preposterous plot twists, as writers struggle to fill that middle with entertaining content, and also helps to demarcate daytime from primetime drama as the latter *is* intended to end (the only question being, when?). Having said this, soap worlds *do* end, of course, and the "death" of the U.S. daytime genre appears to many a fait accompli, the inevitable destiny of this long-standing cultural form (Harrington 2015). In the past 15 years, numerous cancellations have reduced the 13 soaps airing on U.S. broadcast television in 1999 to the four currently airing today (ABC's *General Hospital*, NBC's *Days of Our Lives*, and CBS's *The Bold and the Beautiful* and *The Young and the Restless*). Both mainstream and soap-specific news outlets have featured numerous commentaries on the decline of the genre. Indeed, the disappearance, death, and (occasional) resurrection of entertainment content in general is of growing interest to media scholars, who voice concerns about erratic archival practices (e.g., Wilson 2010), the curation and preservation of online and social media worlds (e.g., Lowood 2009), and what might constitute a "good textual death" in a media context (e.g., Harrington 2012).

204   C. Lee Harrington and Byron Miller

In our analysis, the imaginary worlds of soap operas experience two kinds of endings. One might be thought of as a *shrinking* of the world(s) caused by financial constraints. The golden era of U.S. soaps was the 1980s, marked by lavish budgets, multiple on-location shoots both inside and outside the states, celebrity casting, and on-air celebrations (weddings, picnics, funerals) attended by dozens of characters (read: dozens of actors drawing paychecks). In the past 20 years budgets have been drastically reduced and the effects are felt both off-screen (such as when actors are forced to take pay cuts) and on-screen (such as when serial-killer storylines are crafted to handily reduce a soap town's population; "Budget Cuts Rock Daytime," *Soap Opera Digest* December 16, 2003, 34–35). The impact of budget cuts is regularly discussed in soap magazines, with both critics and fans documenting instances of world shrinking: for example, when the wedding reception of a popular couple is inexplicably held in a small foyer and attended by a mere handful of guests ("Winners and Losers," *Soap Opera Weekly*, December 12, 2006, 6) or when certain sets are oddly mobilized:

> [The] "no vacancies" sign at the Beacon [Hotel] seems permanently lit. And while we don't know many cops (like [the character of] Mallet) who could afford to make a chic boutique hotel home, if using one set and a closet full of varied linens keeps the budget down, we're all for a little suspension of disbelief
> (in reference to CBS's *Guiding Light*; "That's Hot!"
> *Soap Opera Digest*, November 21, 2006, 75)

More meaningful than soap worlds *shrinking* is the second kind of ending— those same worlds *dying*. Soaps have an advantage over primetime television in their ability to plan for death (cancellation) in advance. Unlike primetime shows that are cancelled unceremoniously, daytime soaps receive advance warning from network executives, thus allowing the creative team time to craft a meaningful finale. The executive producer of ABC's *All My Children*, Julie Hanan Carruthers, describes her aims as the show prepares to end after 41 years:

> For our final month of broadcast, our goal, top of the list, was to respect the viewers, particularly the people who have watched the show for decades, with the families and the characters that they love, and offer some hope and promise for the future. Things that we felt may not have been right in the past, we wanted to make right. [Plotting the last month] was an opportunity to set up [the world of] Pine Valley in a way that everyone was proud of [...].
> ("Fond Farewell," *Soap Opera Digest*, September 6, 2011, 36)

Daytime executives, along with their primetime peers fortunate enough to negotiate endings in advance (e.g., AMC's *Breaking Bad*), aim to achieve

Mapping the Daytime Landscape   205

narrative coherence in the show's final episode by bringing the story to a "natural" death (Harrington 2012). Explains head writer Jean Passanante on the finale of *As the World Turns* (CBS):

> We don't burn the house down or anything! What we wanted to suggest is that there's a place for these characters in our imagination, always [...] you deal with all these fundamental experiences. Birth, death, love and marriage—all those things are reflected in the last episode.
>
> (McClure 2010b, 44, 46)

Soap magazines function to document the end of soap worlds and offer a space for those worlds to be mourned. Documentation consists of backstage industry reports, descriptions of actors' plans after cancellation, and compilations of story ends. Not surprisingly, narrative ends receive the most attention. For example, an article titled "Fade to Black" (*Soap Opera Digest*, November 21, 2000, 88–89) offers brief capsule summaries of what happened in the "action-packed finales" of 25 years' worth of cancelled soaps:

> [*The Doctors*, 1963–1982]: Felicia and Paul were unmasked as Billy's killers. Jeff and Adrienne tied the knot. Maggie agreed to marry Matt—again.
>
> [*Ryan's Hope*, 1975–1989]: Jack and Leigh tied the knot. Pat asked Faith if he was Grace's dad. Maeve sang "Danny's Boy" one more time.

On more rare occasions, the end of physical settings is documented, as in a feature announcing, "When these soaps were cancelled, these iconic locales perished with them" ("Gone but Not Forgotten," *Soap Opera Digest*, July 29, 2008, 83). Here, on-set photographs are accompanied by brief spatial 'memories' such as: "*Another World* fans remember well the lushly appointed Cory Mansion, the most stately estate in Bay City."

More meaningfully, as noted, magazines provide a space for mourning the end of soap worlds. Lead articles include commentary by executives, actors, and fans and feature titles such as "A Fond Farewell" (McClure 2009), "That's a Wrap" (McClure 2010a), and "Last Merry Go-Round" (McClure 2010b). Actor Robert Newman, who spent more than two decades playing Josh Lewis on *Guiding Light* (CBS) remarked on one of the last days of filming:

> Just the other day, I started feeling this sort of tug at my heart a little bit and getting scripts and thinking, "Oh well, that's the last of it." I think it's somewhere between 3,000 or 3,500 episodes [I've been in] over 24 years. To think I'm on the last five or six is pretty weird.
>
> (McClure 2009, 63)

The ending of *As the World Turns* (1956–2010) inspired an in-depth, four-part "behind the scenes" series in *Soap Opera Digest*[12] chronicling the

206 *C. Lee Harrington and Byron Miller*

show's final days: Part I examined the 1950s, Part II the 1960s, Part III the 1970s and 1980s, and Part IV its final years. The cancellation news was mourned by viewers—one wrote, "I'm so sad it's ending. It's been a constant in my life [...]. I'm losing my TV 'friends' of 18 years"—and signaled the death of the last U.S. soap opera still produced by a major soap company (Proctor & Gamble) (Kiesewetter 2010). While the four remaining soaps on the air are drawing a steady audience, the genre as a whole has witnessed the ending of numerous fictional landscapes.

Conclusion

Our chapter has focused on how fan magazines help viewers map the imaginary worlds of U.S. daytime soaps. Offering a unique media window (Wolf 2012, 2) into the fictional towns dotting the soap opera landscape, fan magazines aid viewers in inventing, living in, and ending soap worlds. As such, they also aid viewers in the ongoing cultural project of developing and embodying an "as if" (rather than "just so") perspective: the ability to "embrace complementarities, to be capable of living simultaneously in multiple worlds without experiencing cognitive dissonance" (Saler 2012, 13). While media fandom is often (still) dismissed as a deliberate and misguided suspension of rationality, it is instead a "willing activation of pretense" that facilitates a specific post/modern skill set: the ability to "question essentialist interpretations of the world" (Saler 2012, 28, 21).

We conclude with a consideration of the type of imaginary worlds that most soap operas represent and the changing role of soap magazines in fans' ability to access those worlds. Drawing on J. R. R. Tolkien's notion of primary versus secondary worlds (itself derived from Coleridge's ideas of primary versus secondary imagination; see note 7), Wolf (2012) notes that "secondariness is a matter of degree" (27) based on the extent of reliance the secondary (or imaginary) world has to the primary (or real) world. In contrast to many science fiction or fantasy-based landscapes, most imaginary worlds of U.S. daytime soap operas continue to evidence (as they did when radio soaps launched in the 1930s) a strong reliance on real life. With a few notable exceptions—such as NBC's *Passions* (which featured witches and a talking doll) and ABC's *Port Charles* (which evolved to focus on vampirism)—most U.S. soaps portray a parallel life to that of the viewers through mimicking the geographies and temporalities of everyday lived experience.

To a non-soap-viewer, this may seem an absurdist claim. U.S. soaps are well known (and widely mocked) for characters that experience multiple weddings, multiple episodes of amnesia, multiple relatives that return from the dead, and multiple run-ins with mob bosses, drug kingpins, evil overlords, and dirty politicians. But as Allen (1985) noted three decades ago, soaps aim for emotional rather than narrative realism. Viewer pleasure centers not on *what* happens on-screen (plot twists) but rather on how the characters and communities populating soap towns *react to* what happens. As such,

Mapping the Daytime Landscape   207

emotional authenticity trumps narrative realism. The imaginary soap towns created by writers and directors—and expanded in fan magazines—function to provide a (mostly) credible setting for soap stories to unfold. Hence, viewers' and journalists' nit-picking over details of weather, travel time, and set decoration is geared toward enhancing that credibility, and the most outlandish of soap plots (involving heaven, the Wild West, or aliens descended to earth) are either interpreted *within* the confines of the imaginary world (how long should it take a character to fly to a fictional Mediterranean island?) or "given a pass," so to speak. In short, the degree of imaginative and affective separation between U.S. soap worlds and the primary world is designed—deliberately, consciously, and creatively—to be narrow.

Earlier we spoke of the shrinking and ending of soap worlds. Not only are there fewer soap worlds for fans to visit and experience, but there are also fewer windows or portals into those worlds. As the genre has contracted over the past 15 years, so have the ancillary industries that support it—fan magazines, dedicated soap cable channels, fan conventions, and so on. In terms of print magazines, only three continue regular publishing (*Soap Opera Digest*, *ABC Soaps In Depth*, and *CBS Soaps In Depth*), while others have succumbed to the same fate (cancellation) as many of the shows they followed, including *Soap Opera Update* (1988–2002), *Soap Opera News* (1997–1999), *NBC Soaps In Depth* (1997–1999), and *Soap Opera Weekly* (1989–2012). But as old portals close, new ones open. As fandom as a whole has migrated online, so have the location of numerous new windows, including online sites launched by print sources and fans' creative re-visioning of soap landscapes through blogs, vlogs, and fanfic. U.S. soap worlds are alive and well. We may just need to be savvier travelers to find and visit them.

Notes

1. See one fan's recent attempt to map Westeros (posted and retrieved May 8, 2015): http://www.slate.com/blogs/browbeat/2015/05/08/westeros_in_google_maps_what_the_game_of_thrones_continent_would_look_like.html.
2. Fans might be in luck here: a group of British architects is raising funds to build a full-scale replica of Minas Tirith, one of *Lord*'s famed cities, to be located in southern England and function as a fully livable city (*Time*, August 31, 2015, 10).
3. Saler defines contemporary virtual worlds as "acknowledged imaginary spaces that are communally inhabited for prolonged periods of time by rational individuals" (2012, 6).
4. The bible was posted on the blog "We Love Soaps" in March 2010: http://www.welovesoaps.net/2010/03/original-bible-as-earth-turns-part-1.html.
5. We thank Melissa Scardaville for access to her collection of 511 issues of *Soap Opera Digest* and 441 issues of *Soap Opera Weekly*. The authors met to review a small subset of magazines and discuss a coding scheme. They then divided the larger collection between them and examined each magazine to identify specific instances of world-building. After evaluating all magazines, the authors met to

208   *C. Lee Harrington and Byron Miller*

clarify common themes; those themes are discussed in the remainder of this chapter.

6. Settings can change over time. When *Guiding Light* (CBS) debuted as a radio serial in 1937, it was set in a Chicago suburb named Five Points. A decade later, the show was briefly set in Chicago itself; shifted to Selby Flats, California, in 1949; and settled on its current location in Springfield in 1968 (*Soap Opera Digest*, February 3, 2004, 72).
7. Primary imagination occurs unconsciously, "as we conceptualize the world around us and our place in it," but secondary imagination is "conscious and deliberate, not done merely out of habit or necessity but as a creative act" (Wolf 2012, 22).
8. Blocking is an instrumental part of rehearsals involving precise positioning and movement of actors, lights, cameras, and props.
9. Attempted crossovers that fail are often about legal ownership of characters and production companies' unwillingness to "play nice" (Kelley 1999, 45).
10. In contrast to *General Hospital: Night Shift*, the short-lived spin-off *Port Charles* (ABC) was set in the same town as *General Hospital* but featured characters no longer appearing on *Hospital*.
11. See Harrington (2015).
12. The series appeared in the following issues: August 24, 2010; August 31, 2010; September 14, 2010; September 21, 2010.

References

Allen, Robert C. 1985. *Speaking of Soap Operas*. Chapel Hill and London: The University of North Carolina Press.

Churchill, Douglas W. 1937. "Hollywood Witnesses a Skirmish of Giants." *New York Times*, February 14, 165.

Flores, Elaine G. 2000. "It's about Time." *Soap Opera Digest*, December 19, 74–76.

Flynn, Lauren, and Devin Owens. 2008. "Fake Locale vs. Real Locale." *Soap Opera Digest*, May 27, 80.

Gonzales, Racquel. 2010. "From Daytime to Night Shift: Examining the ABC Daytime/SOAPnet Primetime Spin-off Experiment." In *The Survival of Soap Opera: Transformations for a New Media Era*, edited by Sam Ford, Abigail de Kosnik, and C. Lee Harrington, 191–200. Jackson: University Press of Mississippi.

Harrington, C. Lee. 2012. "The Ars Moriendi of US Serial Television: Towards a Good Textual Death." *International Journal of Cultural Studies* 16 (6): 579–595.

———. 2015. "Time, Memory and Aging on the Soaps." In *Ageing and Old Age in TV Series*, edited by Anita Wohlman and Maricel Oro-Piqueras, 25–48. Bielefeld, Germany: Transcript.

Harrington, C. Lee, and Denise D. Bielby. 1995. *Soap Fans: Pursuing Pleasure and Making Meaning in Everyday Life*. Pittsburgh, PA: Temple University Press.

Kelley, Adam. 1999. "The Out-of-Towners." *Soap Opera Digest*, July 27, 44–46.

Kiesewetter, John. 2010. "'As the World Turns' Ends Run Friday." *Cincinnati Enquirer*. http://www.cities-times.com.

Lowood, Henry. 2009. "Memento Mundi: Are Virtual Worlds History?" iPRES2009—The Sixth International Conference on Preservation of Digital Objects, California Digital Library, UC Office of the President. http://www.escholarship.org/UC/item/2gs3p6jx.

McClure, Danielle. 2009. "A Fond Farewell." *Soap Opera Digest*, September 22, 62–66.

———. 2010a. "That's a Wrap." *Soap Opera Digest*, September 21, 76–79.

———. 2010b. "Last Merry-Go-Round." *Soap Opera Digest*, September 21, 45–47.

McMillan, Graeme. 2014. "New 'Star Wars' Expanded Universe Plans Greeted with Resignation, Nostalgia." *Hollywood Reporter*. http://www.hollywoodreporter.com/heat-vision/new-star-wars-expanded-universe-699082.

Porter, Dennis. 1977. "Soap Time: Thoughts on a Commodity Art Form." *College English* 38 (8): 782–788.

Saler, Michael. 2012. *As If: Modern Enchantment and the Literary Prehistory of Virtual Reality*. New York: Oxford University Press.

Wilson, Mary Jeanne. 2010. "Preserving Soap History: What Will It Mean for the Future of Soaps?" In *The Survival of Soap Opera: Transformations for a New Media Era*, edited by Sam Ford, Abigail de Kosnik, and C. Lee Harrington, 140–153. Jackson: University Press of Mississippi.

Wolf, Mark J. P. 2012. *Building Imaginary Worlds: The Theory and History of Subcreation*. New York: Routledge/Taylor & Francis.

Part V

Material Culture and the Creative Self

16 In Reverse

Declining Automobility and the Accidents of Progress

Marcin Mazurek

> The history of the automobile can ultimately be read as a morality play about the withering of a historical project.
>
> —Wolfgang Sachs (1992)

The Car Is Dying

Few objects of everyday use embody social ideals and concerns to such a degree as the motor car. From a status symbol of consumerist prosperity to a sinister harbinger of environmental doom to an icon of national identity, the car has remodeled our social reality. In the process, it has given rise to a multitude of cultures and subcultures, which today do more than just gather their often involuntary or unaware participants: they are ideological battlefields where both social and technological paradigms, not always immediately identified as related to the automotive milieu, are confronted and contemplated.

This chapter concentrates on the cultural appropriation of three recent features of social life reflected in the cultures of automobility that have redefined our understanding of the motor vehicle. These features include increased proenvironmental awareness, greater need for personal safety, and the growing intrusion of digital technologies. Their combined influence has resulted in an almost apocalyptic withering of the traditional location of the motor car, which, as this chapter will argue, is turning into a mobile laboratory whose functions and dysfunctions are more likely to be addressed with the use of a computer rather than a screwdriver or a wrench. And even though throughout their history cars have always strived to be safer and more comfortable, never before has this process taken place at such an expanse of the only factor capable of utilizing their true potential: the driver.

The car is on the wane and so are its traditional meanings. Drawing on a number of contemporary cultural theorists, the chapter analyzes two contrasting approaches to present-day automobility. The first one revolves around various forms of digitalization, which has turned driving from a mechanical to a more computer-oriented experience, changing forever the position of the driving subject. The second approach, represented, among others, by Paul Virilio's accident theory, points to the futility of our obsession

214   *Marcin Mazurek*

with safe, comfortable, and proenvironmental automobility. Here, driving culture is located in the broader narrative of progress, whose secret history, as Virilio has it, is permeated by the shadow of the universal catastrophe, to which the car is by no means immune.

Thus, out of the background of the dichotomy between the convenient and the catastrophic, there emerges a changing perception of the car's social meaning. By appeasing its catastrophic potential through safety options and electronic convenience, the car evolves as an object of everyday life following the line of social promotion. From being perceived in terms of what Mark Hansen refers to as a "machine reduction of technology," which basically treats it as a mere tool of daily convenience (2003, 8), it is elevated into what Jean Baudrillard appoints as "a partner in a general negotiation of life-styles" (1988, 13).

The car, therefore, seems to be dying in two ways. Firstly, it withers as a tool subjected to the physical competence of its human master, who thus far has determined its functioning. Secondly, it is the very experience of driving that wanes, as it is now controlled by invasive electronics, lifestyle obsessions, and environmental requirements. In effect, this brings about first the death and then a sinister resurrection of the driving subject, who experiences a deposition from a master to a partner and, then, more and more often, to a slave.

Autonomy in Decline

In a contemporary car the driver is no longer left to contemplate his or her relationship with the car (and the road) in solitude. Instead, he or she is accompanied by a number of electronic assistants keeping the automobile within prescribed lanes, maintaining a safe distance from the vehicle in front, switching lights and wipers on when the right time comes, and making sure that when the parking maneuver turns out to be problematic, the car will happily park itself in a spot that it will first find. On top of that, there is an impressive number of satellite navigation systems, on-board cameras, and tens of sensors monitoring almost everything—from the car's interior temperature to unfastened seatbelts to tire pressure—and always prepared to signal a warning reminder. The pretenses of safety and convenience seem to have turned the modern car into a mechanical-electronic Big Brother, slowly but gradually depriving the driver of almost any sense of predigital autonomy. Once the master of the machine, the driver is now a mere component of its complex self-monitoring systems.

In other words, we are witnessing an evolutionary change in the position of the driving subject resulting from a new technological paradigm informed by the ideals of safety and convenience. And regardless of whether the change in question is inspired by redefined concepts of contemporary masculinity or demands for higher technical efficiency, one thing seems certain: Western culture's traditional relation with the car and, by extension,

In Reverse 215

with the whole culture of automobility is gone. Instead, it has been replaced by a new collection of sociotechnological ideals that, as Jean Baudrillard observes, produce "a transformation of the subject [...] into a driving computer, instead of the demiurge drunk with power," while "the vehicle [...] becomes a bubble, the dashboard a console, and the landscape all around unfolds as a television screen" (Baudrillard 1988, 13).

This metamorphosis seems to bear two major consequences. The first one is obvious: contemporary automobiles are much safer, more comfortable, and environmentally friendly than their pre-electronic predecessors. Always ready to make the journey more relaxing and less harmful to the environment, the modern car is oozing with relevant devices, from particulate filters to sophisticated air-conditioning systems or such inventions as Citroen's recent introduction of perfume diffusers in selected versions of its cars. In terms of safety, electronic interference is even more widespread: antilock brake systems, tens of air bags, or advanced traction-control devices are likely to appease even a novice driver in arduous conditions. But of much greater importance for our considerations is the second of the aforementioned consequences: the degrading autonomy of the human subject behind the wheel.

In the context of contemporary cultural debates revolving around the relationship between the human and the technological, the question of human dethronement is by no means a novelty. From Bruce Mazlish's theory of "the fourth discontinuity" (1993) to Scott Bukatman's concept of "terminal identity" (1993) to various critical appropriations of technological singularity (e.g., Kurzweil 2005), the contemporary critical landscape is full of voices announcing the end of the independent subject. Most of these voices, however, seem to locate human declining autonomy along the lines of the ever more ubiquitous computer technologies, and very few associate the phenomenon with the supposedly banal activity of driving. Thus, in order to better illustrate the link between declining autonomy and automobility, a broader philosophical reflection appears necessary.

This is because the dethroning tone reverberating across a number of contemporary discourses in fact signifies a broader cultural operation at work: a serious reappropriation, if not a straightforward crisis, of one of the most significant Western notions—namely, that of progress. Rooted in Cartesian philosophy, the notion of progress has always exceeded that of simple development. Progress—understood as the ultimate telos of the whole series of Western sociocultural, economic, and scientific phenomena—has traditionally been defined against culture's other—namely, nature. And even though Descartes himself advocated a meticulous study of natural laws as the main way to fully understand the universe and its mechanics, every now and then the real purpose behind this study was revealed:

> For these notions have made me see that it is possible to attain knowledge which is very useful in life, and that [...] it can be turned into a practice by which, knowing the power and action of fire, water, air,

216   *Marcin Mazurek*

> stars, the heavens, and all the other bodies that are around us [...], we
> could put them to all the uses for which they are suited and thus make
> ourselves as it were the masters and possessors of nature.
>
> (Descartes 2006, 51)

The rhetoric of mastery and possession is far from being coincidental. The ultimate goal behind scrutinizing nature's laws appears to be a two-stage operation, necessarily simplified here: the first stage assumes gathering a substantial amount of knowledge on nature's workings only to be subsequently used—and this is stage two—in order to minimize that very nature's restricting influence. To put things crudely, Descartes seems to have a cunning plan to first learn about nature's secrets only to use them against all possible natural inconveniences, in what is inevitably a gesture of separation from the constrains of the organic and the biological.

Much as it is not the purpose of this chapter to even briefly analyze the history of Western conceptualization of nature and/or culture, suffice it to mention that the nature–culture binarity has not only become the key framework for a number of ensuing discourses (psychoanalysis or feminism, to mention just two) but also a peculiar sort of philosophical battlefield in which the power of progress—seen here as the messenger of *culture*—was measured against the level of human liberation from the limits of biological and organic determinism stemming from *nature*. To put things simply, the greater the victory over nature is, the bigger is the step of progress toward a higher level of culture, with technology serving here as a primary tool of nature's defeat. Culture's triumph in the battle of domination is thus executed through its technological potential. In the context of car culture, this particular observation is especially topical: Audi, one of the world's leading car manufacturers, has traditionally advertised its automobiles with a motto reading, "Vorsprung durch Technik" ("Advantage through Technology"). And even though the advantage in question, especially when spotted on a commercial billboard, is primarily associated with free market competition and Audi's technological superiority over other car producers, one may read the slogan in a broader cultural context, in which the advantage is not only over Opels or Fiats, but also over the very concept of nature itself.

The cultural outcome of this peculiar victory is in fact a paradoxical one as, in the long run, it narrates another step in removing natural/bodily participation from the picture of automobility. With the sense of disorientation corrected by satellite navigation, fatigue handled by lane assistants, and poorer eyesight improved by bi-xenon lights, the driver's bodily engagement with the machine becomes gradually obsolete, as he or she is now preoccupied with absorbing data rather than struggling with physical difficulties of car travel. Baudrillard's aforementioned observation of "a transformation of the subject [...] into a driving computer" is in fact a testimony of the subject's withering autonomy, which has been substituted by its unavoidable participation in the constant process of information exchange with the motor vehicle. Taking the line of degrading human self-sufficiency to a hypothetical extreme, already as early as 1988 Baudrillard envisaged the future of the car, which, prophetically, seems to have become our present reality:

> However, one can conceive of a subsequent stage to this one, where the car is still a performative instrument, the stage at which it becomes an informing network. That is the car which speaks to you, which informs you spontaneously of its general state and yours (eventually refusing to function if you are not functioning well), the advising, the deliberating car, a partner in a general negotiation of life-styles; something (or some*one*, since at this stage there is no more difference) to which you are *wired*, the communication with the car becoming the fundamental stake, a perpetual test of the presence of the subject *vis-à-vis* his objects—an uninterrupted interface. (Baudrillard 1988, 13–14, italics in original)

In other words, the fate of the car is sealed by highlighting its transformation into the next stage of cultural development, where the car offers a practical exercise in what Baudrillard sees as the key activity of the late capitalist/postmodern society: simulation. Deprived of its mechanical materiality and stronger bodily engagement typical of the pre-electronic era, the automobile becomes indeed a perfect "bubble"—a self-sufficient capsule effectively separating the subject from the outside world, framed by biological constraints—a capsule that reduces the subject to a "terminal of multiple networks" (Baudrillard 1988, 15, 16) whose primary function is to process an endless flow of information and adjust behavioral reactions accordingly. It is not the outside world that dictates "the logic of driving" (Baudrillard 1988, 12), but rather the signs and symptoms of that world filtered through and interpreted by sophisticated on-board equipment whose signals, warnings, and orders produce desired reactions.

The declining sense of human autonomy over the mechanical milieu seems thus to be reaching a concluding moment. The perpetual control of the driver's behavior combined with the car's self-diagnostic capabilities clearly relocates the predigital position of the moving subject, placing it now among other components of its cyber-mechanical structure. Paradoxically, the death of the car announced at the beginning of this chapter seems to be caused by the fact that—through its technological complexity and the modes of communicating—the modern car is strangely alive, slowly but gradually promoting itself from the mere means of transportation to the partner of the traveling experience, in equal measures capable of making it safer or more enjoyable or of interrupting it for reasons known only to itself. The declining autonomy of the driver seems thus to go along with the growing autonomy of the car.

218 *Marcin Mazurek*

Are we dealing, then, with the death of the car or with its electronically mediated resurrection? If we opted for the first choice, an obvious comment seems necessary: it is the death of the car as we know it, or at least have known it, since the beginning of the industrial era. This is because the death of the car is, at the end of the day, the death of traditional human relationship with it, accompanied by withering of the emotional investment that once characterized the automobile. As Baudrillard aptly summarizes this transformation: "[n]o more power, speed, appropriation phantasies linked to the object itself, but a potential tactic linked to its use—mastery, control and command, optimization of the game of possibilities, which the automobile offers as a vector, and no longer as a psychological sanctuary [...]" (1988, 12–13).

Accidents by Progress

Baudrillard is by no means the only postmodern theorist preoccupied with the changing role of the car and the transformation of the driving subject. Paul Virilio seems to echo these views, noticing that "'[d]riving by instinct' has given way to 'driving by instruments' and then to 'automatic driving' anticipating what will probably be the full automation of automobility [...]" (2007a, 112). His views on cultural operations through which the subject is first denaturalized and then—by way of evolution "[f]rom travel to transfer, from transportation to transmission" (2007a, 158)—relocated into the realm of simulation culture (of which the driving process becomes the ultimate symbol), coincide with Baudrillard's conviction of the bodiless disposition of automobility today.

But where Baudrillard and Virilio differ is in the account of the dark side of the metamorphosis "[f]rom travel to transfer." For Baudrillard, the ultimate separation of the subject "at an infinite distance from his original universe [...] in the same position as the astronaut in his bubble" (Baudrillard 1988, 15), is in fact only the beginning of a completely new level of the subject's development, the level of simulation and hyper-reality in which the subject's body must be abandoned in favor of the mind's enhanced potential to acquire, interpret, and process an infinite stream of data. Paul Virilio, on the other hand, although very often formulating his views in accordance with Baudrillard's ideas of hyper-real simulation, identifies a rather different consequence of the progress symbolized by automobility. Not so much preoccupied with the future of the "logic of driving," Virilio points to a disturbing possibility not that often contemplated in the discourse of automobility-related progress: the possibility of an accident.

In fact, for Virilio, there is no such thing as the *possibility* of an unfortunate collision or other automotive disaster. On the contrary, the accident is an inevitable consequence of progress, a vital component of each new technology, particularly when transportation machines come into play.

In Reverse 219

For Virilio, derailment is an inseparable element of the invention of railway, just as the car crash constitutes a morbid shadow of car travel:

> Just as the catastrophe of the shipwreck was introduced by navigation, where the vessel disappears in its element, so also has accelerated traffic triggered and developed a new catastrophe, the collision: that is, the disappearance of one vehicle into another [...] (2007a, 113). The shipwreck is consequently the "futurist" invention of the ship, and the air crash the invention of the supersonic airliner, just as the Chernobyl meltdown is the invention of the nuclear power station. (2007b, 5)

Controversial and even cynical as such views may appear, they nevertheless seem to bear at least two major consequences. The first one is rather commonsensical—if accidents are and have always been inseparable from human involvement with technology, then instead of fearing them we should rather expect their sinister presence in our lives, seeing them not as coincidental exceptions or fatal aberrations in the history of Western development, but rather as almost ordinary and predictable components of everyday life. No longer a matter of divine punishment, technical imperfection, ill design, or unlikely anomaly, the accident constitutes a regular and common event, gloriously indifferent toward our sense of shock, denial, or fear. To put things crudely, the accident, as an indivisible part of any industrial technology, is the price that Western society pays for its sociotechnological development, according to the rule of "[...] the more powerful and high-performance the invention, the more dramatic the accident" (Virilio 2007b, 31).

To make matters worse, or perhaps just more realistic, if we follow Virilio's logic, things are unlikely to be improved in the future. Against all the institutionalized and private efforts and actions of what is often referred to as "risk society," whose main preoccupation is the management and prevention of possible dangers and hazards brought about by industrial development, there is little hope that the accident will ever be eliminated. True, the basic premises of risk society are mainly concerned with "global dangers like those that arise for all of humanity from nuclear fission or the storage of radioactive waste" (Beck 1992, 21), but, as Ulrich Beck, one of the leading theorists of risk society, maintains:

> Questions of the development and employment of technologies (in the realms of nature, society and the personality) are being eclipsed by questions of the political and economic "management" of the risks of actually or potentially utilized technologies—discovering, administering, acknowledging, avoiding or concealing such hazards with respect to specially defined horizons of relevance. (1992, 19)

Virilio's account of the inevitability of the accident seems thus to stand in serious opposition to the premises of risk culture. Naturally, there is

220   Marcin Mazurek

no denial that the process of "discovering, administering, acknowledging, avoiding or concealing" risks (and hence potential accidents) has become one of the dominating practices in contemporary Western life, and the desperate attempts to minimize their effects strongly influence almost all spheres of social existence and even, as Beck maintains, introduce new types of social stratification. But if we adopt Virilio's standpoint, all these efforts—though probably reducing the number of impending disasters—are in the final analysis futile, precisely because of the speed at which new technologies emerge and outline their own accident options, against which the risk/accident management strategies often seem ineffective or simply delayed. As Virilio stubbornly reminds us, offering a car-related example:

> If we take the realm of private car ownership, for example, the way the carnage on the highways has become commonplace is Freudian proof that the accumulation of traffic accidents largely puts an end to "chance"—and the multiple security systems our vehicles are equipped with don't alter this fact one iota: in the course of the twentieth century, the accident became a heavy industry (2007b, 12).

Virilio's "accident rule" thus assumes a slightly apocalyptic tone—in fact, questioning the implicit assumption that the ultimate goal of progress is a worry-free life. Since each new technology—still understood as the instrument of progress—brings about a new set of potential calamities, then what we are likely to encounter in the future is not only an impressive collection of improvements, but also an equally impressive collection of disasters and catastrophes. In terms of car culture Virilio himself is in no doubt that "[t]o invent the family automobile is to produce the pile-up on the highway" (2007b, 10).

Putting obvious benefits of technological development aside, progress is then something that is in almost equal measures to be anticipated as well as feared. In fact—and this is the second of the aforementioned consequences of our technological dependence—to think of progress in historical terms is to unveil the secret history of the accident. In other words, the accident is, by definition, inscribed in the history of technology, constituting its silent but irreducible core. Hence, to think of the future of progress is to prepare not so much for technological wonders but rather for as yet unspecified tragedies. For Virilio, the history of progress is a history of technological misfortunes that the Western culture still tends to see in terms of unlucky anomalies—unfortunate *incidents* rather than inevitable *accidents*—and today this bitter conclusion is more visible than ever before: "Indeed, after the twentieth century and the sudden *capitalization of tragedies and catastrophes of all kinds*, we really should draw up the bankruptcy report on a technoscientific Progress that the nineteenth-century positivists were so proud of" (2007b, 12, italics in original).

In Reverse 221

The reason behind "the bankruptcy report on [...] Progress" is not only related to the number of casualties of industry-related accidents, although even with reference to car crashes only, the numbers are staggering: it is estimated that in the course of the twentieth century about 60 million people were killed and that, each year, about 1.2 million die and well over 20 million are injured in car-related accidents worldwide (Featherstone 2005, 3). If one dared to carry these morbid statistics further, one would notice that the daily death toll of car crashes significantly exceeds 3,000 people—more than the total number of victims of all of the 9/11 attacks.

But Virilio locates his skepticism toward progress elsewhere. For him, the proliferation of technologies resulting in the proliferation of accidents is likely to produce what he refers to as the *integral* accident—the global accident consisting of numerous local accidents whose integrated consequences are going to be truly apocalyptic:

> Once upon a time the local accident was still precisely situated in the North Atlantic or the *Titanic*. But the global accident no longer is and its fallout now extends to whole continents, anticipating the integral accident that is in danger of becoming, tomorrow or the day after, our sole habitat, the havoc wreaked by Progress then extending [...] to the whole of geophysical space [...]. (2007b, 11)

Paradoxically, in a rather Freudian manner, Virilio identifies a sense of sinister expectation of "the havoc wreaked by Progress," as if the ultimate telos of progress were supposed to materialize itself in definitive destruction rather than in the successful fulfillment of the Enlightenment Project. He illustrates this collectively unconscious anticipation through, among other things, the popularity of horror and catastrophic movies produced by the "Hollywood dream machine" (Virilio 2007b, 38). But his real appeal is the necessity to redefine the very notion of progress in a way that would reveal its true character—chaotic, profit driven, accident prone, and potentially deadly on a global scale. This new notion of progress should essentially be based on a reformulated approach toward the accident—no longer treated as a waste product or side-effect of progress but rather as its strategic component, in the long run forcing Western society to ask the questions of scope, character, and limits of progress itself: "[f]ar from urging some 'millenarian catastrophism,'" says Virilio, "there is no question here of making *a tragedy* out of an accident with the aim of scaring the hordes as the mass media so often do but only of finally taking accidents *seriously*" (2007b, 11–12, italics in original).

How should we then start "taking accidents seriously" and begin our conceptual rearrangement of the accident as the foreseeable component of progress? Virilio offers a rather surprising solution advocating the founding of the museum of accidents. Its purpose, of course, would not be to promote accidents as mere objects of gloomy fascination or twisted curiosities of

222   Marcin Mazurek

technology's dark side, but instead to radically increase the level of public awareness of the potential threats interwoven into the very fabric of technological development and hence help prevent a much bigger disaster:

> In order to avoid shortly inhabiting the planetary dimension of an integral accident, one capable of integrating a whole heap of incidents and disasters through chain reactions, we must start right now building, inhabiting and thinking through the laboratory of cataclysm, the museum of the accident of technical progress. (2007b, 24)

The museum of accidents serves thus as the first step toward a radical redefinition of progress. Its main purpose would be to heighten public knowledge not so much of the possibility of the accident but rather of its inescapable inevitability. Once this catastrophic potential becomes commonly accepted, the very idea of progress has to be given a critical reexamination in the course of which its deadly disposition is first revealed and then possibly handled or controlled. This is because, if we remain as helpless when confronted with the forces of progress as we have been so far, the multiplication of ensuing technologies and the resulting accidents are likely to cause the integral accident whose consequences might be really devastating and thus should be avoided at all cost.

Conclusion: Domesticating the Threat

Virilio's essentially pessimistic account of the very concept of progress manifested through disasters rather than achievements seems to provoke at least two major doubts. If progress, whose path is marked by technological calamities, is likely to culminate in some sort of an apocalyptic event, how are we supposed to react to it, now that we have been made aware of its potentially deadly telos? Are we supposed to abandon the idea and stop thinking or dreaming of a better future achievable through technology? Or shall we perhaps redefine our approach to technological development by withdrawing from potentially risky projects? Virilio does not seem to answer any of these questions, perhaps sensing that any effort to reduce the speed of social or technological advance would at best be classified as utopian if not merely absurd.

The second doubt, however, concerns the presence of the accident in the Western culture, which is by no means a novelty: accidents, even those of the modern type, have accompanied Western social life at least since the beginning of the Industrial Revolution. Thus, if we look at Virilio's idea from a broader historical perspective, his postulate of the Accident Museum is perhaps unnecessary, if not futile. After all, the museum's mission to develop a more skeptical attitude toward the very concept of progress would imply that, by and large, the members of Western society still approach progress with enthusiasm rather than criticism and remain forever blinded by the glorious prospect of trouble-free existence achieved through the uninterrupted production of new technological innovations—of which the contemporary automobile is perhaps the best example, a living proof of advantage over the forces of nature gained through technology. But Western society no longer seems to be that naïve: our fascination with disasters and catastrophes is caused not only by a sense of mere awe but also, if not in the first place, by a deeper critical reflection, a sort of collective existential curiosity about what the end—of our lives and of our cars—might look like.

The accident does not need a museum to be doubly present in our culture. Apart from real-life catastrophes, the accident is perhaps the single most popular event—constantly narrated, represented, and relived in media culture, suffice it to mention any news program, most of which usually begin with some sort of an accident report and many of which include automobile accidents. As J. G. Ballard grimly noted, "The car crash is probably the most dramatic, perhaps the only dramatic, event in most people's lives apart from their own death, and in many cases the two will coincide" (2012, 30). If to those observations we add the unstoppable popularity of the "Hollywood dream machine," constantly producing horror and science-fiction movies that not only depict spectacular cataclysms—whether they be man-made environmental disasters, multiple car crashes, or hordes of men-eating zombies—but also teach us how to survive them, the picture will be almost complete.

This is because the accident has always been a significant part of Western history. After a century of two world wars, countless local conflicts, a number totalitarian regimes and global-scale terrorist attacks—all possibly interpreted as accidents in the history of technology—it seems barely possible that its fateful shadow will ever be forgotten or ignored by even the highest hopes of modernity. Nor does it seem even remotely likely that these hopes—today materialized by the tens of electronic components installed in our cars, all preoccupied with our safety, comfort, or environmental friendliness—will ever be fully capable of protecting us from the more sinister threats produced by our own culture—threats that we almost literarily invite every time we start the engines of our cars.

References

Ballard, J. G. 2012. "1970: Lynn Barber. Sci-fi Seer." An interview with Lynn Barber. In *Extreme Metaphors. Interviews with J. G. Ballard 1967–2008*, edited by Simon Sellars and Dan O'Hara, 22–35. London: Fourth Estate.

Baudrillard, Jean. 1988. *The Ecstasy of Communication*. New York: Semiotext(e).

Beck, Ulrich. 1992. *Risk Society. Towards a New Modernity*. London: Sage.

Bukatman, Scott. 1993. *Terminal Identity. The Virtual Subject in Post-Modern Science Fiction*. Durham, NC: Duke University Press.

Descartes, Rene. 2006. *A Discourse on the Method of Correctly Conducting One's Reason and Seeking Truth in the Sciences*. Oxford: Oxford University Press.

Featherstone, Mike. 2005. "Automobilities. An Introduction." In *Automobilities*, edited by Mike Featherstone, Nigel Thrift, and John Urry, 1–24. London: Sage.

224 *Marcin Mazurek*

Hansen, Mark. 2003. *Embodying Technesis. Technology beyond Writing*. Ann Arbor: University of Michigan Press.

Kurzweil, Ray. 2005. *The Singularity Is Near: When Humans Transcend Biology*. New York: Viking.

Mazlish, Bruce. 1993. *The Fourth Discontinuity: The Co-Evolution of Humans and Machines*. New Haven, CT: Yale University Press.

Sachs, Wolfgang. 1992. *For the Love of the Automobile: Looking Back into the History of Our Desires*. Oakland: University of California Press.

Virilio, Paul. 2007a. *Negative Horizon*. London: Continuum.

———. 2007b. *The Original Accident*. Cambridge, England: Polity Press.

17 Living Dolls—A Food Studies Perspective

Nina Augustynowicz

Living dolls can be provisionally defined as women who undergo multiple body modifications with the intention to liken themselves to Barbies. These idealized and idolized dolls inspire appearance adjustments and changes that range from the relatively harmless practice of wearing abnormally colored contact lenses to the extremes of major surgical intervention such as breast augmentation, rhinoplasty, and ribs removal. Among chief physical characteristics of living dolls are the following: slim bodies with unnaturally enlarged breasts, narrow waists and fuller hips, toned legs, perfectly smooth skin, immaculate complexion, long shiny hair, and enormous glassy eyes. Valeria Lukyanova is an embodiment of this trend, which has earned her wide recognition. Her metamorphoses are made public thanks to social networking and services allowing self-publishing and self-promotion, resulting in "morbid fascination" (Rhodan 2014) and a "virtual firestorm" (Sandberg 2013) among her audiences.

This chapter attempts to put forward a cursory analysis of the living doll Valeria Lukyanova within the methodological framework of food studies. While cultural research usually approaches this phenomenon with the tools of body studies, applying the food studies perspective allows us to focus on aspects other than the doll's extraordinary looks. Taking the human Barbie's dietary patterns as the main clue, the chapter reaches beyond the consideration of body modifications. By broadening the theoretical perspective, it rehearses continuity between two seemingly unrelated phenomena: a contemporary woman posing as the iconic fashion toy and the nineteenth century fasting girl. The analysis of attitudes toward food and consumption reveals that the practices of living dolls share similar cultural energy with Victorian female fast practitioners. Assuming the food studies perspective shows that Lukyanova, with her background in the human Barbie phenomenon, inscribes herself in the same cultural pattern of self-denial eventually stemming from the mind versus the body opposition.

Living Dolls and Food Studies

By locating Valeria Lukyanova within the multidimensional paradigm of eating disorders, food studies[1] offer a critically fruitful disciplinary perspective

226 *Nina Augustynowicz*

on her living doll practices. Since it deals with the cultural practice of consumption, food studies can be considered a subfield of cultural studies distinguished owing to its object of interest (Ashley et al. 2004, 1–26). It is also closely bound with body studies, and that is why the latter's leading scholar, Susan Bordo (2003), can be taken as a representative of both, with her work on the axes of influence in anorexia nervosa from the beginning included in food studies publications. The compromising position is to link these disciplines on the visceral level on which the pathologies that affect the very materiality of the human Barbie's body, such as life-threatening emaciation, are functionally brought about by food disturbances. The food studies perspective takes into consideration not only the Ukrainian doll's alterations to appearance and anatomy, however invasive and dazzling they might be; it makes it possible to account also for her dietary aberrations. As it is her eating habits that allow Lukyanova to achieve the desired waist size, the analysis of her dieting practices should take precedence over the study of their end result: the shape of her body. In other words, with the methodological framework of food studies, examination of living doll practices operates on a level deeper than with other theoretical approaches. What is more, taking the food studies perspective allows us to focus on the roots of self-denial and serves as a lens in dealing with the many-sided phenomenon of the human Barbie.[2]

In her existence as a living doll, Lukyanova draws from the available cultural repository of female self-denial, probably without being directly acquainted with her Victorian ancestors. Fasting girls of the nineteenth century were women who claimed to be engaged in long-term abstinence from solid food.[3] They can be perceived as some sort of early celebrities who appeared on both sides of the Atlantic, were popularized in the press, and had people visiting them as attractions, which allowed them to capitalize on their performance: for instance, they gladly accepted small gifts and other offerings from those impressed with their apparent abilities and agreed to have their resemblances made for a fee. Although they were usually bed ridden or invalided to some degree, there is already a considerable overlap between these characteristics and the Ukrainian Barbie's behavior. The similarity is taken further when we look at a representative of these Victorians, Sarah Jacob. One of the visitors noted her unusual appearance:

> [T]he little girl was dressed up in the most imposing and fantastic way possible. Her hair, which is profuse, was brushed back Eugenie-style; she wore a necklace of large beads with cross attached. She also had a white silk ribbon round her neck, fastened by a brooch (or "at least a tassel and a small narrow little victorine as well"); an embroidered white nightdress; a blue ribbon round right wrist, and a black-and white one round left; and her hands were enveloped in warm gloves.
>
> (Fowler 1871, 15)

Living Dolls—A Food Studies Perspective 227

Lukyanova, habitually dressed in revealing and eye-catching clothing, resembles Jacob even in her passion for flamboyance. Thus, eating habits remain the initial and primary concern in establishing the continuity between this modern-day doll and Victorian fasting girls. Nonetheless, other features that the human Barbie shares with them have become discernible thanks to seeing the fasting connection first. The fact that a phenomenon significantly resembling living doll practices was reported two hundred or so years back lets us see Lukyanova and her like in another light—as points on a continuum instead of exclusive events.

Lukyanova, as a living doll, taps into an existing cultural potential for exploiting and sensationalizing female food refusal. The Victorian period, when the fasting girls originate, is widely taken to be the time when anorexia nervosa and eating disorders emerged as concepts. Along with their birth, the notion of pathological bodily mimesis came into play. The idea that eating disorders can be infectious, so convincingly described by Athena Vrettos (1995), has since then transmuted into the modern phenomenon of so-called 'wannarexia.' Moreover, the virulent nature of these disturbances has transformed them into a virtual epidemic spread by media imagery promoting thinness. A much simpler access to channels of disseminating information stands behind this change. The easy availability of social media tools, of which Lukyanova often takes advantage when publishing photos of her emaciated body, allows her to gather popularity and viewership. Despite the fact that the Victorian fasting girls had a more limited range of means at their disposal, they similarly used what was available to them (e.g., press advertisements with their resemblances) to publicize their cause. Circulation of such images, be it in the nineteenth century or now, contributes to boosting the communicable nature of eating disturbances. Although separated from the nineteenth century girls by almost two hundred years, Lukyanova still generates similar dysfunctions. Nevertheless, we cannot immediately assume that all the traits ascribed to fasting girls have remained the same. The continuum has been affected by advancements with respect to gender relations, socioeconomic conditions, and access to technology. Claiming that twenty-first century living dolls are no novelty is not equal with stating that, due to their repetitive natures, they are not a topic worthy of consideration. Quite the opposite is true. Spotting the similarities draws the lines along which the nineteenth century notions of promoting female food abstinence have been developing up till the present day, influencing the shape of today's popular culture.

Living Dolls as Hyperbolic Images

Lukyanova's perfection is pathological because it is unnatural. This generates a contradiction in how she is approached by her audience. In theory, her looks correspond with the standards of feminine appearance, so she is appealing for many. The interest concerns both a desire to emulate, as noted

228   *Nina Augustynowicz*

before, and physical attraction. What she represents is not immediately perceived as pathological. The uncanny perfection she strives to achieve in appearance, however, often breeds hostility and even disgust. The discrepancy in the impressions Lukyanova creates shows that, in the case of living dolls, perfection and pathology are not opposite terms. Her features are simultaneously ideal and aberrant, which produces the confused reactions. Lukyanova's legs are way too long and her hourglass figure is overdone, as if she were laced in a corset; her skin is unblemished, porcelain, and plasticky, while her eyes have this eerily blank stare reminding us of the lifeless glass orbs set in a doll's face. She is simultaneously the perfect woman and an otherworldly, nonhuman freak.

Her creepily perfect shape seems to fit flawlessly in Susan Bordo's consideration of the potential dangers inherent in exaggerating existing cultural standards, by which we should understand the domestic, sexualized ideal of passive femininity with nineteenth century origins. In other words, Lukyanova's hyperbolic version of femininity can be a way of throwing the oppressive norm in the face of her audience. The overstated curves of her body and pretty face amplify the standards so much that they are rendered ineffective. Yet, paradoxically, this way of disabling the power of the dominant cultural imagery involves a risk of actually strengthening it by spreading images based on it. The circulation of photos and videos of the human Barbie contributes to both defusing the overdone norms and solidifying them by inviting imitation. This is what Lukyanova does herself in tutorials in which she actively encourages copying her. However, even though inflating features of femininity, such as as slimness and doll-like face, entails the subversive potential of exposing the beauty requirements as harmful, it is done at the expense of enfeebling the body. The price Lukyanova pays for holding a magnifying glass to the ideal of womanhood is emaciation and violence done to her own material existence.

The confused reactions of displeased audience are noted in the press coverage of the human Barbie. In fact, many of the stories reporting on Lukyanova and other living dolls appear to be bitter accounts of a wronged voyeur. An article in *GQ* magazine immediately calls Lukyanova and her way of practicing over-the-top femininity. Then it moves on to commenting on her from the perspective of a disgusted viewer whose male gaze unexpectedly becomes frustrated. The feeling results from not getting the visual satisfaction that was supposed to come from somebody dubbed a Barbie. The journalist writing the article openly admits that Lukyanova's "features are the features we men playfully ascribe to ideal women; it's how we draw them in manga and comics and video games" (Idov 2014). He is right, up to a point, for the word *playfully* hardly describes the realities of the female form with reduced mobility and minimal eating. As he goes on to say, "[e]xcept we don't expect them to comply with this oppressive fantasy so fully. As a result, she almost throws our idea of a supervixen back in our face" (Idov 2014). This sounds much like the laments of someone who does not like his

Living Dolls—A Food Studies Perspective 229

or her dominant rhetoric to be exposed. The journalist's indignation is thus a proof that Lukyanova's hyperbolic femininity is effective in emphasizing the standards of female appearance. However, at least in this case, the doll does not succeed in communicating that her strategy entails an attack on the materiality of her own body.

Revealing the workings of the male gaze is one thing, whereas openly confronting the mechanisms is quite another. The journalist states that the human Barbie's appearance and—in particular, short videos featuring her— are an experiment on the viewer, a sort of a stare-down contest. Does this mean the Ukrainian doll engages in feminist resistance strategies? Embodying what is wrong with the Western-born ideal of femininity, Lukyanova asserts: "[e]ven though people call me Barbie, I never tried to look like a doll. I just like everything beautiful, feminine and refined. It just so happens that dolls are based on the image of refined girls" (Idov 2014). Saying so, she implies that doll-like appearance is a natural consequence of following feminine perfection, covertly accusing the standard of being inherently harmful and unhuman. Moreover, she implicitly recognizes that her body has become a warning and a "graphic cultural text" (Hekman 1998, 63). As such, it functions as a site to play out cultural tensions surrounding the ideal of womanhood; in particular, it can operate as an open protest against female subjugation. Lukyanova's official website, *Humanbarbie.org*, defines her cause as helping women to "increas[e] confidence in their own voice and convictions, develop life-skills, and improv[e] the ability to identify paths and resources within their communities that can contribute to positive change and break cycles for a lifetime." Be it naïve, it seems that she is trying to put forward a comprehensive strategy in which her doll-like appearance is only one of the elements. Nevertheless, as it was succinctly summarized by Susan Hekman (1998) in reference to Butlerian theory of the body, a perspective that does not take into consideration the materiality of the body, its emaciation and painful distortions, "cannot fashion a feminist politics that can adequately deal with this reality" (69). Thus, Lukyanova's feminist resistance is bound to fail.

Abstinence and Social Role

Drawing on the work by anthropologist Mary Douglas (1966), food studies views nourishment as external influence on the body. A person may either accept or disavow the foods he or she consumes. These two basic reactions apply also to ideas absorbed together with the eating habits, which are determined by culture and society. In this framework, food refusal occurs when the intake of nourishment is treated as contamination and a source of possible degeneration. Food, along with the cultural constructions it carries, is not allowed to cross the body boundaries, which, in turn, delineate personhood. In the mode of thinking in which ingesting food denotes violation of boundaries, emptiness of the stomach is perceived as desirable purity.

230 *Nina Augustynowicz*

The access to the mouth, through which external influence can enter, is strictly guarded not to admit alien, unwanted norms and worldviews that could shape the body. When this becomes the dominating conceptualization, allowing food in comes to mean simply physically stuffing the body. Instead of genuinely feeding it by providing spiritual nutrition to the mind, it is a form of indiscriminately taking it into oneself. Consequently, food is viewed as an unneeded addition or a necessary evil at best, which brings no benefits and thus should be shunned. With these convictions, "food is transformed from physical sustenance into a vehicle of morality" (Counihan 1999, 99). Abstinence then follows as an act of defiance and a form of revolt against the ideological influence. Refusal results directly from a desire to turn the body into a vehicle of moral purity and a testimony to one's spiritual aspiration. If eating means succumbing to external pressures, then being empty expresses the ability to distance oneself from the surrounding influence. This is the ultimate goal of food abstinence.

The human Barbie, though it might not seem so at first owing to her showy looks, observes this logic. At some point, both Luyanova's attention and that of her audience started moving to diet: as she got thinner and was accused of anorexia,[4] she revealed she had begun a regimen of liquids only and commented on quantity restrictions that she was imposing on herself even with regard to nonsolid food. Furthermore, in the human Barbie's case, prolonged abstemious eating is coupled with extensive gym training. The overall impression of a very slender physique resulting from these two is enhanced by the striking difference between her tiny waistline and bigger than D-cup breast implants. All of these strategies serve to shape a body that attempts to deny coming in contact with nourishment. However, even such forms of achieving conceptual purity were apparently insufficient. Thus, Lukyanova currently builds her public image on the claim that she has now resorted to the practice of breatharianism (i.e., living off air, sun energy, cosmic micro-food, etc.), depending on the definition. Basically, however, she claims to be abstaining from food completely while still being able to function normally, which is in direct conflict with the laws of human biology, as proven by years of development in medical science. She explains her controversial decision to undergo prolonged fasting by saying that it leads to having more energy and to feeling more "pure emotions"—an emptiness-based narration she delivers with much conviction in the face of increased interest from the public.

Interestingly, the claims Lukyanova makes about her total abstemiousness are similar to those made by the Victorian fasting girls. These young women insisted that they possessed the ability of prolonged fasting and often maintained they did not accept any nutrition apart from some liquids or minute portions of fruit. What is more, they also posited that they were followers of breatharianism. In the nineteenth century the concept was even given a scientific explanation: there was a belief in a possibility to extract the substances necessary to survive directly from the air itself. This solution coexisted, however, with the indignation of the medical authority at the

Living Dolls—A Food Studies Perspective 231

fasting girls. In the doctors' opinion, their abstinence was meant to mock the regard for the basic principles of the newly born nutritional science. Nevertheless, nutritional science developed amid conflicts as to almost every aspect of dietary regulations—how much protein a human body requires; whether animal protein is vital; the recommended frequency of bowel movements; whether fiber is necessary and, if yes, in what quantities; whether autointoxication can occur—that shook the field all century long. Curiously, these and other similar points of contention continue to trigger heated discussions despite the commonly held belief that in a calorie-obsessed society there are no secrets left and all the processes happening in the digestive tract are well expounded.

Even though the technologies that the Ukrainian doll applies to promote her claims about total abstinence from food are different from the ones used by the Victorian fasting girls, the claim she makes remains controversial. The audience, offended by the hoax, has repeatedly accused the human Barbie of fakeness. Interestingly, she regards the criticism as appreciation. This must indicate that there is a serious difference between how the dolls themselves and those actively engaged in criticizing them define and valuate naturalness in appearance. What the audience take as forms of rightfully pointing out her inadequacies (or, in this case, they should be called *over*adequacies), the human doll receives as utmost praise for her work and effort put in perfecting the image. This fundamental aporia may be related to the public reactions professional competitive eaters (so-called 'gurgitators') and, to a lesser degree, obese and overweight people's experiences in modern Western societies. A recent Bakhtinian analysis of the benefits that society as a whole derives from and through the gaping mouths of these overeaters suggests the existence of a successful social strategy at play. Adrienne Johnson posits that in such cases superficial disgust is followed by more deeply located feelings of marvel at performing the undoable (2011, 280–284). Thus, in spite of the initial repulsion caused by even witnessing the act of stuffing oneself with a staggering number of hotdogs or any other countable foodstuffs, the fact that such carnivalesque infringement on decorum causes fascination and is gaining a wide audience remains. It seems that people's reaction toward the overdone, out-of-bounds body and ridiculous diet of the human Barbie occurs along the same lines. When it comes to the cultural representations of the obese, being able to see oneself in contrast with them is crucial. As discussed by Alice Julier (2003, 555–556), having one's good features underlined in relation to them is the social function of these people. The same mechanism may be at work in the case of Lukyanova, whose unrealness is needed so as to redefine the audience's stable positioning within the norm.

Spiritualism and Cartesian Duality

The reactions that the fasting girls got were varied. They were treated like living miracles by some. Their audience approached them with Christian

232   Nina Augustynowicz

reverence and admired them for their efforts at striving for moral perfection. Nonetheless, they also met with harsh opposition and ridicule from the medical authority representatives. Their ability to refuse nutrition was linked to anorexia mirabilis, a medieval phenomenon of prodigious fasting in the name of God. Most importantly, they were associated with spiritualism because, aside from rejecting food, they claimed to have psychic powers such as contacting the dead, mind reading, and clairvoyance. These, along with complete resignation from taking in food, were constantly mocked and tested by doctors, who actively sought to expose them as frauds. Quite predictably, physical examinations, if they were allowed, showed that they ate. Yet the Victorian fasting girls can still be thought of in terms of female empowerment through constantly challenging the medical authority. All in all, it seems that Lukyanova shares, with her predecessors from the nineteenth century, the essential feature of not eating—but what about mystic abilities?

The Ukrainian Barbie also claims to have many paranormal abilities. Among them, she describes herself as a spiritual leader who travels in time, has contact with aliens, and is able to go through out-of-body experiences. In a short documentary, *Space Barbie* (2013) produced by *Vice*, which is otherwise filled with unintelligible mumbo-jumbo about past selves and other planets, she boldly announces things such as, for instance, "for a long time I thought I was from Venus." Also, she admits seeing spirits from other dimensions. Even her nails are said to be decorated with patterns from the twenty-first dimension. Together with her girlfriends (who also resemble Barbies, though to a lesser degree than she does), she performs rituals that look much like spiritual séances. The participants chant mantras together in circle, surrounded by rows of candles. This is also what the fasting girls did: they were used as mediums, embraced by the followers of highly popular Spiritualism. Just as the Victorian abstemious eaters, who wanted to commercialize their abilities, she seems to employ the hype created by her abstinence to her own goals, only now using slightly different means to do so. Moreover, Lukyanova says spiritual ideas do not get sufficient attention and that she uses her attractive appearance as a tool to draw attention to more important things, which might be quite a clever ruse. And when she says "more important," it is clearly visible that she alludes to the Cartesian duality.

The cases of fasting girls were understood as powerful arguments in the discussion of the relation between mind and body. The women were seen as almost disembodied spirits who advocated transcendence and escape from the prison of the flesh, even though they were adorned with colorful ribbons and wreaths and wore nice clothes. Here the same holds true: even though Lukyanova's attention to her own body is perceived as profound love and devotion to it, it is the mind she wants to purify through the attention to body. What may be seen as a cult of the body is actually an attempt to escape its confinement, and the doll's struggle for perfection is bound to end in

Living Dolls—A Food Studies Perspective   233

failure as self-satisfaction leads to degeneration in this framework. Moreover, what in popular understanding is perceived as excessive worship of the bodily sphere is actually a manifestation of a fundamental rejection of this realm and a turn toward attaining nonmaterial existence. The true perfection for the doll is to shed the body by transforming it into an object that can be controlled by the mind without them coming in close contact, like a puppeteer remotely pulling the strings. In the documentary, Lukyanova discusses one of the dimensions she has visited, which is populated by sexless creatures—her ideal. While telling the story, she is dressed as some space Wiseman with a long wizard beard to match her hair. This is no longer about looking beautiful at this point. She dreams of a world without the body, and her gradual alienation from it makes people perceive her as an alien. In the words of the *GQ* article: "instead of a doll-obsessed girl from a small town in a Soviet country you get a racist space alien." And we cannot forget she is also a lecturer on out-of-body experiences. With these self-proclaimed goals and ambitions, Lukyanova is something more than an overblown picture of the beauty standards.

Final Remarks

Fasting girls, both the Victorian and contemporary ones, are often condemned for apparent deceptiveness. This is illustrated by an anecdote from when the human Barbie met the living Ken. To digress for a moment: the existence of a human Ken does not necessarily suggest that fascination with doll-like appearance is not limited to women. Quite the opposite: gender is a powerful factor in the incidence of the trend, if only for the fact that emaciation accompanying the transformation into a creature resembling a Barbie is strongly linked with playing out the norm of feminine qualities. For these reasons, exactly, the gendered character of living dolls requires a separate analysis centered around the role of the standards of womanhood, possibly incorporating the new tendency exemplified by the appearance of persons such as Justin Jedlica, the Ken in question. After the meeting, he was displeased with Lukyanova and said she was fake. This is not the only disapproving comment concerning her credulity. She admits having had a breast augmentation done, but nothing more. In the documentary, she states that journalists accuse her of deception; in another place she is called a two-faced liar, and later she fears being exposed. A considerable amount of time is spent on disproving the nonbelievers and persuading them it is neither Photoshop nor surgical interventions but rather just skillfully applied makeup and lighting or also good genes. Deception was also a major question for the fasting girls: doctors tested if they really did not eat in all seriousness, and some of them died as a result of the experiment, even though postmortem examinations showed they had obviously eaten. They were ridiculed as going out at night to eat in secret, but, still, new fasting girls appeared who would stick by the same story. Now when the deception is in optical

234   *Nina Augustynowicz*

illusions of makeup, other feminine paraphernalia, and surgical restructuring of the body, the role of medical authority is becoming less and less important. Maybe now scientific opinion is too strong to be challenged, and the process of secularization and medicalization that began in nineteenth century culture is in this manner shown as complete.

It is quite possible that the aspect of class is a factor in the case of fasting girls, be it Victorian or contemporary. In the nineteenth century, they tended to appear in peripheral locations and came from poorly educated, secular families without access to medical care; now it is the working class families of Russia, Ukraine, and other Eastern European countries where these dolls are raised (for instance, Angelica Kenova, Lolita Richi, Alina Kovalevskaya, and Anastasiya Shpagina). This is necessarily only a proposition requiring further study, but it might be true that their bizarre eating habits are partly motivated by the struggle to become popular and wealthy—and to put in practice the marriage plot, which necessitates possessing all the right female attributes. Observing the frustrated fates of women not entirely conforming to the standards of femininity in this economy of social relations may lead these girls to strive for perfection with doubled efforts.

Recently, some changes have been noticed in Lukyanova's image—in the pictures she is sharing now she is wearing less makeup and she seems a bit more natural, but also even thinner. A likely interpretation, against the idea that she might simply be getting better, is that additional living doll practices become unnecessary when not eating becomes the focus and takes center stage. An emaciated, anorexic body is a sufficient tool to isolate oneself and gain control over the unruly body.

The analysis of Valeria Lukyanova's strategies, taken to be an exemplary living Barbie, shows clearly that her phenomenon is nothing new, as it can be traced back to the Victorian fasting girls, who operated on similar principles despite their markedly less striking appearance. Claims to being able to sustain oneself solely thanks to some unidentified particles reaped from the air we breathe link the cases across centuries, which in turn leads to noting further similarities. This offers a vision not only of a small-town girl striving to achieve the exaggerated traditional ideal of femininity while at the same time ridiculing it, but also of a dramatic desire to separate the body and the mind, giving the latter full dominance. Obviously, this study is limited in its scope and does not postulate that the perspective of food studies is the only one available that is capable of yielding insight into the phenomenon of living dolls. Conversely, it openly calls for a more systematic examination of the strategies applied by these women from the vantage point and with the use of tools offered such disciplines by media studies or gender studies. Nonetheless, the continuities spotted, thanks to drawing attention to the nutritional and eating-related aspects of the behavior and appearance, are formed on the basis of food studies research and, in consequence, help the troubled field to overcome its issues with having a real impact on popular materialities.

Living Dolls—A Food Studies Perspective   235

Notes

1. Food studies is a rapidly growing field of research, and, as admitted by Carole Counihan and Penny van Esterik in their introduction to the third edition of the now-iconic collection *Food and Culture* (2003), it offers complementary but also independent methods for phenomena not easily included in body studies. The scholars recognize the upward trend that has been noted since the late 1990s and enthusiastically speak of both the expansion and diversification occurring in the discipline (1). Conversely, Kyla Wazana-Tompkins (2013, 2) rejects this standpoint, claiming that even if it happens, the development of food studies is of negative consequences, as it leads to the field's turn toward increasingly narrower topics. In her view, this reflects the elitism and trivialization of the discipline—an inevitable effect of its recent evolution. Food studies is centered around the examination of nourishment in its numerous aspects and does not concentrate on any particular theoretical perspective. This often leads to methodological ambiguities and unnecessary overproduction of ultimately indistinguishable frameworks of study. Nevertheless, this worrisome bent is not all there is to this discipline. It still has strong redeeming qualities, such as the liberating sense of interdisciplinarity essential for the examination of a sphere as ubiquitous and simultaneously ripe with equivocations as food and eating and, on the other hand, good sociohistorical insight into food practices exemplified by, for instance, the scrutinizing works of Sidney Mintz. In addition, using the case of the human Barbie to underline the direct preoccupation of food scholars with the materiality of food consumption may actually benefit food studies as well, by demonstrating that its insights do apply to popular culture matters on a very practical, down-to-earth, and at the same time extremely fundamental level.
2. Other approaches to the human Barbies are not only possible but also encouraged; researchers working within the framework of media studies and psychologists would probably have a lot to say about other facets of the living doll phenomenon, by, for instance, commenting on the sustained ability to attract media attention and mechanisms behind prolonged food refusal.
3. According to Joan Jacobs Brumberg (1988, 1999), these women were dubbed girls no matter how old they actually were (1988, 61), which emphasizes the condescending approach to them, seen also with respect to ignoring the realities of eating disturbances. Brumberg's investigation into the causes of anorexia nervosa presented in *Fasting Girls* was a clear inspiration for the chapter.
4. Being accused of having anorexia is an interesting turn of phrase that suggests that the attitude toward eating disorders has not changed much since the Victorians scorned them as imaginary; surely, nobody would be accused of having cancer or a cold, for that matter.

References

Ashley, Bob, Joanne Hollows, Steve Jones, and Ben Taylor. 2004. *Food and Cultural Studies*. New York: Routledge.

Bordo, Susan. 2003. *Unbearable Weight: Feminism, Western Culture, and the Body*. Berkeley: University of California Press.

Brumberg, Joan Jacobs. 1988. *Fasting Girls: The Emergence of Anorexia Nervosa as a Modern Disease*. Cambridge, MA: Harvard University Press.

236 *Nina Augustynowicz*

———. 1999. *The Anthropology of Food and Body: Gender, Meaning, and Power*. New York: Routledge.

Counihan, Carole, and Penny Van Esterik. 2003. "Why Food? Why Culture? Why Now? Introduction to the Third Edition." In *Food and Culture. A Reader*, edited by Carole Counihan and Penny Van Esterik, 1–15. New York: Routledge.

Douglas, Mary. 1966. *Purity and Danger. An Analysis of the Concepts of Pollution and Taboo*. London and New York: Routledge.

Fowler, Robert. 1871. *A Complete History of the Case of the Welsh Fasting-Girl (Sarah Jacob) with Complete Comments Thereon; and Observation on Death from Starvation*. London: Henry Renshaw.

Hekman, Susan. 1998. "Material Bodies." In *Body and Flesh: A Philosophical Reader*, edited by Donn Welton, 61–70. Malden, MA: Blackwell Publishers.

Idov, Michael. 2014. "Is Human Barbie Valeria Lukyanova a Feminist?" *GQ*, April 9. Available online at http://www.gq.com/story/valeria-lukyanova-human-barbie-doll.

Johnson, Adrienne Rose. 2011. "The Magic Metabolisms of Competitive Eating." In *Taking Food Public: Redefining Foodways in a Changing World*, edited by Psyche Williams-Forson and Carole Counihan, 279–292. New York: Routledge.

Julier, Alice. 2003. "The Political Economy of Obesity: The Fat Pay All." In *Food and Culture. A Reader*, edited by Carole Counihan and Penny Van Esterik, 546–562. New York: Routledge.

Rhodan, Maya. 2014. "Is the 'Human Barbie' Sexy? A GQ Writer on Meeting the Real-Life Doll." *Time*, April 7. Available online at http://time.com/52026/is-the-human-barbie-sexy-a-gq-writer-on-meeting-the-real-life-doll/.

Sandberg, Patrick. 2013. "Living Doll." *V Magazine*. Available online at http://www.vmagazine.com/site/content/261/living-doll.

Space Barbie. 2013. Produced by Vice. Film. Available online at http://www.vice.com/video/space-barbie-full-length.

Valeria's homepage. http://www.humanbarbie.org/.

Vrettos, Athena. 1995. *Somatic Fictions: Imagining Illness in Victorian Culture*. Stanford, CA: Stanford University Press.

Wazana-Tompkins, Kyla. 2012. *Racial Indigestion: Eating Bodies in the 19th Century*. New York: New York University Press.

18 Contemporary Toys, Adults, and Creative Material Culture
From *Wow* to *Flow* to *Glow*

Katriina Heliakka

Introduction: Toy Play in the Age of the Ludic Turn

In the time of the *ludic turn*, as proposed by Brian Sutton-Smith (1997), the cultures of play are in convergence. Although the industry of traditional toys is faced with fears relating to the digitalization and dematerialization of play culture, physical toys are surviving due to unique tactile and manipulable qualities that still cannot be grasped by digital or even hybrid playthings. The presumption is that a toy with an outstanding play value will endorse a *wow* effect. Once utilized in play, the toy gives the player a secondary wow, which results in an experience of *flow*. Popular play patterns are used to cultivate mass-marketed toys and, in this way, add certain value to artifacts that have previously been considered trivial objects, at least from the perspective of adult use. Finally, when the player has creatively cultivated the toy, she or he has given it an added (auratic) value, *glow*.

This chapter addresses the material life of toys from the perspective of temporal and spatial trajectories of adult-created toy stories. Drawing on contemporary research on adult engagement with playthings, the chapter presents the evidence of the existence and the multifaceted dimensions of object play at a mature age. Part of the analysis is dedicated to the nature of play in an adult–toy interaction. Contemporary toys such as dolls, action figures, and soft toys are given narratives in the form of backstories. In play, these narratives are challenged, creatively cultivated, and finally circulated through social media platforms. In other words, character toys as categorized here are used in various play activities such as collecting, customizing, and creating visual and animated stories (including play patterns, e.g., toy tourism, photoplay, and transmedia-inspired play). As my research demonstrates, personalized play content and the documenting and sharing of it create both engagement with toys and mimicking of the aforementioned play patterns. Play practices of adults who use toys during leisure time (whom I also discuss as 'everyday players') show that uses of toys are activities partaken not only in domestic spheres, but also in public spaces and social contexts. Contemporary mass-marketed toys are frequently being used as creative, social tools by adult players. Their activities suggest not only that the playgrounds of material play culture expand in parallel with play that

238   *Katriina Heliakka*

occurs in context of digital, social media, but also that these different realms of play culture are being reinforced by each other.

Toys in Play

Toys derive meaning in play. Toy play as a type of *object play* functions as an umbrella term for many forms of 'playful behavior' interested in the material and three-dimensional aspects of play, ranging from manipulative exploration to mimicry and from storytelling to creative interaction etc. Through toy play, people of every culture in every location have mastered their cognitive abilities and grown toward a creative practice (Heljakka 2015b).

The central quality of a toy is its *playability*. Every toy proposes its own action, depending on the possibility behind its design. When it comes to their play potential, toys are usually goal directed or open ended. Alleged *precisive toys* (Heljakka 2013b, 128; orig. Kalliala 1999) are thoroughly produced for preprogrammed play and therefore closed in their playing patterns. Again, open-ended toys such as dolls, action figures, or soft toys rarely have prescribed instructions of use, even though they might suggest play patterns in connection with transmedia-tied narratives (so-called media play) or serve emotional needs of the players by inviting their owners to bond with them, personalize and anthropomorphize them, and, finally, to build long-term relationships with these toy objects, which come with a face.

Toys are most often defined solely as objects related to childhood. According to the Oxford English Dictionary, a toy is "a material object for children or others to play with (often an imitation of some familiar object); a plaything; also, it can be something contrived for amusement rather than for practical use." In my interpretation, this definition opens up to the possible inclusion of adults.

Play scholar Brian Sutton-Smith has expressed a concern for modern toys as limiting themselves mostly to the ideals of romanticism and commercialism (1997). He has spoken of toys as artifacts that support solitary forms of play as opposed to social play. Furthermore, Sutton-Smith says that children's and adults' play are quite different—that of children being open, or creative, and that of adults being closed, or reactive (19).

The idea of the toy as a commercial and romanticized object that promotes solitary play mainly among children produces false assumptions about toy play. Also, the notion of the reactive nature of adult play limits the view on the possibilities of human–toy interactions. Object play at mature age is a multifaceted activity of a wide scope that relies on the variety of play contexts and engagements with toys. Mature play presents toys as material and deliberately designed—playable—artifacts that function as a point of departure for experiences related to *wow* and *flow* and that generate creative play that enables the formation of a *glow* effect in adult play.

Adults, Toys, and Creative Cultures of Play

In the thinking of anthropologist Jean-Pierre Rossie, toys can never really be explored without reflecting on their use (2005). Toys, as ludic objects, are first and foremost artifacts that derive meaning in play. The ideal user for a toy is anyone who puts this object into play.

The play patterns that are relevant for the scope of my study are the material, digital, and social practices around toys. In the following, I will discuss how toys combined with play acts enable creativity that is manifested both solitarily and socially. I am taking creative object practices as a starting point for examining contemporary adult play with character toys: dolls, action figures, and soft toys.

Research in object practices built around adult toy play, e.g., sensory engagement and creative manipulation with character toys such as dolls or action figures is scarce or underdeveloped even in contemporary interest in toy cultures. However, my previous research focusing on play with *Blythe* dolls (2012), *Uglydolls* (2013a), and *My Little Pony* (2015a) shows that material artifacts continue to have deep significance for the players of today. Adults use popular play patterns to cultivate mass-marketed toys and, in this way, add certain value to these playthings. By studying temporal and spatial trajectories of adult-created toy stories both online and offline, it becomes possible to understand how human interactions with toys manifest as multifaceted and complex object relations that involve creative and productive aspects.

A player's personality and environment may lead to unique interpretations of a particular toy regardless of the intentions of the toy manufacturer (Ferris Motz 1992, 223). Gender, age, experience, socioeconomic status, race, expertise, and sociocultural factors all are of importance for the interpreter (Ash 2006, 292–294)—in this case, the player. The interpretation and later appropriation of the toy, seen in this light, is affected by the player's age and background.

It is rare for an adult to admit to 'playing' with a toy. Yet the practices acted out in relation to toys such as collecting, creative manipulation, personalization, and storytelling can hardly be categorized outside of ludic interaction. The negative assumptions related to the fear of being labeled or stigmatized as infantile prevail: adult toy play is often disguised behind various activities that are categorically thought of as hobbies, such as *collecting*. Even dolls are sometimes not referred to as things for play, but rather as *collectibles*. This discursive accentuation does not, however, place dolls, soft toys, or figurines outside of the sphere of play, not even in the case of adult toy owners and collectors.

In Groos's meaning, hobbies of adults usually resemble activities characteristic for play, but they often aim beyond the intrinsic value of play (Groos and Baldwin 2010, 248–249). This places these activities in the realm of *allotelic* play (Klabbers 2009), in contrast to the traditional way of seeing play as *autotelic* or self-motivated. As noted, adults who admit to having a

240 *Katriina Heliakka*

toy hobby do not necessarily understand (or want to communicate) their practices with playthings as *play*. In other words, it is much more common to hear about adults 'hobbying' with dolls, doll houses, or other miniatures (see, e.g., Heljakka 2013b).

Even though adult toy play may manifest both as an autotelic or allotelic activity, it is often symptomatic for adults to wish that their engagement with objects results in outcomes. In this way, adult play with toys is often creative and productive in nature. "'Object practices,' such as modeling, collecting, making and modifying, bring to the fore the physical artifacts and processes by which popular culture both remembers and recreates itself" (Rehak 2013, 43 in Geraghty 2014).

In the case of adults, toys are often considered and valued based on their looks. Therefore, it is important to note that toys may be playable simply based on their capacity to function as aesthetically pleasing objects that may be *displayed* either individually or as part of a group of (other) objects. However, in adult play with contemporary character toys, the object practices do not limit themselves to accumulation or even displaying of the playthings, but rather demonstrate a willingness to alter and personalize mass-produced character toys. In adult toy play, playthings acquire new meanings as action or manipulation adds player-created content to the narratives surrounding the toy. Sometimes, the personalization—physical alteration of a toy—is of more importance for the player than the original mass-marketed and transmedially connected storyline or backstory associated with it. On the other hand, these aspects of toy play are often intertwined with the transformation of a toy's 'personality,' character, and a narrative present in play.

The evidence for the continuous popularity of nontechnological toys is, for example, character toys (see, e.g., Heljakka 2013b). Paradoxically, what seems to sustain this popularity are the technological devices and social media-oriented play practices that enable the extending of play with physical playthings: play patterns carried out with the help of technological devices such as mobile phones or digital cameras and shared on social media have gained popularity in all age groups. In some cases a three-dimensional toy without embedded technological features is employed in transgenerational play that manifests mainly in digital contexts and platforms: the toy stories created and cultivated in the play scenarios involving physical play materials are often shared with other players through digital means. In this way, the solitary play practices, through uses of technology and social media platforms, enter the social sphere of play.

Photographic play (photoplay) seems to be one of the most popular play patterns among mature toy users, but other creative activities of toy fans and hobbyists, such as customizing, crafting, and creating continuous narratives, exemplify further forms of socially shared, creative play behavior. In an increasingly ludic society, the emergence of toy play activities at mature age has become more perceptible precisely due to these developments in digital and social media environments. Through still and animated images

Contemporary Toys, Adults, and Creative Material Culture 241

and textual and verbalized narrations of toys that are shared online, contemporary players demonstrate the importance of digital culture and social media to the inherently material culture of traditional toys. In digital realms, by documenting and showcasing their inventiveness and playful interactions with toys, adult players come to contribute to promoting skill-building and learning through toy play, paralleling the idea of twenty-first century skills (Heljakka 2015b).

Wow, Flow, Glow and Afforded Values of Toys

Anything can be a plaything (such as the classic example of a cardboard box illustrates), but a good toy affords repeated playful exploration. In other words, a good toy has *play value*. As Sotamaa affirms, with good playthings a child not only derives useful experiences from objects, but also "learns to learn" (1979, 11). Didactic and entertainment goals are, however, not always the same. To the player, the play value of a toy does not necessarily relate to its pedagogic capacities. Nor does play value necessarily relate only to the mechanical features of a toy—some dolls, soft toys, and action figures may be quite limited in the ways they can be manipulated physically (e.g., through posing). Even though a sophistically articulated toy offers great play value in terms of poseability, for some players, its play value is a result of something else—for example, the overall aesthetics or narrative dimension (backstory, connection to transmedia storytelling). Sometimes it is hard to predict what constitutes perceived value in a toy: the positive meanings given to the toys may increase their play value in the mind of their owner. Old toys may retain their play value even if play with them would happen on a purely visceral level.

"Curiosity is the name given to the playful manifestation of attention which results from this tendency" (Groos and Baldwin 2010, 93). Curiosity leads us to explore the possibilities that a toy offers—in other words, its *affordances*. Ultimately, curiosity is also what leads to creative play (including challenging their designed affordances) with toys at an adult age.

The toy designer may ask himself or herself whether the toy in development will have affordances—action possibilities that limit and guide the player toward certain activities (Kudrowitz and Wallace 2010). By designing playful affordances and integrating these action possibilities into the toy, the designer may suggest various ways of use for the player. For example, when considering the playthings addressed in this chapter—namely, character toys—the designer may encourage the player to pose the toy (by designing movable joints), to engage in hair play (by giving the toy hair that affords styling), or to change the eye color of the toy (by giving the player the chance to change the eye 'chips').

In other words, a toy should *allow* play on many levels and allow both manipulation and imaginative play. Toy designers design suggestions for play, or affordances, into toys. In use, the play(ful) affordances are interpreted

242   Katriina Heliakka

and sometimes challenged in the acts of play. Finally, through the outcomes of play (e.g., play scenarios perceivable to others either when participating in play or when viewing documented play through socially shared photo-play or videos involving toys), the observed and employed affordances are again turned into further *invitations of play*, which may attract new players to participate socially.

Most toys fulfill the requirement of playablity and some manage to convey play value by affording different play patterns, but only a few make the player 'go *wow*.' The play potential of the toy is actualized in the playful engagement (the play acts) with the toy. If designed well, the suggestion of playability, the promises of play value, and the potential affordances of the toy are fulfilled, and the player, putting the toy into play, experiences a flow-like state of mind. In play, creative acts of the player narrativizing or physically manipulating the plaything give the toy an auratic glow.

The logic behind the idea of the *wow–flow–glow* continuum on the level of adult relationships with toys communicates that toy designers give the toy affordances that potentially wow the players and encourage them to object practices that enable a flow state of mind, which again may result in a sustainable *glow*, a player added value on the toy.

Wow and *flow* are concepts associated with the writings of Henry Jenkins (2007) and Mihaly Csikszentmihalyi (1975). Glow is a term I employ to describe the last stage of the trajectory of the relationship between the player and the toy, and it is most comparable to Walter Benjamin's concept of *aura* (1968, orig. 1936).[1]

Henry Jenkins defines *wow* as an old vaudeville term that describes a peak experience. He writes: "Consider the singular beauty of the word 'wow'. [...] Imagine the particular enthusiasm it expresses—the senses of wonderment, astonishment, absolute engagement" (2007, 1). In Jenkins's terms, the *wow* relates to "putting on a show" (4). One of the toy designers I have interviewed describes *wow* as "the unexpected, the surprising element or of something that has not been done before" (Heljakka 2013b, 83). Levy and Weingartner consider the wow factor to be "some promotable feature that, combined with a market need, delivers obvious excitement" (2003, 144).

Furthermore, the most cleverly designed playthings are able to channel a wow experience not only once, but multiple times. *Double-wow*[2] in a plaything thus extends beyond the first encounter with the toy and wows the player again once the object is employed in play. Hidden features such as the unobvious articulation of the jointed limb of a doll or a sound chip that activates only on occasion, prolong the predesigned wow-ability of the toy. On the other hand, *wow* can be a result of how the player has altered the toy (e.g., through customization).

When exploring the dimensions of contemporary play, one needs to understand one of the most central concepts linked to it—namely, the one of *flow*. The flow experience consists of challenging activity, a merging of action and awareness, clear goals and feedback, concentration, the paradox of control,

Contemporary Toys, Adults, and Creative Material Culture   243

and loss of self-consciousness and track of time. The flow experience is a highly rewarding state of doing (Battarbee 2004, 55).

In Csikszentmihalyian terms, the peak experience of flow may also be a result of cherished objects we keep in our homes (Csikszentimihalyi and Rochberg-Halton 1981). In toy play, the flow state of mind results from engaging and satisfactory toy experiences that may happen in connection with the silent dialogues carried out with the toys, as well as with actual manipulation of the toy objects. For example, the joy of dis*playing* toys in aesthetic arrangements may generate a feeling of flow. In advanced play scenarios, character toys are arranged either as groups or singular artifacts on shelves, dioramas, or dollhouses that often make use of objects appropriated in play, such as miniatures or other types of souvenirs. Photoplay in the intimacy of the play spaces in these domestic environments or pilgrimages taken with toys to famous locations such as touristic sites further enhance the experience of flow. Although the flow of play may include humorous aspects, it is important to note that players also enjoy simultaneous feelings of excitement, challenge, and losing track of time.

Player-Generated Glow in Adult Engagement with Toys

As Margolin notes, contemporary design regards longevity as a desired value in products (2002, 49). The life cycles of toys have to do with both their material and conceptual durability. Toys should not be grown out in a fast pace, but they should grip the imagination and the imagination must outgrow them, as Sutton-Smith postulates in *Paradoxes of Toys* (n.d.).

Although at times, adults receive toys as gifts, acquiring toys at adult age is often a result of economical (and ecological) thinking. When toys are purchased for a child, there is often an underlying thought that the child at some point will outgrow the plaything, which is then recycled, disposed, or packed away to reenter once the child has matured and perhaps has children of his or her own. Consequently, adults are more considerate in building their toy worlds according to more long-term goals than is the case for children as toy consumers. Toy characters are added to adult-owned collections based on more sustainable ideas and expectations on long-term relations: toys are expected to communicate longevity in terms of continuous play value and an ability to invite the player to repetitious and enthralling 'replay.' In other words, toys that fulfill their promises of play by wowing their player and inviting him or her to a flow state of mind, have a good chance of being given an added value to them in play—a glow.

The auratic glow of adult relationships with toys manifests itself in different ways, mostly in the narrative dimensions and signs of physical manipulation of the toy object. One example of player-generated glow is made visible, for example, in the art of photographer Mark Nixon. In his *Much Loved* (2013), the glow of the torn and tattered teddy bears and other plush animals may be read viscerally on the level of the photographs, and narratively in the toy stories shared by their owners in the book. Whereas Nixon's

244 *Katriina Heliakka*

toy stories build on nostalgia and long life cycles of toys with a history, the glow in association with contemporary playthings results from play acts and player-added value of the present.

As Jenkins explains, play is changing media and media is changing play (2010). As demonstrated earlier, one of the most notable developments in play culture is the presence and active role given to media technologies and socially shared aspects of play. In terms of toy play, perhaps one of the most interesting developments is how mobile devices such as cameras are constantly employed in contemporary toy play. Toy play scenarios are photographed and videoed and then shared on social media. Photo management applications such as Flickr and Instagram enable the formation of playful communities and function as a platform for visually (and digitally) shared play. As visual images may be grouped, commented, and categorized according to their themes and popularity, player-generated glow is made visible and thus communicable in more perceivable ways than before.

Toys may be portrayed with artistic aspirations in mind and therefore enjoyed from an aesthetic viewpoint. Artistic enjoyment is, according to Groos, the highest and most valuable form of adult play (Groos and Baldwin 2010, 234–235), but the plaything as a creatively cultivated and an artistically photographed artifact affords other kinds of playful enjoyment as well. This relates to the joy that the player gets not only from photographing or filming the toy, but also from being able to share this form of ludic engagement with other players. Once a toy player shares his or her engagement with toys through social media, this engagement turns into an invitation to social play directed to fellow players. Many contemporary toy players who are present in social media appear to gain pleasure from 'flickering' through the photography as shared on the photo management application site. Flickering through the photographs (or videos) of other players may encourage the viewer to acquire a certain toy and to become a creative toy player. Seen in this way, it is possible to consider social media applications as the world's largest toy catalogs and, furthermore, as 'shop windows' through which contemporary toy cultures are preserved, perceived, and constantly cultivated as new players are inaugurated in the increasingly participatory play patterns of players of all ages.

An analysis of contemporary play patterns as expressed in documentations of play such as singular or serial products of photoplay or play videos in which toys function as vehicles for storytelling illustrates the importance of creative and productive acts for contemporary adult toy players. In other words, players tend to treat toys in increasingly creative—sometimes even subversive—manners compared to the original idea of the designer. By exploring mature player engagement with toys, we may find out more about the creativity expressed in connection with contemporary playthings and object practices in reference to them.

A trend that connects with DIY (do it yourself) and maker cultures—the personalization of toys—represents one important direction of creative play practices of the past years and, as such, is an example of how players add glow to mass-produced toys of various types. Through personalization, toys are

Contemporary Toys, Adults, and Creative Material Culture 245

given new, individual, and customized looks through the handicraft conducted by the player. For example, a large fan audience of the Blythe doll customizes and personalizes dolls for reselling purposes and some produce unique dresses and accessories for Blythe to sell to other doll enthusiasts (Heljakka 2015b). Similar practices are shared by My Little Pony players (Heljakka 2015a), who wish to extend the original toy characters either materially or narratively. Customization practices are of interest to the 'toying artists' as well as the 'everyday players' of today (Heljakka 2013b). One example of an artist who has received international attention by using My Little Pony as her material platform to create *My Little Pop Icons*, or toy portraits of fictional and actual 'characters' of pop culture, is Finnish artist Mari Kasurinen (Heljakka 2013b, 384). Everyday players who do not have professional goals to use toys in their creations may nevertheless have similar interest in cultivating contemporary toy characters either as subjects of their fan art (toys as inspiration) or as physical objects that may be reinterpreted through physical alteration (toys as raw material).

Afterglow: Conclusion

In the time of the ludic turn physical toys continue to engage players of different ages. My studies in the field of adult toy play[3] have proven that playthings carry on to have meaning in adulthood, not only as aesthetically appreciated and collectable artifacts but also, more importantly, as objects that encourage their players to enjoy solitary and socially shared play time in offline and online playgrounds. Furthermore, through the popular processes related to toy play, players improve their manipulative skills and acquire new ones through creative self-expression of various kinds. At the same time, adults enjoy imaginative scenarios enabled by physical toys and have an interest in forming long-term relationships with their character toys.

Thus, toys should first and foremost be designed in ways that invite play, afford various ways to play—toyed with in many ways—and to be played with repetitively. Del Vecchio proposes that such toys should be invented to "provide a multidimensional experience for the child (and adult)" (2003, 165).

Well-designed toys serve players on many levels. Toys that stimulate the imagination due to their material, visual, and narrative features have a good chance to wow their audience. Toy designers seek to deliberately design potential 'wow-ness' into new toy objects. If a toy manages to communicate a wow effect to the audience, there is a possibility that a player will acquire the toy and get into a flow state of mind while playing with it. Through manipulative acts such as creative customization and personalization, as well as activities aiming at the narrativization of the toy such as photoplay, the plaything may attain an *auratic glow*, transforming the toy in terms of its physical appearance and its narrative dimension. In sustainable toy relationships, the toys that have accumulated the most glow as cherished and well-played objects cast an afterglow that is unreplaceable by yet 'unplayed' toys: they have a chance to reenter the sphere of play by wowing new players again and again.

Figure 18.1 Blue toys in photoplay. (Photo by Katriina Heliakka.)

Figure 18.2 Seiren of the sea—artistic photoplay. (Photo by Katriina Heliakka.)

Figure 18.3 Toys in a game session within a diorama. (Photo by Katriina Heliakka.)

Notes

1. It needs to be noted here that these theoretical concepts stem from methodologically different areas of study: *wow* (cultural studies), *flow* (psychology), and Benjamin's aura from aesthetic theory. As Miriam Bratu Hansen writes, *aura* may be described "as an elusive phenomenal substance, ether, or halo that surrounds a person or object of perception, encapsulating their individuality and authenticity" (Bratu Hansen 2008, 340). My appropriation of the term is based on the idea of individuality and authenticity—the personal and unique 'glow' given to a toy object while employed in play. This glow may be perceived either directly in the artifact or, for example, an outcome of toy play, such as a product of photoplay, or, for example, a piece produced by a 'toying artist.' For more on toying artists, see Heljakka (2013b).
2. For this term, I am indebted to toy designer Dan Klitsner of KID Group LLC, who shared the idea of double-wow in a personal meeting in San Francisco, September 2013.
3. This study has been funded by the Academy of Finland and Tekes—the Finnish Funding Agency for Technology and Innovation—and is a part of the research projects Ludification and the Emergence of Playful Culture (276012) and Hybrid Social Play (2600360411).

References

Ash, Dan. 2006. "New Experimental Aesthetics and Popular Culture." In *Popular Culture. Theory and Methodology. A Basic Introduction*, edited by Harold E. Hinds, Jr., Marilyn F. Motz, and Angela, M. S. Nelson, 271–308. Madison: University of Wisconsin Press.

Battarbee, Katja. 2004. *Co-experience. Understanding User Experiences in Social Interaction*. Helsinki: Publication Series of the University of Art and Design Helsinki A 51.

248 *Katriina Heliakka*

Benjamin, Walter. 1968. "The Work of Art in the Age of Mechanical Reproduction." In *Illuminations*. New York: Schocken Books.

Bratu Hansen, Miriam. 2008. "Benjamin's Aura." *Critical Inquiry* (34): 336–375.

Csikszentmihalyi, Mihaly. 2000. *Beyond Boredom and Anxiety: Experiencing Flow in Work and Play*. San Francisco: Jossey-Bass.

Csikszentmihalyi, Mihaly, and Rochberg-Halton, Eugene. 1981. *The Meaning of Things. Domestic Symbols and the Self*. Cambridge: Cambridge University Press.

Del Vecchio, Gene. 2003. *The Blockbuster Toy! How to Invent the Next BIG Thing*. Gretna, LA: Pelican Publishing Company.

Ferris Motz, Marilyn. 1992. "Seen through Rose-Tinted Glasses. The Barbie Doll in American Society." In *Popular Culture. Theory and Methodology. A Basic Introduction*, edited by Harold E. Hinds, Jr., Marilyn F. Motz, and Angela, M. S. Nelson, 211–234. Madison: University of Wisconsin Press.

Geraghty, Lincoln. 2014. *Cult Collectors. Nostalgia, Fandom and Collecting Popular Culture*. London and New York: Routledge.

Groos, Karl, and Elizabeth L. Baldwin. 2010. *The Play of Man*. Memphis, TN: General Books.

Heljakka, Katriina. 2012. "Aren't You a Doll. Toying with Avatars in Digital Playgrounds." *Journal of Gaming and Virtual Worlds* 4 (2): 153–170.

———. 2013a. "Lelutarinointia Tuubissa: Leikkijä ja liikkuvat Uglydoll-kuvat." ["Toys on the Tube: Players and Animated Uglydoll Images"]. *Wider Screen* (2–3). Available online at http://widerscreen.fi/numerot/2013-2-3/lelutarinointia-tuubissa-leikkija-ja-liikkuvat-uglydoll-kuvat/.

———. 2013b. *Principles of Adult Play(fulness) in Contemporary Play Patterns. From Wow to Flow to Glow*. Espoo: Aalto University Publication Series, Doctoral Dissertations.

———. 2015a. "From Toys to Television and Back—My Little Pony Appropriated in Adult Toy Play." *Journal of Popular Television* 3 (3): 99–109.

———. 2015b. "Toys as Tools for Skill-building and Creativity in Adult Life." *Seminar.net. International Journal of Media, Technology and Lifelong Learning* 11 (2). Available online at http://seminar.net/images/stories/vol11-issue2/5_Katriina_Heljakka.pdf.

Jenkins, Henry. 2007. *The Wow Climax. Tracing the Emotional Impact of Popular Culture*. New York: New York University Press.

———. 2010. "Toying with Transmedia: The Future of Entertainment Is Child's Play." In *Sandbox Summit Lecture at MIT*. May 18. Available online at http://video.mit.edu/watch/toying-with-transmedia-the-future-of-entertainment-is-childs-play-9605/.

Kalliala, M. 1999. *Enkeliprinsessa ja itsari liukumäessä. Leikkikulttuuri ja yhteiskunnan muutos* [*The Angel Princess and Suicide in a Slide*]. Helsinki: Gaudeamus Yliopistokustannnus University Press.

Klabbers, Jan H. G. 2009. *The Magic Circle: Principles of Gaming and Simulation*. Rotterdam: Sense Publishers.

Kudrowitz, Barry M., and David R. Wallace. 2010. "The Play Pyramid: A Play Classification and Ideation Tool for Toy Design." *International Journal of Arts and Technology* 3 (1): 36–56. Available online at http://www.inderscienceonline.com/doi/abs/10.1504/IJART.2010.030492.

Contemporary Toys, Adults, and Creative Material Culture 249

Levy, Richard C., and Ronald O. Weingartner. 2003. *The Toy and Game Inventor's Handbook. Everything You Need to Know to Pitch, License, and Cash-In on Your Ideas*. New York: Alpha (A Member of Penguin Group).

Margolin, Victor. 2002. *Politics of the Artificial. Essays on Design and Design Studies*. Chicago: University of Chicago Press.

Nixon, Mark. 2013. *Much Loved. Photographs*. New York: Abrams Image.

Oxford English Dictionary. 2016. "Toy," *OED*. Available online at http://www.oed.com/view/Entry/204133?rskey=WAfskC&result=1#eid.

Rossie, Jean-Pierre. 2005. *Toys, Play, Culture and Society. Anthropological Approach with Reference to North Africa and Sahara*. Stockholm: SITREC.

Sotamaa, Yrjö. 1979. "Some General Aspects Concerning the Development of Playthings." In *Playthings for Play. Ideas of Criteria on Children's Playthings*, edited by Karlheinz Otto, Käthe Schmidt, Yrjö Sotamaa, and Juhani Salovaara, 11–14. Berlin: AIF, and Finland: Ornamo.

Sutton-Smith, Brian. n.d. *Paradoxes of Toys*. Notes accessed at the Brian Sutton-Smith Archives, the Strong National Museum of Play.

———. 1997. *The Ambiguity of Play*. Cambridge, MA: Harvard University Press.

19 From Stuff to Material Civilization— Toward a Materiality of Childhood

David James

There is considerable interest in the study of 'stuff' (Miller 2010), often intentionally loosely defined, but usually meaning discrete objects with a particular focus on the meaning of stuff used by people. This chapter aims to try to develop an analysis of stuff, but drawing on the wider conceptions of materiality (Dant 2006) and material civilization (Braudel 1981). It will be argued that 'stuff,' understood as material culture and objects, is not enough to provide an adequate account of the importance of the material world for children and hence conceptualizations of childhood. As part of the material turn, there is a need to look closely at the material infrastructure of daily life in historical context and with a much keener eye kept on materiality as technology that determines the place, space, and flow of children through the period known as childhood. This chapter will focus on the everyday technologies of childhood to develop links between the anthropological approach to the analysis of things, and the historical and sociological approaches to the study of technology. The examples of water and toys will be explored to focus on the important relationships between the background of material civilization and the more discrete popular material artifacts in the lives of children.

Stuff, Material Civilization, and Materiality

Stuff matters, and matters a lot, especially to babies, infants, and children. To be, to learn how to be, and to continue being and becoming part of the world all involve the obvious, evident, never discrete interaction with the loosely defined stuff. Stuff is the recognition that objects and things should be a key consideration in any exploration of the social world. Stuff could be clothing, toys, furniture, transport, food, and the meanings that people attach to them in specific cultural contexts. The study of how humans use, think about, and interact with material objects spans a number of disciplines and is often called material culture. Due to material culture being a relatively recent arrival as an area of academic study, the study of stuff or material culture can therefore be considered an undisciplined discipline (Miller 1998, 2009). The lack of a clear definition is intentional in order to maximize its potential to inquire into "what it is to be human within the diversity of culture" (Miller 1998, 20).

From Stuff to Material Civilization—Toward a Materiality of Childhood 251

Stuff is therefore broadly aligned with the study of material culture. This approach often focuses on discrete objects or collections of objects (for example, clothing, Coca Cola, or furniture). An important aspect of the study of this stuff is the meaning given to objects—for example, the meaning and practices in relation to religious artifacts. Indeed, material culture or the study of stuff tends toward the immaterial meanings given to interactions with things by people. It is intended here to re-embed stuff in physical materiality. In order to extend the study of stuff to have greater emphasis on physical materiality, four interrelated concepts will be explored: material culture, materiality, material civilization, and technology.

Material culture can be considered as synonymous with the study of stuff and particularly with the project of looking at the meaning of stuff as it is embedded in human culture. Daniel Miller further argues that beyond the study of material culture as the study of stuff is a grander project seeking "to demonstrate the consequences of the universal for the particular and of the particular for the universal" (2010, 10). There is here an important two-way motion that relates to wider human meaning and comes out of consideration of the detail. This process is so important that "[t]he best way to understand, convey and appreciate our humanity is through attention to our fundamental materiality" (Miller 2010, 4). To convey our humanity needs us to consider our materiality. Material culture and materiality are strongly interwoven terms but often having a clear focus on the meaning of things. To move away from the meaning of things and back toward the things, consideration of a wider materiality or material civilization is to be explored before returning to a slightly recast version of materiality.

Things are, however, not as simple as the broad stuff as material culture or stuff as materiality. This is in two senses, both of which are interrelated. First, stuff should also be conceived of as the basis for human interactions that make up a material civilization and, second, as technology that is designed by humans to have a purpose. All of this stuff forms part of the rich layer that Braudel (1981) majestically calls material civilization. He uses this term to allow historians to capture what is important in people's everyday lives in the past, but openly admits to its ambiguity. Material civilization does, however, start to capture the sheer volume of material interactions that humans are involved in. Attempting to capture the whole volume of material interactions and their specificity to everyday life makes material civilization a useful concept, for all its acknowledged ambiguity. For Braudel (1981, 23), material civilization is "lying underneath the market economy: this is that elementary basic activity which went on everywhere and the volume of which is truly fantastic. This rich zone, like a layer covering the earth, I have called for want of a better expression material life or material civilization." The emphasis is here on everyday human activity with each other and with the materials of daily life, but always looking toward the wider expanses of space that make up a market economy. This is the silting up and layering of human activity into the *longue durée* of time captured in

252 David James

the historian's data. From these dense and constant basic activities Braudel can write about agriculture, markets, the economy, towns, and civilizations, all made up of these human activities of which material interaction makes up an important part. These form the basic activities of human social life. So for Braudel the fabric of everyday life is woven out of human interaction with things, the consequence of which allow us to link up wider spaces of interaction and the longue durée of ongoing interaction.

Braudel is very useful in looking toward the wider meanings and implications of material life. In particular, he brings in the quantity of these material interactions. This "rich zone" of "basic activity" with the material world can be joined with the study of material culture and materiality to allow us a greater focus upon many particular instances, which is trying to capture the universal in the singular and the singular in the universal that Miller aims for. For example, the daily material interaction with particular types of clothing is also part of wider economic relations of production and consumption. It is probably better to settle for groups of things rather than the literally singular, but that is a pragmatic way of avoiding too much ontological baggage and discussion (see Baker, 2008, for further discussion). This also allows the term 'material civilization' to have an important role in providing the wider spatial and temporal context to the study of materiality.

There is a large literature on material culture spanning anthropology, cultural studies, and sociology that is now a well-developed field (see, for example, Appadurai, 1986; Csikszentmihalyi and Rochberg-Halton, 1981; Dant 1999, 2006, and Miller, 1998, for some key starting points and considerations). Material culture tends toward meaning and, in many studies, the cultural meaning of things. This moves away from what Miller calls our "fundamental materiality" and the promise identified earlier of outlining the key elements of material civilization. There is a drift away from the things themselves. One way to try to stem the flow toward the meaning of things is to use the concept of materiality that emphasizes physicality alongside material culture or stuff that emphasizes meaning.

For Boivin (2008, 26), materiality "emphasises the physicality of the material world—the fact that it has dimensions, that it resists and constrains, and that it offers possibilities for the human agent (or organism) by virtue of a set of physical properties." In a similar way, for Dant (2005, 6), "[m]ateriality constitutes an environment for human being with which individual human subjects engage; sometimes materiality remains environment, sometimes it is interacted with directly as distinct objects and sometimes material objects are taken up as tools that extend human instrumentality." Materiality is here both the environment and material objects. These material objects may also be technology and there is an important emphasis upon physicality and material interaction. By invoking the human body in this relationship it avoids the immediate turn from things to meaning. This more physical emphasis for materiality can rebalance the shortcomings of moving too quickly from stuff to meaning within studies of material culture.

From Stuff to Material Civilization—Toward a Materiality of Childhood 253

So far, stuff is material culture, part of the slightly wider and more physical materiality, and the much wider and at times opaque concept of material civilization. We must also consider the ever present layer of stuff as technology, simple and complex, ancient and modern. In this way stuff can be more directly related to material culture, materiality, material civilization, and, very importantly for the current argument, technology. Much materiality that we interact with on a daily basis is also technology. Not all of it, but much of it. In order to try to work out what this might mean for a materiality of childhood, the mundane example of bath time will be used. In what follows, the importance of materiality and physicality will be emphasized with an eye to round upon the often neglected technological angle to materiality.

Of Plastic Ducks and Bathwater

Some of Latour's (2005) advice to those who are unsure about where to start a study is to start in the middle of things. A child is sitting in a bath, playing with floating yellow toy ducks; the child is intent on playing, and ignoring the shampoo that is shortly to be wielded by the parent. We have here, if we ignore the things, part of the standard conceptualization of the child in the sociology of childhood that emerged in the 1990s. It is bath time as a social relationship. The discourses of hygiene and cleanliness can be invoked, as can ideas about care and what good parenting might be; the child may even be evil or good. The child is in the center, the social (family, parent) is around the child, and the meaning of the social for the child and the child for the social is what matters for the social scientific enterprise. One is left with the social interactions between children, parents, carers, and the ill-defined and opaque wider society formulated through discourses. But nowhere in this possible account of the child in his or her social world, in our bath time example, is there a look at the water, the toys, the bath, the taps, the heating of the water, the shampoo, or the room in which this takes place. There is no real account of things, just a detailed account of the meaning of social things for each other. Material civilization, materiality, and technology are left out. This is, of course, somewhat unfair on the now wide-ranging approaches in the sociology of childhood, but helps us to think more carefully about the importance of materiality.

At this point another piece of advice from Latour can be taken to ensure that we move toward a sociology of associations rather than a sociology of the social. One can arrive at a detailed description of this situation, the actors in their networks; indeed, one can reach the point where the description is saturated enough so as to become the explanation of what is going on (Latour 2005). All of the actors can have their agency made thin and the associations traced, gravity for the water flow, solidity for the container of the bath, dexterity of the fingers for the playing action with the toy ducks, the floating properties of the toy ducks, brightness for the color of the toy.

254   *David James*

We can provide this detailed description, and we can indeed follow the actors, slowly and methodically, but this can only be taken so far. It is at this point that we should avoid boredom and ignore Latour's advice to keep the world flat and start jumping around a little. This allows us to cover more ground.

Background Materiality and Technology

Much discussion of materiality focuses on discrete objects to the detriment of what can be termed background materiality. Background materiality is humanly produced and provides the framework and substance by which humans live an on-going life in the world; it is what makes the longue durée human. In our example of the bath, the water is the key background item and yet also the star attraction of the social event of bath time. Water is elemental, soft, wet, yet forceful, and able to be enrolled in all kinds of human projects, from irrigation to transport to the aesthetic show of wealth in beautiful wasteful fountains or excess showering, or, as we have here, a child having a bath. Human channeling and control of water clearly shows the interaction of materiality with technology. All human civilizations have a close relationship with water. Water is directly channeled through, around, or near human settlements through various mechanisms of storing and controlling the flow of water. The arrival of water from a tap is a complex, ongoing everyday aspect of material civilization that brings together materiality and technology. The use of human technology to channel water into this bath necessitates our conceiving of technology and materiality as intertwined. The channeling of water relies upon three key aspects of technology. Using Arthur (2009), we can identify these as the use of effect, combination of these effects, and that something happens so that a program is followed and executed. We can simply define technology as the use of effects in combination to do something.

In the bath, we have the use of effects, gravity and water as a liquid that can flow, so that water does something and arrives in the bath. It also requires the combination of starting and stopping the flow technologies, such as the tap and the plug, which in our bath time example are close to the bath. We here have the use of gravity and, to extend the complexity, pumps to channel the water from the reservoir through pipes into taps and, when turned on, into a bath, perhaps with a younger child-friendly plastic bath within a bath. There is the use of effects, the combination of technologies (pipes, taps, etc.) and doing something. There is lots of doing through the harnessing of effects taking place here: the water staying in the bath with a plug at the bottom; the softness and wetness of the water, allowing the child to sit in it; the massive network of pipe technology (the infrastructure of water supply) that allows water to flow out of taps in bathrooms. The technology of the bath is the outcome of "the programming of phenomena to our purposes" (Arthur 2009, 51).

From Stuff to Material Civilization—Toward a Materiality of Childhood 255

Physicality

To hop back into the bath, rather than thinking how the water in the bath got there and stays there, one can explore the idea of the ready-to-hand duck for the child—the duck in the hand, the duck as splashing water displacement device, as something that bobs. This physical contact between the child and the toy duck involves what Dant (2005, 111) calls "material interaction," which is "the socially acquired human skills for recognising in the form of the things what can be done next with them." This has a similarity to the affordances (Gibson 1977) for interaction that are present when people and things (or environment) are together. (Are they ever not?) It is the relationship between the senses, the body and the object—the physical nature of the yellow plastic toy duck, its perception as an object with potential, and the realization of this potential—that makes for the play with a duck in the bath activity. There may also be a parent doing some socializing about playing with toy ducks in the bath, by showing how a duck can be pushed under before popping out again. The physicality of this material interaction is part of the changing of cognition, which over many years of material encounters shapes our bodily actions to our material environment. Our repertoire of bodily actions is made in partnership with our material environment. Mauss's (1973) techniques of the body are a further way to explore the human–material interactions. The important point is that the jump should not be made from people to how people think about things or give meaning to things before identifying the physical interaction with things.

Agency, Determinism, and Things

Moving back toward some of the concerns of the sociology of childhood allows us to see something of the different perspectives on things and their importance for childhood. There are the natural toys of the natural Rousseauian child that embody innocence, the wooden blocks or appropriately scaled natural things of the Montessori school of early childhood education, even the ready-to-hand objects of childhood identified by Margaret Mead in her *Coming of Age in Samoa* (1928). Questions of agency emerge from the things themselves to move the argument on and away from ideas about different types of toys. The toys themselves have agency or are determining of the material interactions that can take place. This provides a point of tension with more recent accounts within the new sociology of childhood that emerged in the 1980s and 1990s (James and Prout 1997). These accounts emphasized that children need to be conceived of as having more agency than they are usually given credit for, and, further, that politically they should have greater agency. The question of agency is important for addressing the contribution that a more materially informed study of children and childhood can offer. A more materially informed study of childhood questions the extent to which freedom and agency are present in

256 *David James*

these material interactions but in a different way from that of traditional forms of singular technological determinism.

These ducks, these plastic yellow ducks, move us toward a more modern conception of childhood, where the dominant technological forms determine the shape of the childhood and the nature of the child (Postman 1983). For Postman, childhood starts to disappear when the world of the child as shaped and formed by the printing press gives way to the TV screen. It is not technological determinism here that should be doubted, but rather the identification of one form of technology as having a singular dominant role in determining human interactions and ideas. A more careful consideration would have to admit to technological determinism (stronger or weaker varieties), but within a plurality of material and technological interactions.

That is, however, to go too far too fast, we should settle on the yellow plastic duck for a moment. It allows us to contemplate the universality of plastic as the material context of childhood, represented by the simple forms that much of this plastic takes. The yellow plastic duck brings us directly to the material—the plastic material—and also requires us to account for its presence. It is a modern material with certain properties. It is the programming of a phenomenon for our purposes. The properties of oil when transformed make it malleable, strong, and difficult to break and able to float. We can also color plastics easily. The yellow plastic duck is the combination of form, function, and meaning. It therefore becomes a toy that floats and can be bobbed and used to splash with by a child. It has programmed properties, which have intended playful outcomes. Here materiality and technology come together. Our simple ensemble of parent, child, bath, yellow toy duck, and water together in the bathroom forms an interactive element or layer of the material civilization of which Braudel speaks.

Points of Departure for a Materiality of Childhood

The bath time example shows the importance of material civilization and technology that underlies even simple material interactions. It further shows that there is an inherent materiality to any account or conceptualization of childhood. Yes, children are socialized and develop a sense of self, have an identity, and interact with others, but all of this goes on with and never without the constant materiality and always within the context of a specific material civilization. This shows how background materiality forms an important part of a seemingly simple event: bath time.

This idea is reflected in a four-layer model or framework for a materially informed study of childhood. It would look something like Figure 19.1, with a need to ensure that materiality, technology, and physicality are adequately attended to.

All of these elements are encountered and go to make up a wider field— that rich layer of human life with things called material civilization. The intention is to try to look at the different elements to develop a way of

From Stuff to Material Civilization—Toward a Materiality of Childhood   257

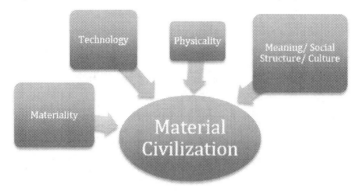

Figure 19.1 Framework for a materiality-informed study of childhood.

analyzing childhood that attends to materiality as well as to questions of meaning, social structure, and culture.

The first aspect or layer is the materiality that underlies and is present in all human social life. Next comes the layer of technology, which includes much but not all materiality. Technology covers much materiality, especially in the modern world, and should be understood as the use of effects in combination to do something, or the programming of phenomena to our purposes. It does not usually cover mountains or hills or rivers (except when mountains are thrown into the sea to make land for airports or rivers are dammed to produce power), but does cover much materiality that humans have had an involvement in; considering children and toys, it is the playful end of things and technology (alongside the military end of things as well) that often leads to what is sometimes called the cutting edge of technology.

The third element in our model or framework is physicality—there is always a human interaction with technology and materiality, but not necessarily all of the time. Even reading involves physicality; it is not a direct entry from the material object of the book to a world of symbols and the meaning made in the mind. There is a pragmatics at play here. The physical bodily action of reading is the key link between things and people.

The final layer is meaning. This is the major area that has been the focus of much social science: meanings seen on an individual level, on an interaction level between people, and on an aggregate level paying particular attention to power relations between people. It is on this level that much of the study of childhood has been based and, in political terms, quite rightly so. It has focused on power differences, the importance of discourses—be they legislative or ways of conceiving and thinking about possibilities for action or intervention (the evil child, the innocent child, etc.)—and the importance of laws. Many of these elements have an important material aspect to them, but the importance is often played down as questions of power and meaning predominate. The law is an instrument, at times interpretative, but usually

258   *David James*

with an administrative impact that relates to the making and following of rules in concrete material situations.

Each aspect of this model is not necessarily separate; this is not geology—humans are not nice sedimentary rocks that build up slowly over time, although many may wish to view childhood in this way. There is an important dynamic element here in which different parts of the model interact with each other at the same time. For example, being repulsed by dirty water in a bath with a scum on it, pulling the plug, and watching and hearing the water gurgle down the plughole have all the elements of materiality, technology, physicality, and meaning in a seeming instant. In terms of analysis and making sure that all elements are discussed, it is a useful framework or tool for thinking about how to include materiality in the study of childhood.

Questions and Doubts

It is difficult to carve up the materiality of the world, to slice it and dice it so that it can be tackled and made analyzable. The material civilization that covers all human life in groups provides awe and some deeper understanding of the nature of things, but becomes slippery when the task turns to analysis. Indeed, Braudel found himself swiftly moving to the world of meaning and aggregates rather than tackling the direct materiality of the world. There is also the difficulty of the visible, the invisible, the ready-to-hand or not. Key problems are raised of how and what to study using this framework. Miller (2010) acknowledges the difficulty of what stuff can add when it crosses many already well-established disciplines, all with their regional ontologies and questions of concern. Indeed, ontological and epistemological questions come to the fore as uncertainties emerge about where to start and what to focus on. At times it seems that these are insurmountable problems for a coherent and focused approach. Nibbling at the edges of the standard approaches to studying social life is what emerges from a response of partial resignation, and despair, to these problematic questions of what and how to study a thoroughly material world. Further despair emerges when considering that the major challenge to most social science delivered by Latour (2005) and actor-network-theory flounders on the questions of what, how, and in what detail to study things, now that the standard picture has been made implausible. The difficulty is a lack of an obvious link between this material turn and how we take account of things, and common human problems or policy dilemmas.

Conclusion

Despite these uncertainties, there are a number of strengths to using the materially informed framework for the study of childhood outlined in this chapter. There is an important contribution to be made to existing areas of study. It is sensitive to historical context by its awareness of the power of materiality, in the form of material civilization and technology, to provide

From Stuff to Material Civilization—Toward a Materiality of Childhood 259

the medium in which children live their lives. Further, it can capture the important volume of both background and ready-to-hand materiality that shapes our possibilities for acting. Human action does not take place without a material context.

A materially informed study also provides a way of tempering singular forms of technological determinism with a more generalized deterministic contextualism that is particularly aware of the key shaping role of materiality as technology. Equally, taking account of technology is a particular strength that is missing from a number of studies that focus more on the meaning of things in the material culture tradition. It has an opportunity to add and contribute to, rather than replace, material culture by attending to things and the material interaction, and what people do with things before jumping to the meaning. In short, it outlines a way to take stuff seriously. Most political, policy, and empirical concerns about children and childhood have key material elements to them. Discussion about the extent to which screen technologies dominate the lives of contemporary children or provide important new risks are all related to a thoroughgoing materiality. There is therefore an important contribution to be made by a materially informed study of children and childhood. This materially informed model for studying childhood can provide a clear account of the material stability of everyday life and contribute to the wider politically and policy relevant study of children.

References

Appadurai, Arjun, ed. 1986. *The Social Life of Things*. Cambridge: Cambridge University Press.

Arthur, Brian W. 2009. *The Nature of Technology: What It Is and How It Evolves*. Harmondsworth, England: Penguin.

Baker, Lynne Rudder. 2008. "A Metaphysics of Ordinary Things and Why We Need It." *Philosophy* 83 (1): 5–24.

Boivin, Nicole. 2008. *Material Cultures, Material Minds*. Cambridge: Cambridge University Press.

Braudel, Fernand. 1981. *Perspective of the World, Civilization and Capitalism 15th–18th Century: Structures of Everyday Life*. London: Collins.

Csikszentmihalyi, Mihaly, and Eugene Rochberg-Halton. 1981. *The Meaning of Things: Domestic Symbols and the Self*. Cambridge: Cambridge University Press.

Dant, Tim. 1999. *Material Culture in the Social World*. Buckingham, England: Open University Press.

———. 2005. *Materiality and Society*. Maidenhead, England: Open University.

———. 2006. "Material Civilization: Things and Society." *British Journal of Sociology* 57 (2): 289–308.

Gibson, James J. 1977. "The Theory of Affordances." In *Perceiving, Acting, and Knowing: Toward an Ecological Psychology*, edited by Robert Shaw and John Bransford, 67–82. Hillsdale, NJ: Lawrence Erlbaum.

James, Allison, and Alan Prout, eds. 1997. *Constructing and Reconstructing Childhood: Contemporary Issues in the Sociological Study of Childhood*. London: Falmer Press.

260　David James

Latour, Bruno. 2005. *Reassembling the Social: An Introduction to Actor-Network-Theory*. Oxford: Oxford University Press.

Mauss, Marcel. 1973. "Techniques of the body." *Economy and Society* 2 (1): 70–88.

Mead, Margaret. 1928. *Coming of Age in Samoa: A Psychological Study of Primitive Youth for Western Civilisation*. London: Harper Collins.

Miller, Daniel, ed. 1998. *Material Cultures: Why Some Things Matter*. London: UCL Press.

———, ed. 2009. *Anthropology and the Individual. A Material Culture Perspective*. Oxford: Berg.

———. 2010. *Stuff*. Cambridge, England: Polity Press.

Postman, Neil. 1983. *The Disappearance of Childhood*. London: W. H. Allen.

Contributors

Nina Augustynowicz is a Teaching Assistant at the Institute of English Cultures and Literatures, University of Silesia, Poland. Her research interests include food studies, Victorian studies, and cognitive studies. She is currently working on her PhD dissertation on the study of scientific and religious conceptual metaphors of food in nineteenth century Britain and the U.S.

Grzegorz Czemiel is Assistant Professor in literary studies at Maria Curie-Skłodowska University in Lublin, Poland. He specializes in contemporary Northern-Irish poetry and literary theory. His research focuses also on cartography, translation, urban studies, and philosophy, particularly Speculative Realism.

Mayannah N. Dahlheim is Editor-in-Chief of the bilingual small press Von Reuth Publishing in Regensburg, Germany. She holds a PhD in English Literature (postcolonial studies) from the University of Duisburg-Essen (2016) and an MA in English literature and philosophy from the University of Regensburg (2008). Previous to her work as editor, she was a researcher and lecturer at the University of Duisburg-Essen and the University of Regensburg. She retains an avid academic interest in the shifts in semiotics and signification triggered by the digital age, as well as liminal spaces, cultural interfaces, and postimperial dynamics of present-day societies.

C. Lee Harrington is Professor of Sociology and Social Justice Studies at Miami University. She has coauthored books on soap opera fan culture (*Soap Fans*, 1995) and on global TV distribution (*Global TV*, 2008) and has coedited anthologies on popular culture, fan culture, daytime soap opera, and issues related to culture, media, and aging. She has published in journals such as *Feminist Media Studies, Popular Communication, International Journal of Cultural Studies, Poetics*, and *Communication, Culture & Critique*.

Katriina Heljakka is a toy researcher and a doctor of arts in visual culture with an MA in art history and MSc. She currently holds a post-doc researcher position at the University of Turku (digital culture studies) and continues her research on toys and the material and digital cultures of

262   *Contributors*

play. She is an author of *Principles of Adult Play(fulness) in Contemporary Toy Cultures. From* Wow to Flow to Glow (2013, Alto University).

David James is Senior Lecturer in Sociology and Course Leader for Sociology and Criminology degree routes at University Campus Suffolk. His evaluation work has examined social policy interventions for young people, youth perspectives on education, and city center policing practice. He has a wide interest in social theory and social change, particularly its links to technology. Current interests include the sociology of childhood, material culture, and materiality.

Karolina Lebek is Assistant Professor in literary and cultural studies at the Institute of English Cultures and Literatures, University of Silesia, Poland. Her research focuses on theories of materiality and representation of things in cultural practices, literary conventions, and narrative storyworlds, especially in connection to the fantastic. She is a coeditor of *Inside-Out: Discourses of Interiority and Worldmaking Imagination* (2012) and is currently working on a book about catalogs of curiosities in the context of theories of wonder and natural philosophy in seventeenth century England.

Joanne Lee is an artist, researcher, writer, and publisher with a curiosity about everyday life and the ordinary places in which she lives and works. Much of her activity emerges through a serial publication, the Pam Flett Press, which explores the visual, verbal, and temporal possibilities of the 'essay' via the opportunities for production that arise in dialogue with creative and critical friends. She is senior lecturer in graphic design at Sheffield Hallam University (www.joannelee.info).

Frédérik Lesage is an Assistant Professor in the School of Communication at Simon Fraser University (SFU). He completed his PhD research at the London School of Economics and Political Science (LSE) in 2009 on the topic of art/science research in the field of high-performance computing and taught at King's College London, the LSE, and the University of Cambridge. His current research interests are focused on applying mediation theory to our understanding of how consumer-driven creative digital tools like Photoshop are designed and used. His research has recently been published in international journals including *Digital Creativity, Journal of Broadcasting and Electronic Media, Fibreculture,* and *Convergence.*

Nicolás Llano Linares is a PhD candidate in communication studies at São Paulo University (Brazil). His research interests include media theory, food discourses, and the intersection between visual and national culture. He is one of the editors of *Antropologia & Comunicação* (2014) and an active member of the research group GESC3: Semiotic Studies in Communication, Culture and Consumption (USP). He also works as a regular collaborator with various cultural publications and as a translator of Latin American and Portuguese literature.

Contributors 263

Joanna Maciulewicz is Assistant Professor in Literature and Literary Linguistics at Adam Mickiewicz University in Poznań, Poland. Her research interests include eighteenth century literature, theory of the novel, and book history as well as English, Australian and New Zealand literature and literary theory.

Anna Malinowska is Assistant Professor in literary and cultural studies at the Institute of English Cultures and Literatures, University of Silesia, Poland. Her research interests embrace critical theory, popular culture, material culture, and love studies, but specifically focus on the formation of social and cultural norms, cultural narratives, and the social-aesthetic codes of cultural production. She is an author of many publications in English and Polish.

Marcin Mazurek is an Assistant Professor at the Institute of English Cultures and Literatures, University of Silesia, Poland. His research interests are in postmodern theory, consumer culture, and film studies. He is the author of *A Sense of Apocalypse. Technology, Textuality, Identity* (Peter Lang, 2014).

Byron Miller is an Assistant Professor of Sociology at Miami University. His research focuses on interracial romance, family, and the social determinants of health.

Marcin Sarnek is Assistant Professor in literary and cultural studies at the University of Silesia, Poland, where teaches American history and culture, American literature, and multimedia. He has written on the presence of cryptographic technologies in American society and their privacy-related applications, attempting to situate these not only within their constitutional framework, but also within a wider spectrum of cultural sensitivity *to them*. He is now working on a book about copyright and creativity issues within the video games industry.

Joanna Soćko is a PhD candidate in the Department of Comparative Studies, University of Silesia, Poland. She graduated from interdisciplinary humanistic studies and took part in a number of research projects at the University of Silesia, including research on Darwinism in literature and spectrality in contemporary humanistic thought. Her main academic interests embrace literary theory and contemporary religious (so-called 'postsecular') reflection. Currently, she is a principal investigator of a research project "The Category of Materiality in R. S. Thomas's Poetry" funded by the Polish National Science Center. She is an author of many articles in English and Polish for journals such as *Fa-art* and *Wielogłos* and has edited collections published by University of Silesia Press, the Institute of Literary Research of the Polish Academy of Sciences Press, and Ashgate.

Bartosz Stopel is Assistant Professor in literary studies at the Institute of English Cultures and Literatures, University of Silesia, Poland. He is an author of several articles and book chapters, including journals from the European Reference Index for the Humanities list. Since 2015 he has been the principal investigator in a research grant entitled "From Mind to Text: Continuities in Cognitive Science, Aesthetics and Literary Theory" funded by the Polish National Science Center. His research interests include mainly literary theory, literary aesthetics, and cognitive approaches to literary studies.

John Storey is Emeritus Professor of Cultural Studies at the Center for Research in Media and Cultural Studies, University of Sunderland, UK. He has published extensively in cultural studies, including eleven books. His work has been translated into Arabic, Chinese, Dutch, German, Indonesian, Japanese, Korean, Persian, Polish, Portuguese (Brazil and Portugal), Russian, Serbian, Slovenian, Spanish, Swedish, Turkish, and Ukrainian. He is also on the editorial/advisory boards in Australia, Canada, China, Germany, Lithuania, the Netherlands, Spain, the UK, and the U.S. and has been a visiting professor at the Universities of Vienna, Henan, and Wuhan and a senior fellow at the Technical University of Dresden.

Lucia Vodanovic is Senior Lecturer at LCC (University of the Arts) and course leader of the MA in arts and lifestyle journalism. She completed her MA and PhD in cultural studies at Goldsmiths College, where she also worked as visiting lecturer. Her research interests revolve around issues of obsolescence, ephemerality, social aesthetics, and the wider discussion of how knowledge is produced and transmitted. She is coeditor of *Disturbios Culturales* (Ediciones UDP), and her work has also been featured in journals such as *Travesia: the Journal of Latin American Cultural Studies*, *M-C Journal*, *Journal of Visual Art Practice*, and others.

David Walton is Senior Lecturer and coordinator of cultural studies at the University of Murcia and has taught courses on popular culture, postmodern culture, the history of thought, and literary and cultural theory. He currently teaches courses on cultural theory and cultural practice at the undergraduate level, and comparative postmodern literature and culture at the master's level. He is a founding member, and currently president, of the Iberian Association of Cultural Studies (IBACS), which is dedicated to the promotion of the area on the Iberian Peninsula. He has organized a number of conferences and published widely in cultural theory, cultural studies, and visual culture. Recent books include *Introducing Cultural Studies: Learning through Practice* (Sage, 2008) and *Doing Cultural Theory* (Sage, 2012); his latest publication (with Juan Antonio Suárez) is *Culture, Space and Power: Blurred Lines* (Lexington, 2015). Recently, he has also published chapters and articles on new sexualities, the satire of Chris Morris, graffiti culture, the interfaces between philosophy and cultural studies, and road racing on the Isle of Man TT.

Index

'Adventures of a Pen' (it-narrative) 58–62

'Adventures of a Quire of Paper' (it-narrative) 57, 60–2

acceleration 36–7

accident: theory of 213–23

actant (quasi-object) 48

actor-network-theory 48, 258

Adobe Photoshop 5, 76; digital imagining and 84–5; 'You Suck at Photoshop' (video tutorial) 81–3; as both tool and commodity 77, 79–80, 84; see also middlebroware

Adorno, Theodor 32, 120

affordance(s) of objects: aesthetic 27; formal 26; semiotic/signifying 6, 182, 184; social 2, 3, 8, 37, 164, 180; as toys 241–2, 255

After Finitude (Quentin Meillassoux) 47

agency of things/ objects 2–3, 25–6, 37; in speculative realism 42, 44–7, 50; as social actors 253, 255

Alford, Henry 150–1

All My Children (soap opera) 195, 197, 199, 204

Allen, Rob 30

Allen, Robert 206

Amazon Kindle 91

Andersen, Hans Christian 21

Anderson, Wes 167–70, 175–6

Animobile (InterAction educational project) 136

anorexia nervosa 226–7, 235n

Another World (soap opera) 195, 205

anthropocentric fetishism 46

anthropocentrism 42, 44–5, 49

anticonsumerism 149–50

apophany 111

Appadurai, Arjun 1, 3, 35, 45–6, 256

arche-fossil (Quentin Meillassoux) 47

architecture 32, 133–4, 185

Areopagitica (John Milton) 56

Aristotle 49

artisanal products 150

As the World Turns (soap opera) 195, 198, 203, 205

astronomy 109–110

Attridge, Derek 44

aura (Walter Benjamin) 242, 247n

Austin, J. L. 164

Austin, Joe 119, 126

automobility 213–18

autonomy: from commoditization 78; of the driver 214–17; of objects 49

baby boomers 145

Bachelard, Gaston 110, 192n

Bal, Mieke 114

Ballard, J. G. 223

Banksy 119, 122–3, 125–6

Barthes, Roland 17–18, 157, 159

Baudrillard, Jean 31, 214–18

Beck, Ulrich 219–20

Beer, David 79–80

Benjamin, Walter 114, 125, 242, 247n

Bennett, Jane 44–5

Berg, Thijs van den 30

Berman, Ed 133; see also InterAction

Betts, Raymond F. 37

Birds (Aristophanes) 106

Blackbourn, David 113

Bledsoe, Matt 82

Blythe dolls 239, 245

bobo gentrification 151–2

bobos (bohemian bourgeoisie) 143, 145–6, 148–152, 153n

Bobos in Paradise (David Brooks) 143

body studies 225–6, 235n

Bogost, Ian 44–5

bohemian bourgeoisie see bobos

Boivin, Nicole 252

The Bold and the Beautiful (soap opera) 196–8, 200–1, 203

266   Index

Bordo, Susan 226, 228
Bourdieu, Pierre 14, 143, 150
bourgeoisie 144–5, 147, 152–3; *see also* bobos (bohemian bourgeoisie)
Bourriaud, Nicolas 114
Brandeis, Louis 97–98
Brassier, Ray 44
Braudel, Fernand 251–2, 256, 258
breatharianism 230
Bron/ Broen [*The Bridge*] (TV series)158
Brooks, Darin 197
Brooks, David 143–6, 152
Brooks, Peter 164
Brown, Bill 159, 162
Brugger, Peter 112–13, 115
Bruno, Giuliana 168
Bryant, Levi R. 44–6
Bukatman, Scott 215

Callois, Roger 105
Carter, Paul 114
Cartesian duality 231–2; *see also* Descartes
cartography 167–9, 175–6; *see also* cinemaps; maps
Cawelti, John G. 160, 163
Certeau, Michel de 1, 122
Chesterton, G.K. 165
childhood: materiality of 253, 255–9
Christensen, Julia 110
Christie, Agatha 158–9
cinemaps 167–8, 169, 171, 175
classificatory imagination 80–1, 85
collecting 94, 237, 239–40
commodification 1, 5, 46, 56, 61, 63
commodity 45, 147–50, 152, 153; identity as 96; privacy as 100; tool and/or 77–82, 84–5; *see also* digital commodities
commodity camaraderie 77–80
commodity fetishism 33, 45–6, 148
complex television 179, 182–3
Conley, Tom 168, 171
conspicuous consumption 143, 148–52
consumer 14–15, 31, 147–9, 151, 194, 243
consumer behaviour 90, 143, 148, 152
consumer culture 6, 55
consumer goods *see* consumer products
consumer objects 123
consumer patterns 145, 148, 150, 194
consumer products 76, 144, 149, 152
consumer society 55
consumerism 147, 149–53; *see also* anticonsumerism

consumption 5, 7, 84, 147, 252; of culture 88–92, 120, 139, 168; of food 225–6, 235n1; *see also* conspicuous consumption; mass consumption
convergence: of cultures 35, 237
copyrights 88, 100 *see also* intellectual property rights
correlationism 44, 47–8
counterculture 16, 144–6
Cozens, Alexander 107–8
creative class 143, 146–7, 152, 153n; *see also* bobos
crime fiction *see* detective fiction
Croft, Susan 132
Csikszentmihalyi, Mihaly 46, 242–3, 252
cultural hegemony 125–6
cultural infrastructure 25, 27–9
cultural materialism 25
cultural studies 13; materiality and 18, 20–1, 23, 44–5; the popular and 120, 125, 194, 226, 252; speculative realism and 50–1
cultural transfer *see* transfer
culture industry 16, 120
customization 29–31, 242, 245

Dahaene, Stanislas 72
Dali, Salvador 108
Dant, Tim 252, 255
The Darjeeling Limited (Wes Anderson) 169–73
Days of Our Lives (soap opera) 196–7, 200, 203
deceleration 71
demonstration (demo) 79, 81–2
Descartes 215–16
detective fiction 7, 157–9, 161, 164–5
detective narrative *see* detective fiction
diegesis 161
digital assets 88; definition of 89–90; rights to resell 92; collecting and 94; inheritance of 95–6
digital commodities 5, 78
digital culture 72, 76, 79, 82, 88, 241
digital economy 92–3
digital heritage 94, 96
digital imaging 76, 79–81, 84–5
digital inheritance 6, 88–91, 94–6, 100, 100n5
digital media 56, 72, 78, 85, 88–9, 91, 96
digital natives 65–6, 90–1
digital property 89, 91, 97; *see also* digital assets

Index 267

digitized consumers 88–9, 91–2
distinction (Pierre Bourdieu) 14, 143, 150 152
Douglas, Mary 229
Doyle, A. C. 158
Durkheim, Emil 2

Eisenstein, Elizabeth 63
Elam, Keir 182
embodied cognition 66
emotional realism 206
'The Emperor's New Clothes' (Hans Christian Andersen) 21–2
Enzensberger, Hans Magnus 113
ephemerality 5; in architecture 133; of social media content 88, 90–1; of writing 58, 61–2
Espagne, Michel 33
An Essay Concerning Human Understanding (John Locke) 55
EULA (end-user license agreement) 91–2
The European Court of Justice 92
evocative object 171

fabula and 161, 163–5; *see also sjużet*
Facebook 70, 95–6, 100n1, 101n5
fan culture 30
fandom 7, 199, 206–7; *see also* fan culture
fantasia 108
fasting girls 226–7, 230–4
first-sale rights 92, 96, 100n3
Fisher, Mark 49
Fiske, John 6, 15, 30, 120, 126
Florida, Richard 143–6, 151–3; *see also* creative class
flow 237–8, 241–3, 245, 247n1
fluid materiality 136, 140
folk culture 15–16
food studies 225–6, 229, 234, 235n1
Fornäs, Johan 33
Foucault, Michel 106, 115, 116n
Frank, Lawrence 157
Franzen, Jonathan 63
friction 92
Friesen, Norm 114
Frith, Simon 16
Fun Art Bus (InterAction project) 133
The Fun Palace (urban project by Cedric Price) 134–6, 140, 141n5, 7

Gamboni, Dario 107
Game of Thrones (TV series) 193
Gass, William 115

Gehl, Robert 79
General Hospital (soap opera) 196, 201–3
General Hospital: Night Shift (soap opera) 196, 201
Generation Z 88–91
'The Genuine Memoires and Most Surprising Adventures of A Very Unfortunate Goose-Quill' (it-narrative) 61
Giddens, Anthony 28–9
Giedion, Siegfried 114
glow 237–8, 241–5, 247f
Gorman, Dave 105
Gorvey, Carry 138
GraffARTi 124, 126; *see also* graffiti
graffiti 119–27, 128n2, 129n3–9
Gramsci, Antonio 16, 120
The Grand Budapest Hotel (Wes Anderson) 169–70
Graves-Brown, Paul 20
the great outdoors (Quentin Meillassoux) 47
Greenberg, Clement 32
Greenblatt, Stephen 34
Guetta, Thierry 123
Guiding Light (soap opera) 194, 196, 204–5, 208n6

Hall, Stuart 120, 126
handwriting 66–9, 71–2, 73n3
Hansen, Mark 214
haptic(s) 66–9, 71–2, 73n3
Harman, Graham 44–45, 48–9
Harré, Rom 180
Harris, Marvin 27
Hebdige, Dick 26
hegemony 16, 119–20, 126; counter-hegemony 122; *see also* cultural hegemony
Heidegger, Martin 49, 159
Hekman, Susan 229
heritage 88, 91, 138–9; *see also* intangible heritage; digital heritage
heritage studies 138
Higgs, Jessica 132
hip vs square (Norman Mailer) 145
Hirst, Damien 126
Hitch, Tory 82
Hodder, Ian 1
human Barbie 225–31, 233, 235n2
Hume, David 43, 47
hybridization 31–32

268 Index

Illouz, Eve 31
imaginary worlds 193, 194; of daytime soap operas 196, 197–9, 202–4, 206–7
Inferno (Arthur Strindberg) 111–12
infrastructure 27, 34, 36, 77, 80, 134, 250, 254; *see also* cultural infrastructure, legal infrastructure
inheritance 5, 90, 92, 94, 96; *see also* digital inheritance
intangibility 90, 138, 140
intangible heritage 132, 138–40
intellectual property rights 88, 93
InterAction (artistic group) 132–3, 135–8, 140; *see also* Cedric Price
interdisciplinary research 114
intimacy 68–71; as privacy 98
it-narratives 55–63
iTunes 91

Jameson, Fredric 31, 125
Janson, H. W. 108
Jenkins, Henry 35, 242, 244
Johns, Adrian 63
Johnson, Jeri 42
Journals to Stella (Jonathan Swift) 69–70
Joyce, James 41, 50; *see also Ulysses*

Kaltenhäuser, Robert 126
Kant, Immanuel 43, 47–8, 50
Kasurinen, Mari 245
Katz, Linda S. 26
Kentish Town City Farm 132, 136
Klee, Paul 108
König, Johann 107
Kopytoff, Igor 45–6
Kress, Gunther 66

La Calle No Calla [*The Street No Street*] (documentary) 124; *see also* graffiti 124
late modernity 4, 25, 27–9, 33
Latour, Bruno 46–7, 164, 253–4, 258
legal infrastructure 95
The Life Aquatic with Steve Zissou (Wes Anderson) 168–71, 173–4
Lilly, John C. 105
Littlewood, Johan 135
living doll 225, 226–8, 233, 234; *see also* human Barbie
Locke, John 55
The Lord of the Rings (J. R. R. Tolkien) 26, 193

ludic turn 237, 245
Lukyanova, Valeria 225–34; *see also* living doll
Lunenfeld, Peter 77–8

MacDonald, Dwight 32
Mackenzie, Henry 58
Mahon, Peter 42
Mailer, Norman 145
The Man of Feeling (Henry Mackenzie) 58
Mangen, Anne 65–8, 71–2, 73n3
map 167–8, 170–6; in soap opera world-building 194; *see also* cinemaps
Marcuse, Herbert 123, 147
Margolis, Howard 115
Marx, Karl 21, 78
mass consumption 15–16
mass culture 15–16
material agency 7, 44, 47
material civilization 250–6, 258
material culture 1, 3–4, 7, 51, 143, 250–3, 259; popular culture and 13, 25; of toys 241; in *True Detective* 183, 188, 191
material culture studies 20–3
material domain 7, 25
material interaction 255–6
material objects 5, 17–19, 26, 55, 89, 150, 170, 180, 250, 252
material property rights 97
materiality 2–3, 139, 250–9; automobile and 217; of books 58; of the body 226, 229; in crime fiction 165; of writing 57, 63; meaning and 18, 20–4, 66; popular culture and 1, 4, 6, 8, 13, 16–17, 25–6; *see also* fluid materiality; childhood
Mathews, Stanley 135
Mazlish, Bruce 215
McLuhan, Marshall 55, 114
MD House (TV series) 159
Mead, Margaret 255
media software 79–80; *see also* Adobe Photoshop
mediatization 33
Meillassoux, Quentin 44, 47
middlebroware 76–7, 80, 85
Millenials 89–91
Miller, Daniel 21–3, 25–6, 250–2, 258
Milton, John 56
mimesis 108, 182, 227; *diegesis* and 161
Mittel, Jason 179, 181

mobility: in architecture 135, 146; capitalism and 153; cultural 35; of things 45, 62; *see also* automobility
modernization 4, 25, 28
Monastery (Walter Scott) 58
Moonrise Kingdom (Wes Anderson) 168–71, 174
Moore, Kevin 26
Morton, Timothy 44–5
The Murder of Roger Ackroyd (Agatha Christie) 159
The Murders in the Rue Morgue (E. A. Poe) 161–3
My Little Pony 239, 245
The Mysterious Affair At Styles (Agatha Christie) 162

native digital media 88, 100n2
nature 216, 219, 223
New Materialisms 2, 4
Nixon, Mark 243

Obama, Barack 70
objectification 56, 100
Object-Oriented Ontology 44, 50
One Life to Live (soap opera) 195–9, 203
Ong, Walter 61, 66
online video tutorial *see* demonstration (demo)
Orwell, George 23, 148

Pam Flett Press 106, 115–16n
pareidolia 105–6, 108, 114–15
Park, Julie 55
Passions (soap opera) 194, 196–7, 206
pastiche 31
Phaedrus (Plato) 65
physical media 89–90, 92, 100n3
piss-communication 121; *see also* graffiti
Plait, Phil 109
Plato 65
play 237; allotelic play vs autotellic play 239–40; adult play 237–41, 243–45; photoplay 240; media and 244; solitary play vs social play 238; *see also* toys
Poe, E. A. 161–3
poetic artifaction 179–80, 182–3, 191
poetics of objects/things 161, 165; *see also* poetic artifaction
polysemy 26, 55
Pop Art 32, 119, 123, 125

Pope, Alexander 57, 97
popular culture 27–8, 167–9; Adobe Photoshop and 76; buildings and 134; definition of 13–16, 23, 120; graffiti and 122; living dolls and 227; materiality and 1, 4, 6, 8, 13, 16–17, 25–6; play and 240; popular processes and 2, 29–35, 37–8, 182; research and 105, 115; speculative realism and 41, 44, 50; *see also* popular materialism; popular processes
popular materialism 4, 25–7, 182
popular narratives 6–7
popular processes 27, 29, 245; aesthetic 8, 29, 179; distributive 29, 32; *see also* acceleration; customization; hybridization; mediatization; recycle; serialization; transfer
Port Charles (soap opera)196, 206
posthumanism 49
postmodernity studies 28
The Potteries Thinkbelt (urban project) 134
Powell, David 137
Powell, Harriett 137
Price, Cedric 133–5, 138, 140; *see also* InterAction
print(ing) technology 55–6
privacy 96–9
procedural literacy 182
progress, the idea of 215, 220

radio dramas 194
randomness: structure and 135–6, 138, 140
Raunig, Gerald 106, 115
recycle 31–2
Re-staging Revolutions (exhibition) 132
Richards, Keith 16
risk society (Ulrich Beck) 219
Robert, Francois 105
Rogoff, Irit 114
Rossie, Jean-Pierre 239
The Royal Tenenbaums (Wes Anderson) 168, 170

scarcity 93–94
Schaschek, Sarah 31
Schweizer, Harold 36–7
Scott, Jason David 168
Scott, Walter 58
secondary imagination 196, 206, 208n7
secondary worlds 206

270 Index

secondhand market 92–3
secularization 157, 234
semionaut 114
semiotic turn 3
serialization 7, 30–1
Serres, Michel 121–2, 126
Shakespeare, William 14, 59, 67, 106
Sharp, Cecil 15
Shaviro, Stephen 44–5
Shiel, Lisa 111
Silicon Valley (TV show) 148
The Simpsons 106–7
sjužet 161, 164; *see also fabula*
Smith, Laurajane 138
Smith, Paul 30
Snap to Grid (Peter Lunenfeld) 77–8
Snapchat 90–1, 100n1
soap fan magazines 194; *see also Soap
   Opera Digest; Soap Opera Weekly*
Soap Opera Digest 195–207
Soap Opera Weekly 195–207
soap operas 33, 193–6, 199, 202,
   204, 206–7
social determinism 3
The Social Life of Things The (Arjun
   Appadurai) 1, 45
social object(s) 8, 179–80, 182
social objects 8, 179, 180, 182
Space Barbie (documentary) 232;
   see also living doll
speculative materialism 25
speculative realism 4, 41–4, 47, 49–51
squatting 121–2
Steam platform 91, 94
Sterne, Jonathan 77
storytelling 163–4, 179–82, 191,
   194–5; toy play and 238–39,
   241, 244
storyworld 180–2; *see also*
   world-building; storytelling
street price market 93
Strinati, Dominic 3
Strindberg, Arthur 111–12
stuff 250–3, 258–9
Style Wars (documentary) 124
subculture 17, 119, 213
substance 4, 5, 33, 49
Sunset Beach (soap opera) 196
The Supreme Court 97
Sutton-Smith, Brian 237–8, 243
Swift, Jonathan 56–7, 69–70, 97
Szentkuthy, Mikló 114

A Tale of a Tub (Jonathan Swift) 56–7
tangibility 33
technology 5, 67, 80, 148; Adobe
   Photoshop as 84–5; delivery
   technology 90–1; materiality and
   251–9; in Western societies 214,
   216, 218–19, 220, 222–3; of
   writing 55–6
television *see* complex television;
   see soap operas
The Dunciad in Four Books (Alexander
   Pope) 57
The Last Straw (InterAction play) 136
The Young and the Restless
   (soap opera) 196, 199, 201, 203
Todorov, Tzvetan 160
Tolkien, J. R. R. 26, 181, 206
tool 49, 66, 76; car as 214; digital/
   software 5, 76–81; writing 60
toy ducks 253, 255–6
toys: adult toy play and 237–45;
   childhood and 250, 253,
   255–6, 257
transfer 7, 33–5, 180
True Detective (TV series) 179,
   183–91
Turkle, Sherry 171, 180

Uglydolls 239
Ulysses (James Joyce) 41–3
UNESCO 139
urban culture 6, 119, 143, 150

vandalism: graffiti and 126
Veblen, Thorstein 143, 150
Velay, Jean-Luc 65–8, 71–2, 73n3
Venice Biennale (2013) 105
Vinci, Leonardo da 105, 107
Virilio, Paul 36–7, 213, 218–20
Voltaire 68
Vrettos, Athena 227

wannarexia 227 *see also* anorexia
   nervosa
Warner, Marina 108, 110, 112–13
Warren, Samuel 97–8
We Have Never Been Modern (Bruno
   Latour) 46–7
Werner, Michael 33
Westin, Alan 99
Williams, Abigail 69–70
Williams, Emma 3

Williams, Raymond 120
Winnicott, D.W. 111
Wolf, Mark J.P. 180, 193–4, 200, 206
Wood, Denis 176
Woodward, Christopher 113
Woodward, Ian 180–1
world-building: technoculture and 78; objects and 179–82, 191; US soap operas and 193–8; *see also* storytelling

wow effect 237–8, 242–3, 245, 247n1
writing materials/tools 55–60

'You Suck at Photoshop' (YSP) *see* Adobe Photoshop
YouTube 79 80–2

Zoo Aviary (urban project) 134

Žižek, Slavoj 22